Cracking the
TOEFL® CBT

THE PRINCETON REVIEW

Cracking the TOEFL® CBT

BY GEORGE S. MILLER

2000 EDITION

RANDOM HOUSE, INC.
NEW YORK

Princeton Review Publishing, L.L.C.
2315 Broadway
New York, NY 10024
E-mail: comments@review.com

ISBN 0-375-75469-5

Editor: Lesly Atlas
Production Editor: Kristen Azzara
Production Coordinator: Robert McCormack

TOEFL is a registered trademark of the Educational Testing Service, which does not endorse this book.

Manufactured in the United States of America on partially recycled paper.

9 8 7 6 5 4 3 2 1

2000 Edition

ACKNOWLEDGMENTS

The author would like to thank Lesly Atlas, Kristen Azzara, Tim Dougherty, Tommy Furuhata, David Kelley, Jacqueline Jendras, Stephanie Martin, Robert McCormack, Matthew Reilly, Evan Schnittman, Alex Weiner, Chris Warnasch, and Iam Williams.

CONTENTS

Foreword

No other educational system in the world offers the degree of diversity and flexibility that is found in the United States. A vast array of educational opportunities is offered among both public and private institutions, allowing each student to pursue his or her particular academic and social goals in the environment that best suits that individual.

Students in the United States typically begin school at around six years of age and study for six years in elementary (primary) school, three years in junior high (middle) school, and three years in senior high (secondary) school. It takes a total of twelve years for students to complete both their primary and secondary education, after which they may go on to a college or university for postsecondary study.

POSTSECONDARY EDUCATION: AN OVERVIEW

Postsecondary education in the United States is unique. In most countries of the world, higher education is operated or controlled by one central ministry of education or some other centralized government agency. In the United States, each individual state regulates those institutions within its borders. The federal government has no direct control. Quality and uniformity of degrees and programs are achieved through private, nongovernmental accrediting agencies that tie the state systems together.

In each state there are both public (state-run) and private colleges and universities. Private institutions may either be independent or have a specific religious affiliation. The degree of influence such affiliation has on the academic program and student life varies from one college to another. Most colleges in the United States are coeducational, meaning that they accept both men and women students; however, a small number of institutions accept only men or only women.

There is no direct relationship between public and private schools and cost. Some private institutions cost more than public institutions, and vice versa. Costs vary tremendously from school to school. For example, tuition at Harvard—a private university—is around $20,000 per year, not including living expenses. On the other hand, it is possible to study at a junior (two-year) college for as little as $5,000 per year plus living expenses.

Most public institutions have two rate structures: one for students who are legal residents of the state, and another for students from other states or countries. Private institutions charge the same tuition for all students.

DEGREES

Postsecondary education in the United States is provided by two-year junior or community colleges and four-year colleges and universities. Universities offer more postgraduate courses than colleges, including the doctorate degree. There are four basic degrees offered by United States colleges and universities:

1. The *associate's* degree is usually an Associate of Arts (A.A.) or an Associate of Science (A.S.), and is offered primarily by junior or community colleges. This degree requires two academic years of full-time study to complete. Students can pursue either a technical or an academic course of study. Technical programs are considered "terminal" (they end after two years of study), and they typically prepare individuals for a trade or profession. Students pursuing an academic program will usually transfer to a four-year college or university after receiving their associate degree.

2. The *bachelor's* degree is the first degree earned at a four-year United States college or university; it generally requires four years of full-time academic study.

3. The *master's* degree is the first postgraduate degree earned at a college or university. Depending on the field of study, this degree requires one to two years of academic study beyond the bachelor's degree.

4. The *doctorate* is the highest degree offered at universities. It requires two years of full-time study beyond the master's degree, plus a dissertation based on original research.

The first two years of a bachelor's degree program consist of general education courses. During the final two years, students specialize in their chosen major field of study. Most institutions recognize that students' interests may change as they expand their academic horizons, so they allow individuals to change their majors at any time without losing credit for courses already completed. It may be necessary for a student to complete a few extra courses to satisfy the requirements of a new major, but credit for all courses successfully completed is never lost.

Students may also transfer (or change) institutions during their postsecondary studies, usually without loss of credit for courses previously taken. Transfer credit, however, is not automatic. Whether or not a college or university allows credit for prior study at a different institution is at the discretion of the particular school.

ACADEMIC CALENDARS

The academic year in the United States is approximately nine months long, beginning in September and ending in June of the following year. Most colleges and universities also have short-term summer programs during which students can complete one or two courses toward their degree.

There are four basic academic calendar systems:

1. *Semester* calendar of two terms in the academic year (fall and spring semesters), each consisting of approximately fifteen weeks of classroom instruction. There may also be an optional summer session offering a limited selection of courses.

2. *Trimester* calendar of three ten-week terms (fall, winter, and spring) in the nine-month academic year. An optional summer session offering a limited course selection may also be offered.

3. *Quarter* calendar of four ten-week terms year-round (fall, winter, spring, and summer); students generally attend three of the four sessions, but have the option of attending all four if they wish to expedite their academic program.

4. *4-1-4* calendar of two two-month terms with a one-month "intersession," during which students generally concentrate on a specialized project. There are several variations on this calendar, including 4-4-1 and 5-1-5.

When selecting an institution for study in the United States, you should consider nine basic factors:

1. Your financial resources—How much money do you have per year for your education? The yearly costs vary greatly from state to state and from school to school.

2. Your academic record—Each college or university has its own requirements for admission. Universities such as Harvard, M.I.T., and Stanford are highly selective and accept only the top students from the best schools. Be sure to select an institution that accepts students within the range of your academic achievements. However, be assured that if you have successfully completed secondary school, you will find an institution in the United States that will accept you as a student for postsecondary studies.

3. Your major field of study—No single school offers all the fields of study that are available in the United States. Be sure the college or university to which you apply offers the program you wish to pursue.

4. Location of the institution—Physical and social conditions vary greatly from one region to another in the United States. There are large, mid-size, and small colleges in both major urban areas and in smaller towns. Life in a large city is very different from that in a small town. Colder climates in winter are found in the north and east of the country, while the southern portions are more temperate. Every prospective student should have an idea of what kind of setting to expect when arriving in the United States to begin studies.

5. Size of the institution—The student population at colleges and universities can vary from as little as 500 to more than 10,000. The size of an institution influences its social and educational atmosphere.

6. Accreditation—Is the institution accredited? *Accreditation* means that a given institution has been investigated by a team of experts and found to meet the minimum requirements of the accrediting agency. It is not recommended that international students attend a nonaccredited school, for several reasons. First, students should be sure they are getting the best possible quality education for the investment of time and money. Second, if a student initially enrolls in a nonaccredited school and later wishes to transfer to an accredited institution, the new school may not allow credit for past studies. And finally, many countries will not recognize degrees from nonaccredited institutions for purposes of employment or professional licensing.

7. Applicability—Will the degree earned at a particular college or university be recognized by employers, educational institutions, and/or the government in your home country?

8. Living facilities—Does the institution offer dormitory facilities? Living in an on-campus residence hall can be more convenient, reduce the stress of cultural adjustment, and make finding friends easier than if you live off campus in an apartment. Apartment accommodations, on the other hand, allow a greater degree of independence.

9. Type of institution—The last factor to consider is the type of institution you wish to attend. There are both private and public colleges and universities. Some institutions accept only men or only women, but the vast majority are coeducational. Some private schools are operated by, or affiliated with, religious organizations. Is attending a university with high "prestige" important to you, or will a lesser-known institution that provides a solid education be acceptable? Do you want a college that emphasizes academics, one that affords an active social life, or a school that falls somewhere in between?

THE APPLICATION PROCESS

Once you have decided which institution you would like to attend, the next step is to obtain an application and apply for admission. You may contact the school directly and request an application for enrollment, or you may use a service such as ELS (English Language Services) Language Centers' Academic Placement Service, which will help you select a suitable college or university and then handle all paperwork related to your application.

It is important that you begin the application process far in advance of the term you wish to attend. Many universities have deadlines after which they will not accept applications for that semester or year. Sometimes it takes several months for an admissions officer to process an application; applications for postgraduate study can take as long as six to nine months to process.

Although the forms from different schools may appear to differ greatly, the documents necessary to complete an application are much the same regardless of the college or university. All institutions require the following:

1. An application form. Be sure to answer all questions thoroughly; an incomplete application could delay the entire admissions process.

2. Transcripts of all academic work you have completed, showing courses taken and grades received. An original official copy and a certified English translation are required.

3. A financial statement demonstrating that you have sufficient funds at your disposal to support your study and living expenses in the United States.

4. An autobiography of yourself, in English, with a statement of your educational goals in the United States.

5. Many institutions require a statement of good health from a physician, in English or with an official English translation.

6. Demonstrated proficiency in English. This requirement may be fulfilled in several ways. The TOEFL (Test of English as a Foreign Language) is the most widely accepted test of proficiency; it is a standardized test that is administered worldwide. An alternative to taking the TOEFL is first to enroll in an English as a Second Language (ESL) program. There are numerous such programs in the United States, many situated on college campuses. ELS, for example, has twenty-three Language Centers located throughout the United States. Students in ELS's intensive English program study six hours per day, five days per week in consecutive four-week sessions until they reach the desired proficiency level. Some United States colleges and universities accept completion of the ELS program and other ESL programs in place of the TOEFL as proof of English proficiency.

A student who has been accepted to a college or university or to an intensive English program will receive two documents: a letter of acceptance and a Form I-20. The Form I-20 is a United States government form filled out by the accepting institution, which gives a student the right to go to the nearest United States Embassy or Consulate and request an F-1 student visa. The visa officer has the sole authority either to grant or deny the visa.

In making a decision, there are two main things a visa officer considers. First, applicants must prove that they have sufficient financial resources to live and study in the United States without working, at least for their first academic year. Second, the visa officer must be convinced that the students will return to their home countries upon completion of their degree programs.

The Choice Is Yours!

As you can see, the educational alternatives in the United States are many and perhaps even overwhelming. However, the great variety of programs and institutions means you can receive as much education as you want if you work for it and can figure out how to pay for it.

The United States has a long tradition of welcoming international students into its colleges and universities. Most institutions, both large and small, have services in place to assist international students in making the transition—whether academic, cultural, or social—as smooth as possible.

—Nora Saidi
Director of ELS Academic Placement Service

What Is the TOEFL CBT?

The computer-based Test of English as a Foreign Language (TOEFL CBT) is a standardized test administered by the Educational Testing Service (ETS), a huge, tax-exempt private company located in New Jersey. ETS is the same testing organization that administers the GRE, SAT, LSAT, and a bunch of tests in other fields, including hair styling, plumbing, and golf. The TOEFL CBT is supposedly designed to test a non-native English speaker's proficiency in American English. However, it really tests how well you take a multiple-choice exam. In any case, all the expressions, idioms, and grammar tested in the TOEFL CBT are those most common in America, *not* in England or other English-speaking countries.

What Does the TOEFL CBT Measure?

It is unclear exactly what the computer-based Test of English as a Foreign Language measures. Clearly, a person fluent in English will perform better on the test than would a person only somewhat familiar with the language. However, how well you speak English is not the only factor that determines your TOEFL CBT score. Some people get very nervous when taking a test and don't get the score they deserve. Others always do well on tests even when they don't study. Standardized tests aren't the most reliable measure of proficiency in *any* subject. So what is *really* tested by the TOEFL CBT? Well, one might say, the TOEFL CBT measures your performance on the TOEFL CBT.

This book will help improve your TOEFL CBT score by showing you how to look for shortcuts, avoid common mistakes, and practice taking the test. These skills are just as important to your TOEFL CBT score as studying English.

For many of you, taking a computer-based test is a new experience. Fortunately, you have this book to help you prepare.

How Important Is the TOEFL CBT?

The importance given to your TOEFL CBT score varies greatly from school to school. Although ETS does not intend for TOEFL CBT scores to be used by universities as cutoffs (for example, rejecting all applicants with scores below 250), usually that is exactly what happens. Another result of a low TOEFL CBT score might be that a college will admit you but not allow you to register until you have taken a semester or two of English courses. If you're taking the TOEFL CBT in order to apply to a college or university, find out how your scores will be evaluated and used. The majority of colleges and universities in the United States, and many in Canada, require TOEFL CBT scores from all international applicants. Approximately 950,000 students worldwide, from those applying to college to those applying to doctoral programs, will take the TOEFL CBT this year.

Why Is the Test Given on a Computer?

Until summer 1998, the TOEFL was only available as a paper-and-pencil test. Those persons administering the test often were unfamiliar with the TOEFL, and at best, could barely answer any question posed. Recently, ETS realized the enormous financial benefits they could reap from transforming the paper-and-pencil TOEFL test to the Computer-Based Test (CBT). It now saves money on printing test materials, renting facilities, and processing answer sheets. It also almost doubled the test fee from $55 to $100.

Honestly, ETS doesn't really care how good your English is. When the paper-and-pencil test was still offered, you had the option to review the material after taking the test. Now, with the TOEFL CBT, ETS makes it impossible for you to:

- know which answers you got wrong

- see the test or questions again

- learn from your mistakes

- be sure the computer accurately determined your score

Cracking the TOEFL CBT is a great tool to help you prepare for the new TOEFL CBT. However, since the TOEFL CBT is a computer-adaptive test, you will have to overcome the instincts you have developed in school for taking a paper-and-pencil test. No longer can you simply turn back a page and revisit a question whose answer you suddenly remember. Once you have clicked on an answer choice and confirmed your decision, say "good-bye," because you will never see that question again. *Cracking the TOEFL CBT* will help you change all of your pencil-and-paper test-taking techniques.

How Does the TOEFL CBT Work?

Computer-adaptive tests use your performance on one question to determine which question you'll be asked next. The TOEFL CBT begins with ETS assuming that you have the average score in a particular section. You'll be asked a question of difficulty that represents this score level. If you answer correctly, the computer adjusts your score to a new level, and your next question will be more difficult. If you answer incorrectly, your score will drop and your next question will be less difficult. Additionally, the amount that your score changes with each new correct or incorrect answer is reduced as you move further into the test. Therefore, by the end of the test, the computer will have effectively zeroed in on your TOEFL CBT score. That is what ETS claims, anyway.

On the computer-based TOEFL, only the Listening and Structure sections are computer-adaptive. Again, this means that how much credit you get for a harder question depends on how you've done on earlier questions. If you've correctly answered all of the previous questions, you're going to get more credit for answering a hard question correctly. If you missed the answers to a bunch of questions before you worked your way "up" to that harder question, you will get less credit for answering it correctly. Simply put, your responses early in a section will have a greater impact on your final score than your responses to those later in the section. So be *extra* careful when answering the first five or so questions in a section.

Never try to figure out how difficult a question is. Concentrate on working carefully on each question that you get. You'll learn a lot more about pacing as well as other general TOEFL CBT strategy techniques in the following chapters.

ARE THERE DISADVANTAGES TO THE TOEFL CBT?

Yes! There are several disadvantages to the TOEFL CBT.

◆ The cost rises from $55 to $100.

◆ The test is longer, and therefore more exhausting.

◆ Testing appointments at Sylvan Learning Centers are limited.

◆ Some question types are more difficult.

◆ A 30-minute essay (the Writing section) is mandatory

ARE THERE ADVANTAGES TO THE TOEFL CBT?

It's not all bad, folks....

◆ You have more time to answer the questions! There is no longer a 12-second interval between the Listening section questions that there was for the paper-and-pencil test. You get to work at your own pace!

◆ You can take the TOEFL CBT any day of the week at any time a Sylvan Learning Center is open. There is no deadline for registration. However, since the seats fill up quickly, we recommend that you register one or two weeks before you want to take the TOEFL CBT.

◆ The atmosphere is quiet and comfortable, and you can actually hear the speakers in the Listening section.

◆ You can receive your scores faster and ETS will send them to up to four academic institutions, rather than just three. (You can always pay for additional score reports).

◆ Selecting an answer is easier on the computer. No more annoying ovals to fill in with a number 2 pencil.

HOW IS THE TOEFL CBT STRUCTURED?

The TOEFL CBT is divided into four sections and lasts approximately four and one-half hours. ETS refuses to commit to specific question numbers. According to ETS's logic, because the TOEFL is now computer-adaptive, and the number and difficulty of questions depend on your performance, it is impossible to say exactly how many questions and how much time you will have in any one section. However, you can count on the following:

Section 1: Listening		
Part A (short conversations)	11–17 questions	
Part B (6 to 9 lectures and long conversations)	16–45 questions	
	Total:	30–50 questions
	Time:	40–60 minutes
Section 2: Structure		
Sentence completion and Error Identification	20–25 questions	
	Total:	20–25 questions
	Time:	15–20 minutes
Break	Time:	10 minutes
Section 3: Reading		
4 to 5 passages	10–13 questions each	
	Total:	44–60 questions
	Time:	70–90 minutes
Section 4: Writing		
1 written essay	Time:	30 minutes
Approximate number of questions:	94–135	
	Total Time:	Approximately 4 and one-half hours

Keep in mind that the total time takes into account the mandatory tutorials that explain the computer, question types, and all other procedures. Even though your performance on the tutorials has *no* impact on your final score, they are tiring and time consuming. You should move through them as quickly as possible in order to save energy for the actual test questions and to avoid test fatigue.

HOW IS THE TOEFL CBT SCORED?

The highest score on the new TOEFL CBT is 300. Each of the three sections is given a scaled score from 1–30: Listening (1–30), Structure and Writing (1-30), and Reading (1–30). Your final score is the combined, scaled scores from each section, multiplied by 10. Each section is each worth one-third of the total score.

Your mandatory 30-minute essay will be evaluated by two individual graders who will assign your essay a score from 0 (the lowest) to 6 (the highest). A third reader will grade the essay if there is more than a 1-point discrepancy in scoring.

Immediately after completing the TOEFL CBT, you will have the opportunity to see your *rough* score on the computer screen. The Listening score and the Reading score will be shown immediately. However, your combined Structure and Writing score will be approximated because the essay will not yet have been sent to the individual graders. The computer will then guide you step-by-step in selecting up to four academic institutions to which your scores may be sent.

If you think you did poorly on the TOEFL CBT and do not wish your scores to be sent to any schools, you have the option of canceling your scores. However, you must choose to cancel the scores before seeing them. In this case, you will not receive a refund, and you'll never know what your scores were.

WHEN DO I GET MY SCORES?

Your score will be sent to your address and the academic institutions you have selected 14 days after the test. ETS makes it clear that your scores will not be available any earlier. Additional score reports cost $11 US for each, and need to be ordered with a special form found in the back of the TOEFL CBT bulletin. The scores are valid for two years from the day you take the test. If more than two years have elapsed since the last time you took the test, you will need to take the test again. Although your scores are confidential, ETS has the right to use them anonymously for any research or project it might concoct.

WHERE DO I TAKE THE TOEFL CBT?

You will take the TOEFL CBT at a Sylvan Learning Center. Scattered all over the United States (see Appendix C in the TOEFL CBT bulletin), each Sylvan Learning Center is a test-administrating business. The test is given at individual testing stations similar to partitioned study areas you might find in a library. The testing rooms are under camera surveillance, which eliminates most cheating techniques. There is a 10-minute break between the Structure and Reading sections, but you can actually take a break at any time you want. Just remember, if you decide to take a break during the actual test, the time is still running. We do not recommend taking additional breaks beyond the 10-minute break provided.

How Do I Register For the TOEFL CBT?

By Phone:

The easiest way to register is by phone. You must have a valid Visa, Master Card, or American Express card.

Step 1: Call ETS at 1-609-771-7100 to get a free copy of the TOEFL CBT Bulletin.

Step 2: Fill out the CBT Voucher in the center of the bulletin. This is the information you will need to supply over the phone. The test will cost $100 US.

Step 3: Call 1-800-GO-TOEFL (1-800-468-6335). This is the general number to the Sylvan Learning Centers where you will be taking the test. (There is a list of Sylvan test centers in Appendix C in the TOEFL CBT bulletin). Supply the information on your CBT Voucher.

The operator will give you a confirmation number, test date, the time you must report to the test center, address, and identification requirements. *Do not lose your confirmation number!*

By Mail:

Paying by check is a little more complicated.

Step 1: Call ETS at 1-609-771-7100 to get a free copy of the TOEFL CBT bulletin. You may also write for a bulletin at the following address:

TOEFL Office
P.O. Box 6151
Princeton, New Jersey 08541-6151

Step 2: Complete the CBT Voucher located in the center of the bulletin and mail it to the appropriate address. (Look inside the envelope for the mailing labels). Be sure to enclose your check or money order payable to TOEFL.

Step 3: In approximately 4 weeks, ETS will send you a TOEFL CBT voucher with a confirmation number. *Do not lose your confirmation number*.

Step 4: Call 1-800-GO-TOEFL (1-800-468-6335) to reserve your time and date. Give them your confirmation number so they know you have paid.

Sylvan Learning Center testing sites fill up very quickly, so register as soon as possible

CAN I RESCHEDULE?

Yes, but you must call 1-800-GO-TOEFL (1-800-468-6335) by noon at least five business days in advance and pay a $20 US penalty. You will need to supply the operator with your confirmation number when you call.

CAN I TAKE THE TOEFL CBT MORE THAN ONCE?

Definitely—but only once per month. If you take the TOEFL CBT more than once per month, the second test will *not* count, you will *not* be able to see your score, and you will *not* get a refund. Don't despair if you have to retake the test. Since ETS only reports the scores you want them to, it is to your advantage to take the test more than once and then submit your best scores to the schools or institutions to which you are applying.

CAN I STILL TAKE THE PAPER-AND-PENCIL TEST?

No! Once the TOEFL CBT becomes available in a country, the paper-and-pencil test is eliminated. The TOEFL CBT is available in the United States, Mexico, and selected other countries as of summer 1998. All other countries will gradually go to the TOEFL CBT by the year 2000.

WHAT IS THE PRINCETON REVIEW?

The Princeton Review is a test-preparation company based in New York City. We have branches in more than fifty cities across the country and the world. We've developed the techniques found in our books and courses by analyzing actual exams and testing their effectiveness with our students. We don't want to waste your time with a lot of unnecessary information. It would be foolish for us to try to teach you every rule of English grammar or every subtlety of spoken English. Those things aren't what will raise your score.

What we will teach you is how to approach the test. Once you learn to think like the people who write the test, you'll learn what sorts of questions come up most often and what a right answer looks like. You'll learn to use your time effectively, avoid problems along the way, and find answers to questions you may be unsure of.

You need to do only two things: Trust the techniques, and *practice*.

Are There Any Ways to Practice the TOEFL CBT?

If you feel that you have adequately covered all the information in the book and could use more practice, ETS still makes available practice paper-and-pencil TOEFL tests. Also, you can order a CD-ROM that has practice questions. However, the practice CD-ROM is much shorter and mainly focuses on the new and more difficult question types. This makes the TOEFL CBT CD-ROM much harder than the actual test you will take on site. You may obtain the CD-ROM on-line at www.TOEFL.org or by calling ETS directly at 1-800-446-3319. An order form is located on page 19 of the TOEFL CBT bulletin.

The Princeton Review also offers a highly successful TOEFL CBT preparation course at many of its sites. The course is famous for its small classes, personal attention, and most importantly, excellent results. For information about course offerings in the United States call 1-800-2REVIEW.

For course information in the following countries call The Princeton Review in:

Hong Kong: (011) 85-2-517-3016
Mexico: (525) 564-9468
Montreal, Canada: (514) 499-0870
Japan: (011) 81-3-3463-1343
Korea: (011) 82-2-554-7763
Saudi Arabia: Call in the United States at (413) 584-6849
Singapore: (011) 65-235-5222
Spain: (341) 571-3849
Taiwan: (011) 88-6-2751-1293
Thailand: (011) 66-2215-6479
Toronto, Canada: (800) 495-7737
Turkey: (011) 90-212-257-7042

1

The Basics

WHY PRACTICE FOR THE TOEFL CBT?

ETS will tell you that it is not possible to learn English in a short period of time. While this is true, what you *can* learn in a short period of time is how to take an exam.

Would you rather take the test in *this* situation:

You wake up tomorrow morning to discover that the test is being given in an hour. You rush to the test center, unprepared, upset, and out of sorts. You arrive at the test center nervous and unsure of what to expect. You begin the test, misread the instructions, and make time-consuming mistakes. Unfamiliar with the computer-based TOEFL, you make more silly mistakes, which continue to lower your score.

Or this one?

After preparing for the test, you arrive at the test center on time, confident and relaxed. You know what to bring with you. You know how long the test will take. There are no surprises. You don't waste your time or your brainpower trying to familiarize yourself with the new TOEFL CBT test. You are completely used to all question types and are not intimidated by the changes ETS has made. Your score reflects your confidence.

There is no reason to panic over the new TOEFL CBT. Nothing can alleviate your stress more than knowing what to expect. Don't let your score be affected by the unknown! Prepare and get ready to improve your score.

HOW MUCH CAN I EXPECT MY SCORE TO IMPROVE?

As with any new endeavor, the more you practice the better you become. A great deal depends on what your score was to start with. Generally speaking, if you're scoring pretty well to begin with, then your score will not improve as much as it would if you were starting with an average-to-below-average score. However, every little bit helps!

HOW TO USE THIS BOOK

What this book sets out to do is to train you for the TOEFL CBT in the most efficient way. There is not a lot of memorizing, but as with any study aid, it is best to allot a few hours each day for a few weeks before the test. You'll want time to find your strengths and weaknesses. You'll want to practice the techniques and do the drills a little at a time. Do not try to finish everything in a weekend!

In addition to the information in the book, here are a couple of general pointers to help you become as familiar as possible with spoken and written English:

- ◆ **SPEAK!** Don't be intimidated by English. Try to converse with native English speakers as much as possible. If you have a friend or teacher who is an English speaker, practice with that person. Have conversations on the telephone. Learn the idiomatic expressions, feel the rhythm of the language, and get to know how Americans express themselves. Nothing can improve your English more than speaking with real people in real situations. The most important thing you can do is *speak, speak, speak!* Got it?

◆ **LISTEN!** Turn on the radio and television. This is a fun way to improve listening comprehension! Try to understand what is being implied in a conversation or discussion. Talk shows can be great sources of conversation.

◆ **READ!** Buy newspapers and magazines. Get used to skimming articles to find the main ideas. Pay attention to captions under pictures. You never have to read any long passages on the TOEFL CBT, so look for short paragraphs that are informational or conversational.

◆ **BE POSITIVE!** Set reasonable goals and stick to them. Your English *will* improve if you believe. Eliminate your fear.

These are some of the most interesting and natural ways to practice. Make it your goal for the next few weeks to spend as much time as possible *speaking, listening* to, and *reading* English.

CAN I REALLY IMPROVE MY SCORE?

Yes! Yes! Yes! ETS always says that no one teaching method can help prepare someone for the TOEFL CBT. Remember, although native speakers will do better on the TOEFL CBT than will non-native speakers, the more familiar you are with a standardized test, the easier it will be to raise your score. Everyone can learn how to take a standardized test. The first step in doing better on the TOEFL CBT is realizing this.

Trained Princeton Review staff, who have carefully researched through exhaustive analysis all available TOEFL material, developed the strategy and teaching methods for use on the TOEFL CBT. Our focus is on the basic concepts that will enable you to attack the TOEFL CBT problems, strip them down, and solve them as quickly as possible. The sooner you accept the fact that the TOEFL CBT is not a regular test, but a standardized test with standardized "logic," the more your score will improve.

All right, now let's get down some general strategies for taking the TOEFL CBT.

POE (Process of Elimination)

Perhaps the best thing about ETS's standardized TOEFL CBT is that the correct answer is always in front of you, right? You never have to fill in a blank, or come up with the answer on your own. Because there are usually three times as many wrong answers as there are right answers, it's often easier to eliminate the wrong answers than to pick the correct one. By identifying and eliminating the "incorrect answers" it is easier to click on the correct answer.

Wrong Answers

Eliminate wrong answers to find the correct answer.

ETS has labeled the wrong answers as "distractors." The definition of "distract" is to draw attention away from one object, and focus it on another. This is exactly ETS's goal: to draw your attention away from the correct answer, and focus it on a wrong one. This ETS strategy keeps you from earning points accidentally. Once you are able to recognize ETS's distrators, your score will greatly improve! It makes sense!

Improve Your Odds

Use POE to improve your chances of clicking on the on the best answer.

Every time you are able to eliminate an incorrect choice on the TOEFL CBT, you improve your chances of clicking on the best answer. The more you use POE, the better your odds. Think about it. If you guess on any question, you have a one-in-four chance of getting the best answer. When you eliminate just one choice, you are now down to one-in-three. Eliminate just two answers and you now have a 50/50 chance of guessing the best answer. In the Listening and Structure sections, you have to click on an answer before the next one appears. If you don't know the answer you'll have to guess, so guess intelligently. This indirect way of finding the correct answer helps you avoid the traps that ETS wants you to fall in. POE is a powerful testing tool!

In the Reading section, every question is worth the same. Logically, you will want to learn how to skip the more difficult questions and leave them for last. However, you must answer every question by the end of the Reading section. It is very important to know that you are not penalized for guessing. Use POE and make your best guess.

Pacing

Be extra careful at the beginning of the Listening and Structure sections.

In the last chapter, you learned a little about the way an adaptive TOEFL CBT operates. On the TOEFL CBT, only the Listening section and the Structure section are computer adaptive, meaning that the difficulty of each question is based on how you answered the previous question. For example, if you answer question 4 correctly, question 5 will be a little bit more difficult. However, if you answer question 4 incorrectly, question 5 will be easier and your final score may be lowered.

Remember, you must be *extra careful* at the beginning of the Listening and Structure sections of the TOEFL CBT. It is at this point where the computer determines your level. The first several questions of these two sections impact your final score more than later questions do.

If you make a careless mistake early on, it might take you five or six questions to get back to the same level. The jumps the computer makes at the beginning of the Listening and Structure section are drastically steeper than the increments it makes at the end of the test.

Take your time! The most important matter is accuracy. But be careful—just because you are not supposed to rush doesn't mean you can look out the window for five minutes, or daydream about your weekend. Remember, during the Listening section, the 12-second interval between questions on the old paper-and-pencil test has been eliminated. Although you can take as long as you want to answer the questions, you can't go back once you have clicked on the "Answer Confirm" icon. During the Structure section, the questions also disappear forever once you have clicked on the "Answer Confirm" icon. In both cases, keep on working. For any question that takes more than two minutes, use POE, guess and go on! Only in the Reading section can you go back and answer those questions you skipped.

As you may have noticed from the chart in chapter 1, you have around 4 and 1/2 hours to complete:

- Several tutorials describing the computer, the different sections, and question types

- Approximately 94 to 135 questions

- A 30-minute mandatory written essay

That's a lot to accomplish. You will be mentally and physically exhausted by the time you get to the last section. Don't give in to fatigue. Prepare to reward yourself when you finish. Stick with it. Never just answer a question to "get through" and "get it over with."

Practice Using a Computer

A major obstacle facing many foreign students taking the TOEFL CBT is their fear of computers. Computers are easy to use, especially at a Sylvan Learning Center. ETS has made it impossible for you to accidentally erase your score, crash the computer, or delete any information. In fact, they make a great effort to explain how to move, point, and click a mouse. Mandatory computer tutorials explain the different question types that will appear on the TOEFL CBT. Although prior computer skills are not required to be able to take the TOEFL CBT, familiarizing yourself with a computer before signing up for the TOEFL CBT will greatly increase your confidence.

Try to familiarize yourself with the computer.

THE WEEK OF THE TEST

By the week of the test you should be confident in your test-taking abilities. Keep in mind that you are not really memorizing information for this exam. By the week of the test you should have reviewed most of the information in this book. It's a good idea to save some practice test material for the last week. When you work on this practice material during the last week, be sure to time yourself, and try to complete an entire section in one sitting. It's important to get a feel for the amount of time you will have for each section so that it will not come as a surprise to you on test day.

Don't cram a great deal of studying into the last week. If you were running a marathon, would you run five marathons the week of the race? Of course not. That would leave you exhausted on the day of the race. The same is true with test practice. You want to feel confident and prepared, not exhausted and sick of test questions. The last week you should try to stay well-rested and healthy, and review just enough to keep your level of confidence high.

The night before the exam, plan to eat a light meal, maybe see a movie. *Don't study*. All you will learn that last night is how to be nervous. You're well prepared, so relax and get a good night's sleep.

The Day of the Exam

Be sure to bring with you:

- Photo identification—This basically means your passport. However, if your passport picture doesn't resemble your current look, expect some trouble. There are no exceptions. The administrators at the Sylvan Learning Center are no-nonsense and will not hesitate to throw you out if they suspect something is wrong.

- Confirmation number—The confirmation number was given to you by the friendly operator if you registered by phone, or is listed on your CBT Voucher if you registered by mail.

- A watch—The time remaining for each section is always in the upper left corner of the screen. However, it isn't a bad idea to bring your own time source.

Think positive!

- A positive attitude—This is perhaps your biggest advantage to cracking the TOEFL CBT.

You are not allowed to bring anything into the Sylvan testing rooms. No food, drinks, tobacco, paper, pencils, beepers, cellular phones, pagers, pens, calculators, books, pamphlets, dictionaries, and so forth are allowed. Only during the Writing section will the administrators give paper to you. At some Sylvan Centers, lockers are available to store your stuff in, but they are *small*, big enough for a small purse! You have one official 10-minute break between the Structure and Reading sections; however, you can leave at any time provided that you sign in and out. Time will still run if you are in the middle of a test section. If you must, take a break during the tutorials. It is important that you eat before you start the test. Being hungry or tired in the middle of the exam will likely affect your score. Even though you cannot bring food into the room, you may want to bring a snack to eat during your break.

Before each section of the TOEFL CBT, you will go through a tutorial, which basically teaches you about the computer and the different test questions you will encounter. Move through them quickly as to not waste your energy and brainpower. The test centers are also monitored by closed-circuit television. Ignore them. You won't be doing anything wrong, so block them out.

Now relax and feel confident. You are well prepared and will do your best.

Think positive! Think positive! Think positive! Think positive! Think positive! Think positive!

PART **II**

Listening

THE BASICS

In the Listening section of the TOEFL CBT, you will have to answer approximately 30 to 50 questions in 40 to 60 minutes. There are two sections to this part of the test.

Part A: In this section you will hear short conversations between two speakers. A third speaker will then ask you a question about what was said. There are about 11 to 17 questions in Part A.

Part B: In this section you will hear either a long conversation between two to four speakers, or a lecture given by one person. In both cases, another speaker will ask you a series of questions about what was said. There are anywhere from 6 to 9 listening passages and a total of about 30 to 40 questions.

WHAT IS IT SUPPOSED TO TEST?

ETS says that this part of the test offers you "an opportunity to demonstrate your ability to understand spoken English." According to ETS, the information it obtains from your performance on this section is supposed to help a school determine if your English is good enough to understand what is going on in your classes.

WHAT DOES IT REALLY TEST?

Before you feel too grateful for the opportunity to demonstrate your English skills, think for a minute about what this section really measures. If you wanted someone to "demonstrate his ability to comprehend" any spoken language, what would you do? You would probably try to have a conversation with that person.

What you probably *wouldn't* do is make him wear headphones and sit in a room full of computers with 15 other people and answer a bunch of multiple-choice questions that have nothing to do whatsoever with anything relevant. That kind of test measures:

- how well you hear
- the ability to comprehend non sequiturs
- the ability to stay calm under pressure

But does it measure your ability to understand spoken English? Not very well. The one thing the TOEFL CBT Listening section does with total accuracy is measure how well you do on the TOEFL CBT Listening section. Nothing more.

How to Tackle the Listening Section

It is true that someone who speaks English well will probably score better on the Listening section than someone who barely speaks English. If you are using this book, your English must already be pretty good. The techniques presented in this section will help you improve your score on the Listening section.

This chapter will teach you how to use some of the weaknesses of the Listening section to help you rather than hurt you. We'll also show you how to use the process of elimination (POE) to find the right answers, *even if you didn't understand what you heard.*

How Much Will Your Scores Improve?

That depends on how much you practice and on your consistency when you do it. If you use the techniques, your scores will improve, but remember:

- It's easier to improve starting with a medium score than with a high score. The Listening section, like the Reading section, is scored on a scale of 1 to 30. If you are already scoring somewhere between 25 and 30, there is not that much room for improvement. On the other hand, if you're doing that well, your scores don't need to improve very much to satisfy the requirements of just about any institution.

- If you improve your listening abilities, *and* learn the techniques, your score will improve even more.

Start praticing your conversational English today!

If you have planned well in advance, you may have a few months to prepare for this test. In the Conversational English chapter, we've included some suggestions for ways to work on your listening skills. Get started as soon as possible!

Conversational English

2

PRACTICING LISTENING TO ENGLISH

As is often said in the English language, "practice makes perfect." In other words, if you want to learn to do something well, you should do it over and over again until you have mastered it. If you wanted to, say, learn to play the piano, or help lead your basketball team to the finals, you would probably put in several hours of practice per week. The same goes for learning a new language. Here are a few activities you can practice to help prepare you for the Listening section of the TOEFL CBT.

- Talk on the telephone (in English, of course). Speaking on the phone eliminates facial expressions, gestures, and any other clues as to what the person on the other end of the line is saying. The same is true for the Listening section; you can rely only on the speakers' voices to answer the questions.

- Listen to talk shows and news reports on the radio. Like the telephone, the radio eliminates physical clues that help you determine what the speaker is saying.

- Practice speaking English where it is difficult to hear. If you have friends with whom you can practice speaking English, go to noisy places to do it, such as restaurants or nightclubs or even train stations.

VOICE EMPHASIS

When speaking to people face to face, visual clues help you understand not only the words they use, but also the meanings of the words. Facial expressions, hand gestures, and body posture can all help you understand what a person is saying. However, in the TOEFL CBT Listening section, you can't see the speaker, so you are forced to rely solely on vocal cues.

In spoken English, people place emphasis on certain words in a given sentence to convey additional meaning beyond the dictionary definitions of the words. The most common way to place emphasis on a word is raising or lowering the pitch or volume of one's voice. This will enable that word to stand out from the rest of the sentence. One of the things that vocal emphasis can tell you is which information in the sentence the speaker considers to be the most important.

What's important?

In the following sentence, every word is stressed equally.

Jane's red bag is on the table.

However, when emphasis is placed on specific words in the sentence, the intention of the speaker changes slightly.

Jane's red bag is on the table.

When the sentence is spoken with emphasis placed on the word *Jane's*, that word becomes the most important in the sentence. In other words, the primary goal of the speaker is to communicate the ownership of the bag. The person the speaker is talking to probably thought the bag belonged to someone else, and the speaker wants to clear up the misunderstanding.

Jane's **red** bag is on the table.

When the emphasis is on *red*, the color of the bag is what's important. The other person likely thought that a different bag was being discussed, probably of another color.

Jane's red **bag** is on the table.

Now the emphasis is on the actual item. The other person may have thought that something else belonging to Jane was on the table, such as a red book or a red sweater.

Jane's red bag **is** on the table.

The emphasis is on *where*. The other person may have just said, implied, or thought that the bag was not on the table.

Jane's red bag is **on** the table.

The speaker wants to make clear that the bag is on—not under, next to, in front of, or behind—the table. The other person probably misunderstood the location of the bag.

Jane's red bag is on the **table**.

Again, the speaker clarifies the location of the bag for the other person. In this case the other person was probably confused about *what* the bag was on. He or she might have thought that the bag was on something else, such as the cabinet, the stairs, or the bed.

Voice Emphasis Drill

Directions: For the following drill, play the recording that came with this book. You will hear the sentences printed below read with emphasis on different words. For each sentence, circle the word or words that were stressed; then, on the line below the sentence, jot down a couple of words to express the implied meaning of what the speaker said. (You will have about ten seconds to do this, so don't worry about writing complete sentences). If the drill moves too quickly for you, you also have the option of pausing the disk between sentences. When you're done, check your answers on page 47–48.

1. Louis always recycles his newspapers.

   _____

2. Louis always recycles his newspapers.

   _____

3. Louis always recycles his newspapers.

   _____

4. Louis always recycles his newspapers.

   _____

5. Louis always recycles his newspapers.

   _____

6. Diane will arrive at three o'clock on Tuesday.

   _____

7. Diane will arrive at three o'clock on Tuesday.

    _____

8. Diane will arrive at three o'clock on Tuesday.

    _____

9. Diane will arrive at three o'clock on Tuesday.

    _____

10. Diane will arrive at three o'clock on Tuesday.

    _____

11. What do you want?

    _____

12. What do you want?

    _____

13. What do you want?

    _____

14. This test is pretty easy.

    _____

15. This test is pretty easy.

    _____

16. This test is pretty easy.

    _____

17. This test is pretty easy.

    _____

What's Understood?

In spoken English, it's sometimes acceptable to speak in ways that violate the rules of written grammar. One of the most common violations is speaking in incomplete sentences. This is possible because one speaker can use the context supplied by the other speaker, without having to repeat it.

There's an elephant at our front door.

What's at our front door?

An *elephant!*

It's *where?*

At the *front door!*

At *whose* front door?

Ours!

If you looked at any of these "sentences" by themselves, they wouldn't make any sense, but since you know what the first speaker said, the meaning is clear.

What's Implied?

Many words in English take on additional meaning when spoken aloud. You can often recognize these constructions because if you took their meaning literally, the sentence wouldn't seem to mean anything. Many of these expressions use exaggeration or sarcasm to make the point.

You **could** help me with the dishes.

The speaker doesn't mean that the other person "has the ability" to help with the dishes. The emphasis on *could* carries with it the implication that the speaker believes the other person *should* help with the dishes. The speaker is being sarcastic. The other person would probably respond by apologizing and would immediately start to help.

You can say **that** again.

Again, the speaker uses a form of *can*, but not in the sense "have the ability to." That meaning would make the sentence illogical. Here the meaning of the sentence is that the speaker agrees strongly.

It **can't** be eleven o'clock already!

Another use for *can*. The speaker doesn't mean that it's impossible for it to be eleven o'clock. Rather, the speaker knows it is eleven o'clock and is very surprised by how quickly time has passed. Depending on the context, the speaker is either happily or unhappily surprised by the time.

Do you need a little help?

*Help? I need a **miracle**!*

Are you hungry?

*Hungry? I'm **starving**!*

In each case, the person answering the question uses exaggeration to mean: Yes, I certainly do! or I certainly am . . . but much more than you can imagine!

EMPHASIZED EXPRESSIONS

Following are some expressions you might find on the TOEFL CBT that have special meanings *only when they are emphasized.*

We'll be lucky if . . .

We'll be lucky if we get there by the year 2000!

This means: We're encountering so many obstacles that whatever we're doing may take a very long time.

You'll be lucky if you get out of here alive!

He'll be lucky if he has two cents left to his name.

We might as well . . .

We might as well be in Timbuktu.

This means that we are in such a remote place, it's as if we were many miles away in Timbuktu.

We might as well walk to New York from Kansas!

This means that our means of transportation is so bad that it would be the same if we walked an impossibly long distance. This statement makes clear it is an impractical scheme.

Only . . .

The word "only," when emphasized, answers the question, "Yes," "Of course," or "Yes, a lot!"

Did you have fun at the dance?
I *only* danced my feet off!

Did you really want to spend time with me?
I *only* drove a whole hour to see you!

Does Sam know anything about American politics?
He's *only* read everything that's ever been published about it!

If only . . .

If only means "I really wish."

If only I had known before now!

If only I had a million dollars!

Did/was/is

When the second speaker emphasizes the auxiliaries *did, was,* or *is* in response to the first speaker, the second speaker is expressing surprise.

I just got home from the concert.
So you *did* go.

David really enjoys his new car.
So he *did* buy a new one.

Professor Weiner really helped me with those math problems.
Oh, so he *did* help you.

Don't you love Michael's new musical arrangements?
So, those *are* his arrangements.

Did you see Andrew and his new girlfriend at the hockey game?
So, they *were* there.

We all noticed that you weren't in class on Monday.
So, it *wasn't* cancelled.

Can always . . .

The speaker uses *can always* to remind you that you still have another alternative.

If you don't like the party, you *can always* go home.

You *can always* change your mind.

Can't . . .

Can't is emphasized to indicate the speaker's surprise in a particular situation. The speaker means: I know that it *is* true, but I can't believe it!

It *can't* be eight o'clock already!

This *can't* be my last dollar!

That *can't* be our bus pulling out of the station!

CLICHÉS

All of the following are clichés (a phrase or expression that has become overly familiar or commonplace) that appear on the TOEFL CBT and are used to express simple ideas. We've grouped them by meaning in order to make them easier to learn.

I don't know.

I couldn't tell you.

I wouldn't know.

I haven't the vaguest.

I haven't the foggiest.

I haven't any idea.

Who knows?

It's a mystery to me.

Don't look at me.

Don't ask me.

It's over my head.

You got me.

Beats me.

Don't do it!

I wouldn't if I were you.

Oh no you don't!

Cut it out!

Not here you don't.

Better leave well enough alone.

Forget it!

Don't bother.

You can't be too careful.

Question/Suggestion

How about . . . ?

Why not . . . ?

What about . . . ?

What would you say to . . . ?

What do you think about . . . ?

Would you mind if . . . ?

Shouldn't you . . . ?

Agreement

To say the least.

That's putting it mildly.

You can say that again.

That's for sure.

Don't I know it.

Now, that's an idea.

There you go!

Now you've said something (. . . I agree with, whereas you didn't before.)

I'll say.

I couldn't agree with you more.

Count me in.

Why not!

Do I ever!

You bet!

Disagreement

I doubt it.

Probably not.

Not likely.

I wouldn't say that.

Don't bet on it.

Don't count on it.

Don't be too sure.

I don't think so.

No way.

Never.

Not in a million years.

Thank you!

Thanks!

I appreciate it.

Thanks a lot.

I don't know how to thank you.

You're a lifesaver.

I'll never be able to repay you.

I'm grateful.

You're welcome!

It's the least I can do.

Forget it.

Don't mention it.

Never mind.

It doesn't matter.

No problem.

What did you say?

Pardon me?

Excuse me?

Sorry?

What?

Surprise/Disbelief

Isn't that something!

I can't believe that . . .

My goodness!

How about that!

It/He/She's too good to be true!

We made it!

You're kidding!

You're joking!

Come on!

It can't be!

Who says?

To think I . . . !

No! You don't say!

Homonyms

Another trap you need to know about when listening is homonyms—words that are spelled differently, but sound alike. These are used to fool you. Write a short sentence or phrase after each one to familiarize yourself with the differences. Because your sentences will vary, ask an English speaker to check them for you to make sure that you got them right.

This is by no means a complete list. We have not included every definition for each word—just the most common definition. Keep a list of any homonyms you miss when studying and see if you can keep them straight in the future.

new: not used. "I bought this *new* dress today with the money I earned."

Your sentence _____

knew: past tense of know. "I *knew* that you were going to show up at the party!"

Your sentence _____

flower: daisy, tulip, rose. "I love to grow *flowers* in my garden."

Your sentence_____

flour: ingredient in baking. "I need two cups of *flour* for the cake."

Your sentence _____

sew: use a needle and thread. "I want to *sew* the rip on these jeans."

Your sentence_____

so: who cares? "*So* what? I really have no interest in what you are saying."

Your sentence_____

won: defeated an opponent. "We *won* the game by 2 to 1."

Your sentence_____

one: the number 1, or alone. "There is only *one* girl on the softball team."

Your sentence_____

plain: simple, unadorned. "This dress is too *plain*—there are no designs on it."

Your sentence _____

plane: airplane, for flying. "We flew to Europe in that new *plane*."

Your sentence _____

sea: ocean. "We swam in the *sea* today."

Your sentence _____

see: to view, use your eyes. "I *see* that you are wearing the sweater I gave you for your birthday."

Your sentence _____

wood: material from a tree. "The furniture is made out of *wood*."

Your sentence _____

would: subjunctive or conditional mood of "will". "I *would* like a new table."

Your sentence _____

hour: a sixty-minute time period. "This class is one *hour* long."

Your sentence _____

our: possessive form of we. "We like *our* new teacher."

Your sentence _____

red: the color. "Stop at a *red* light."

Your sentence _____

read: finished reading. "I *read* a whole book last night."

Your sentence _____

wait: to pause, stop. "*Wait* for me—I'll be right there."

Your sentence _____

weight: heaviness. "The *weight* of this package is three pounds."

Your sentence _____

maid: someone who cleans. "The *maid* will clean your room."

Your sentence _____

made: past tense of *make*. "I *made* the bed myself."

Your sentence _____

way: direction. "Which *way* should we go?"

Your sentence _____

weigh: to figure out how heavy something is… "Did you *weigh* these vegetables?"

Your sentence _____

hole: an empty space. "Last week, I dug a big *hole* to plant those seeds."

Your sentence _____

whole: entire ."He ate the *whole* pie before anyone else could even have a piece."

Your sentence _____

by: near "Her house is by the shopping mall."

Your sentence _____

buy: to purchase. "I want to *buy* a new car."

Your sentence _____

sail: on a boat. "The *sail* catches wind and pushes the boat."

Your sentence _____

sale: a discount, bargain. "I bought this coat on *sale* and saved a lot of money."

Your sentence _____

sense: as in common sense. "That advice makes good *sense*."

Your sentence _____

cents: pennies, money. "The phone call cost twenty-five *cents*."

Your sentence _____

reflex: unconscious movement. "I pulled my hand out of the water in a *reflex*."

Your sentence _____

reflects: casts back an image. "The lake *reflects* the trees perfectly."

Your sentence _____

soul: spirit. "The Buddhists believe the *soul* is reincarnated."

Your sentence _____

sole: only. "He was the *sole* survivor of the train accident."

Your sentence _____

son: male child. "She has one *son* and two daughters."

Your sentence _____

sun: the earth revolves around it. "The *sun* is very hot today!"

Your sentence _____

I: me, myself. "*I* am taking a vacation next month."

Your sentence _____

eye: what you see with. "My *eyes* are bothered by cigarette smoke."

Your sentence _____

banned: not allowed "Short skirts are *banned* at her school."

Your sentence _____

band: a music group. "The *band* at the party played only the most popular songs."

Your sentence _____

hire: to employ someone. "I need to *hire* a tutor to help me with my studies."

Your sentence _____

higher: more elevated. "Put the books on a *higher* shelf."

Your sentence _____

worn: past tense of *wear*. "Have you *worn* those shoes yet?"

Your sentence _____

warn: to caution. "I *warn* you—he's a tough teacher."

Your sentence _____

jeans: denim pants. "Levi's are my favorite *jeans*."

Your sentence _____

genes: units of inheritance. "He inherited blue eyes from his mother's *genes*."

Your sentence _____

cell: the smallest unit of living matter. "The amoeba consists of a single *cell*."

Your sentence _____

sell: to make a sale. "I want to *sell* this old car and buy a new one."

Your sentence _____

pale: light in color. "Jane is *pale*—she hasn't been to the beach."

Your sentence _____

pail: a container. "She carried two *pails* of milk from the barn."

Your sentence _____

tale: story. "That was some *tale* Jack told us."

Your sentence _____

tail: at the end of an animal. "Don't pull the cat's *tail*!"

Your sentence _____

scene: where something takes place. "That *scene* in the movie was filmed in New York City."

Your sentence _____

seen: past tense of *see*. "I've *seen* that movie three times!"

Your sentence _____

fair: festival, carnival. "The town *fair* is held every summer."

Your sentence _____

fare: cost. "The round trip *fare* by airplane is $200."

Your sentence _____

here: this place. "Come *here* right now!"

Your sentence _____

hear: listen. "Did you *hear* what I said?"

Your sentence _____

principal: the head of a school. "*Principal* Jones supervises the whole school."

Your sentence _____

principle: belief. "Stand by your *principles*."

Your sentence _____

weather: what it's like outside. "The *weather* report calls for rain."

Your sentence _____

whether: if. "I need to know *whether* you will go."

Your sentence _____

die: to become dead or expire. "The man will likely *die* from his severe injuries."

Your sentence _____

dye: used to color things. "What *dye* did you use to get that interesting purple color?"

Your sentence _____

Idioms

Idioms are words or phrases that do not translate literally. For example, "break down" may not mean to break something in a downward motion, but to lose control. Many different idioms are tested on the TOEFL CBT, in both the Listening section and in the Reading section. Start studying idioms now—make a list of those you have trouble with and practice using them.

Of course, nothing beats practicing conversation with native English speakers—it's the easiest and most natural way to learn English idioms. But for now, we've divided the list of the most commonly tested idioms into three sections. Work on a section at a time and test yourself on each set after you've finished going over them.

Section 1

break down—a collapse of physical and/or mental health; failing to work:

> When she heard that her pet iguana had escaped, Mary Lou *broke down* and cried in front of the whole class.

> After their car *broke down*, Marty and James had to walk five miles to the nearest service station.

break in—to enter forcibly; with an item of clothing, it can mean to wear in and make comfortable:

> The thief *broke into* the museum and stole all the artwork.

> I finally *broke in* those shoes—but not before they gave me some terrible blisters.

breakthrough—a sudden achievement:

> The new vaccine represented a significant *breakthrough* in the battle against the virus.

break up—to separate or collapse; to divide and disperse:

> In 1969, the Beatles officially *broke up* after playing together as a band for more than a decade.

clear away—to free from something:

> When all this trouble *clears away*, he'll be able to go back to school.

> If you *clear away* the dishes, I'll wash them.

clear out—to leave a place, usually quickly:

> The fire marshal ordered the people to *clear out* of their homes due to the possibility that the brush fires would spread.

come about—to happen:

> The train wreck *came about* as a result of the engineer's negligence.

come across—to find or meet by chance:

> We *came across* my grandmother's old diary while cleaning out the attic.

come down with—to get sick:

> When she *came down with* a terrible case of laryngitis, Kathy Lou Kelly wasn't able to perform at the benefit concert.

come up with—to produce something or have an idea:

> It was Juan who *came up with* the scheme to trick Mrs. Huxtable.

come from—to derive or originate from:

> The English language *comes from* many sources, such as Greek and Latin.

come of—result from:

"Nothing good will *come of* that sort of behavior," my mother always said.

come out—to disclose:

The news finally *came out*—cholesterol is not as bad for you as scientists originally believed.

come through with—to succeed in doing:

The union finally *came through with* an offer to negotiate rather than strike.

come to—to regain consciousness; add up to:

After Dorothy *came to*, she saw that she was in her own bed in Kansas.

That dress and those shoes will *come to* about $100 dollars.

come to terms with—to understand or absorb mentally:

She had trouble *coming to terms with* her dog's death—it seemed so sudden.

do without—to get along without:

During the drought, residents had to *do without* long, luxurious showers.

drop in/drop by—to visit casually and sometimes unexpectedly:

After the movie, we'll *drop in* and see if Margie is home.

On your way to the dorm, *drop by* the library to see if the book is on reserve.

fall back on—to turn to for help:

Fortunately for John, after he lost all his spending money, he had some savings to *fall back on*.

fall behind—to fail to keep up with:

Mark had *fallen behind* so badly in his studies, it seemed he'd never be able to finish all his work and pass his courses.

fall for—be taken in by; duped:

I can't believe that John *fell for* that trick—it was so obvious.

fill in—to substitute for:

Mary Jones will *fill in* for Patty Smith during the race, as Patty is too ill to come today.

fit in—to make time for; to conform:

The doctor will *fit you in* at about 3 o'clock for an appointment with her.

Teenagers often try to *fit in* with their friends by wearing the same style clothes and listening to the same music.

give away—make a gift of:

> The store was *giving away* a new scarf with every purchase in order to bring in more customers.

give in—to surrender:

> In Hesse's *Siddhartha*, the main character's father finally *gives in* and allows his son to leave home.

give up—to stop; to yield to; to part with:

> I finally *gave up* smoking after years of hearing all the health warnings.

> Nellie wouldn't sign the legal papers yet—she wasn't sure if she wanted to *give up* her right to a trial.

go along with—to agree to:

> The president would *go along with* the decision to hire more people if the department could bring in more revenue.

go down—when referring to food this means it can be swallowed and digested:

> Ice cream was the only food that would *go down* easily after her operation.

go far—to succeed:

> Laura would *go far* with her hard work and intelligence.

go on—to proceed with; to happen;

> "I don't want to *go on* a diet again in my lifetime!" exclaimed Bob.

> The speaker *went on* for almost three hours before stopping.

go through with—to do:

> Few people thought that the mayor would *go through with* his plans to close all the city's homeless shelters.

go under—to fail:

> Due to the poor economy, ten businesses have *gone under* in our town in the last year.

go up—be erected:

> The building *went up* in a few months and soon there were tenants in the apartments.

hang on—to hold on to; to wait or persevere:

> Indiana Jones managed to grab onto the cliff and *hang on* for dear life.

> The receptionist told me to *hang on* while she consulted her appointment book.

hang around—to loiter:

> On a hot summer day, the kids like to just *hang around* at the beach.

hang up—to end a telephone conversation by putting the receiver down:

Police tell you to just *hang up* if you get an obscene phone call.

heat up—to increase in pressure:

The debate *heated up* significantly when Congressman Smithers mentioned plans for rezoning in the area.

Idiom Drill—Section 1

Directions: Choose the answer choice that best answers each question. Then check your answers on pages 48–49.

1. (Woman) I heard that the award ceremony was wonderful.

   (Man) Yes, John broke down when he won the humanitarian award.

   What does the man mean?
   - (A) John's award was broken.
   - (B) John got emotional when he won.
   - (C) John only received one award.
   - (D) The award was humanitarian.

2. (Man) Will you help me clean the kitchen?

   (Woman) Sure. You clear away the dishes and I'll wash the pots.

   What does the woman want the man to do?
   - (A) Wipe off the dishes.
   - (B) Take the dishes off the table.
   - (C) Take the pots away.
   - (D) Put the dishes away.

3. (Man) It's so sad that Harvey isn't feeling well.

   (Woman) What a bad time for him to come down with chicken pox!

   What does the woman mean?
   - (A) Harvey was coming over with chicken.
   - (B) Harvey has chicken pox.
   - (C) Harvey fell down.
   - (D) Harvey is having a bad time.

4. (Woman) When did that new movie house open?

   (Man) I don't know—it seems like it went up in a week!

   What does the man suggest?

   (A) The movie house was built quickly.
   (B) The movie house is very tall.
   (C) He doesn't understand the woman's question.
   (D) It opened a week ago.

5. (Woman) Have you heard about the principal's new plan to make the school day longer?

   (Man) She'll never go through with it!

   What does the man mean?

   (A) He likes the principal's plan.
   (B) The principal went through the school.
   (C) Her plan is possible.
   (D) The principal will not carry out her plan.

6. (Man) How long have you been working on that paper?
   (Woman) Three hours—I give up!

   What does the woman want to do?

   (A) Give the man the paper.
   (B) Stop working on the paper.
   (C) Throw the paper up in the air.
   (D) Work longer.

7. (Man) Did you see John's new haircut?

   (Woman) I don't know if that crazy style will fit in with his conservative friends.

   What does the woman suggest?

   (A) John's haircut is not like any of his friends' haircuts.
   (B) John's hair won't fit his head.
   (C) John's friends are too conservative.
   (D) She hasn't seen John's haircut.

8. (Woman) What time do you want to wake up?

   (Man) Well, I'll set the alarm to go off at eight in the morning.

   What does the man want to do?

   (A) Put off the alarm.
   (B) Eat in the morning.
   (C) Wake up at eight in the morning.
   (D) Get a new alarm.

9. (Man) Did you hear about that new vaccine?

   (Woman) What a breakthrough for people with that sickness!

   What does the woman mean?

   (A) It's good news for people with that sickness.
   (B) People with that sickness will get sicker.
   (C) The vaccine is broken.
   (D) Scientists are not through with their study.

10. (Man) What do you want to do today?

    (Woman) It's hot outside, let's just hang around.

    What does the woman suggest?

    (A) That they do nothing.
    (B) That they go home.
    (C) That they walk around.
    (D) That they hang pictures.

Section 2

keep in touch with—to stay in communication with:

Please *keep in touch with* us after you move to France.

kill off—to put to death:

The use of that pesticide will *kill off* ants as well as fleas.

lay aside—to give up or set aside:

The mayor warned the students to *lay aside* their angry feelings toward the rival school on the day of the big soccer game.

Jan *laid aside* some money for just such an emergency.

lay off—to terminate someone's employment:

The Brindley Corporation had to *lay off* ten percent of its employees due to decreased sales.

laid up—sick in bed or out of the action:

Mr. Rodriquez was *laid up* for several weeks with a terrible flu.

leave out—to omit:

"Don't *leave out* Aunt Mary from the wedding invitations!"

leave up to— to allow to decide:

"I'll *leave* your punishment *up to* you to decide," Principal Skinner told the kids.

live up to— to fulfill:

We expect that Jim will *live up to* our plans to become the first member of the family to attend college.

live down—to bear the embarrassment:

He'll never *live down* the shame of forgetting all his lines in the class play.

move on—to go in another direction:

"It's time for you to *move on*," Susan told her friend, who wanted to quit her job as an editor.

off limits—restricted:

That area is *off limits* to cars, due to efforts in our community to cut down on pollution.

on the mark—exactly right:

"Boy, were you *on the mark* about Irene—you were the only one who thought that she'd play so well in that concert."

overkill—excess:

You really didn't need to prepare fifteen pages for that report—it really was *overkill*.

over with—finished:

I was so relieved to be *over* with the TOEFL after six months of study.

pass by—to overlook:

Marie was upset that the committee *passed* her *by* and chose a different finalist.

pass through—to go through:

To get to New England by car from that town, it is necessary to *pass through* New York.

pass up—to refuse:

> We couldn't believe that Jose would *pass up* an opportunity to travel all around the country for free.

pour in—to arrive in a large amount:

> Cards and letters came *pouring in* to offer help and money after the news report about that young girl's need for an operation.

pull out—to take out:

> The United States *pulled* its last troops *out* of Vietnam in 1973, although soldiers had been leaving for years.

pull off—to do something in spite of problems:

> Jake could hardly believe that Amanda could *pull off* that deal after she'd made such a big mistake.

pushover—someone who is easily taken advantage of:

> That Mrs. Jones is a real *pushover*—she always lets you hand in papers late if you ask.

put down—to insult; to suppress:

> I can't believe the way John *puts down* his mother when she's standing right there.

> The leaders *put down* a rebellion in their country by appeasing the different groups.

put up—to allow or go along with:

> Mr. Smith doesn't *put up* with any troublemakers in his class—they are immediately punished.

run by—to tell someone about:

> Maria asked her accountant to *run* those figures *by* her one more time before she signed the contract.

send back—to return:

> President Clinton vetoed the bill and *sent* it *back* to Congress for changes.

Idiom Drill—Section 2

Directions: Match the idiom with its definition. Then check your answers on page 49.

1.	pushover	a)	to refuse
2.	pull off	b)	to overlook
3.	pass up	c)	to bear an embarrassment
4.	pass by	d)	to do in spite of problems
5.	over with	e)	to terminate someone's employment
6.	off limits	f)	to stay in communication with
7.	live down	g)	restricted
8.	laid up	h)	someone easily taken advantage of
9.	lay off	i)	sick in bed
10.	keep in touch with	j)	finished

Section 3

sign in—to sign your name to enter a place:

Visitors must *sign in* at the front desk before going into the main auditorium.

speak out—to state publicly:

Jones was afraid to *speak out* when he saw his boss stealing supplies—he didn't want to get in trouble.

speak up—to speak more loudly; to state publicly:

"Please *speak up*—the rest of the group cannot hear you," Ms. Montgomery told Peter.

Activists argue that we all have the responsibility to *speak up* wherever we see injustice, or no change will ever take place.

speed up—to increase one's speed:

I have been practicing my reading comprehension with the hope that I will *speed up* and finish more passages in the time allotted.

step in—to intervene:

The Town Board was forced to *step in* and put a stop to the development in the area when it was judged to be unsafe.

stick to—to persist:

"*Stick to* your morals and you'll do a good job," my grandfather always advised.

stick around—to stay:

I think I'll *stick around*—there's no reason to head home yet.

stop by—to make a brief visit:

Could you *stop by* the grocery store on your way home from work and pick up a loaf of bread?

stop up—to clog or prevent from moving:

The grease and hair *stopped up* the sink and Jan had to call a plumber to fix it.

Traffic was *stopped up* for miles due to that horrible five-car accident.

think better of—to change your mind:

Mark had considered dropping out of school to work, but a discussion with his parents made him *think better of* it, and he decided to stay in school.

think nothing of—to do without care:

Some people in that town *think nothing of* throwing all their garbage into the river—don't they know the long-term effects?

think over—to consider:

Every time Steven writes a paper he has to *think over* his topic for a few days before he even begins to write.

think through—to consider all the effects:

"You obviously did not *think through* what would happen to you if you pulled that fire alarm," Principal Skinner told Marie.

tied up—busy; unavailable for use:

Mr. Jones cannot come to the meeting this afternoon—he'll be *tied up* downtown until 7:00 p.m.

Since most of their money was *tied up* in long-term investments, Jan and Mark couldn't spend any of it.

turn down—to refuse; to lower:

The Smiths were *turned down* for a loan because of their poor credit history.

The volume on the speakers was *turned down* because it was so late at night.

turnoff—something that disgusts a person:

"Guys who only talk about themselves are such a *turnoff!*" the magazine article proclaimed.

turn over—transfer:

By law, attorneys must *turn over* evidence to the court so that both sides may have a chance to review it.

turn to—to go to for guidance or inspiration:

Many teenagers *turn to* their friends and family to help them decide where to attend college.

turn up—to find or uncover:

It's always a good idea to browse the shelves in a library when you are doing a research paper—you never know what you may *turn up*.

up against—confronted with:

In spite of being *up against* strong opposition from the larger British forces, the United States won the Revolutionary War.

up to date—current:

Her clothes are always so stylish and *up to date*—she must read all the fashion magazines.

wake up—to rouse from sleep or inactivity:

The young Americans of the 1960s sent a *wake up* call to the country to get involved and work for change.

Young children may *wake up* at any time in the middle of the night.

Idiom Drill—Section 3

Directions: Choose the answer choice that best completes the sentence. Then check your answers on page 49.

1. "Pick one topic and _____ it throughout your term paper."

   (A) stick around
   (B) step on one's toes in
   (C) stick to
   (D) pull out of

2. "I'm in a real rush now, but _____ later and I'll have more time to talk."

   (A) stop by
   (B) drop out
   (C) turn over
   (D) turn off

3. Jane was _____ with work and couldn't be here.

   (A) up to date
   (B) tied up
   (C) filled up
   (D) touched up

4. Smitty felt that people who were rude were a real _____.

   (A) turnoff
   (B) turn down
   (C) turn over
   (D) stop up

5. Patty always sets her alarm so that she can _____ at 8:00 a.m.

   (A) think over
   (B) write down
   (C) think through
   (D) wake up

6. The beginning of the second book brings the reader _____ with what happened in the first book.

   (A) up over
   (B) up to date
   (C) up against
   (D) think over

7. At our school no one would even think to _____ against the administration for fear of getting in trouble.

   (A) step in
   (B) sign in
   (C) speak out
   (D) step up

8. Always a quiet boy, John was too shy to _____ in class.

   (A) speed up
   (B) step down
   (C) speak up
   (D) step in

9. "Why don't you _____; I'm sure that Mr. Smith will be here any second."

(A) step up
(B) sign in
(C) stick around
(D) think better of

10. Americans _____ being able to buy anything they want in a large convenience store; in other countries, it is not always so easy.

(A) think over
(B) think through
(C) think better of
(D) think nothing of

ANSWERS TO DRILLS

Voice Emphasis Drill

1. *Louis*—The other person thought that someone else recycles his or her newspapers.

2. *always*—The other person implied that Louis hadn't recycled them at some time in the recent past; the speaker is surprised.

3. *recycles*—The other person thought that Louis did something else with his newspapers.

4. *his*—The other person thought that Louis recycled someone else's newspapers.

5. *newspapers*—The other person thought that Louis recycled something else.

6. *Diane*—The other person thought that someone else was coming.

7. *will*—The other person thought or implied that Diane wasn't coming.

8. *arrive*—The other person thought that Diane would be doing something else at three o'clock—leaving, for example.

9. *three o'clock*—The other person thought that Diane would arrive at a different time.

10. *Tuesday*—The other person thought that Diane would arrive on a different day.

11. *what*—The other person asked for something unusual or something which the speaker didn't understand.

12. *you*—The other person was talking about what someone else wanted, which is not what the speaker is interested in.

13. *want*—The other person was talking about what they have to do, or what they don't want, or something else entirely.

14. *this*—The speaker wants to make it clear that while this test may be easy, she finds other tests difficult.

15. *is*—The speaker anticipated a difficult test and therefore is surprised that it turned out to be so easy.

16. *pretty*—The speaker doesn't believe that the test is as easy as the other person implied.

17. *easy*—The speaker is disagreeing with the other person who found the test more difficult than the speaker did.

Idiom Drill—Section 1

1. B

2. B

3. B

4. A

5. D

6. B

7. A

8. C

9. A

10. A

Idiom Drill — Section 2

1. H

2. D

3. A

4. B

5. J

6. G

7. C

8. I

9. E

10. F

Idiom Drill — Section 3

1. C

2. A

3. B

4. A

5. D

6. B

7. C

8. C

9. C

10. D

3

Part A—Short Conversations

THE BASICS

In Part A of the TOEFL CBT Listening section, your task is to listen to short conversations, and answer a question based on what is either stated or implied. The conversations will not be repeated. In other words, you have one chance to listen and remember.

> You will not see the four answer choices until after the short conversation is finished.

Unfortunately, because this section is computer adaptive, it is impossible to say exactly how many short conversations you will hear. There are approximately 11 to 17 questions in Part A. Once you have listened to each short conversation, you will be able to read the question asked about it. The questions appear at the top of the computer screen, just above the answer choices. You may also take as much time as you wish to answer each question. The 12-second interval found on the old paper-and-pencil test has been eliminated. (Note: Don't take *too* much time. Remember, the clock is running.)

TUTORIAL

Volume

Prior to beginning the Listening section, ETS will provide a tutorial introducing the new TOEFL CBT. Put on the headset provided by the Sylvan Learning Center to learn how to adjust the volume. Normally, the volume will be preset to an audible level. However, if you need to raise or lower the volume, do it right away. You do not want to waste valuable time adjusting the volume during the test.

Time

The time remaining is shown in the upper left-hand corner of the screen. You have the option of turning off the time by clicking on the Clock icon in the lower left corner of the screen. However, we strongly recommend that you leave the clock on. If you do turn off the clock, you will not be able to see how much time you have remaining and, consequently, will have difficulty pacing yourself. *Fortunately, the clock does not run while any of the conversations are being spoken.* The time displayed in the upper left-hand corner is the time remaining for you to answer the questions. The time *does* run if you click on the Help icon. However, once you finish this book, the Help icon will not be necessary.

> The time shown in the upper-left hand corner is the time remaining for you to answer the questions.

Directions

After the tutorial, the Listening section begins and the clock starts running. The first item to appear on the screen is the directions. You should learn the directions prior to the test so you don't waste valuable time reading them. When you click on the "Dismiss Directions" icon located on the right side of the screen, the directions will disappear and you will immediately be given the first question. The directions will look something like this:

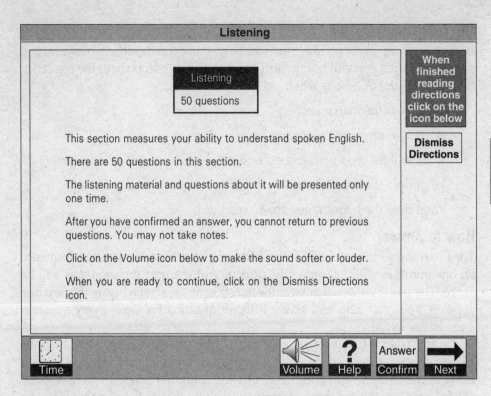

Listening

Listening

50 questions

This section measures your ability to understand spoken English.

There are 50 questions in this section.

The listening material and questions about it will be presented only one time.

After you have confirmed an answer, you cannot return to previous questions. You may not take notes.

Click on the Volume icon below to make the sound softer or louder.

When you are ready to continue, click on the Dismiss Directions icon.

When finished reading directions click on the icon below

Dismiss Directions

Time   Volume   Help   Answer Confirm   Next

Look to see how many questions you will have to answer!

After you see the general Listening section directions, the specific directions for the short conversations will appear. They look very similar to the general Listening section directions. Click on the "Dismiss Directions" icon to immediately begin the test. Do not waste your time reading the directions. The clock is running.

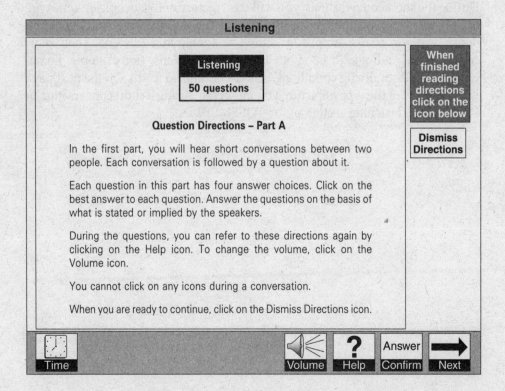

Listening

Listening

50 questions

Question Directions – Part A

In the first part, you will hear short conversations between two people. Each conversation is followed by a question about it.

Each question in this part has four answer choices. Click on the best answer to each question. Answer the questions on the basis of what is stated or implied by the speakers.

During the questions, you can refer to these directions again by clicking on the Help icon. To change the volume, click on the Volume icon.

You cannot click on any icons during a conversation.

When you are ready to continue, click on the Dismiss Directions icon.

When finished reading directions click on the icon below

Dismiss Directions

Time   Volume   Help   Answer Confirm   Next

Question Types

In Part A of the TOEFL CBT, you will hear short conversations between two people, and then you will hear a third person ask a question about the conversation. Most of the questions will be as follows:

What does the man mean?

What is inferred by the woman?

What will the man probably do next?

What does the woman say about . . . ?

What does the man suggest the woman do?

How to Answer

The Listening section of the TOEFL CBT is adaptive, meaning your performance on one question will determine the difficulty of the next question you will be asked. Therefore, you must answer the question on the screen before the next one appears. You can't skip and save a difficult question for later. Every question must be answered.

You can't skip a question.

On the TOEFL CBT you are able to read the question, along with the four answer choices. After clicking on the best answer, you then *must* click on the two icons in the bottom right hand corner of the computer screen. The first is the "Next" icon on the far right. After you click on "Next," you must click on "Answer Confirm." You may change you answer at any time *before* you click on "Answer Confirm." However, once you click on "Answer Confirm," you will never see that question again.

Pictures

During the short conversations, you will see a picture of two people in some type of university setting on the computer screen. The two students will be holding books, walking across campus, or sitting at a table in a cafeteria. Their short conversations will *always* be about academic situations, (for example, homework, a professor, living conditions, class rules, and so forth). On the next page is an example of the type of picture you might see during a short conversation in Part A of the Listening section of the TOEFL CBT.

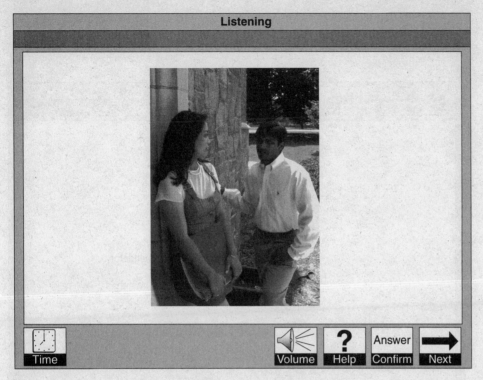

Time	Volume	Help	Answer Confirm	Next

Keep in mind, however, that the pictures ETS shows you in Part A of the Listening section serve only as "distractors." In some cases ETS will even use the same picture for different conversations. You do *not* need to look at the picture on the computer screen. Where the students are located, how they are dressed, what they are holding in their hands, and the color of their hair has absolutely *no* relevance to the question. The picture does not provide any visual information such as facial expressions, gestures, or emotional state that pertains to the upcoming question. Looking at the picture will not make answering the question any easier. In fact, it will make the question more difficult. Humans are much more visual than auditory; we are less inclined to listen if we can see. In other words, do *not* look at the picture. It will only divert your attention away from the conversation.

In the Listening section, the pictures are "distractors." Do not waste time looking at them.

After the short conversation is heard, the picture will disappear, and the question will appear along with the four answer choices. Look at the example below.

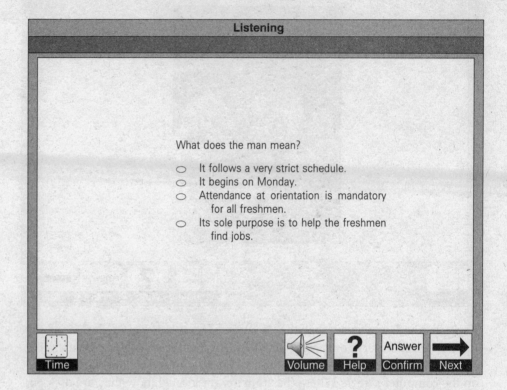

WHAT MAKES PART A SO DIFFICULT?

Probably the biggest disadvantage you will face in the Listening section is that you are unable to read the questions before you actually hear the conversation. Also, on most tests (and on the Reading section of the TOEFL CBT), if you come across a difficult question, you can skip it and come back to answer it later. That's usually a very good strategy. You've spent most of your life approaching questions this way, particularly in school, so it seems perfectly natural. What's not natural is the situation you'll find yourself in during the Listening section. First, you are shown an illogical picture of two strangers to represent the speakers of the short conversation you will hear, and then you'll hear (and read) the question. Be sure to listen to the conversation carefully; once it is finished, you'll never hear it again.

Say What?

Somewhere in the early part of the Listening section, you hear a statement that sounds something like this:

"Question number six. Hey, that's the blah over blah blah bee blah!"

In other words, you have no idea what the speaker said. Now, while you're trying to remember when in your English studies you ever heard *"blah blah bee"* (or was it *"bee blah blah"*?), you hear *". . . blah blah,* don't you think?"

You panic. You only heard part of what the speakers said and now you have just a few words to base your answer choice on.

No Context

The short conversations that ETS gives you in Part A of the TOEFL CBT do not accurately depict real conversations. As we've already pointed out, in real, face-to-face conversations you rely on many visual factors, such as facial expressions and hand gestures, to help you understand what the other person is saying. Also, knowing something about the person or the topic gives additional meaning to the words used. Furthermore, if he or she uses some words or expressions that you're not familiar with, you can use the context of the rest of the conversation to help figure out what they mean.

All of these cues are absent in Part A of the TOEFL CBT Listening section. The largest hurdle to get over in order to do well on this section is the lack of context. For the questions in Part A, the information presented is completely isolated. The questions can be about anything. However, there is some good news. The questions you will be asked are almost always about what the *second* speaker means, what he will do, or what he infers. Luckily for you, you can rely on what the first speaker says to help orient yourself as to what the main idea of the conversation will be about. Then listen closely to what the second speaker says to help you answer the upcoming question.

The Good News

Although there are some problems with the TOEFL CBT, one of the test's weaknesses can make your job much easier. To help you understand how this works, we're going to explain some of the reasons why the TOEFL CBT is constructed the way it is.

Most tests you take in school are not multiple choice. The primary reason for this is that teachers don't like them. Teachers don't like multiple-choice tests because they don't do what tests are supposed to do: Provide some meaningful indication of how much a student has learned. Here's why. Complete the following sentence.

> When I haven't had time to prepare for an exam, I would have the best luck if my teacher asked me to
> - ○ write an essay
> - ○ answer questions orally
> - ○ write short answers to pointed questions
> - ○ choose the best answer from among four options

Most people would pick "Choose the best from among four options." Why? Because on a multiple-choice test you don't necessarily have to *know* the right answer; you can eliminate some answer choices, and then guess! Remember that the correct answer is *always* in front of you on the computer screen.

On multiple-choice tests, the answer is always in front of you!

ETS's Dilemma

Let's say that two people are taking the TOEFL CBT. One of them speaks English almost fluently. The other hardly speaks English at all. The one who hardly speaks English has a lot of trouble understanding the words on the recording and hears something like this:

Question number 12.

(woman) Will Mary blah bee blah blah Sunday?

(man) Sunday blah bee blah Mary's blah blah.

(narrator) What does the man mean?

Now look at the answer choices. Remember, the only words this person understood were *Sunday* and *Mary*.

- ○ School is in session nine months out of the year.
- ○ Hats are not usually worn during dinner.
- ○ Mary rarely works on Sunday.
- ○ The operation was very expensive.

So which answer would he choose? "Mary rarely works on Sunday" of course, because it contains the words he recognized from the question. "Mary rarely works on Sunday" is also the right answer, so this person who hardly understands English just answered the question correctly.

This presents ETS with a problem. Of course the person whose English is very good is also going to answer the question correctly. He will understand the question word for word. According to this particular question, both test takers now have the same level of English proficiency. If this happens on too many questions, it is a disaster for ETS. It means the test is a failure.

ETS had to come up with a way to keep people from guessing correctly on too many of its questions. Now look at the same question with different answer choices:

Question number 12.

(woman) Will Mary blah bee blah blah Sunday?

(man) Sunday blah bee blah Mary's blah blah.

(narrator) What does the man mean?

- ○ Sunday is a day Mary often works.
- ○ Mary rarely works on Sunday.
- ○ Some days Mary's work is awful.
- ○ Mary has had a terrible cough since Sunday.

Would you be able to tell which is the right answer? Probably not. Now, most of the answer choices contain those same two words that you could hear in the statement, so it would be hard to choose among them. Although the statement remained the same, this question just became much harder. Nothing has changed but the answer choices.

The first example was much too easy to have ever appeared on an actual TOEFL CBT. Too many people would correctly guess the answer. To fix this, ETS had to change the answer choices so that the wrong answers don't seem so wrong. In fact, ETS tries to make the wrong answers sometimes look *better* than the right answers. In other words, ETS creates "distractors" to divert your attention from the correct answer. Let's look at how they do it.

A Brief Lesson In Question Writing

First ETS comes up with the short conversation:

> (woman) Will Mary be in on Sunday?
>
> (man) Sunday is usually Mary's day off.
>
> (narrator) What does the man mean?

and the right answer:

> ⬭ Mary rarely works on Sunday.

Now comes the hard part for ETS. It has to come up with three wrong "distractors" that don't *seem* wrong. On many questions, ETS will phrase an answer choice so that it's very close to the right answer but means just the opposite:

> ⬭ Sunday is a day Mary often works.

This wrong answer will attract thousands of test takers who *almost* understood the stem. If you ever see two answer choices that are opposites, chances are, one of them is the correct. Make your best guess and click on it!

Eliminate the opposite answer choice.

ETS will also include answer choices that contain some of the same sounds and words as the stem:

> ⬭ Some days Mary's work is awful.
> ⬭ Mary has had a terrible cough since Sunday.

Some days sounds like *Sunday*; and *awful* and *cough* sound like *off*. These answers will attract those who were able to pick out the sounds of the statement, but didn't understand the sense of it. If answer choices contain these types of "sound-alikes" you can bet they are wrong.

Eliminate the "sound alikes."

But here's the good news. Take a look at what has happened to the answer choices.

- ○ Sunday is a day Mary often works.
- ○ Mary rarely works on Sunday.
- ○ Some days Mary's work is awful.
- ○ Mary has had a terrible cough since Sunday.

Three out of four of them are about the same topic: Sunday. They have to be, or else it would be too easy for you to guess.

QUESTION TOPICS

In Part A of the TOEFL CBT, question types can be put into one of four main categories. The question types below are listed in order of frequency:

- ◆ Meaning questions
- ◆ Infer/imply questions
- ◆ Action questions
- ◆ Detail questions

Remember, you can take as long as you want to answer the questions (but don't take too long). The 12-second interval of the paper-and-pencil test has been eliminated.

1. Meaning Questions

There is basically one type of meaning question:

What does the man/woman mean?

These questions are easy to identify because they contain the word *mean*. Meaning questions always refer to what the *second* speaker has said. The first speaker sets up the conversation with a direct/indirect question or a general statement to which the second speaker responds. The second speaker most likely will use an idiomatic expression, or just simply respond to what the first speaker has asked or stated. In any event, the second speaker holds the answer to the question ETS presents. For example:

Meaning questions contain the word *mean*.

(woman) Have you heard about the new periodical wing that the administration wants to add on to the south side of the library?

(man) Yeah, I can barely wait until it is finished.

(narrator) What does the man mean?

- ○ The library has just opened a new section.
- ○ He is eager to take advantage of the new library wing.
- ○ The new library will be extra crowded.
- ○ The administration wants to close the library.

For meaning questions on the TOEFL CBT, repeat as much of the conversation in your head as possible. Ask yourself the question, "What did the second speaker say?" If there are any words or phrases you don't understand, you can bet ETS is asking about them. In this example, the answer choice "He is eager to take advantage of the new library wing" best represents "Yeah, I can barely wait until it is finished." Focus on the answer choices and use POE. Later in this chapter, you will see more helpful hints to strengthen your POE strategy.

2. Infer/Imply Questions
Some typical infer/imply questions are:

What can be inferred about the woman?

What does the woman imply?

What can be inferred about the conversation?

What does the man imply about . . . ?

These questions are easy to recognize because you will read the word "imply" or "infer" in the question. Basically, to imply something is to express it indirectly, and to infer something is to draw a conclusion from given facts. What makes these questions difficult is that you must click on the answer choice that paraphrases the conversation. Again, the strategy for answering infer/imply questions is to listen to how the first speaker sets up the conversation, and how the second speaker responds. Try to form a picture in your mind as to what they are talking about. For example, you might hear:

To *imply* means to express a thought indirectly.
To *infer* means to draw a conclusion.

(man) I have to stop at the bank before dinner. I'm down to my last few dollars.

(woman) Why bother? I thought we'd use the gift certificates I got for my graduation present.

(narrator) What does the woman imply?

○ Dinner has been canceled.
○ The man will not be able to afford dinner.
○ Dinner will be free of charge.
○ The bank is too far away.

The best answer, "Dinner will be free of charge," correctly paraphrases "Why bother? I'd thought we'd use the gift certificates I got for my graduation present." Later in this chapter, you will see more helpful hints to strengthen your POE strategy.

3. Action Questions

Some typical sample action questions are:

> What does the man/woman suggest the man/woman do?
>
> What will the man/woman probably do?
>
> What will the man/woman probably do next?

These are questions that center on the verb in the conversation. Again, listen closely to the second speaker for clues as to what will happen next. For example:

> (man) I'm just about sick of all this chemistry homework. I don't even have a spare minute to cook.
>
> (woman) Well, if it would help at all, I could run to the cafeteria and pick something up for you.
>
> (narrator) What will the woman probably do?
>
> ○ Help the man with his homework.
> ○ Get some food for the man.
> ○ Find out where the man can exercise.
> ○ Buy some medicine for the man.

The answer choice "Get some food for the man" best paraphrases the woman's statement, "I could run to the cafeteria and pick something up for you." Notice how the first speaker introduces the situation, and how the second speaker responds. Action questions are either about what the *second* speaker will do, or what the *second* speaker recommends the first speaker do. Therefore, try to think of synonyms for the verb the second speaker uses. Use POE to avoid the traps and distractors that ETS presents and click on the answer that best represents what the second speaker will do next. Later in this chapter, you will learn more helpful hints to strengthen your POE strategy.

Answer choices for action questions always begin with verbs.

4. Detail Questions

Recently, ETS has begun to ask more specific questions about the details of the short conversation. Luckily, this is the least-asked type of question. Detail questions may appear in several forms, yet you will be able to recognize them because they refer to specific items mentioned in the conversation. Some typical detail questions are:

> What does the man want to know?
>
> What do the speakers say about . . . ?
>
> What happened to the . . . ?
>
> What does the woman say about . . . ?

Detail questions are those that center on the nouns of the short conversation. For example:

> (woman) John, have you stopped by the registrar to drop off your reservation voucher for a seat at next week's graduation?
>
> (man) You know what my schedule has been like recently, so I just got Jennifer to do it yesterday.
>
> (narrator) What happened to the reservation voucher?

⬭ The woman forgot to give it to Jennifer.
⬭ Jennifer took it to the registrar.
⬭ It was lost at graduation.
⬭ John traded it for a seat.

Detail questions refer to specific items mentioned in the conversations.

When asked a detail question, try to focus on the key words of the question, in this case it would be "reservation voucher." The answer choice "Jennifer took it to the registrar" best answers the detail question, "What happened to the reservation voucher?"

In Part A of the TOEFL CBT, time is on your side. Remember to be extra careful on the first eight questions. They have the most influence on the question types to come that will help improve your score.

Be extra careful on the first eight questions.

THREE POE TECHNIQUES

The following three POE techniques will help you narrow down your choices whether or not you have actually understood what is spoken on the recording.

1. Opposites

When composing the wrong answer choices for a given question, ETS often tries to trap test-takers who *almost* understood the conversation. One wrong answer choice will look pretty similar to the correct answer, but will mean the opposite. For example:

⬭ Sunday is a day Mary often works.
⬭ Mary rarely works on Sunday.
⬭ Some days Mary's work is awful.
⬭ Mary has had a terrible cough since Sunday.

In the example above, "Sunday is a day Mary often works" and "Mary rarely works on Sunday" are what we call opposites; that is, it is impossible for *both* statements to be true. In a typical Listening section, one-fourth of the questions contain opposites. This is good news for you because if there is a pair of opposites in the answer choices, one of them is likely to be the right answer!

Even if you don't understand the question, you still have a 50 percent chance of answering this question correctly. For example, you hear:

> (man) I thought Josh had a huge mid-term final tomorrow. Why is he outside playing frisbee?
>
> (woman) If there's one thing Josh hates, it's cramming for an exam.
>
> (narrator) What does the man mean?

Next, your four answer choices appear. You read:

- ○ Josh does not enjoy studying.
- ○ Josh ate while he studied.
- ○ Studying is a pleasure for Josh.
- ○ Josh doesn't have enough time to study.

In this example, the opposites are "Josh does not enjoy studying" and "Studying is a pleasure for Josh." Now, think of what the woman just said. The answer choice "Josh does not enjoy studying" best represents "If there's one thing Josh hates, it's cramming for an exam."

Now try another one. You hear:

> (Man) I can't seem to find my biology notes. I had them just a minute ago and suddenly they are gone.
>
> (woman) Well, maybe you should try tidying up your desk a bit!
>
> (narrator) What does the woman imply?

Next, your four answer choices appear. You read:

- ○ She thinks his desk is too tiny.
- ○ His desk is too messy.
- ○ He needs to buy a new desk.
- ○ His desk is far too organized.

The opposites are "His desk is too messy" and "His desk is far too organized." If you didn't recognize the opposites, you need to broaden your understanding of the term *opposites*. "His desk is too messy" simply states that the desk is messy, and "His desk is far too organized" implies that the desk is clean. That's enough for them to be considered opposites. So now all you need to do is remember what you just heard. The answer choice "His desk is too messy" best paraphrases the woman's statement, "Well, maybe you should try tidying up your desk a bit!" Use POE to eliminate the other answer choices and click on the best answer.

2. Common Sense/Extreme Answer Choices

The people who write the TOEFL CBT have very conservative tastes. None of their statements or short conversations will contain anything controversial, violent, passionate, or silly.

Remember, you can use common sense and POE to eliminate three types of wrong answers:

Use POE to eliminate extreme answer choices.

Type 1: Answer choices that are too extreme.

Remember Mary?

○ Sunday is a day Mary often works.
○ Mary rarely works on Sunday.
○ Some days Mary's work is awful.
○ Mary has had a terrible cough since Sunday.

The answer choice "Some days Mary's work is awful" is too extreme. ETS would probably say someone's work was "unsatisfactory" or even "bad," but not "awful." Just remember, ETS can't afford to offend anyone: Any answers that might be controversial are automatically wrong.

Type 2: Idioms.

Idiomatic expressions in English mean something different from their apparent meaning. They are a group of words known individually, but together, the words make no sense. For example, "to egg someone on" doesn't mean to put an egg on someone, but to encourage someone to do something bad.

In the TOEFL CBT, the second speaker will frequently use an idiomatic expression. In this case you can eliminate any answer choice that gives a literal translation. Look at an example.

Use POE to eliminate direct translations of idiomatic expressions.

(woman) How did Rob perform in the fall production of Romeo and Juliet last night?

(man) You wouldn't have believed it! He was head and shoulders above the rest of the cast.

(narrator) What does the man mean?

○ Rob is too tall to be an actor.
○ Rob's performance was excellent.
○ Rob was suspended above the stage.
○ No one believed how terrible his performance was.

The answers "Rob is too tall to be an actor" and "Rob was suspended above the stage" directly translate the idiomatic expression "He was head and shoulders above the rest of the cast." Therefore, you may use POE to eliminate these answer choices. The answer choice "No one believed how terrible his performance was" is an opposite of "Rob's performance was excellent." Based on what you just heard the man say, click on one of these two answer choices. The statement "Rob's performance was excellent" correctly answers the question, "What does the man mean?"

Use POE to eliminate answer choices that sound like the short conversation.

Type 3: Sound-Alikes.

Another of ETS's favorite trap answers is what we call a sound-alike. Sound-alikes take some of the words and sounds from the statement or dialogue and rearrange them so that they have a totally different meaning. Remember this example?

- ◯ Sunday is a day Mary often works.
- ◯ Mary rarely works on Sunday.
- ◯ Some days Mary's work is awful.
- ◯ Mary has had a terrible cough since Sunday.

The conversation was:

> (woman) Will Mary be in on Sunday?
>
> (man) Sunday is usually Mary's day off.
>
> (narrator) What does the man mean?

We already found the opposites in these answers, and one extreme answer. So now look at how ETS might trap you with sounds. Notice how many things in the answer choices echo the word *off* in the statement—*often, awful,* and *cough*. In the answer choice "Some days Mary's work is awful," the phrase *Some days* is meant to confuse the test-taker with the sound of *Sunday*. The right answer "Mary rarely works on Sunday," is one of the opposites, is not extreme, and contains the fewest sound-alikes.

After you've found the opposites and extreme answers, choose the answer choice that sounds *least* like what you heard on the tape. You'll notice that many sound-alikes can also be eliminated using common sense.

Summary of TOEFL CBT Listening Part A Strategy

Step 1: Avoid looking at the picture.

Step 2: Listen to how the first speaker sets up the random topic of conversation.

Step 3: Listen *extra* closely to how the second speaker responds. Remember, the question will almost always be about the second speaker.

Step 4: While reading the answer choices, look for those that contain:

- opposite pairs in the answer choices
- answer choices that directly translate idiomatic expressions
- sound-alikes

Step 5: Use POE on as many answer choices as possible and then click on your answer. If you are still undecided, choose the answer choice containing the fewest sounds from the statement or dialogue.

Drill 1

Directions: In this drill, you will hear short conversations between two people. Place the disk that came with this book into your CD player and press play. After you hear the short conversation between the two people and the question, press pause. Then, turn the page and fill in the oval that best answers the question based on what is stated or implied. After you have filled in the oval, press play, and listen to the next conversation. Continue this pattern until the end of the drill. On the TOEFL CBT, you are *not* allowed to see the answer choices until after you hear the conversation. Therefore, *do not* turn the page and read the four choices until you have heard the conversation and the question. Remember, on the TOEFL CBT, the next question will appear after you click on the "Next" icon and the "Answer Confirm" icon. Then check your answers on page 99.

Listening

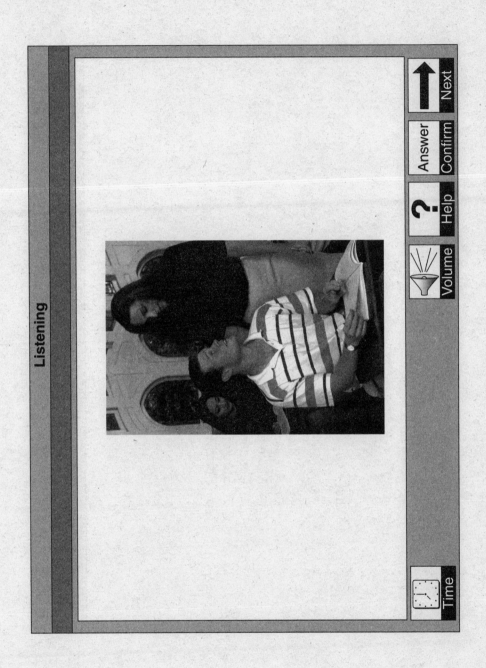

Volume Help Confirm Next

? Help

Answer

Time

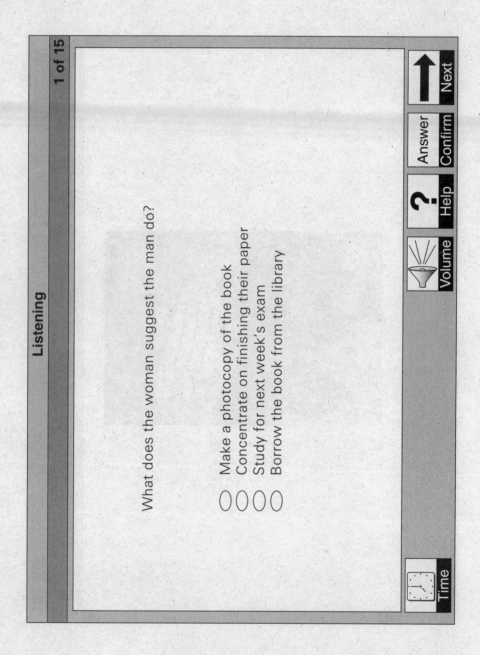

What does the woman suggest the man do?

○ Make a photocopy of the book
○ Concentrate on finishing their paper
○ Study for next week's exam
○ Borrow the book from the library

Volume | Help | Answer Confirm | Next

Time

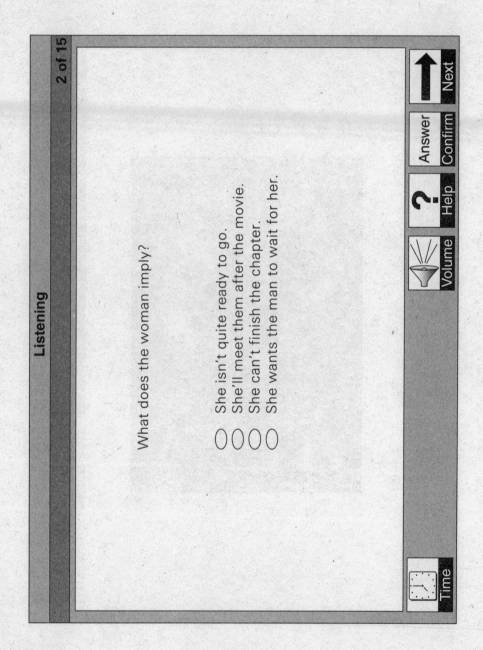

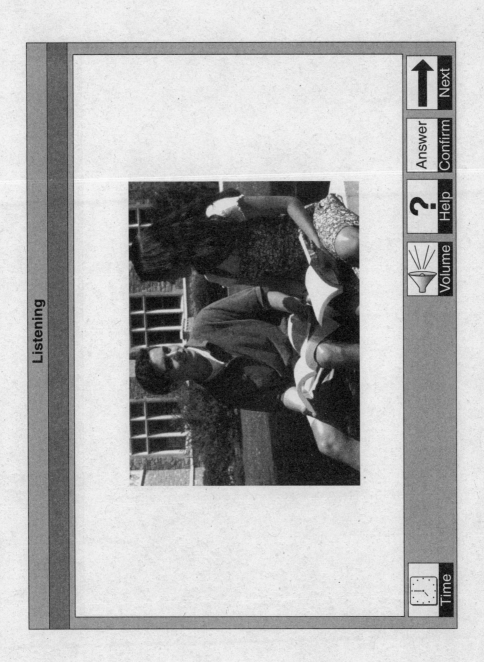

Next

Answer
Confirm

? Help

Volume

Time

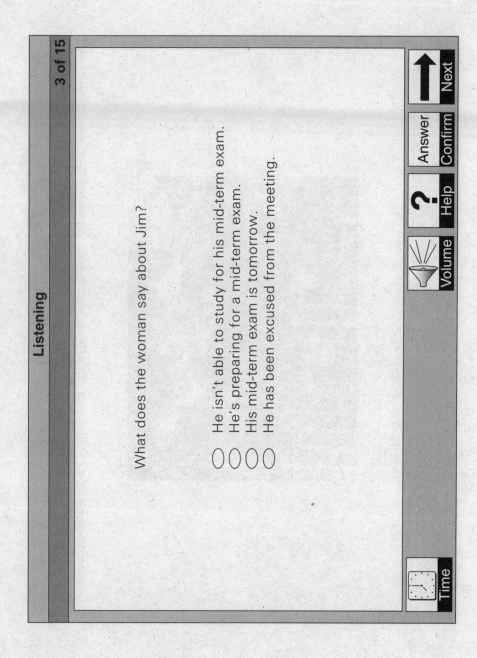

Listening

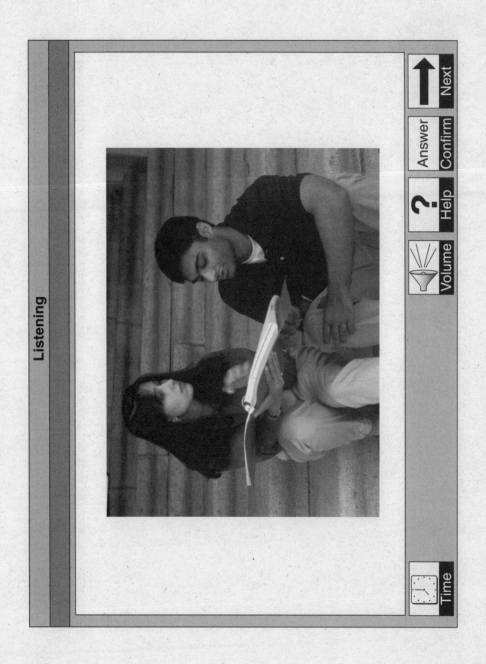

Next

Answer Confirm

? Help

Volume

Time

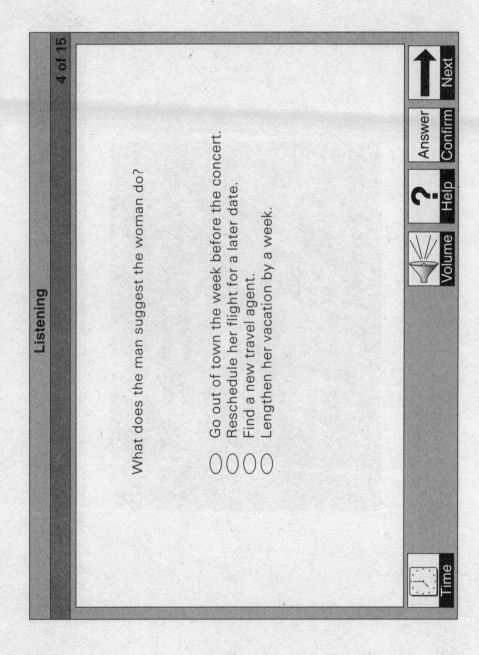

Listening

Volume Help Confirm Next

Answer

Time

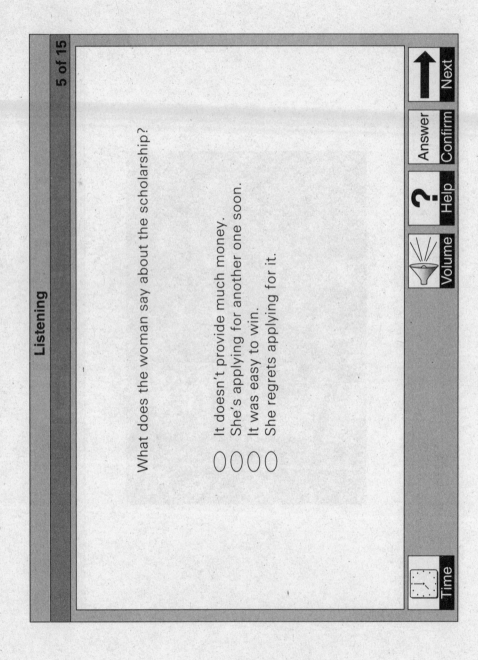

What does the woman say about the scholarship?

○ It doesn't provide much money.
○ She's applying for another one soon.
○ It was easy to win.
○ She regrets applying for it.

Volume   Help   Answer Confirm   Next

Time

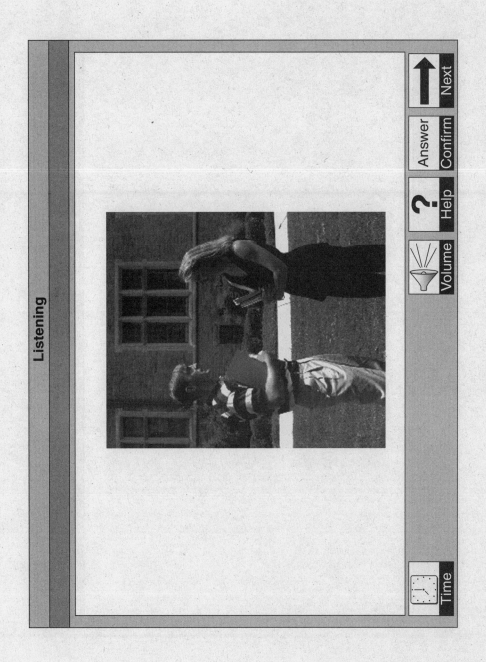

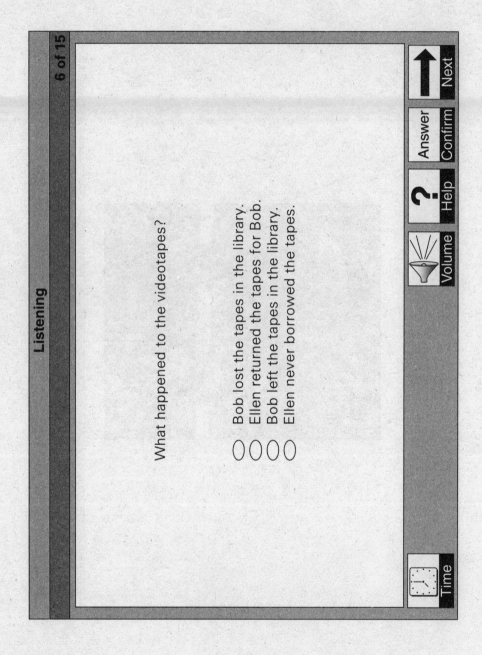

What happened to the videotapes?

○ Bob lost the tapes in the library.
○ Ellen returned the tapes for Bob.
○ Bob left the tapes in the library.
○ Ellen never borrowed the tapes.

Volume   Help   Answer   Next
                  Confirm

Time

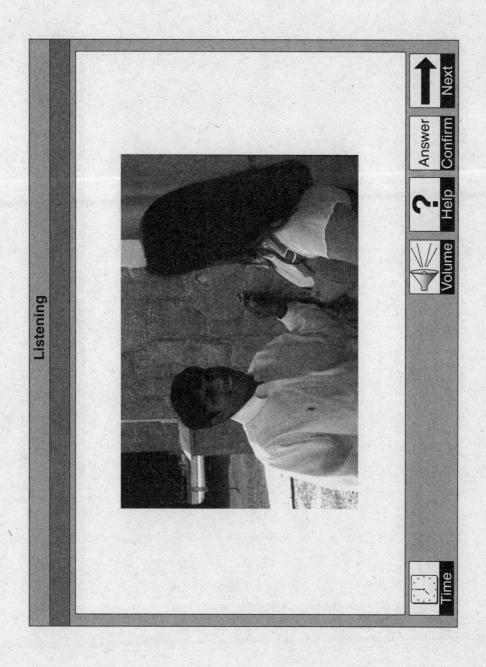

Listening

Volume

? Help

Answer Confirm

↑ Next

Time

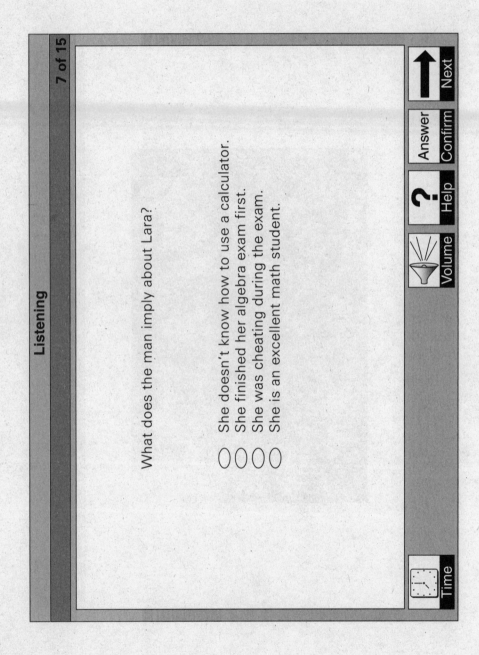

What does the man imply about Lara?

○ She doesn't know how to use a calculator.
○ She finished her algebra exam first.
○ She was cheating during the exam.
○ She is an excellent math student.

Volume | Help | Answer Confirm | Next

Time

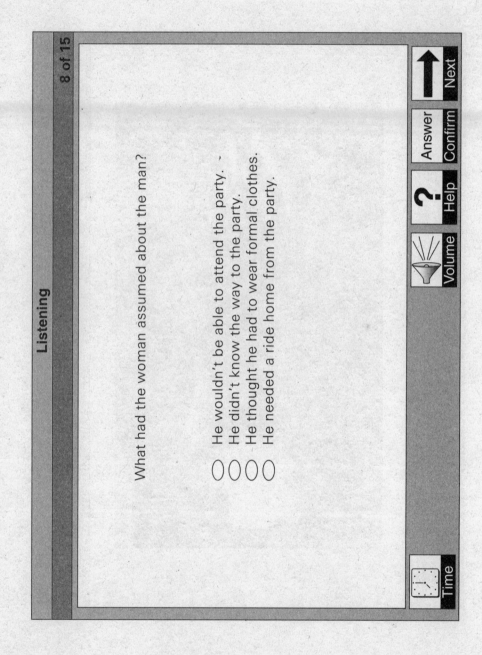

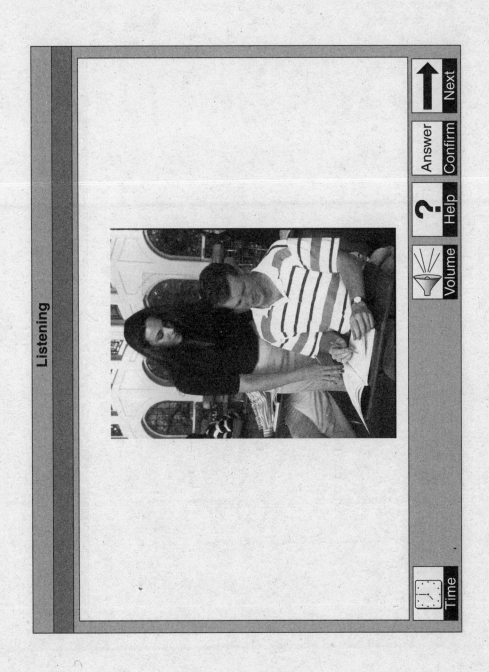

Listening

Next

Answer Confirm

? Help

Volume

Time

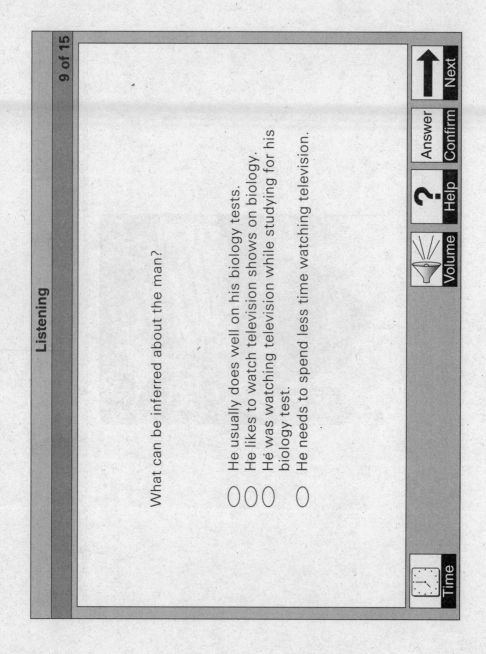

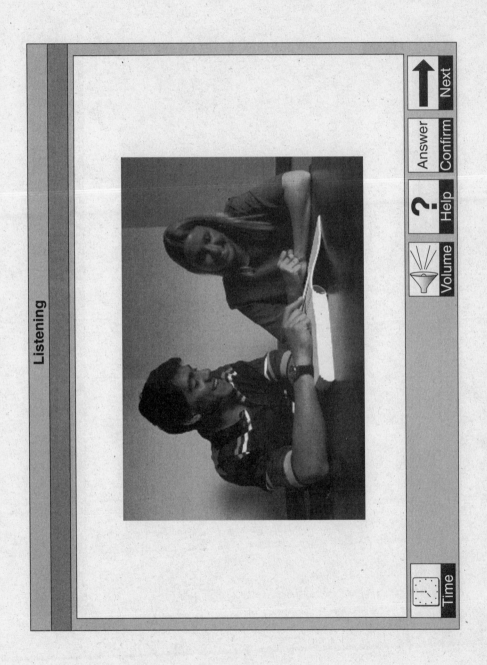

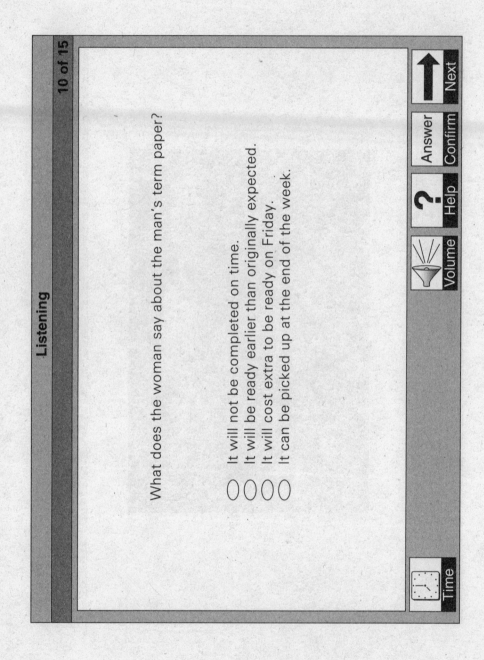

Listening

10 of 15

What does the woman say about the man's term paper?

○ It will not be completed on time.
○ It will be ready earlier than originally expected.
○ It will cost extra to be ready on Friday.
○ It can be picked up at the end of the week.

Volume   Help   Answer   Confirm   Next

Time

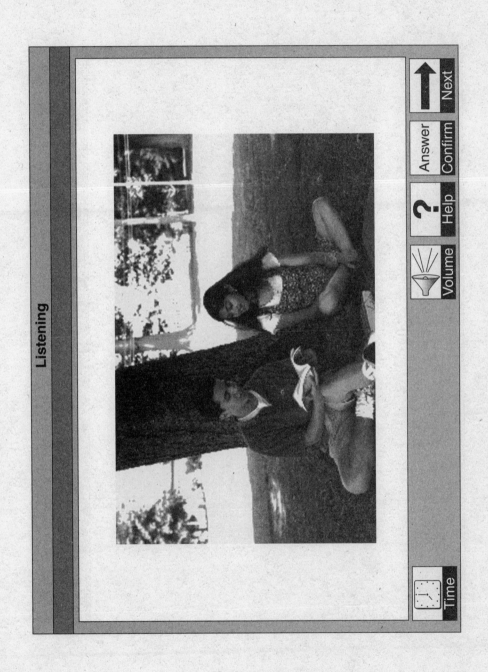

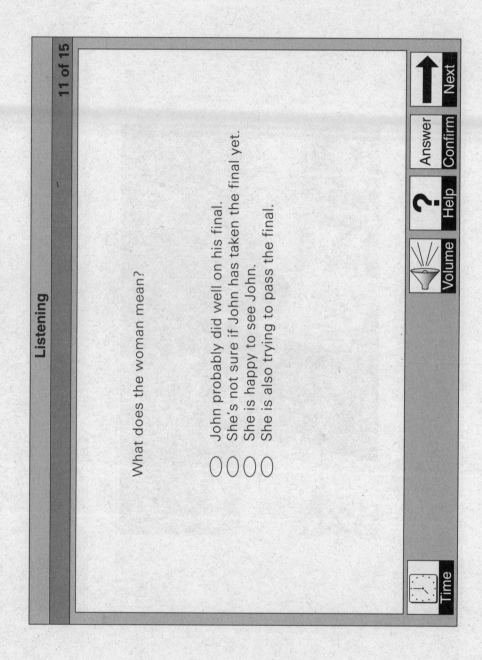

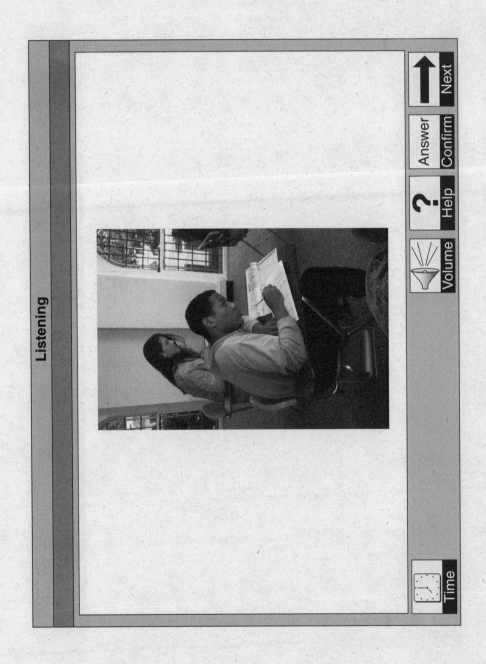

Volume Help Answer Confirm Next

Time

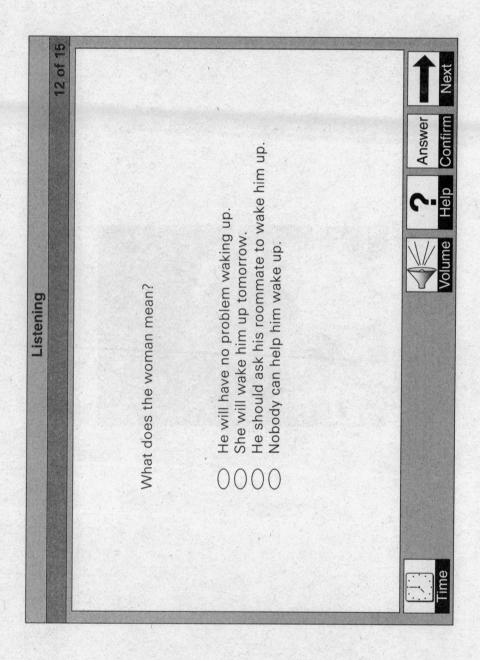

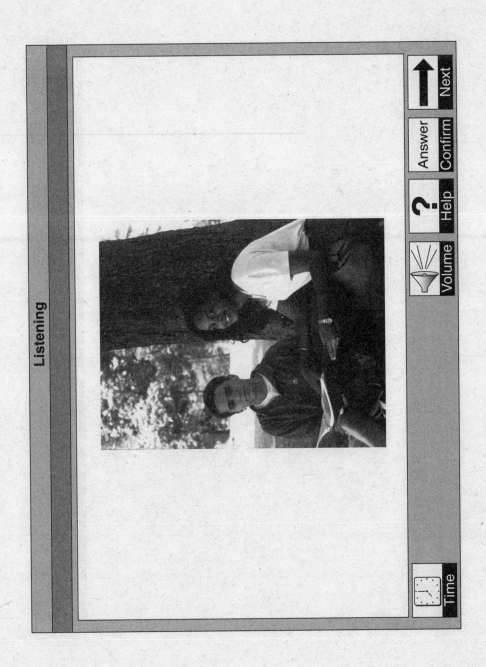

Listening

Next

Answer
Confirm

? Help

Volume

Time

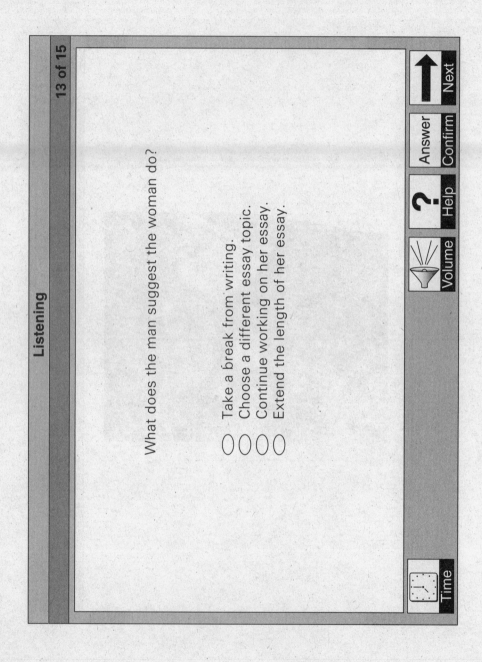

What does the man suggest the woman do?

Take a break from writing.
Choose a different essay topic.
Continue working on her essay.
Extend the length of her essay.

Volume   Help   Answer   Next
                  Confirm

Time

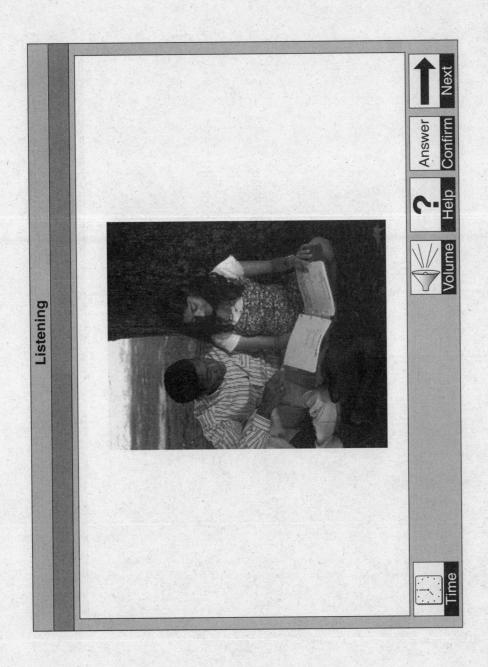

Next

Answer
Confirm

? Help

Volume

Time

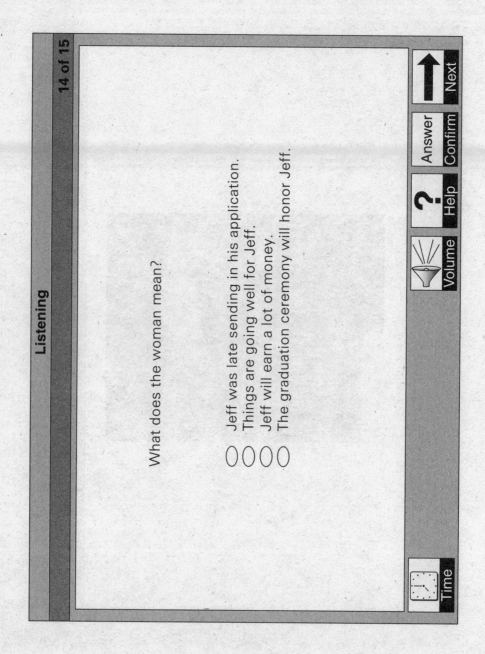

Listening

Next

Answer
Confirm

Help

Volume

Time

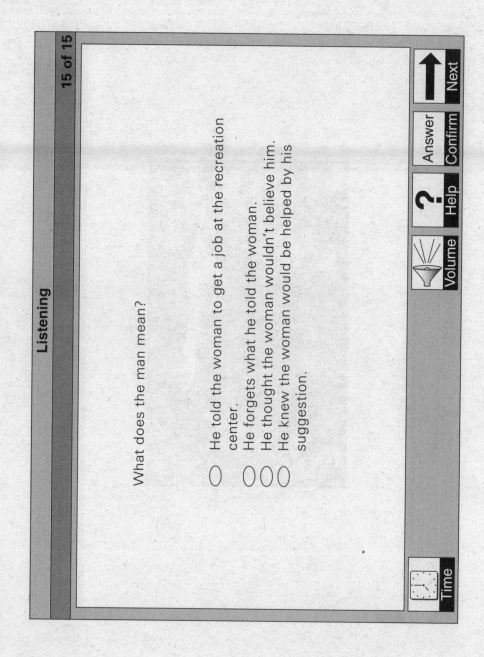

What does the man mean?

○ He told the woman to get a job at the recreation center.

○ He forgets what he told the woman.

○ He thought the woman wouldn't believe him.

○ He knew the woman would be helped by his suggestion.

Volume

? Help

Answer Confirm

↑ Next

Time

ANSWER KEY

1. Concentrate on finishing their paper
2. She isn't quite ready to go.
3. He's preparing for a mid-term exam.
4. Reschedule her flight for a later date.
5. It doesn't provide much money.
6. Ellen returned the tapes for Bob.
7. She is an excellent math student.
8. He wouldn't be able to attend the party.
9. He was watching television while studying for his biology test.
10. It will not be completed on time.
11. John probably did well on his final.
12. He should ask his roommate to wake him up.
13. Continue working on her essay.
14. Things are going well for Jeff.
15. He knew the woman would be helped by his suggestion.

4

Part B—Long Conversations and Lectures

THE BASICS

In Part B of the TOEFL CBT Listening section, your task is to listen to long conversations and lectures, after which you'll be asked questions about the information you just heard. You are *not* able to look at the questions during the long conversations or lectures. Also, neither the long conversations nor the lectures will be repeated. In other words, you have one chance to listen and remember.

Computer-adaptive tests use your performance on one question to determine which question you'll be asked next.

Unfortunately, because this section is computer adaptive, it is impossible to say exactly how many long conversations and lectures you will hear. There can be anywhere from 6 to 9 long conversations and lectures, with 3 to 6 questions each. Once you have listened to the long conversation or lecture, you will be able to read the questions that are asked. They will appear at the top of the computer screen, just above the answer choices. You may also take as much time as you wish to answer each question. The 12-second interval found on the old paper-and-pencil test has been eliminated. (Note: Don't take *too* much time. Remember, the clock is running.)

THE TUTORIAL

VOLUME

You are allowed to adjust the volume for the Listening section at the beginning of Part B. Normally, the volume will be preset to an audible level; however, if you need to raise or lower the volume, do so now. Once you have decided on the volume level, you won't have to think about it during the remainder of the Listening section.

TIME

The time remaining is shown in the upper left-hand corner of the screen. You have the option of turning off the time by clicking on the Clock icon in the lower left corner of the screen. However, we strongly recommend that you leave the clock on. If you do turn off the clock, you will not be able to see how much time you have remaining and, consequently, will have difficulty pacing yourself. Fortunately, the clock does not run while any of the conversations are being spoken. The time displayed in the upper left-hand corner is the time remaining for you to answer the questions. The time *does* run if you click on the Help icon. However, once you finish this book, the Help icon will not be necessary.

The clock stops running while the long conversations or lectures are being spoken.

Directions

Take a look at the directions for Part B:

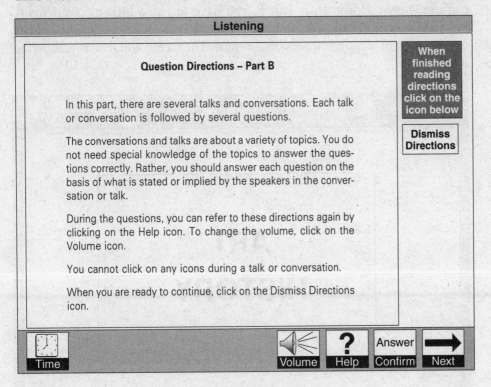

How to Answer

Like Part A, Part B of the TOEFL CBT is computer adaptive, meaning your performance on one question determines which question you will be asked next. Therefore, you must answer a question before the next one appears. You can't skip and save a difficult question for later. Every question must be answered.

During the long conversations, a picture will appear on the computer screen of a professor, and four to six students either sitting around a table or in some other type of university setting. The professor will lead a discussion on an undetermined academic subject. Although the professor will do the majority of the speaking, two or three students *at most* will also participate in the discussion. After the conversation, you will be asked 2 to 4 questions about what was discussed.

During the lectures, a professor will give a talk about various academic subjects such as biology, geography, music, and so forth. The lecture may last anywhere from 2 to 3 minutes. After the lecture you will be asked 4 to 6 questions about what you heard.

After clicking on the best answer, you *must* then click on the two icons in the bottom right-hand corner of the computer screen. The first is the "Next" icon on the far right. After you click on "Next," you must click on "Answer Confirm." You may change you answer at any time *before* you click on "Answer Confirm." However, once you click on "Answer Confirm," you will never see that question again.

Pictures

In Part A of the TOEFL CBT Listening section, you do not need to study the pictures shown. However, in Part B, you have to pay a little more attention. Before you hear a long conversation or lecture, you will see the topic of the conversation or lecture you are about to hear. The screen will look similar to the following.

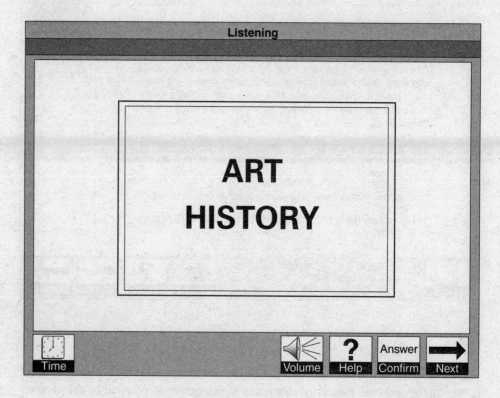

Pay close attention to how the narrator introduces the long conversation or lecture. It might hold valuable information to what the main idea is.

Next, you will see a picture of a professor standing and the lecture or conversation will begin. Do *not* be distracted by the professor. What the professor is wearing, holding, or doing will not be tested. You only have to be concerned with what the professor is saying. Look at the following example.

PICTURE FLIPS

Pay close attention to the picture flips.

Due to the new question types ETS has introduced on the TOEFL CBT, occasionally the picture of the lecturing professor disappears, and a word, diagram, graph, or picture appears on the computer screen. These "picture flips" occur during the lectures of the TOEFL CBT. You *must* pay close attention to what is being said about the word, diagram, graph, or picture that appears on the screen. ETS *will* ask you a question about that word, diagram, graph, or picture in the questions following the lecture. Look at the following example.

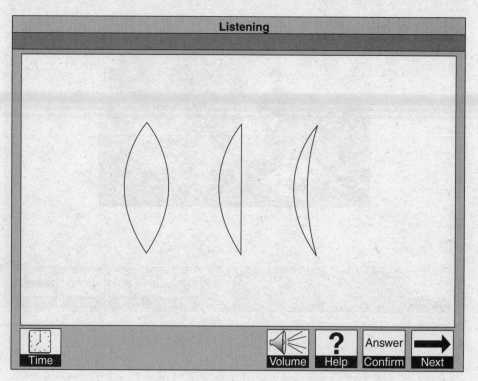

WHAT MAKES PART B SO HARD?

What many test-takers find most difficult is simply remembering what was said long enough to answer the questions. Each long conversation or lecture lasts between two to three minutes and contains a lot of information. Even many native English speakers cannot remember every word.

WHY CAN'T YOU TAKE NOTES?

You may not take notes during the TOEFL CBT.

This part of the test is probably the best proof that the TOEFL CBT is not a very good predictor of how well you could function in an American university setting. Can you imagine a professor at a college or university who forbids you to take notes in class? Of course not! But that's what this section of the TOEFL CBT does.

This restriction exists on no other test administered by ETS, and according to ETS it exists "for security reasons." Is that at all logical? No. It doesn't make much sense to us either.

We believe that it is primarily Part B of the TOEFL CBT Listening section that prompted ETS to decide that you should not be allowed to take notes. Since most of the language in this section is so simple, ETS knows you're not going to have much difficulty *understanding* what was said. What is difficult, however, is trying to *remember* what was said. Perhaps ETS should rename Part B the "memory" section, instead of the "listening" section. The truth is, if ETS allowed note taking in Part B, most people would have no problem answering the questions. In other words, test-takers could easily score too many points on this part of the test.

PACING

In Part B of the TOEFL CBT Listening section, you may take as much time as you wish to answer. Always read each answer choice carefully before choosing. However, just because you have all the time in the world doesn't mean you can let your mind wander and spend two minutes on each question. You need to work efficiently. The time remaining is displayed in the upper left-hand corner of the computer screen. Refer to it to see exactly how much time remains. In the upper right-hand corner of the computer screen, the number of questions remaining is displayed. Keep an eye on the both of them to make sure you don't run out of time. You should try to answer each question in 45 seconds or less.

Pace yourself. Don't spend too much time on any one question.

GENERAL STRATEGY

ETS will only ask 4 to 6 questions about each long conversation or lecture; therefore, you only need to remember 4 to 6 pieces of information. Your short-term memory will be most helpful here. Once you answer the questions, you will never have to use any of the information again. The trick is to figure out which pieces of information you need to remember. Although there is no surefire way to know exactly what ETS will ask, there are some patterns that you can pay attention to.

INTRODUCTIONS

Before the conversations and lectures begin, you will be able to read the introductory academic subject heading. The topics could be about biology, art history, geography, chemistry, history, or any other academic subjects. As you read the topic, the narrator will say several introductory sentences. Listen for any key words that give you clues as to the main topic. For example, you might hear:

> (Narrator) Listen to a professor discuss the side effects of an experimental drug being tested on cancer patients.

Now you have some idea as to what the lecture is about. As you hear the phrases "side effects," "experimental drugs," and "cancer patients," you can safely assume the lecture is something about the various side effects different cancer patients have experienced as a result of taking a new type of drug. This eliminates any new surprises about the topic.

QUESTIONS/DEFINITIONS

A rhetorical question is one usually asked for the purpose of making a point, with no answer expected.

If at any time during the conversations or lectures the speakers pose rhetorical questions or ask the students questions, listen closely for the answers. More than likely, ETS will ask you similar questions after the conversations or lectures are finished. Also, if the speakers at any time define vocabulary words, or if vocabulary words appear on the screen, listen closely and remember the definitions. ETS loves to ask questions about the words they define.

LISTS AND EXAMPLES

The speakers will frequently give lists of items to illustrate or clearly provide details about what they are discussing. They also give examples to support their claims. If you hear lists of words or examples, listen for and remember any specific or unusual details that surround them. ETS might ask questions concerning these lists and examples.

COMPARISONS

From time to time, the speakers will compare two or more objects. Listen closely for the similarities and differences among the objects being compared. ETS might use these comparisons for matching questions.

PROCESSES/CHRONOLOGICAL ORDER

During the long conversations and lectures, be aware of any series of events that are presented or explained in a particular or specific order. ETS might ask you to place the events in chronological order in which they occurred.

QUESTION TYPES

Besides teaching you about volume, time, and how to answer, ETS will also introduce the question types you will encounter on Part B of the TOEFL CBT Listening section. Although they may sound confusing at first, you will become quite familiar with them after finishing our practice questions. There are 4 basic question types.

1. Single Answer Questions

Single answer questions are just like those on the old paper-and-pencil version, except now you are able to read the questions along with the four answer choices. Basically, you are asked to click on one of four choices that best answers the question you are asked. There are two types of single answer questions: main idea questions and detail questions.

Main Idea Questions

The first question you'll encounter in the Part B Listening section will most likely be a main idea question. Main idea questions test how well you understand and interpret the general content of the talk. The answer is *not* directly mentioned; rather, it has to be inferred from other information you hear. These question types do *not* involve pictures. Main idea questions are usually asked in the following forms:

What is the purpose of the talk?

What is the main purpose of the talk?

What is the purpose of the instructor's talk?

What is the main topic of the talk?

What is the professor mainly discussing?

To answer main idea questions, try to remember how the lecture or conversation was introduced. Think about what the general topic of the talk was. Ask yourself which words or phrases were constantly repeated. Then look at your four answer choices, and use POE to eliminate any that introduce any new material *not* mentioned during the conversations or lectures. You will have to rely on your paraphrasing skills. Once you have clicked on your answer choice, you must click on the "Next" and the "Answer/Confirm" icons.

Detail Questions

Detail questions ask for specific facts mentioned in the conversations or lectures. Unlike the short conversations in the Listening section Part A, there are no tricks or traps, such as sound-alikes and idiom interpretations. Three of the four answer choices simply were *not* mentioned in the passage, or were mentioned in association with a topic other than the one asked about. These question types do *not* involve pictures. Detail questions will appear on the TOEFL CBT test as follows:

What does the professor say about the way steamer ships sail?

According to the speaker, why do ants live in colonies?

How does the student manage to take so many courses?

The question types are endless. However, as you read the question at the top of the computer screen, try to remember as much as possible about the topic being asked. Then read the answer choices and eliminate any new information, or any information that was spoken about in regards to another topic. Once you have clicked on your answer choice, you must click on the "Next" and the "Answer/Confirm" icons.

2. Other Single Answer Questions

Other single answer questions may come in two different forms, clicking on one of four letters A, B, C, or D in a picture, or clicking on one of four pictures. In any case, you need to click on just *one* answer choice in the picture before clicking on the "Next" and the "Answer/Confirm" icons.

Clicking on One of Four Letters

There is a good chance that you will encounter at least one of these question types on Part B. Like detail questions, they ask for specific information that you heard during the long conversation or lecture. These question types always refer to a picture, map, or diagram. Look at the following example. At the top of the computer screen you read:

Click on the letter that indicates the location where cork farmers obtain their product.

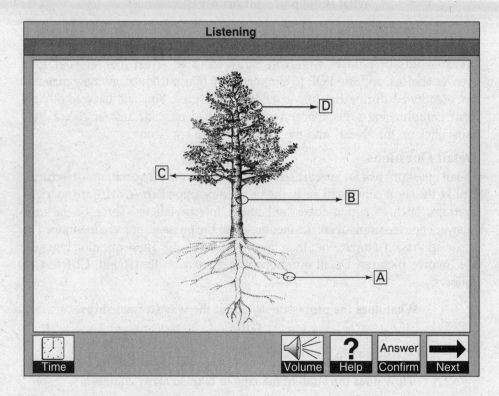

Using your mouse, point and click on the letter that best answers the question. When answering these question types, try to remember the picture you were shown during the lecture. ETS is fairly predictable. If they show you a word, diagram, graph, or picture during the talk, pay *close* attention to what is being said. They will definitely ask you a question about it. However, be sure to answer the question you are being asked. Many students answer hastily and misread the question. Once you have clicked on your answer choice, you must click on the "Next" and the "Answer/Confirm" icons.

Read the question carefully before clicking on the best answer.

Clicking on One of Four Pictures

The only difference between "clicking on one of four pictures" and "clicking on one of four letters" is you have four individual pictures rather than just one picture with four letters. There is a good chance that you will encounter at least one of these question types on Part B. Like detail questions, they ask for specific information that you heard during the long conversation or lecture. These question types always refer to a picture, map, or diagram.

Approach these questions like you would for clicking on one of four letters. Using your mouse, point and click on the picture that best answers the question. When answering these question types, try to remember the pictures you were shown during the lecture. Again, ETS is fairly predictable. If they show you a word, diagram, graph, or picture during the talk, pay *close* attention to what is being said. They will definitely ask you a question about it.

3. Multiple Answer Questions

Multiple answer questions ask for specific facts mentioned in the conversations or lectures. However, they ask you to click on **TWO** choices that best answer the question instead of just one. Interestingly enough, ETS places squares next to the four answer choices rather than ovals. These question types do *not* involve pictures. Unlike the Listening section Part A, there are no tricks or traps, such as sound-alikes and idiom interpretations. Simply, two of the four answer choices simply were *not* mentioned in the passage, or were mentioned in association with another topic other than the one being asked about. Multiple answer questions will appear on the TOEFL CBT test as follows:

Some question types ask you to pick two correct answers.

According to the speaker, what were two ways that early Colonial Americans traveled?

Click on 2 answers.

☐ Covered wagon.
☐ Carriage.
☐ Sleigh.
☐ Wagon.

Time | Volume | Help | Answer Confirm | Next

One simple strategy to remember when answering multiple answer questions is to not click on opposite answer choices. If two statements contradict each other, it is impossible for them both to be correct.

Multiple answer questions are basically detail questions and should be approached as such. As you read the question at the top of the computer screen, try to remember as much as possible about the topic being asked. Then read the answer choices and use POE to get rid of any new information, or any information that was spoken about in regards to another topic. One simple strategy to remember when answer these question types is to *not* click on opposite answer choices. If two statements contradict each other, it is impossible for them both to be correct. Once you have clicked on your *two* answer choices, you must click on the "Next" and the "Answer/Confirm" icons. If you just click on *one* answer choice, you will *not* be allowed to proceed with the test until you click on *two* answer choices.

4. Matching/Order Questions

Matching/Order questions are the most time consuming of all the Part B Listening questions. They require extensive mouse clicking, and moving. Unfortunately, you do *not* get half-credit for getting the question partially correct... It's all or nothing. These questions are also the most difficult because rather than having to remember just one piece of information, you are required to remember many.

MATCHING QUESTIONS

Matching questions ask that you match three items in one category with three items in another category. This question type does *not* refer to a picture that you may have seen; rather, it is based on what is spoken in the conversations or lectures. As referred to in the General Strategy section above, you want to pay close attention to any similarities and differences among objects being compared during the conversations or lectures. ETS might use these comparisons for matching questions. On the TOEFL CBT test, matching questions will be similar to the following:

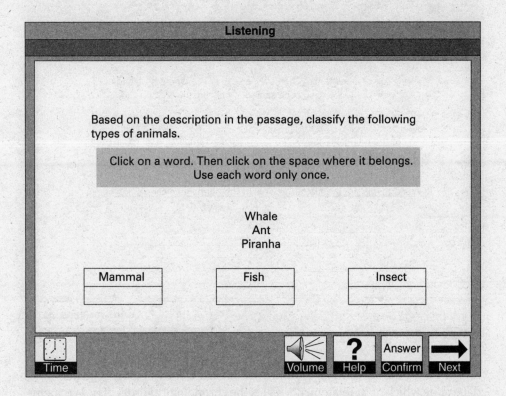

Using the three words in the first category as memory stimulators, try to remember what was stated or implied about each. Most likely they were compared to each other. Click on the first word in the list to highlight it. Then click on the space in which you would like to insert it.

ORDER QUESTIONS

For order questions, you should read all the sentences and determine which of the statements begins the chronological order. Next, determine which of the remaining sentences comes last.

This question type is all about chronological order. ETS gives you approximately 4 sentences and asks you to put them in correct chronological order. Order questions do *not* refer to any picture that you have seen; rather, they are based on what is spoken in the conversations or lectures. As referred to in the General Strategy section above, you want to pay close attention to a series of events that are presented or explained in a particular or specific order. On the TOEFL CBT, order questions will be similar to the following:

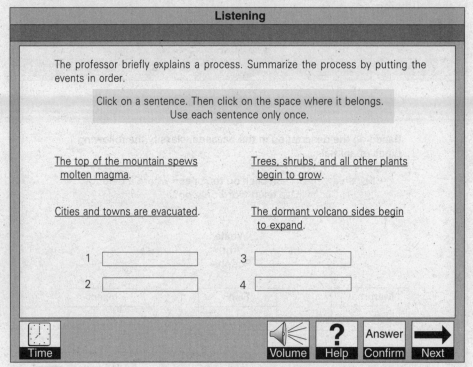

For order questions, you should first read the four or five sentences and determine which of the statements *begins* the chronological order. Try to remember the series of events the professor described in the passage (and use your common sense) to select the best answer. Next, determine which of the remaining sentences come **last**. Your next step is to simply fill in the middle answer choices. After you have made your selections re-read them to make sure they flow in chronological order. You may rearrange them at any time before you click on the "Next" and the "Answer/Confirm" icons.

Drill 1

Now that you have been introduced to strategies and different question types, use what you have learned and practice the techniques. Listen to the following conversation or lecture. Do *not* turn the pages back to review any words, diagrams, graphs, or pictures that might be presented in the lecture. Listen to the lecture only *one* time. After the conversations and lectures are finished, press pause. Then, turn the page and fill in the oval that best answers the question based on what is stated or implied. After you have filled in the oval, press play and listen to the next conversation. Continue this pattern until the end of the drill. On the TOEFL CBT, you are *not* allowed to see the answer choices until after you hear the conversation. Therefore, *do not* turn the page and read the four choices until you have heard the conversation and the question. Remember, on the TOEFL CBT, the next question will appear only after you click on the "Next" icon and the "Answer Confirm" icon. Now get ready to listen to the first conversation.

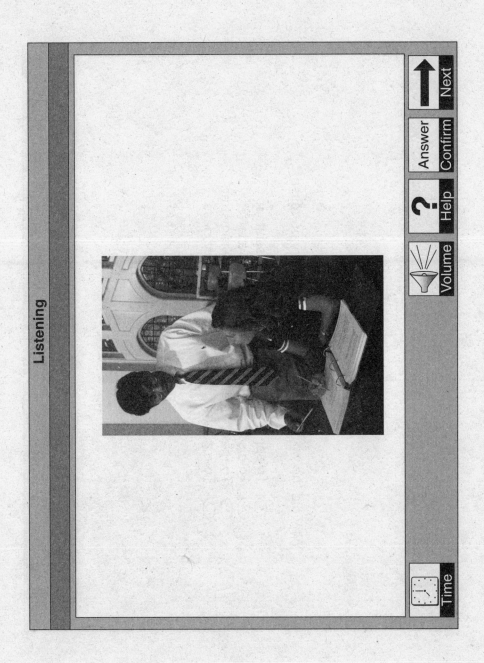

Listening

Next

Answer Confirm

? Help

Volume

Time

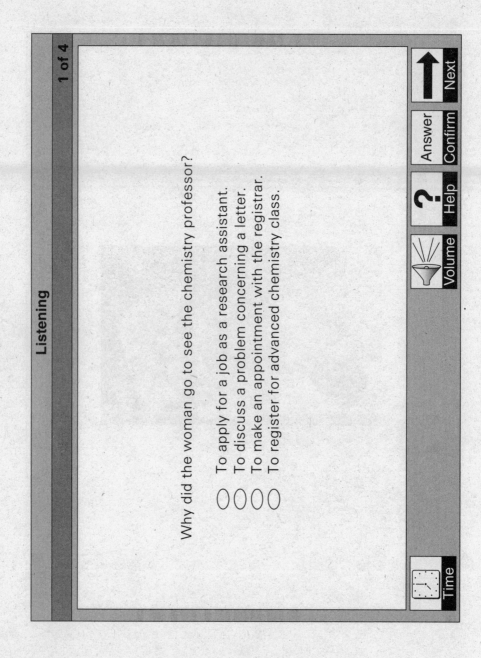

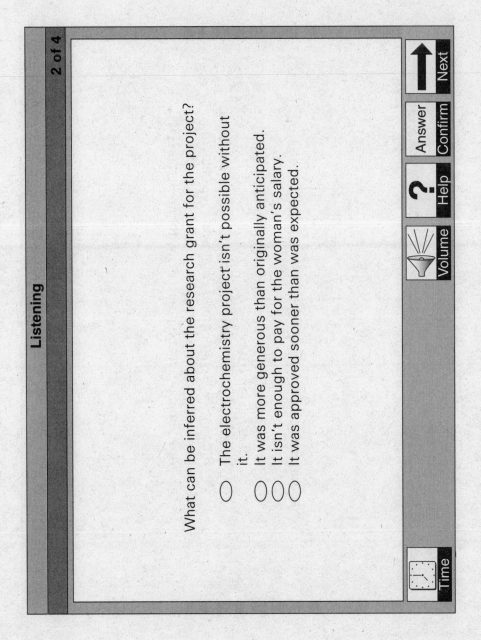

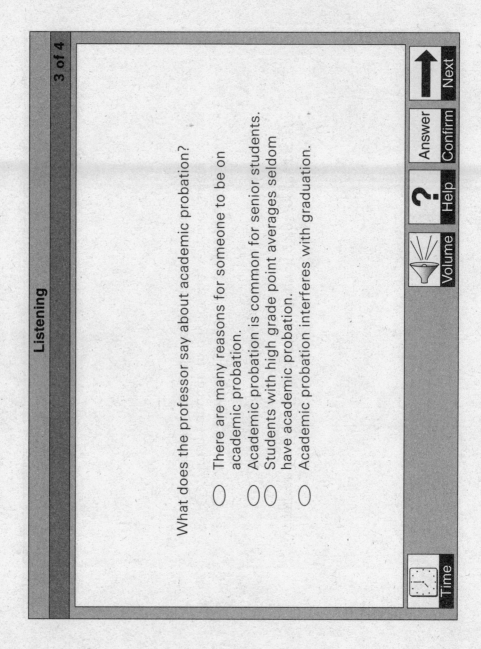

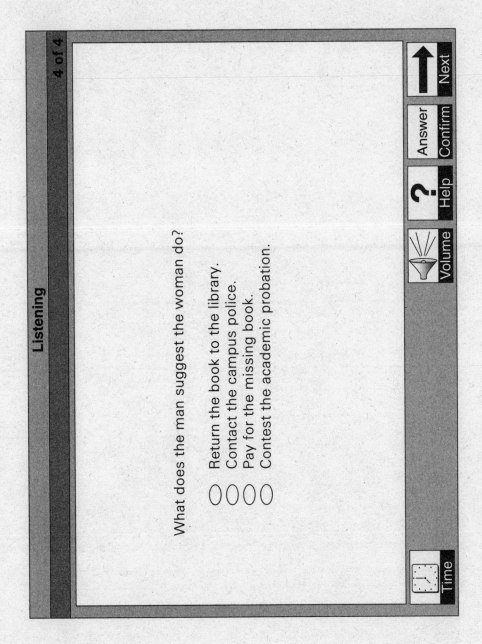

What does the man suggest the woman do?

○ Return the book to the library.
○ Contact the campus police.
○ Pay for the missing book.
○ Contest the academic probation.

Volume

Help

Answer
Confirm

Next

Time

Drill 2

Now that you have been introduced to strategies and different question types, use what you have learned to practice the techniques. Listen to the following conversation or lecture. Do *not* turn the pages back to review any words, diagrams, graphs, or pictures that might be presented in the lecture. Listen to the lecture only *one* time. After the conversations and lectures are finished, press pause. Then turn the page and fill in the oval that best answers the question based on what is stated or implied. After you have filled in the oval, press play and listen to the next conversation. Continue this pattern until the end of the drill. On the TOEFL CBT, you are *not* allowed to see the answer choices until after you hear the conversation. Therefore, *do not* turn the page and read the four choices until you have heard the conversation and the question. Remember, on the TOEFL CBT, the next question will appear only after you click on the "Next" icon and the "Answer Confirm" icon. Now get ready to listen to the first conversation.

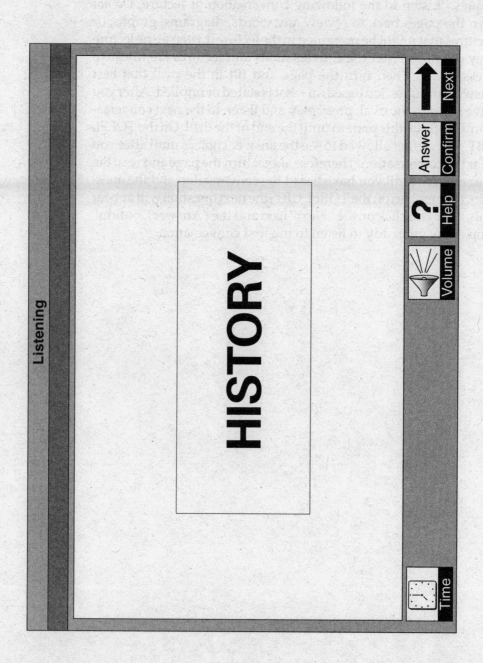

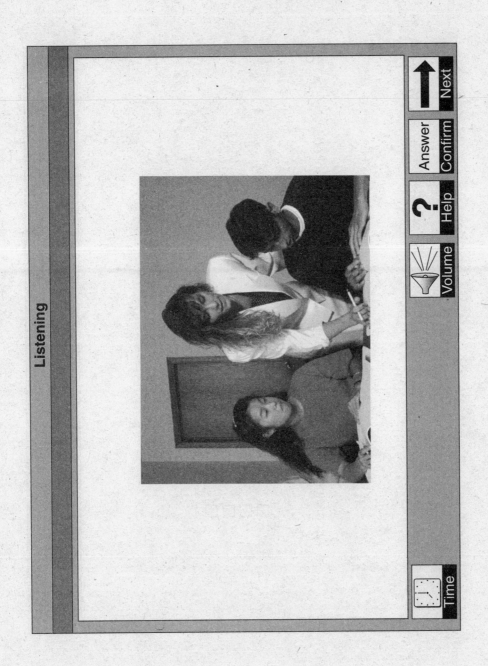

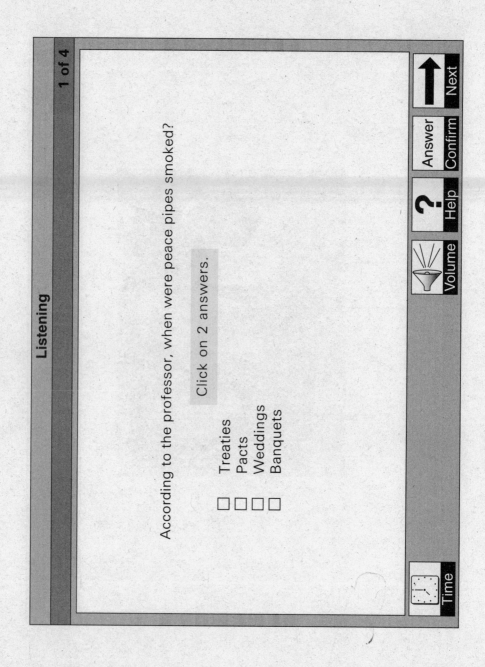

According to the professor, when were peace pipes smoked?

Click on 2 answers.

☐ Treaties
☐ Pacts
☐ Weddings
☐ Banquets

Volume Help Answer Next
               Confirm

Time

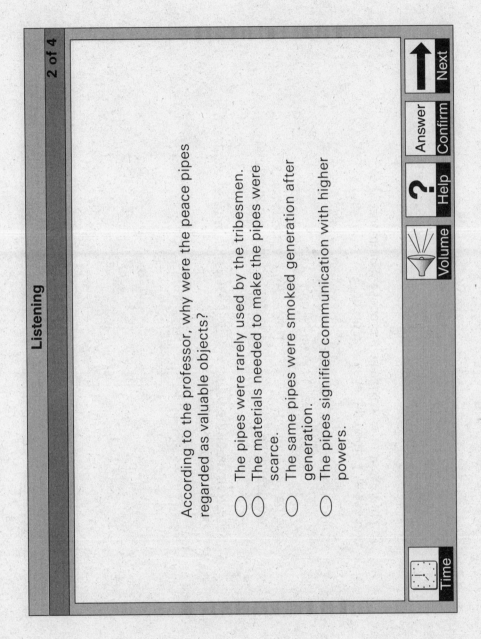

According to the professor, why were the peace pipes regarded as valuable objects?

○ The pipes were rarely used by the tribesmen.
○ The materials needed to make the pipes were scarce.
○ The same pipes were smoked generation after generation.
○ The pipes signified communication with higher powers.

Next

Answer Confirm

? Help

Volume

Time

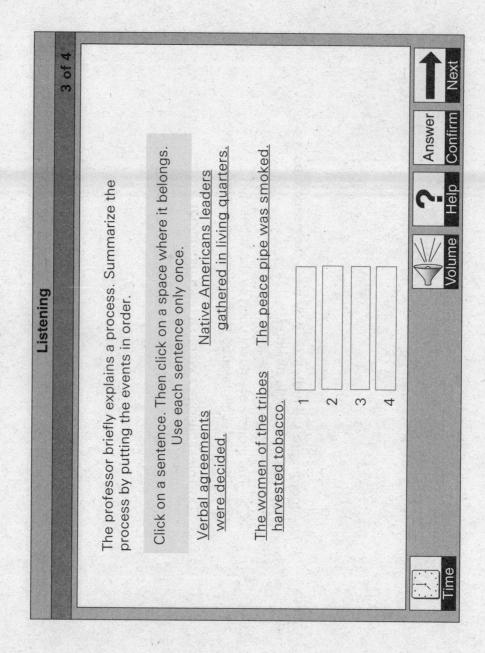

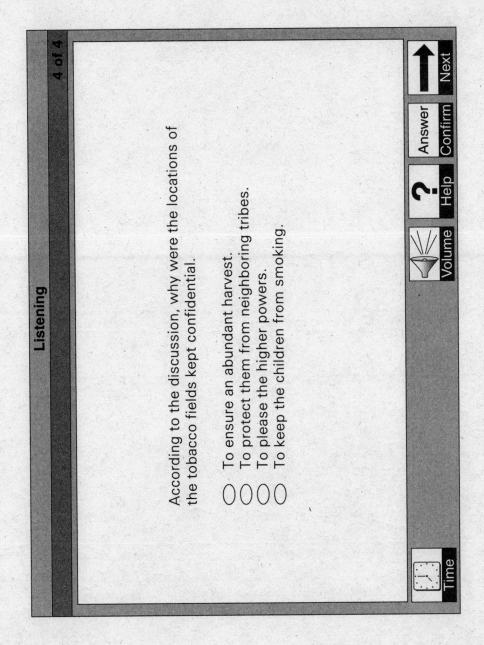

Listening

4 of 4

According to the discussion, why were the locations of
the tobacco fields kept confidential.

○ To ensure an abundant harvest.
○ To protect them from neighboring tribes.
○ To please the higher powers.
○ To keep the children from smoking.

Time

Volume   Help   Answer Confirm   Next

Drill 3

Now that you have been introduced to strategies and different question types, use what you have learned and practice the techniques. Listen to the following conversation or lecture. Do *not* turn the pages back to review any words, diagrams, graphs, or pictures that might be presented in the lecture. Listen to the lecture only *one* time. After the conversations and lectures are finished, press pause. Then, turn the page and fill in the oval that best answers the question based on what is stated or implied. After you have filled in the oval, press play, and listen to the next conversation. Continue this pattern until the end of the drill. On the TOEFL CBT, you are *not* allowed to see the answer choices until after you hear the conversation. Therefore, *do not* turn the page and read the four choices until you have heard the conversation and the question. Remember, on the TOEFL CBT, the next question will appear only after you click on the "Next" icon and the "Answer Confirm" icon. Now get ready to listen to the first conversation.

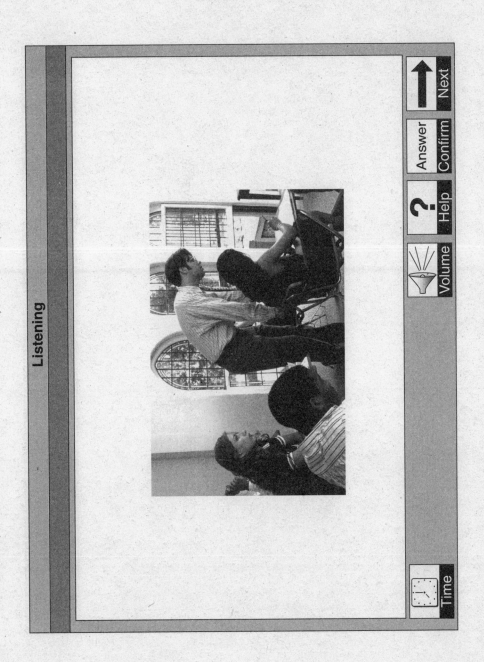

Volume Help Answer Next

Confirm

Time

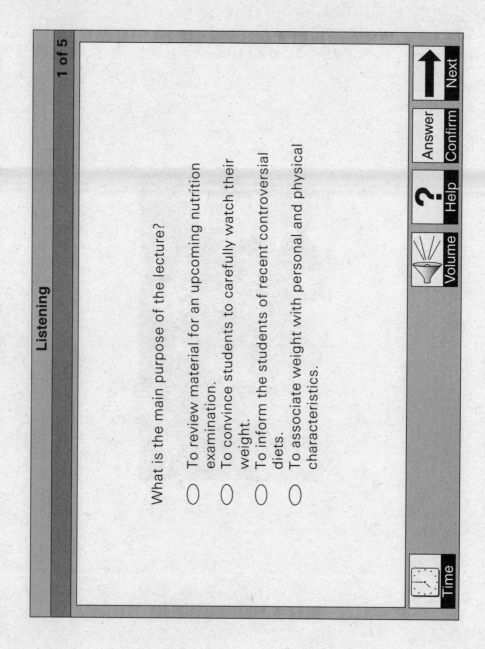

What is the main purpose of the lecture?

○ To review material for an upcoming nutrition examination.

○ To convince students to carefully watch their weight.

○ To inform the students of recent controversial diets.

○ To associate weight with personal and physical characteristics.

Volume

? Help

Answer Confirm

↑ Next

Time

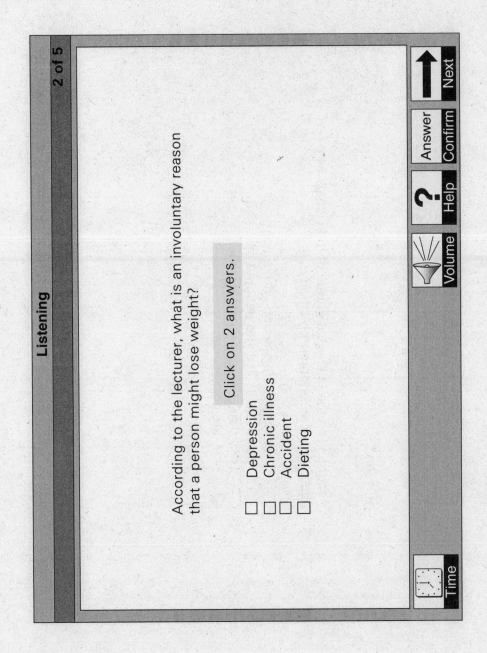

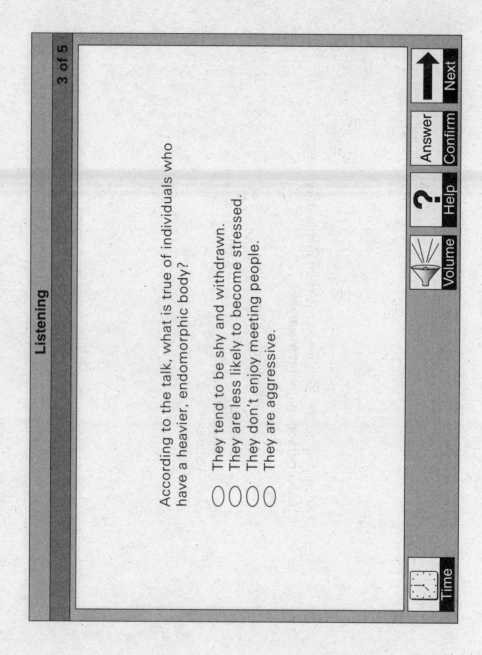

According to the talk, what is true of individuals who have a heavier, endomorphic body?

○ They tend to be shy and withdrawn.
○ They are less likely to become stressed.
○ They don't enjoy meeting people.
○ They are aggressive.

Volume Help Answer Confirm Next

Time

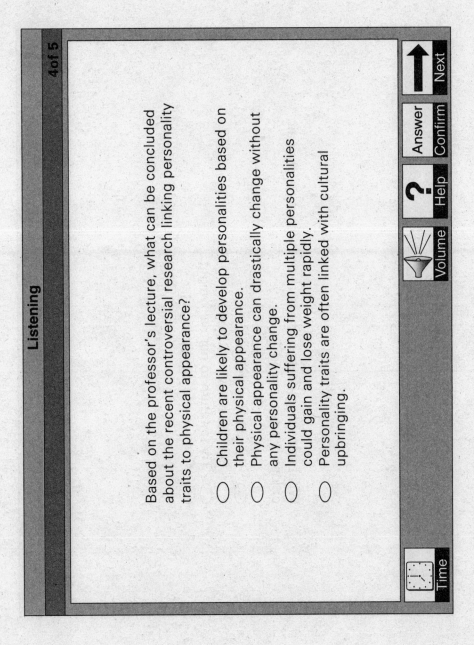

Based on the professor's lecture, what can be concluded about the recent controversial research linking personality traits to physical appearance?

○ Children are likely to develop personalities based on their physical appearance.

○ Physical appearance can drastically change without any personality change.

○ Individuals suffering from multiple personalities could gain and lose weight rapidly.

○ Personality traits are often linked with cultural upbringing.

Next

Confirm

Answer

Help

?

Volume

Time

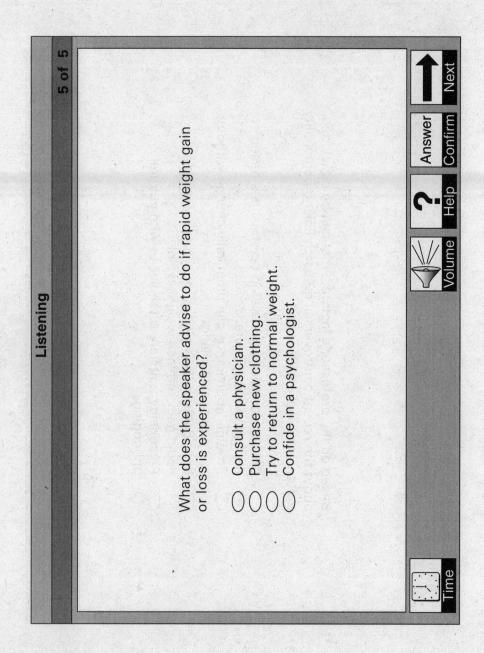

Drill 4

Now that you have been introduced to strategies and different question types, use what you have learned and practice the techniques. Listen to the following conversation or lecture. Do *not* turn the pages back to review any words, diagrams, graphs, or pictures that might be presented in the lecture. Listen to the lecture only *one* time. After the conversations and lectures are finished, press Pause. Then, turn the page and fill in the oval that best answers the question based on what is stated or implied. After you have filled in the oval, press Play, and listen to the next conversation. Continue this pattern until the end of the drill. On the TOEFL CBT, you are *not* allowed to see the answer choices until after you hear the conversation. Therefore, *do not* turn the page and read the four choices until you have heard the conversation and the question. Remember, on the TOEFL CBT, the next question will appear only after you click on the "Next" icon and the "Answer Confirm" icon. Now get ready to listen to the first conversation.

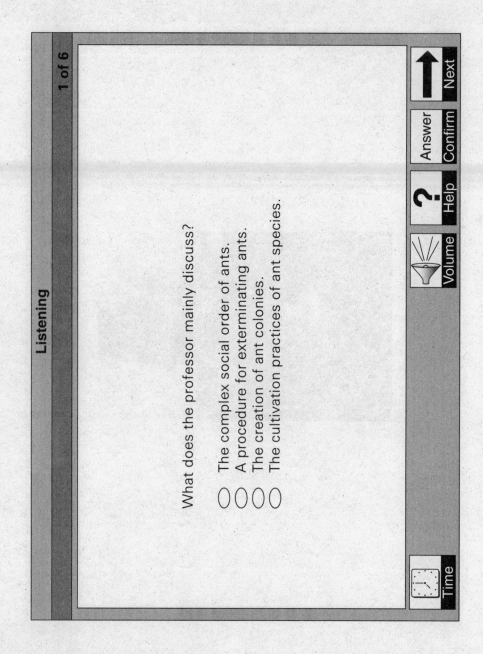

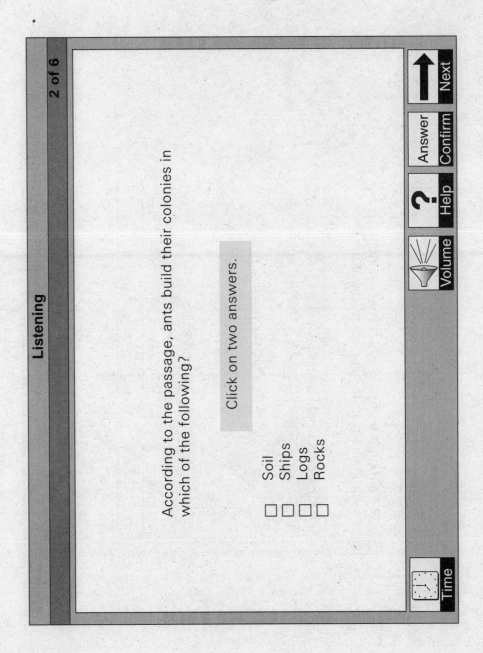

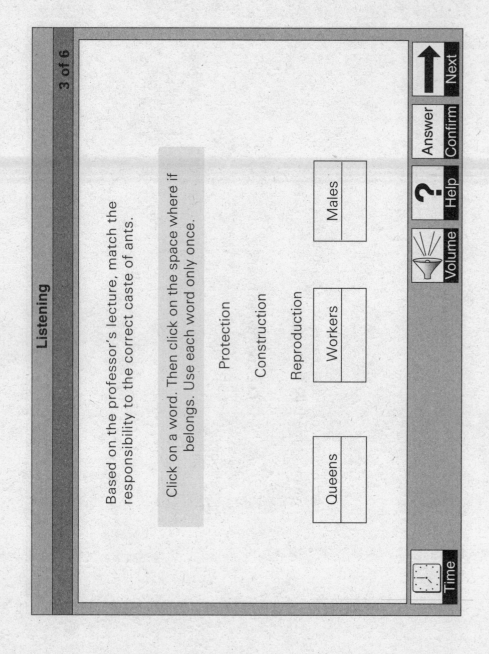

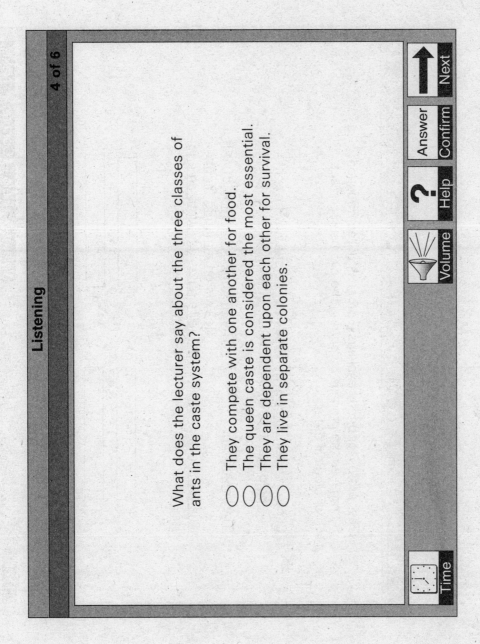

What does the lecturer say about the three classes of ants in the caste system?

⃝ ⃝ ⃝ ⃝   They compete with one another for food.
The queen caste is considered the most essential.
They are dependent upon each other for survival.
They live in separate colonies.

Next

Answer
Confirm

?
Help

Volume

Time

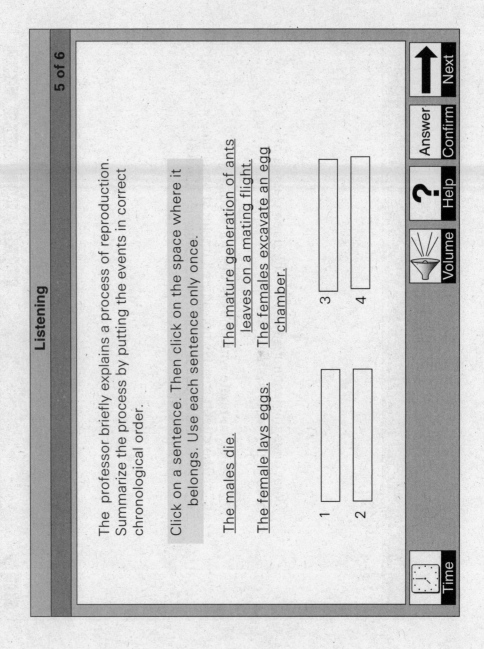

Listening

5 of 6

The professor briefly explains a process of reproduction. Summarize the process by putting the events in correct chronological order.

Click on a sentence. Then click on the space where it belongs. Use each sentence only once.

The males die.

The female lays eggs.

The mature generation of ants leaves on a mating flight.

The females excavate an egg chamber.

1

2

3

4

Time

Volume   Help   Answer
                   Confirm

Next

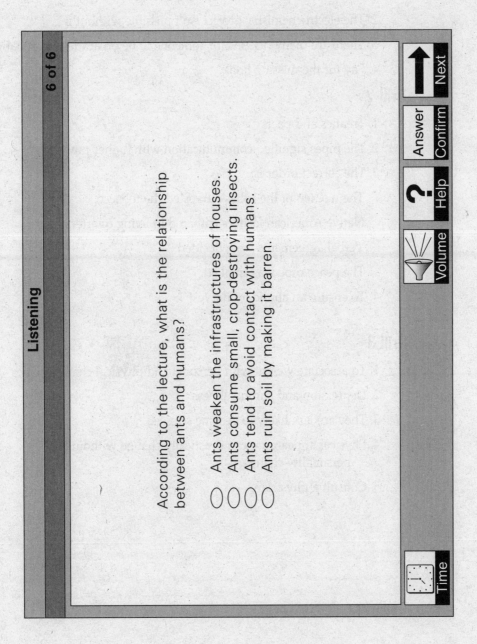

According to the lecture, what is the relationship between ants and humans?

○ Ants weaken the infrastructures of houses.
○ Ants consume small, crop-destroying insects.
○ Ants tend to avoid contact with humans.
○ Ants ruin soil by making it barren.

Time   Volume   Help   Answer Confirm   Next

Answer Keys

Drill 1

1. To discuss a problem concerning a letter

2. The electrochemistry project isn't possible without it.

3. There are many reasons for someone to be on academic probation.

4. Pay for the missing book.

Drill 2

1. Treaties and pacts

2. The pipes signified communication with higher powers.

3. The correct order is:

   The women of the tribes harvested the tobacco.

   Native American leaders gathered in living quarters.

   Verbal agreements were decided.

   The peace pipe was smoked.

4. To ensure an abundant harvest

Drill 3

1. To associate weight with personal and physical characteristics

2. Depression and chronic illness

3. They are less likely to become stressed.

4. Physical appearance can drastically change without any personality change.

5. Consult a physician.

Drill 4

1. The complex social order of ants

2. Soil and logs

3. Protection = Workers

   Construction = Males

   Reproduction = Queens

4. They are dependent upon each other for survival.

5. The correct order is:

   The mature generation of ants leaves on a mating flight.

   The males die.

   The females excavate an egg chamber.

   The female lays eggs.

6. Ants consume small, crop-destroying insects.

PART III

Structure

THE BASICS

The second section of the TOEFL CBT is the Structure section. It tests your basic knowledge of English grammar. The Structure section is computer adaptive, meaning the difficulty of one question depends on whether or not you answered the previous question correctly. Also, you must answer each question before the next one will appear. You will be expected to answer anywhere from 20 to 25 questions in approximately 15 to 20 minutes.

There are two types of questions in the TOEFL CBT Structure section: sentence completion and error identification. No longer are there first 15 sentence completion questions and then 25 error identification questions as on the old paper-and-pencil TOEFL test. Now, ETS presents them one by one in random order. It is impossible to determine how many you will see of each.

DIRECTIONS

The first computer screen you will see in the Structure section of the TOEFL CBT contains the directions. You should learn the directions prior to the test so you don't waste valuable time reading them. By clicking on the "Dismiss Directions" icon located in the upper right side of the screen, the directions will disappear and the first question will appear. The directions will look something like this:

Structure

20 Question

This section is designed to measure your ability to recognize language that is appropriate for standard written English. There are two types of questions in this section.

In the first type of question, there are incomplete sentences. Beneath each sentence there are four words or phrases. You will click on the one word or phrase that best completes the sentence.

> Example: Geysers have often been compared to volcanoes____they both emit hot liquids below the Earth's surface.
> ○ due to
> ○ because
> ○ in spite of
> ○ regardless

The second type of question has four underlined words or phrases. You will click on the one underlined word or phrase that must be changed for the sentence to be correct.

> Example: Guppies are sometimes call rainbow fish because of the males' bright colors.

Now begin working on the Structure questions. When you are ready to continue, click on the Dismiss Directions icon.

When finished reading directions click on the icon below

Dismiss Directions

Time   ? Help   Answer Confirm   → Next

SENTENCE COMPLETION

For sentence completion questions, a sentence will appear in the middle of the computer screen. You must then "click on" one of the four answer choices that is grammatically correct and best completes the sentence. Look at an example.

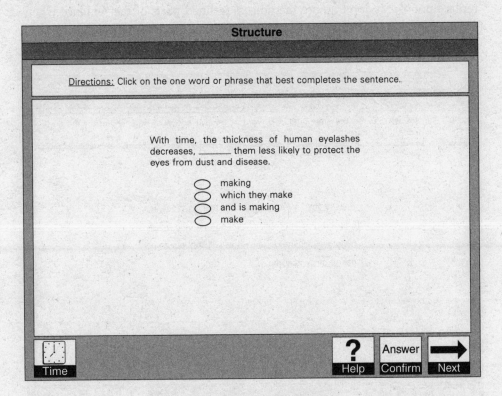

Three of the above four answer choices are incorrect, meaning if they were inserted in the blank, the sentence would *not* make sense in accordance with the standard rules of English grammar. (By the way, the correct answer is "making.")

ERROR IDENTIFICATION

The second type of Structure question you will encounter is error identification. You will see sentences in which four words or phrases are underlined. One of these words or phrases is incorrect and makes the entire sentence grammatically incorrect. The good news in this section is that you are not asked to correct or name the error; you only have to *identify* it. This means that it doesn't really matter if you are not completely sure *why* a particular word or phrase is wrong. Recognizing that it is incorrect is all you need to do. You will not have to supply the correct word or phrase.

For error identification questions, you only have to identify the error, *not* correct it.

One of the most obvious things to keep in mind regarding error identification questions on the TOEFL CBT is that the parts of the sentence that are *not* underlined are *correct* as written. Many times, you can look to the non-underlined parts, the parts you know are correct, and use them to guide you. Articles and adjectives can tell you whether nouns are plural or singular. Pronouns replace nouns. So don't ignore the non-underlined parts of the sentence when you are looking at error identification questions. Look at a typical TOEFL CBT error identification question:

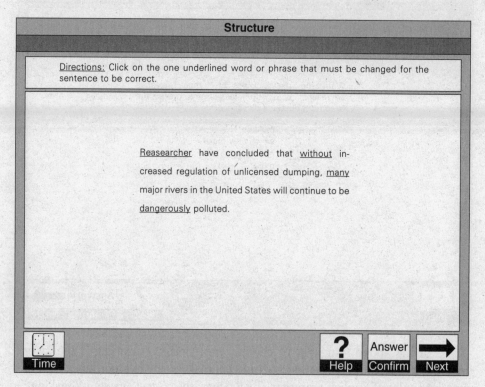

Three of the above four answer choices are correct, meaning they are *grammatically* correct. You want to "click on" the answer choice that is *grammatically incorrect* in accordance with the standard rules of English grammar. (By the way, the correct answer is "Researcher.")

WHAT DOES IT TEST?

ETS says that the Structure section "measures your ability to recognize language that is appropriate for standard written English." The key word here is "recognize." You never have to come up with the answer yourself, you simply have to "recognize" the best answer. Think about it this way. Every day, you go to the same grocery store where you see the same manager. Although you don't know the name of the manager, his face is familiar. If you see that same manager in the subway, at the library, or in the park, you still don't know his name or anything else about him, but you will be able to "recognize" him and know that he works at the grocery store. The Structure section of the TOEFL CBT works the same way. It tests the same grammar rules over and over again.

ETS is not that creative with its questions. Once you "recognize" the limited grammar rules that ETS tests, "recognizing" the best answer is simple. Since ETS uses multiple choice testing, you must simply "click on" one of four possible choices that you "recognize." Once you memorize and practice the different question types, your score will improve significantly. So, the Structure section of the TOEFL CBT simply tests how well you can "recognize" grammar mistakes.

PROCESS OF ELIMINATION (POE)

As you learned in the Listening section, sometimes you aren't quite which answer you should "click on." By eliminating the answer choices you know are wrong, you can greatly increase your chances of "clicking on" the best answer—even if you guess. Guessing and "clicking on" an answer from one of two choices makes your odds of getting the best answer much greater than guessing from four choices.

Use Process of Elimination to rule out wrong answer choices, and as a last resort, *guess.*

HOW MUCH WILL MY SCORES IMPROVE?

This depends on how much you practice. But keep this in mind: If grammar is your strong point, and you are already scoring fairly high, room for improvement is significantly *less* than if grammar is your weak point and you are scoring fairly low. There are a lot of drills in this book. If you use the techniques we teach and practice, practice, practice, your scores will improve.

SCORING

One half of your score for the Structure section is determined by how well you do on the grammar questions—that is, the 20 to 25 sentence completion and error identification questions. The other half of your score is determined by how well you write your essay in the Writing section, formerly known as the Test of Written English (TWE.) The Writing section is covered in chapter 7 of this book.

The computer will immediately determine your score for the grammar part of the Structure section. Your mandatory 30-minute essay will be sent to two individual graders who will assign your essay a score from 6 (the highest) to 0 (the lowest). A third reader will grade the essay if there is more than a 1-point discrepancy. Immediately after completing the entire TOEFL CBT, you will have the opportunity to see your total rough score on the computer screen. The Listening score and the Reading Score will be accurate; however, your Structure and Writing score will be approximated, because the essay will not yet have been sent to the individual graders.

5

Grammar

APPROACHING THE SECTION

Fortunately for you, ETS is not very creative with its question types. They tend to test the same incorrect grammar points over and over. The following is a list of the most common types of errors found in Error Identification questions on the TOEFL CBT Structure section. Each one is described in detail and followed by practice questions like those frequently found on the TOEFL CBT.

Once you have reviewed and learned how to recognize the most common errors, you simply have to "click on" the underlined answer choice that makes the sentence grammatically incorrect.

THE SIXTEEN MOST COMMON ERRORS
Subjects
Verbs
Nouns
Singular and Plural
Articles
Pronouns
Appositives
Adjectives
Adverbs
Subordination
Noun Cases
Passive and Active Modifiers
Gerunds and Infinitives
Prepositions
Conjunctions
Comparisons and Superlatives

SUBJECTS

A sentence is a group of words that expresses a grammatically complete thought. At the heart of every written sentence in English is the main subject and the main verb. The basic parts of a sentence are:

main subject	the noun that does the main action
main verb	the word that expresses the main action

The subject is the part of the sentence that tells you who or what is doing the main verb. On the TOEFL CBT, you should always try to find and isolate the main subject and the main verb. This will greatly increase your chances of using POE to eliminate the incorrect answer choices and selecting the best answer.

> Every sentence *must* have a main subject and a main verb.

The subject of every sentence must be a noun. A noun is a word that names something. However, nouns that function as subjects of sentences are not always a single word. Nouns that act as subjects can take on many forms.

- Nouns: *Astrologers* divide the hemisphere into twelve parts.

- Pronouns: *There* are fewer than 100 panda bears alive in the wild.

  It was Robert Goddard who successfully fired the world's first liquid-fuel rocket.

- Gerunds: *Exercising* is recommended by all health care professionals.

In the TOEFL CBT Structure section, ETS will test your basic knowledge of subjects. The majority of the subject questions are found among the sentence completions. Rarely will you find a question testing subjects in the error identification questions.

The first and most common way ETS tests your basic knowledge of subjects on the TOEFL CBT is by having you identify the noun functioning as the subject. Sometimes the subject is a gerund—a form of a verb, ending in *–ing*, which acts as a noun—but usually the subject is just a regular noun. ETS sometimes tries to confuse you by hiding the subject behind a modifying phrase or by including the main verb in the answer choice. However, always determine whether there is a main subject and main verb. If they are not present, ETS wants you to find them. Look at a typical *subject* question that frequently appears on the TOEFL CBT.

The seventeenth child of slaves, _____ President Roosevelt's policies on Minority affairs.

- ◯ Mary Bethune developed
- ◯ and Mary Bethune was developing
- ◯ because Mary Bethune developed
- ◯ Mary Bethune, to develop

Since modifying phrases must either precede or follow what they modify, you can use POE to get rid of the second and third answer choices. The fourth answer choice does not provide a main verb. The first (and correct) answer choice fulfills main subject and main verb requirements. Look at another typical *subject* question.

_____ among constituents is just one of
the many ways that politicians attempt to
increase their popularity in opinion polls.

- ○ If similarities are found
- ○ Similarities are found
- ○ Finding similarities
- ○ When finding similarities

In this *subject* question, the main subject is missing but the main verb is "is." The first answer choice uses the conditional "if," and ETS never tests conditionals. The second answer choice provides another main verb. Remember, every sentence needs only one main verb. The third (and correct) answer choice provides the gerund *finding* and the noun *similarities* that completes the noun clause.

Another way ETS tests your knowledge of subjects is by using the pronoun *there*. If the subject sentence begins with the word *there*, you must determine what noun the pronoun *there* is referring to. Look at a typical "there" question that frequently appears on the TOEFL CBT:

_____ many viruses that attack the
immune system and leave the victim
vulnerable to infections, malignancies, and
other neurological disorders.

- ○ They are
- ○ Of the
- ○ There are
- ○ The

This question needs a main subject and a main verb. The answer choices "Of the" and "The" lack a main verb. The pronoun in the first answer choice, "They are," cannot refer to "viruses" in a statement of fact. The third (and correct) answer choice supplies the pronoun *there*, which refers to "viruses," and the plural verb *are*, which agrees with "viruses."

ETS may also test your knowledge of subjects by using the pronoun subject *it*, which is used to identify a person who accomplishes something. Look at a typical "it" question that frequently appears on the TOEFL CBT:

_____who was the first African American
writer to win the Nobel Prize for Literature.

- ⊙ Toni Morrison
- ○ When Toni Morrison
- ○ Toni Morrison was
- ○ It was Toni Morrison

This type of question frequently appears on the TOEFL CBT and is easy to recognize. The first two answer choices create dependent clauses and lack main verbs. The third answer choice incorrectly places the verb in front of the relative pronoun *who*. The last answer choice provides a subject, a verb, and a noun for the relative pronoun "who" to modify.

A final way ETS may test your knowledge of subjects is by using the negatives "not only" and "not until." Whenever a sentence begins with this negative, the auxiliary of the verb *must* come immediately before the subject. Look at an example.

<u>Not only</u> <u>are</u> <u>dogs</u> some of the most
　　Negative　aux　sub
loyal animals, but they also provide
safe protection.

Notice how the auxiliary "are" precedes the subject "dogs." This type of negative question would appear as follows on the TOEFL CBT:

Not only _____ some of the most loyal
animals, but they also provide safe
protection.

- ○ are dogs
- ○ dogs
- ○ they are dogs
- ○ dogs are

The first answer choice, "are dogs," is the correct answer. It correctly places the auxiliary before the subject. The second answer choice, "dogs," lacks a main verb. The third answer choice, "they are dogs," repeats the subject. The last answer choice, "dogs are," incorrectly places the subject before the verb.

The only subject questions that sometimes appear in error identification questions simply insert a "double subject" in the form of a pronoun. Look at a typical subject question that frequently appears on the TOEFL CBT in the error identification section.

Many bookstores in <u>most</u> large
American cities <u>they offer</u> gourmet
coffee and food, in addition to
<u>shelves full</u> of <u>popular books</u>.

In this type of question, the pronoun *they* incorrectly repeats the subject, "bookstores."

PRACTICE!

The following exercises contain *subject* questions most frequently found on the TOEFL CBT Structure section. Click on (in this case circle) the one word or phrase that best completes the sentence, or the one underlined word or phrase that must be changed for the sentence to be correct.

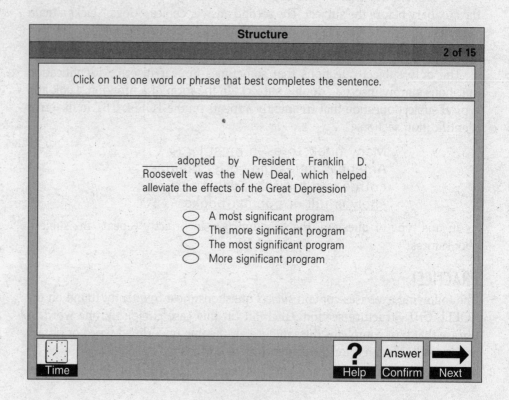

Click on the one word or phrase that best completes the sentence.

_____ more than 60 types of grains, and although they are all edible, only a few types are digestible by humans.

○ There are
○ Of the
○ The
○ They are

Time
? Help
Answer Confirm
Next

Click on the one word or phrase that best completes the sentence.

_____ adopted by President Franklin D. Roosevelt was the New Deal, which helped alleviate the effects of the Great Depression

○ A most significant program
○ The more significant program
○ The most significant program
○ More significant program

Time
? Help
Answer Confirm
Next

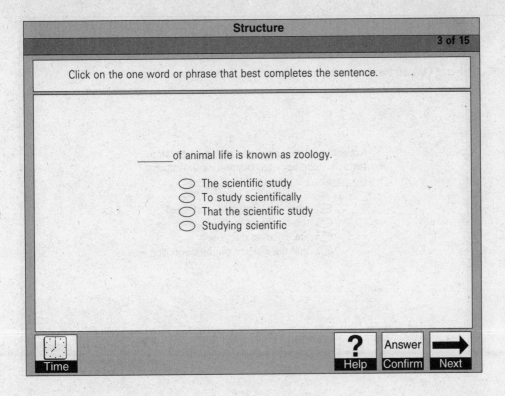

Click on the one word or phrase that best completes the sentence.

_____ of animal life is known as zoology.

○ The scientific study
○ To study scientifically
○ That the scientific study
○ Studying scientific

? Help | Answer Confirm | → Next

Time

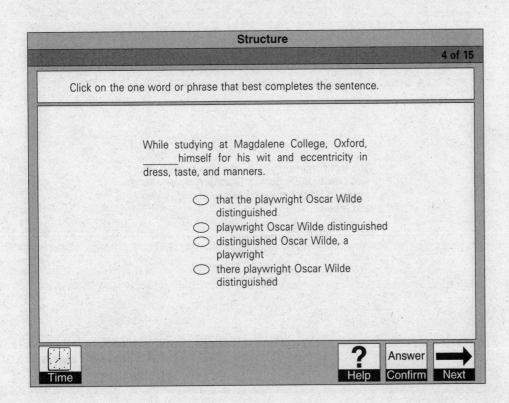

Click on the one word or phrase that best completes the sentence.

While studying at Magdalene College, Oxford, _____ himself for his wit and eccentricity in dress, taste, and manners.

○ that the playwright Oscar Wilde distinguished
○ playwright Oscar Wilde distinguished
○ distinguished Oscar Wilde, a playwright
○ there playwright Oscar Wilde distinguished

? Help | Answer Confirm | → Next

Time

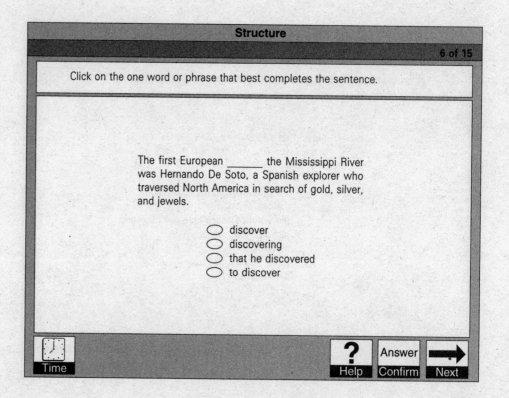

Click on the one word or phrase that best completes the sentence.

Not until a modern physician employs laboratory tests in addition to physical examinations _____.

◯ when the disease is diagnosed
◯ the diagnosis of the disease
◯ are diseases diagnosed
◯ that the disease can be diagnosed

Time Help Answer Confirm Next

Click on the one word or phrase that best completes the sentence.

The first European _____ the Mississippi River was Hernando De Soto, a Spanish explorer who traversed North America in search of gold, silver, and jewels.

◯ discover
◯ discovering
◯ that he discovered
◯ to discover

Time Help Answer Confirm Next

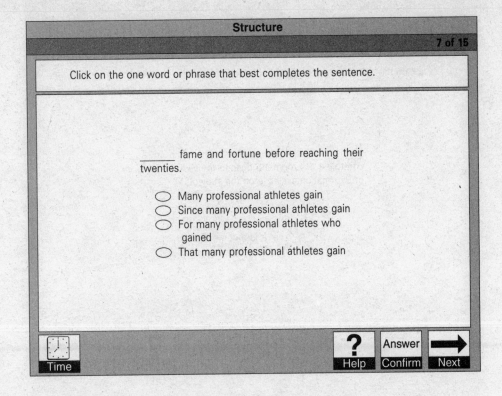

Click on the one word or phrase that best completes the sentence.

_____ fame and fortune before reaching their twenties.

⚪ Many professional athletes gain
⚪ Since many professional athletes gain
⚪ For many professional athletes who gained
⚪ That many professional athletes gain

Time   ?   Answer   Next
        Help Confirm

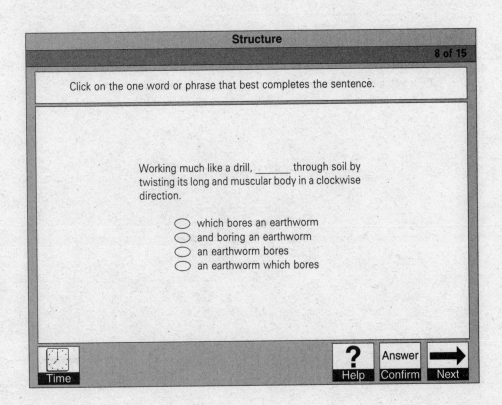

Click on the one word or phrase that best completes the sentence.

Working much like a drill, _____ through soil by twisting its long and muscular body in a clockwise direction.

⚪ which bores an earthworm
⚪ and boring an earthworm
⚪ an earthworm bores
⚪ an earthworm which bores

Time   ?   Answer   Next
        Help Confirm

Structure

9 of 15

Click on the one word or phrase that best completes the sentence.

______ to raise tropical salt-water fish in a controlled environment, despite the vast amount of information available on the subject.

- ◯ Not only is it easy
- ◯ It is not easy
- ◯ That it is much easier
- ◯ Why it is not easy

Time | Help | Answer Confirm | Next

Structure

10 of 15

Click on the one word or phrase that best completes the sentence.

______ the habitual use of any chemical substance to alter states of body or mind.

- ◯ If drug addiction is
- ◯ With drug addiction
- ◯ While drug addiction is
- ◯ Drug addiction is

Time | Help | Answer Confirm | Next

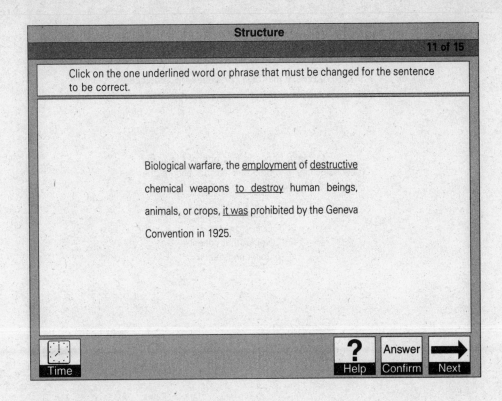

Click on the one underlined word or phrase that must be changed for the sentence to be correct.

Biological warfare, the <u>employment</u> of <u>destructive</u> chemical weapons <u>to destroy</u> human beings, animals, or crops, <u>it was</u> prohibited by the Geneva Convention in 1925.

Time Help Answer Confirm Next

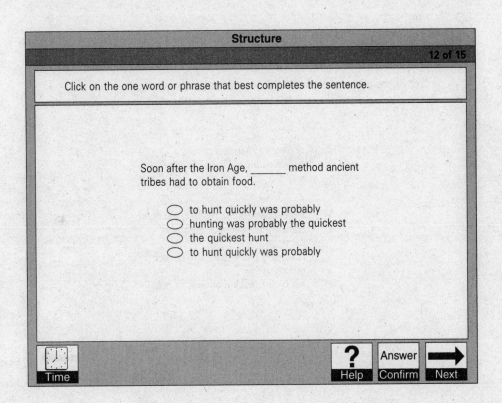

Click on the one word or phrase that best completes the sentence.

Soon after the Iron Age, _____ method ancient tribes had to obtain food.

○ to hunt quickly was probably
○ hunting was probably the quickest
○ the quickest hunt
○ to hunt quickly was probably

Time Help Answer Confirm Next

Structure

13 of 15

Click on the one word or phrase that best completes the sentence.

______ to make honey is just one of the many responsibilities a drone bee has to ensure the survival of its colony.

- ◯ Collection nectar
- ◯ Collect nectar
- ◯ Nectar that collects
- ◯ Collecting nectar

Time | ? Help | Answer Confirm | Next

Structure

14 of 15

Click on the one word or phrase that best completes the sentence.

Although fairly new in their application, ______ relax muscles, adjust blood flow, and alleviate anxiety.

- ◯ biofeedback programs help patients
- ◯ and help biofeedback programs' patients
- ◯ is helping patients in biofeedback programs
- ◯ are biofeedback programs to help

Time | ? Help | Answer Confirm | Next

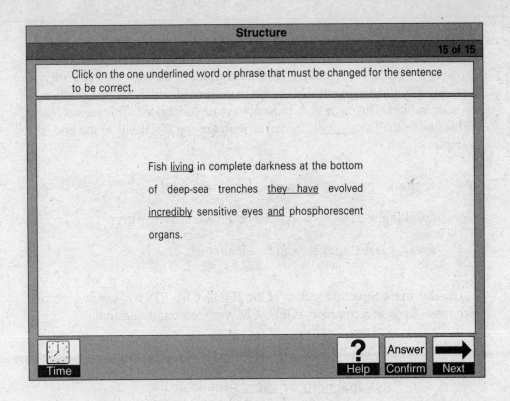

Click on the one underlined word or phrase that must be changed for the sentence to be correct.

Fish <u>living</u> in complete darkness at the bottom
of deep-sea trenches <u>they have</u> evolved
<u>incredibly</u> sensitive eyes <u>and</u> phosphorescent
organs.

Time

? Help

Answer Confirm

Next

Verbs

Try to identify the *main* verb in a sentence. This is the word that indentifies the main action of the main subject. The main verb must always be conjugated.

A verb is an action. Not only does a verb express a physical or mental action, but also a state of being. Even though there may be more than one verb in a sentence, try to identify the *main* verb. This is the word that identifies the main action of the main subject. The main verb must always be conjugated. This means that it will *not* be in the "to _____" form, or with an -ing (by itself) at the end. For example:

to speak	can *not* be a main verb
speaking	can *not* be a main verb by itself
speak, speaks, spoke	can be a main verb

Usually, in the Structure section of the TOEFL CBT, ETS will use an incorrect verb tense. Look at a common TOEFL CBT verb tense test question:

> When he <u>lands</u> on the moon in 1962,
> <u>astronaut</u> John Glenn was considered a
> <u>national hero</u> by <u>every</u> American.

In these types of sentences, ETS will most likely give you a time clause. In this example, the action took place in the past, 1962. Therefore, the verb should be in the past tense, *landed*.

In an English sentence, the subject and the verb must always agree. Singular subjects must take singular verbs, and plural subjects must take plural verbs. ETS will also try to confuse you by inserting long modifying clauses between the subject and the verb to make it difficult for you to know the correct verb conjugation. Look at a common TOEFL CBT subject/verb test question:

> Russia's <u>immense</u> areas of <u>barren</u> tundra
> <u>draws</u> many species of wildlife that depend
> on the foliage for <u>survival</u>.

In these types of sentences, ETS will hide the verb behind a prepositional phrase. What is the main subject in this sentence? Remember, the main verb and the main subject must agree. The subject, "areas," is plural. The main verb, "draws," must also be in the plural form, *draw*. You will also encounter verb questions in the Sentence Completion type of question in the Structure section of the TOEFL CBT. For example:

> During the brief prohibition era, the local
> police force _____ thousands of gallons
> of illegally distilled alcohol.
>
> ○ destroyed
> ○ who destroyed
> ○ destroying that which
> ○ to destroy

This type of sentence needs a main verb. The second and third answer choices create a dependent clause. The infinitive form "to destroy" can not act as a main verb. The first answer choice "destroyed" completes main verb requirements.

Occasionally, ETS will try to confuse you with the passive form of the verb. The passive construction switches the object and the subject, and the "be" verb is added to the past participial verb. Look at a common TOEFL CBT passive test question:

> One of the first grains <u>cultivated</u> in the New World, corn <u>was growing</u> by the settlers <u>who</u> landed on the <u>eastern shores</u> of Massachusetts.

The active sentence would read, "settlers grew corn." When the object and subject are switched the sentence should read, "corn was *grown* by the settlers." The verb *must* be in the past participial form.

PRACTICE!

The following exercises contain the sort of verb questions most frequently found in the Structure section of the TOEFL CBT. Click on (in this case circle) the one word or phrase that best completes the sentence, or the one underlined word or phrase that must be changed for the sentence to be correct.

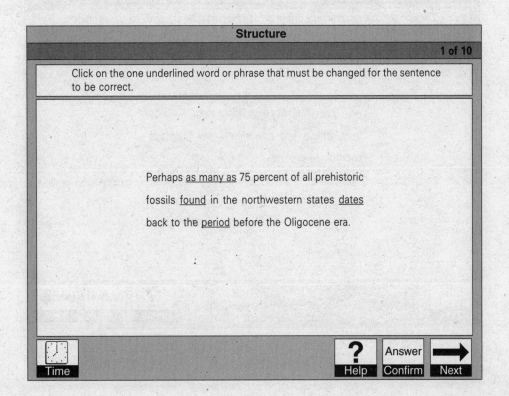

Structure

1 of 10

Click on the one underlined word or phrase that must be changed for the sentence to be correct.

Perhaps <u>as many as</u> 75 percent of all prehistoric fossils <u>found</u> in the northwestern states <u>dates</u> back to the <u>period</u> before the Oligocene era.

| Time | ? Help | Answer Confirm | → Next |

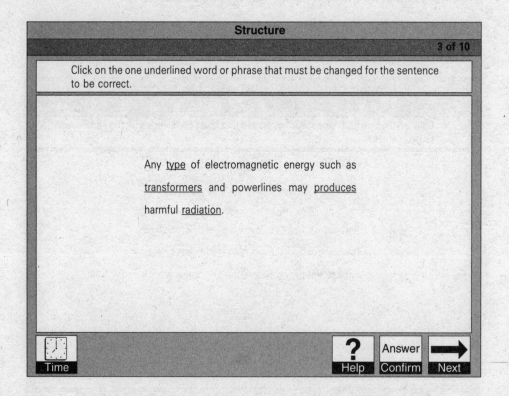

Click on the one word or phrase that best completes the sentence.

Most mammals give birth to live offspring, but a few rare species _____ eggs in the soil until they hatch.

○ to incubate
○ they incubate
○ incubate
○ to have incubated

Time Help Answer Confirm Next

Click on the one underlined word or phrase that must be changed for the sentence to be correct.

Any <u>type</u> of electromagnetic energy such as <u>transformers</u> and powerlines may <u>produces</u> harmful <u>radiation</u>.

Time Help Answer Confirm Next

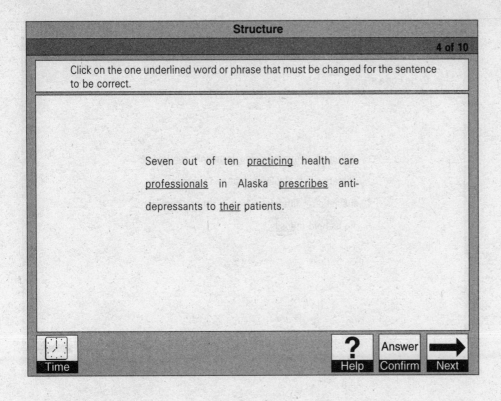

Click on the one underlined word or phrase that must be changed for the sentence to be correct.

Seven out of ten <u>practicing</u> health care <u>professionals</u> in Alaska <u>prescribes</u> anti-depressants to <u>their</u> patients.

Time   Help   Answer Confirm   Next

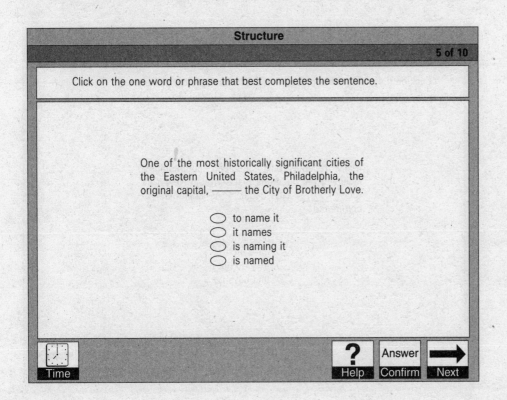

Click on the one word or phrase that best completes the sentence.

One of the most historically significant cities of the Eastern United States, Philadelphia, the original capital, ———— the City of Brotherly Love.

○ to name it
○ it names
○ is naming it
○ is named

Time   Help   Answer Confirm   Next

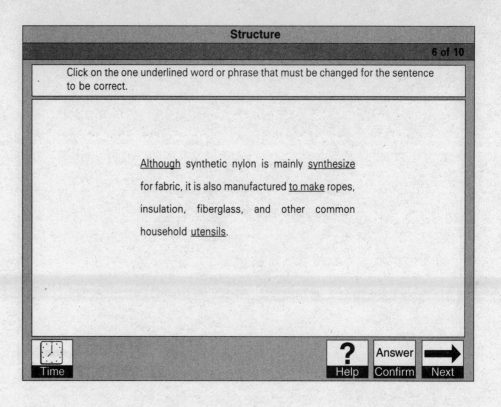

Click on the one underlined word or phrase that must be changed for the sentence to be correct.

<u>Although</u> synthetic nylon is mainly <u>synthesize</u> for fabric, it is also manufactured <u>to make</u> ropes, insulation, fiberglass, and other common household <u>utensils</u>.

Time   Help   Answer Confirm   Next

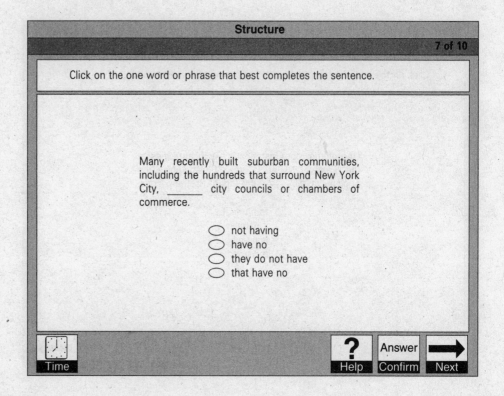

Click on the one word or phrase that best completes the sentence.

Many recently built suburban communities, including the hundreds that surround New York City, _____ city councils or chambers of commerce.

- ⬭ not having
- ⬭ have no
- ⬭ they do not have
- ⬭ that have no

Time   Help   Answer Confirm   Next

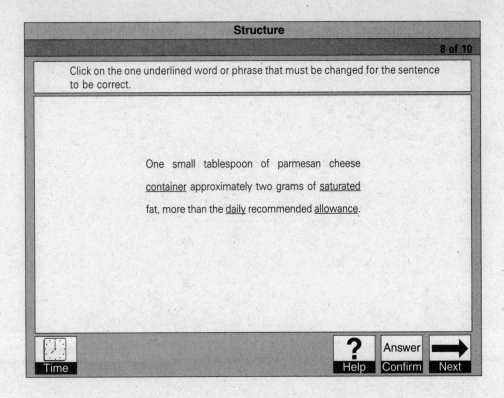

Click on the one underlined word or phrase that must be changed for the sentence to be correct.

One small tablespoon of parmesan cheese <u>container</u> approximately two grams of <u>saturated</u> fat, more than the <u>daily</u> recommended <u>allowance</u>.

Time

? Help

Answer Confirm

→ Next

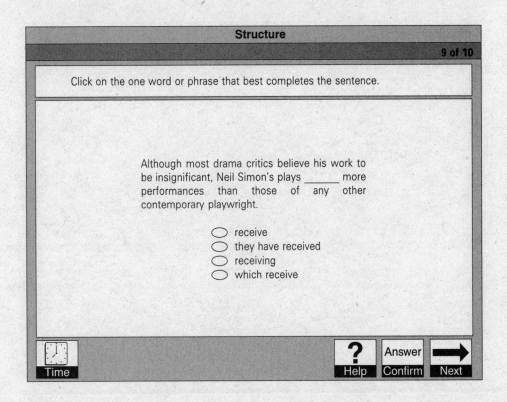

Click on the one word or phrase that best completes the sentence.

Although most drama critics believe his work to be insignificant, Neil Simon's plays _____ more performances than those of any other contemporary playwright.

- ○ receive
- ○ they have received
- ○ receiving
- ○ which receive

Time

? Help

Answer Confirm

→ Next

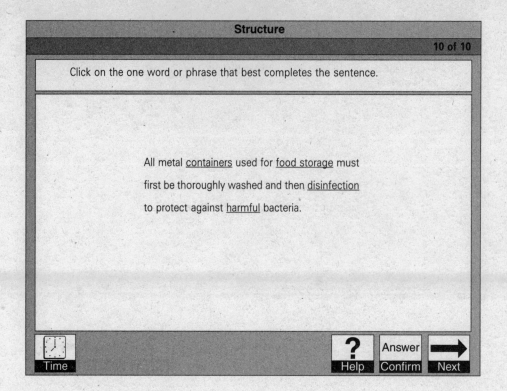

Click on the one word or phrase that best completes the sentence.

All metal <u>containers</u> used for <u>food storage</u> must first be thoroughly washed and then <u>disinfection</u> to protect against <u>harmful</u> bacteria.

Time

? Help

Answer Confirm

→ Next

Nouns

In the subject section above, you briefly encountered nouns that function as subjects. However, ETS also tests your ability to recognize nouns, noun clauses, and gerunds; whether nouns are singular or plural; and the articles that come before nouns. ETS does *not* test capitalization of proper nouns.

Simply, a noun is a word that names a person, place, thing, or idea. On the TOEFL CBT, ETS will test your ability to recognize nouns by incorrectly substituting them with either an adjective or verb. Look at a typical noun question that appears in the Structure section of the TOEFL CBT.

> The <u>current</u> definition of <u>dead</u> is the
> irreversible cessation of <u>all</u> functions of the
> <u>entire</u> brain, including the brain stem.

In this example, ETS has incorrectly substituted the adjective "dead" for the noun "death." If you have trouble distinguishing the adjective form from the noun form, rely on your POE techniques to eliminate the other three answer choices. In this example, the adjectives "current", "all," and "entire" correctly modify the nouns they precede.

PRACTICE!

The following exercises contain noun questions most frequently found on the TOEFL CBT Structure section. Click on (in this case circle) the one word or phrase that best completes the sentence, or the one underlined word or phrase that must be changed for the sentence to be correct.

A noun is a word that names a person, place, thing, or idea.

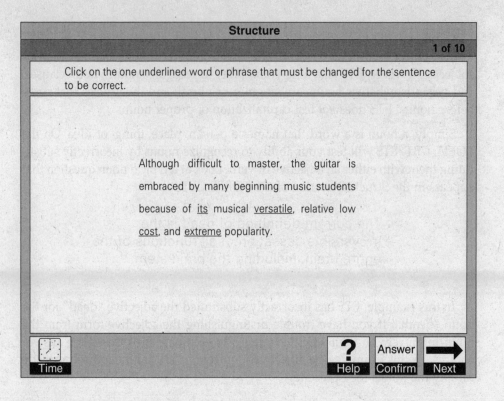

Click on the one underlined word or phrase that must be changed for the sentence to be correct.

Although difficult to master, the guitar is embraced by many beginning music students because of <u>its</u> musical <u>versatile</u>, relative low <u>cost</u>, and <u>extreme</u> popularity.

Time

Help

Answer
Confirm

Next

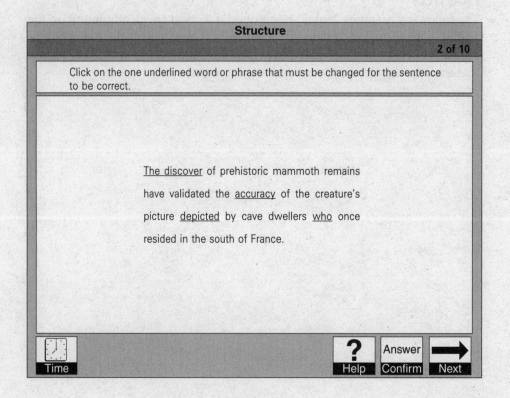

Click on the one underlined word or phrase that must be changed for the sentence to be correct.

<u>The discover</u> of prehistoric mammoth remains have validated the <u>accuracy</u> of the creature's picture <u>depicted</u> by cave dwellers <u>who</u> once resided in the south of France.

Time

Help

Answer
Confirm

Next

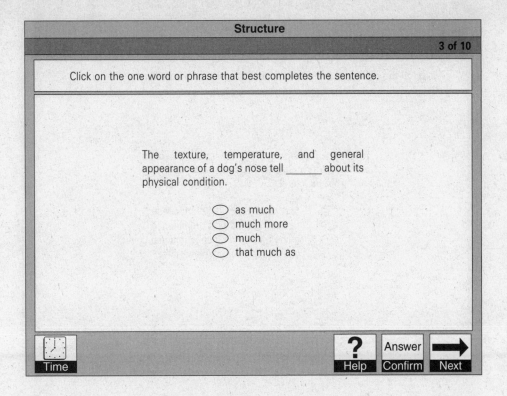

Click on the one word or phrase that best completes the sentence.

The texture, temperature, and general appearance of a dog's nose tell _____ about its physical condition.

- ⬭ as much
- ⬭ much more
- ⬭ much
- ⬭ that much as

Time ? Help Answer Confirm Next

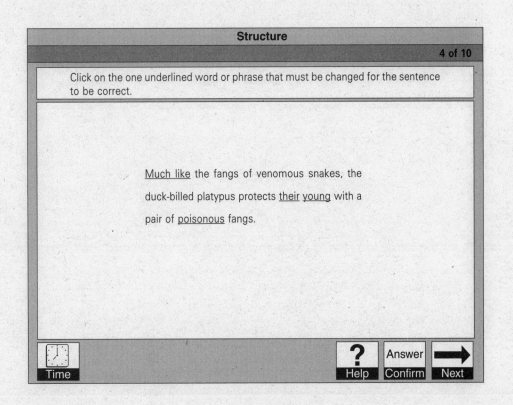

Click on the one underlined word or phrase that must be changed for the sentence to be correct.

<u>Much like</u> the fangs of venomous snakes, the duck-billed platypus protects <u>their</u> <u>young</u> with a pair of <u>poisonous</u> fangs.

Time ? Help Answer Confirm Next

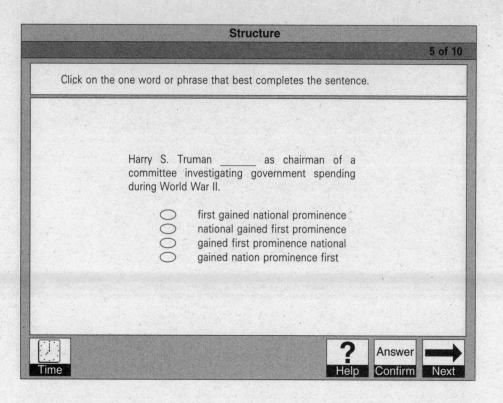

Click on the one word or phrase that best completes the sentence.

Harry S. Truman _____ as chairman of a committee investigating government spending during World War II.

○ first gained national prominence
○ national gained first prominence
○ gained first prominence national
○ gained nation prominence first

Time   ? Help   Answer Confirm   Next →

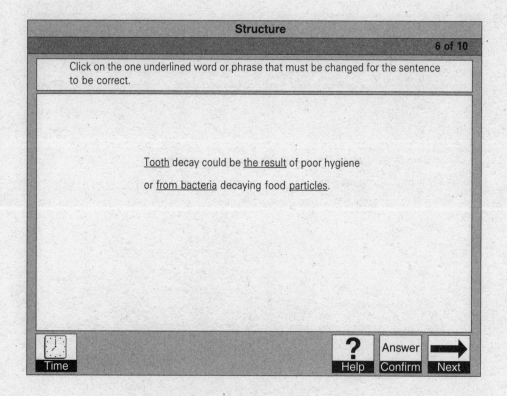

Click on the one underlined word or phrase that must be changed for the sentence to be correct.

Tooth decay could be the result of poor hygiene

or from bacteria decaying food particles.

Time   ? Help   Answer Confirm   Next →

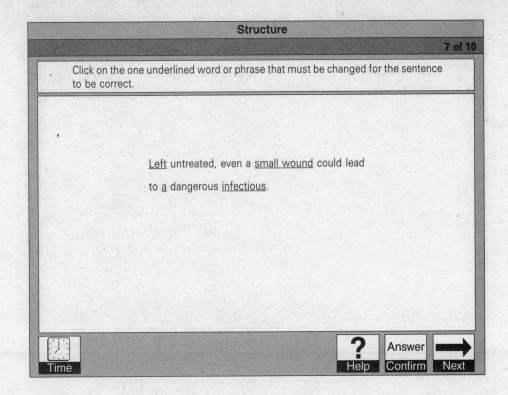

Click on the one underlined word or phrase that must be changed for the sentence to be correct.

<u>Left</u> untreated, even a <u>small wound</u> could lead

to <u>a</u> dangerous <u>infectious</u>.

? Help | Answer Confirm | → Next

Time

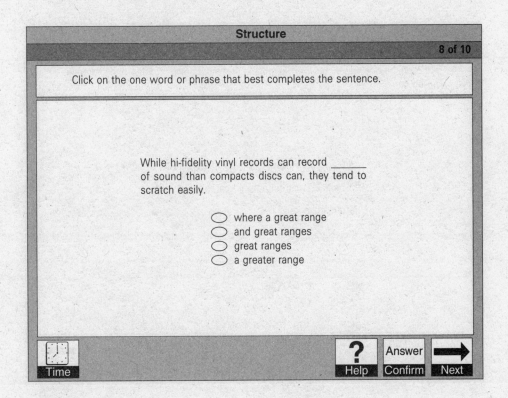

Click on the one word or phrase that best completes the sentence.

While hi-fidelity vinyl records can record _____
of sound than compacts discs can, they tend to
scratch easily.

○ where a great range
○ and great ranges
○ great ranges
○ a greater range

? Help | Answer Confirm | → Next

Time

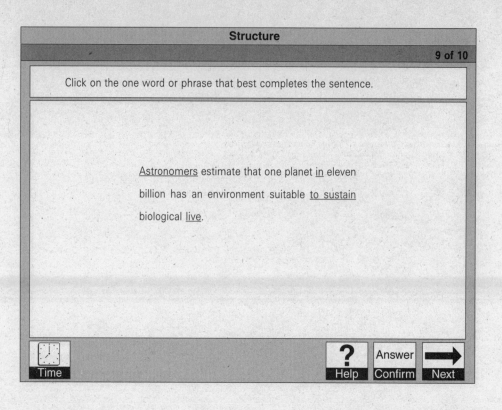

Click on the one word or phrase that best completes the sentence.

<u>Astronomers</u> estimate that one planet <u>in</u> eleven billion has an environment suitable <u>to sustain</u> biological <u>live</u>.

Time   Help   Answer Confirm   Next

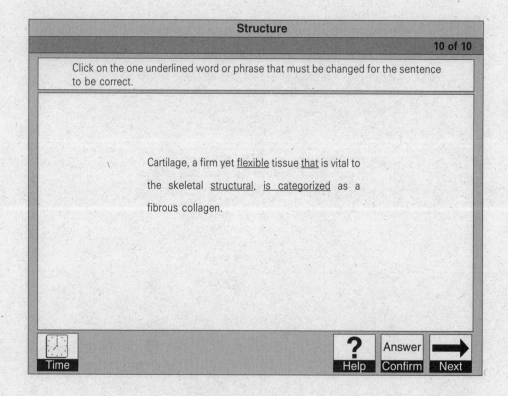

Click on the one underlined word or phrase that must be changed for the sentence to be correct.

Cartilage, a firm yet <u>flexible</u> tissue <u>that</u> is vital to the skeletal <u>structural</u>, <u>is categorized</u> as a fibrous collagen.

Time   Help   Answer Confirm   Next

SINGULAR AND PLURAL NOUNS

ETS will also test your basic knowledge of whether a noun should be singular or plural. The singular and plural noun questions always appear in error identification questions on the TOEFL CBT exam. Ninety-nine percent of the time, ETS will either drop the "s" on words that should be plural, or add the "s" on words that should be singular. Only rarely does ETS confuse irregular plural nouns and irregular singular nouns (feet for foot, people for person, and so forth).

Ninety-nine percent of the time, ETS will either drop the "s" on words that should be plural, or add the "s" on words that should be singular.

How do you know if a noun is singular or plural? It's simple. If the underlined noun is talking about several objects, or referring to an object in general, the noun should be plural. In this case, the underlined noun is often preceded by a quantitative adjective such as several, a few, many, other, various, and so forth. If the underlined noun is referring to just one specific or special object, the noun should be singular. Look at a typical singular and plural question frequently found on the TOEFL CBT.

Earthquakes occur in several geographical

location, many of which are in conjunction

with faults, the areas where opposing

plates pass one another.

The quantitative (meaning "how many") adjective "several" indicates that the noun "location" should be plural. The other underlined nouns in the sentence, "earthquakes" and "faults," are *not* referring to one in particular, and therefore must be plural. Remember that singular nouns must be preceded by the indefinite articles "a" and "an."

Countable and Non-countable Nouns

Some nouns that appear on the TOEFL, such as "children," "tables," or "fish," can be counted and are therefore called *countable* nouns. Others cannot be counted. These nouns are called *non-countable*:

air	water
wheat	equipment
money	gold
petroleum	literature
chemistry	weather
editing	grass

Many nouns refer to abstract ideas instead of concrete things or people. These abstract nouns are rarely countable:

beauty	courage
fear	wealth
determination	blindness
charity	grace
equality	hate

PRACTICE!

The following exercises contain singular and plural questions most frequently found on the TOEFL CBT Structure section. Click on (in this case circle) the one underlined word or phrase that must be changed for the sentence to be correct.

Click on the one underlined word or phrase that must be changed for the sentence to be correct.

Known more <u>for</u> his novels than his poetry, William Faulkner <u>actually</u> published several <u>collection</u> of poems before writing his most famous <u>piece</u> *As I Lay Dying* in 1930.

Time ? Help Answer Confirm Next

Click on the one underlined word or phrase that must be changed for the sentence to be correct.

<u>Occurring</u> predominantly <u>in</u> mountainous <u>area,</u> avalanches are triggered by earthquake tremors, human disturbances, or <u>excessive</u> rainfall.

Time ? Help Answer Confirm Next

Click on the one underlined word or phrase that must be changed for the sentence to be correct.

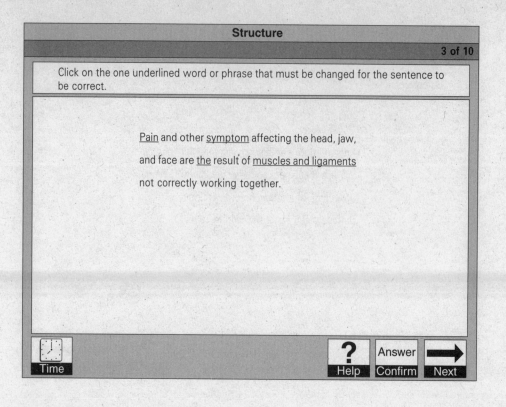

Pain and other symptom affecting the head, jaw,

and face are the result of muscles and ligaments

not correctly working together.

Time   Help   Answer Confirm   Next

Click on the one underlined word or phrase that must be changed for the sentence to be correct.

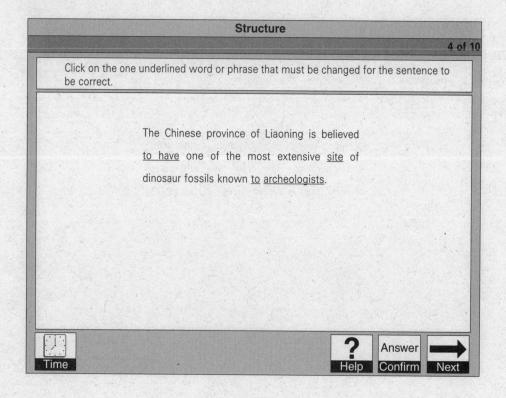

The Chinese province of Liaoning is believed

to have one of the most extensive site of

dinosaur fossils known to archeologists.

Time   Help   Answer Confirm   Next

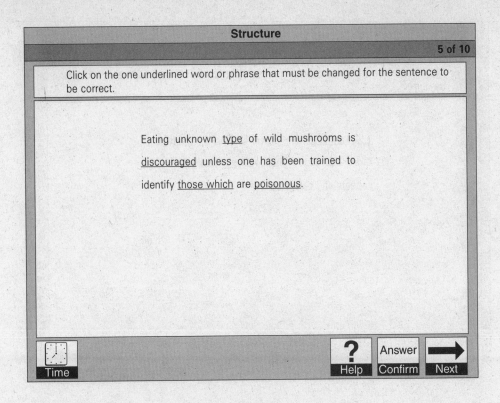

Click on the one underlined word or phrase that must be changed for the sentence to be correct.

Eating unknown <u>type</u> of wild mushrooms is <u>discouraged</u> unless one has been trained to identify <u>those which</u> are <u>poisonous</u>.

Time · Help · Answer Confirm · Next

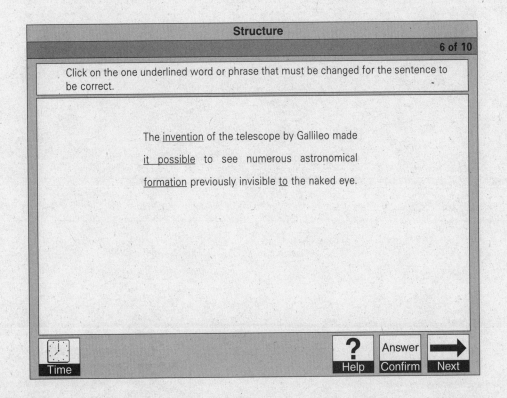

Click on the one underlined word or phrase that must be changed for the sentence to be correct.

The <u>invention</u> of the telescope by Gallileo made <u>it possible</u> to see numerous astronomical <u>formation</u> previously invisible <u>to</u> the naked eye.

Time · Help · Answer Confirm · Next

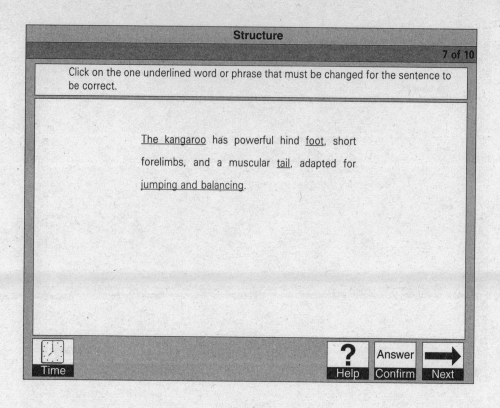

Click on the one underlined word or phrase that must be changed for the sentence to be correct.

The <u>kangaroo</u> has powerful hind <u>foot</u>, short forelimbs, and a muscular <u>tail</u>, adapted for <u>jumping and balancing</u>.

Time   Help   Answer Confirm   Next

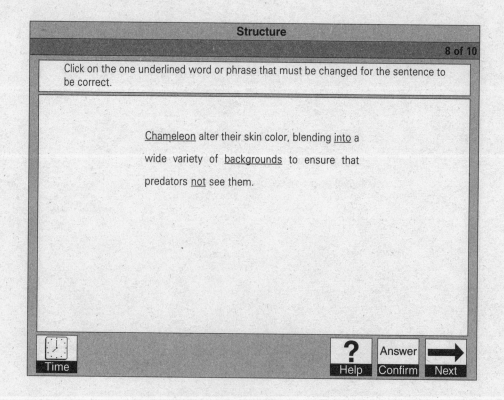

Click on the one underlined word or phrase that must be changed for the sentence to be correct.

<u>Chameleon</u> alter their skin color, blending <u>into</u> a wide variety of <u>backgrounds</u> to ensure that predators <u>not</u> see them.

Time   Help   Answer Confirm   Next

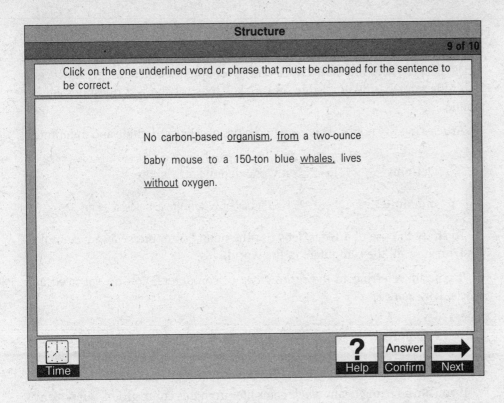

Click on the one underlined word or phrase that must be changed for the sentence to be correct.

No carbon-based <u>organism,</u> <u>from</u> a two-ounce

baby mouse to a 150-ton blue <u>whales,</u> lives

<u>without</u> oxygen.

Time   ?   Answer   Next
       Help Confirm

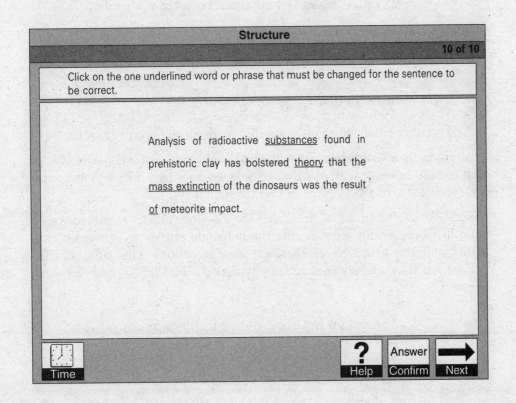

Click on the one underlined word or phrase that must be changed for the sentence to be correct.

Analysis of radioactive <u>substances</u> found in

prehistoric clay has bolstered <u>theory</u> that the

<u>mass extinction</u> of the dinosaurs was the result

<u>of</u> meteorite impact.

Time   ?   Answer   Next
       Help Confirm

ARTICLES

In the Structure section of the TOEFL CBT, ETS tests your knowledge of correct article usage. There are many rules and exceptions to article usage; however, ETS tests your basic knowledge and makes most of the test questions fairly simple.

Articles modify nouns. There are two types of articles, definite and indefinite.

Definite:	There is only one definite article: **the**.
Indefinite:	There are two types of indefinite articles: **a** or **an**

To study the use of articles, let's use the noun "computers" as an example. First, imagine all the computers in the world.

If you are referring to the *entire group* of computers, you do *not* need an article. For example:

Computers cost less than they did ten years ago.

You are simply talking about computers *in general,* not a specific computer.

If you are referring to any *single* computer from this entire group, but not any one in particular, use the indefinite article. Indefinite articles must precede a singular noun!

I want to buy **a** computer for my sister. I don't care what kind.

You are simply talking about any computer, not a specific one.

If you are referring to a *specific* computer, use the definite article.

The computer in front of me isn't working.

You are simply talking about a specific computer, not one in general.

ETS usually tests article usage with error identification questions. Rarely do they test article usage with sentence completion questions. ETS will test your basic knowledge of article usage in four different ways.

First, they will confuse "a" and "an." The indefinite article "a" precedes any noun that begins with a consonant. The indefinite article "an" precedes any noun that begins with a vowel. There are some exceptions to this rule, but ETS will *not* test these exceptions. Look at a typical TOEFL CBT "a" and "an" test question.

> The spider monkey, native to Madagascar, emits <u>an</u> yell so loud that <u>it</u> acts <u>to frighten</u> away <u>potential</u> predators.

Clearly, the indefinite article "an" is incorrectly substituted for the indefinite article "a." Remember, ETS will also test the opposite situation, substituting "a"-for- "an."

Second, ETS will insert the indefinite article "a" for the definite article "the." Remember your rules. Use the indefinite article when referring to a general noun, and a definite article when referring to a specific noun. Remember, it is *impossible* for the indefinite articles "a" and "an" to come *before* a *plural noun*! Look at a typical TOEFL CBT "a" for "the" test question:

Indefinite articles precede singular nouns!

> Usually handed down <u>from</u> one generation
> to the next, hymns <u>were perhaps</u> one of <u>a</u>
> earliest types of music <u>performed</u> by
> humans.

Clearly, the indefinite article "a" is incorrectly substituted for the definite article "the." Not only is the sentence speaking about a specific type of music, but the noun is also plural. Remember, indefinite articles can't precede plural nouns.

Third, in the error identification questions, ETS will also omit the definite ("a" or "an") or indefinite ("the") article. In this case, the two words on either side of the omitted article will be underlined. This gives you a clue that something might need to be inserted. Look at a typical TOEFL CBT article omission test question:

> <u>Rather</u> than <u>purchasing</u> real estate,
> Americans <u>have</u> been investing in mutual
> funds ever <u>since beginning</u> of the 1980's.

The definite article ("the") has been omitted between the preposition "since" and the specific noun "beginning." ETS will also omit the indefinite article "a" as well.

Fourth, ETS will insert an extra definite article ("the") in front of a noun that is speaking in general terms about an entire group, or in front of academic subjects such as mathematics, astronomy, or art. Look at a typical TOEFL CBT definite article addition test question:

> <u>Whether</u> documented or <u>orally</u> transmitted,
> <u>the history</u> is perhaps one of the oldest
> fields of study <u>known to</u> scholars.

In this case, the general noun "history" is *not* specifically referring to anything in particular.

PRACTICE!
The following exercises contain singular and plural questions most frequently found in the Structure section of the TOEFL CBT. Click on (in this case circle) the one underlined word or phrase that must be changed for the sentence to be correct.

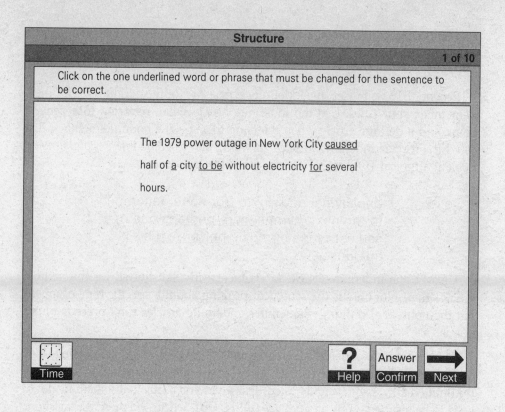

Click on the one underlined word or phrase that must be changed for the sentence to be correct.

The 1979 power outage in New York City <u>caused</u> half of <u>a</u> city <u>to be</u> without electricity <u>for</u> several hours.

Time

Help

Answer
Confirm

Next

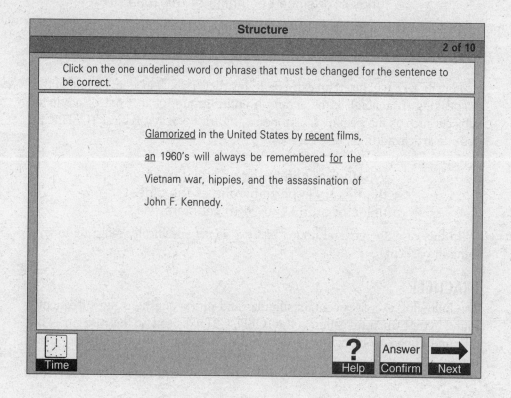

Click on the one underlined word or phrase that must be changed for the sentence to be correct.

<u>Glamorized</u> in the United States by <u>recent</u> films, <u>an</u> 1960's will always be remembered <u>for</u> the Vietnam war, hippies, and the assassination of John F. Kennedy.

Time

Help

Answer
Confirm

Next

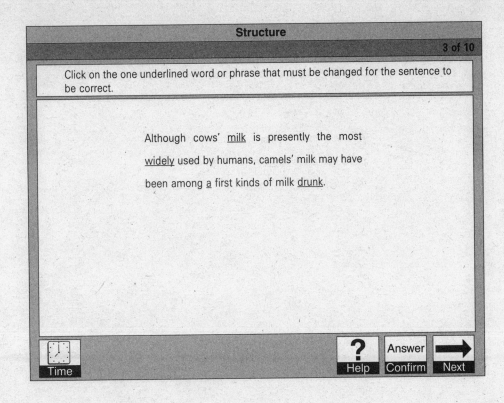

Click on the one underlined word or phrase that must be changed for the sentence to be correct.

Although cows' <u>milk</u> is presently the most <u>widely</u> used by humans, camels' milk may have been among <u>a</u> first kinds of milk <u>drunk</u>.

Time ? Help Answer Confirm Next

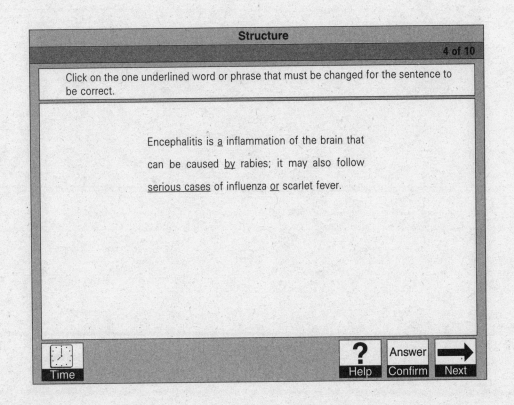

Click on the one underlined word or phrase that must be changed for the sentence to be correct.

Encephalitis is <u>a</u> inflammation of the brain that can be caused <u>by</u> rabies; it may also follow <u>serious cases</u> of influenza <u>or</u> scarlet fever.

Time ? Help Answer Confirm Next

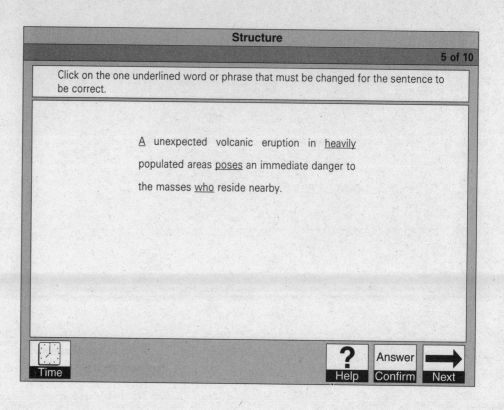

Click on the one underlined word or phrase that must be changed for the sentence to be correct.

A unexpected volcanic eruption in heavily populated areas poses an immediate danger to the masses who reside nearby.

Time   Help   Answer Confirm   Next

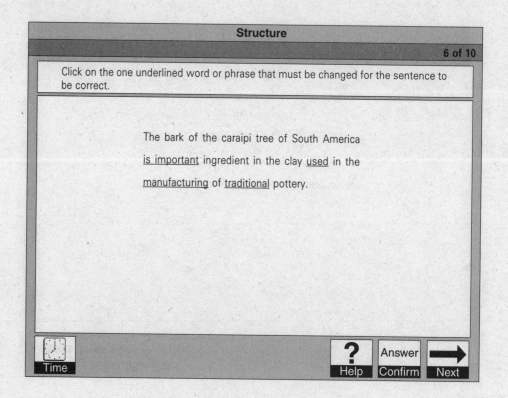

Click on the one underlined word or phrase that must be changed for the sentence to be correct.

The bark of the caraipi tree of South America is important ingredient in the clay used in the manufacturing of traditional pottery.

Time   Help   Answer Confirm   Next

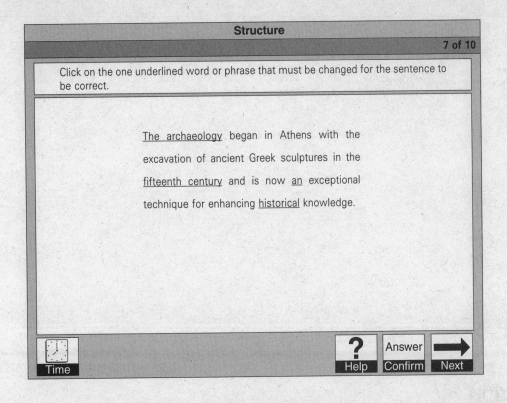

Click on the one underlined word or phrase that must be changed for the sentence to be correct.

The <u>archaeology</u> began in Athens with the excavation of ancient Greek sculptures in the <u>fifteenth century</u> and is now <u>an</u> exceptional technique for enhancing <u>historical</u> knowledge.

Time · ? Help · Answer Confirm · Next

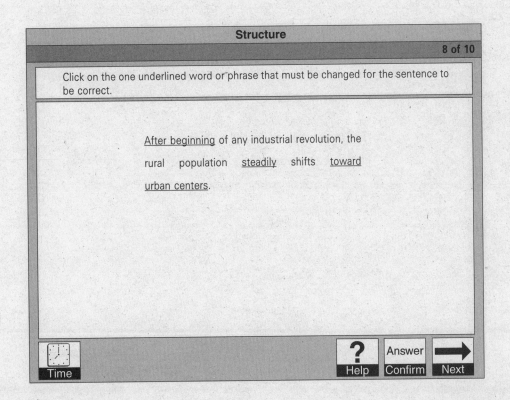

Click on the one underlined word or phrase that must be changed for the sentence to be correct.

<u>After beginning</u> of any industrial revolution, the rural population <u>steadily</u> shifts <u>toward</u> <u>urban centers</u>.

Time · ? Help · Answer Confirm · Next

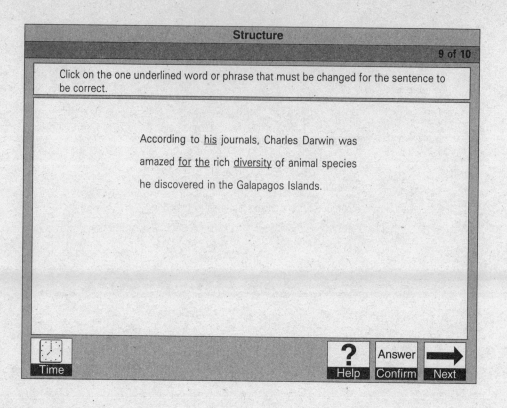

Click on the one underlined word or phrase that must be changed for the sentence to be correct.

According to <u>his</u> journals, Charles Darwin was amazed <u>for</u> <u>the</u> rich <u>diversity</u> of animal species he discovered in the Galapagos Islands.

Time

Help

Answer Confirm

Next

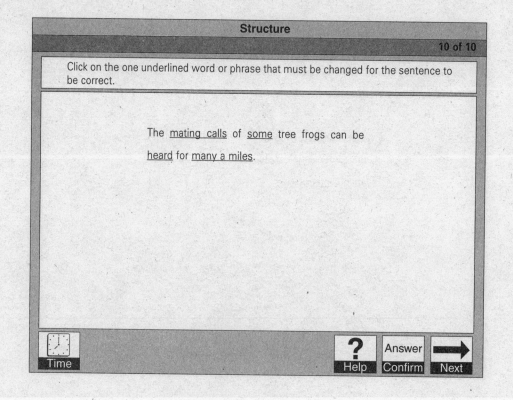

Click on the one underlined word or phrase that must be changed for the sentence to be correct.

The <u>mating calls</u> of <u>some</u> tree frogs can be <u>heard</u> for <u>many a miles</u>.

Time

Help

Answer Confirm

Next

PRONOUNS

A pronoun is a word that takes the place of a noun. It stands for a person, place, thing, or idea *already* stated in a sentence. ETS only tests pronouns in the third person. Fortunately, ETS does *not* test pronouns in the first or second person, or any reflexive pronouns. The list of pronouns ETS tests is as follows:

ETS does not test reflexive pronouns.

Subject	Object	Possessive
he	him	his
she	her	hers
it	it	its
they	them	their
that		
those		

Pronoun questions appear only in the Error Identification questions in the Structure section of the TOEFL CBT. ETS often switches the object pronoun for the possessive pronoun, substitutes a singular pronoun for a plural one (or vice versa), confuses singular and plural possessives, or eliminates the pronoun completely. Look at a typical example that appears on the TOEFL CBT.

> Balancing the ecosystems of Australia's wetlands is an <u>extremely</u> delicate process: even the <u>introduction of</u> an alien insect species could cause <u>serious</u> damage to <u>it</u>.

The singular object pronoun "it" has been incorrectly substituted for the plural object pronoun "them." A pronoun must agree with the noun to which it refers. In this sentence, the pronoun refers to the plural noun "ecosystems." Remember, a pronoun represents another noun already present in the sentence. You have just two simple tasks: Find out if the pronoun agrees with the noun it is referring to, and determine if a possessive is necessary.

Pronouns represent another noun already present in the sentence.

PRACTICE!

The following exercises contain the sort of pronoun questions most frequently found on the TOEFL CBT Structure section. Click on (in this case circle) the one underlined word or phrase that must be changed for the sentence to be correct.

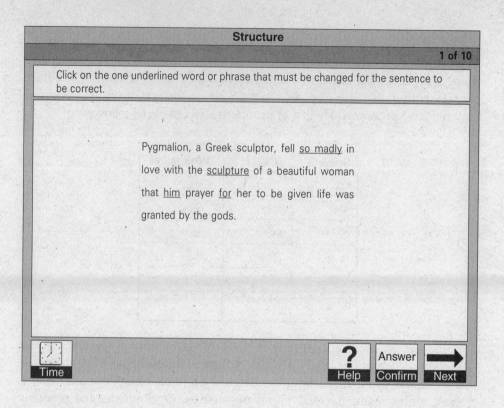

Structure

1 of 10

Click on the one underlined word or phrase that must be changed for the sentence to be correct.

Pygmalion, a Greek sculptor, fell <u>so madly</u> in love with the <u>sculpture</u> of a beautiful woman that <u>him</u> prayer <u>for</u> her to be given life was granted by the gods.

Time   ?
Help   Answer Confirm   → Next

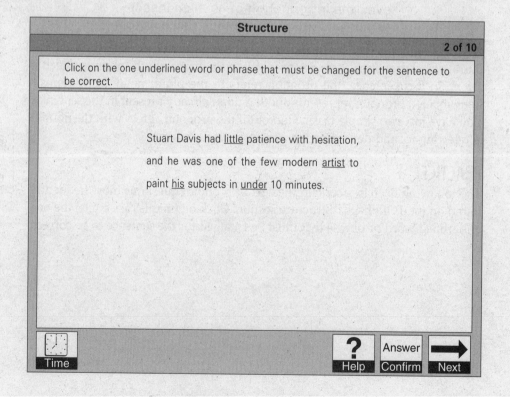

Structure

2 of 10

Click on the one underlined word or phrase that must be changed for the sentence to be correct.

Stuart Davis had <u>little</u> patience with hesitation, and he was one of the few modern <u>artist</u> to paint <u>his</u> subjects in <u>under</u> 10 minutes.

Time   ?
Help   Answer Confirm   → Next

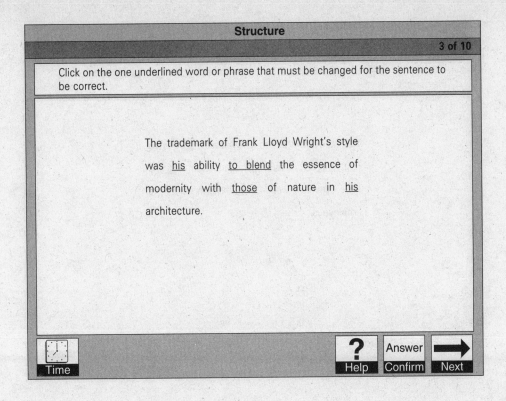

Click on the one underlined word or phrase that must be changed for the sentence to be correct.

The trademark of Frank Lloyd Wright's style was <u>his</u> ability <u>to blend</u> the essence of modernity with <u>those</u> of nature in <u>his</u> architecture.

Time   ?   Answer   Next
        Help Confirm

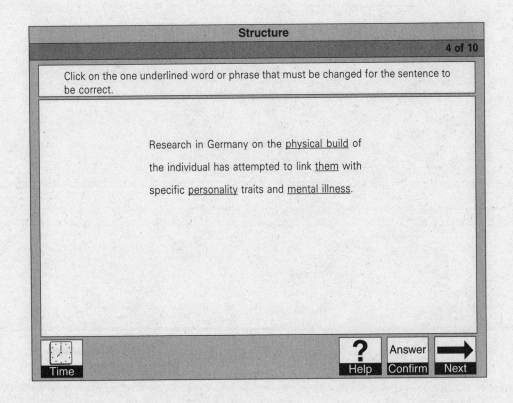

Click on the one underlined word or phrase that must be changed for the sentence to be correct.

Research in Germany on the <u>physical build</u> of the individual has attempted to link <u>them</u> with specific <u>personality</u> traits and <u>mental illness</u>.

Time   ?   Answer   Next
        Help Confirm

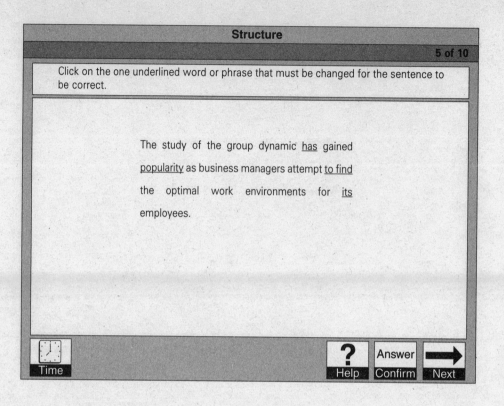

Click on the one underlined word or phrase that must be changed for the sentence to be correct.

The study of the group dynamic <u>has</u> gained <u>popularity</u> as business managers attempt <u>to find</u> the optimal work environments for <u>its</u> employees.

Time   Help   Answer Confirm   Next

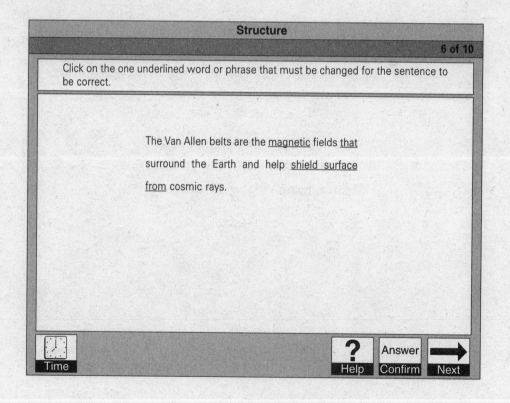

Click on the one underlined word or phrase that must be changed for the sentence to be correct.

The Van Allen belts are the <u>magnetic</u> fields <u>that</u> surround the Earth and help <u>shield surface</u> <u>from</u> cosmic rays.

Time   Help   Answer Confirm   Next

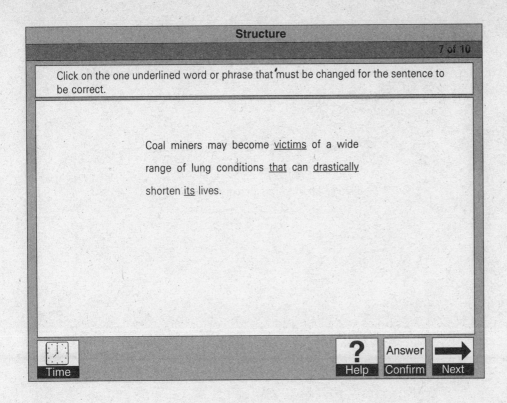

Click on the one underlined word or phrase that must be changed for the sentence to be correct.

Coal miners may become <u>victims</u> of a wide range of lung conditions <u>that</u> can <u>drastically</u> shorten <u>its</u> lives.

Time Help Answer Confirm Next

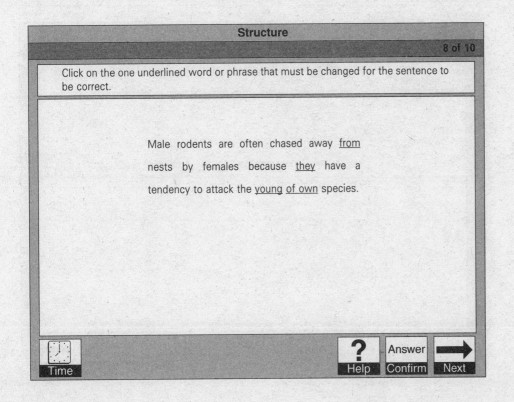

Click on the one underlined word or phrase that must be changed for the sentence to be correct.

Male rodents are often chased away <u>from</u> nests by females because <u>they</u> have a tendency to attack the <u>young</u> <u>of own</u> species.

Time Help Answer Confirm Next

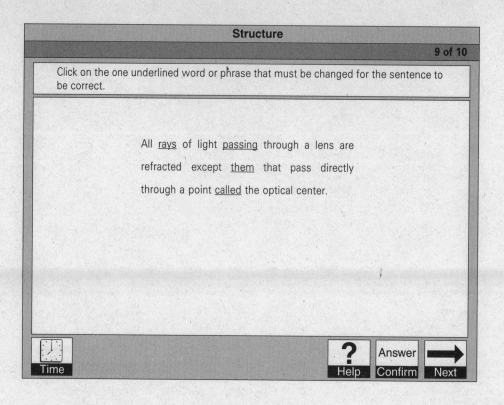

Click on the one underlined word or phrase that must be changed for the sentence to be correct.

All <u>rays</u> of light <u>passing</u> through a lens are refracted except <u>them</u> that pass directly through a point <u>called</u> the optical center.

Time   Help   Answer Confirm   Next

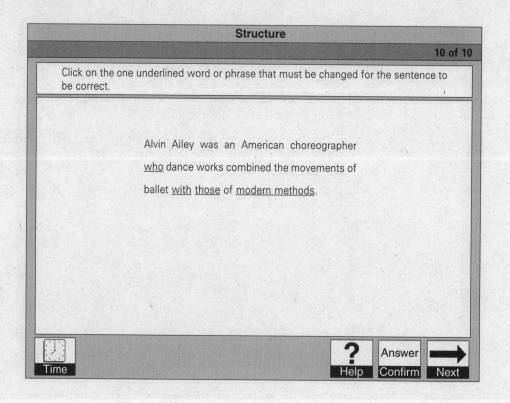

Click on the one underlined word or phrase that must be changed for the sentence to be correct.

Alvin Ailey was an American choreographer <u>who</u> dance works combined the movements of ballet <u>with</u> <u>those</u> of <u>modern methods</u>.

Time   Help   Answer Confirm   Next

APPOSITIVES

Some of the Sentence Completion questions in the Structure section of the TOEFL CBT will test all or a part of the appositive construction. An appositive is simply a noun phrase that repeats the subject. It must be identical to the subject and must provide additional information. A comma must immediately precede and follow the appositive. For example:

> Smallpox, _____, causes a high fever and severe skin eruptions.
>
> ◯ which infecting diseases
> ◯ diseases are highly infectious
> ◯ a highly infectious disease
> ◯ infects disease

To click on the correct appositive answer, use POE to get rid of any answer choice that contains a verb or a relative pronoun (who, that, which, etc). In this case, the first, second, and fourth answer choices contain either relative pronouns or verbs. Only the third answer choice, "a highly infectious disease," correctly restates the subject and follows appositive requirements. It is preceded by a comma and gives you more information about the subject, smallpox.

PRACTICE!

The following exercises contain appositive questions most frequently found in the Structure section of the TOEFL CBT. Click on (in this case circle) the one word or phrase that best completes the sentence.

Structure

1 of 5

Click on the one word or phrase that best completes the sentence.

Claude Monet, ______, is considered to be the founder of Impressionism

- ◯ paints French landscapes
- ◯ is a landscape painter of France
- ◯ a French landscape painter
- ◯ French landscapes are painted

Time | Help | Answer Confirm | Next

Structure

2 of 5

Click on the one word or phrase that best completes the sentence.

The Mississippi, ______ longest river in North America, flows along the border of 10 states.

- ◯ is the
- ◯ the
- ◯ it is by
- ◯ is an

Time | Help | Answer Confirm | Next

Click on the one word or phrase that best completes the sentence.

The jaguar, _____, is similar to the shorter-limbed and stockier leopard.

○ a more adaptable animal
○ adapts more animal
○ is an adaptable animal
○ which adapting animal

Time   Help   Answer Confirm   Next

Click on the one word or phrase that best completes the sentence.

The concept of the greenhouse, _____ plants inside glass houses, is just one of the results of an industrial revolution.

○ for cultivation
○ cultivates to
○ the cultivation of
○ the cultivating

Time   Help   Answer Confirm   Next

Click on the one word or phrase that best completes the sentence.

Viruses, _____, do not carry out the functions
of living cells, such as respiration and growth.

- ◯ microscopic parasites
- ◯ are microscopic parasites
- ◯ parasites are microscopic
- ◯ to parasite a microscope

Time

Help

Answer
Confirm

Next

MODIFIERS

On the TOEFL CBT, ETS will test your basic knowledge about modifiers. In an English sentence, all other words except the subject and noun are called modifiers. Modifiers describe or give more information about the subject, verb, or other modifiers.

> <u>Canada</u>, <u>which has a small population</u>, <u>covers</u>
> Subject   Modifier   Verb
>
> <u>slightly more territory than the United States does</u>.
>   Modifier
>
> <u>Wolfgang Amadeus Mozart</u> <u>wrote</u>
>   Subject   Verb
>
> <u>his first symphony while he was still a very young child</u>.
>   Modifier

As shown in the diagramed sentences above, a modifier is a word or a group of words that describes another word in the sentence. Adjectives and adverbs are just two types of modifiers.

Adjectives

Simply, adjectives modify nouns. They report the *quality*, *quantity*, or *condition* of nouns. In a typical TOEFL CBT sentence, the adjectives will usually precede the noun, follow an adverb, or exist alone after the "be" verb. Adjectives can *not* modify adverbs. Look at the following typical TOEFL CBT sentence with all the modifiers and nouns labeled.

> <u>All</u> <u>flightless</u> <u>waterfowl</u> are <u>still</u> <u>equipped</u> with <u>hollow</u>
> adj.   adj.   noun   adv.   adj.   adj.
> <u>wingbones,</u> giving them an <u>incredibly</u> <u>acute</u> <u>sense</u> of balance.
>   noun   adverb   adj.   noun

Paying attention to the word order will drastically increase your chances of clicking on the best possible answer. Always make sure the parts of speech come in the right order. Look at the following chart.

Word #1	Word #2	Word #3	Word #1	Word #2	Word #3
Adjective			fresh		
Adjective	Noun		fresh	bread	
Adjective	Adjective	Noun	tasty	fresh	bread
Adverb	Adjective		surprisingly	fresh	
Adverb	Adjective	Noun	surprisingly	fresh	bread

Here are the types of adjectives that frequently appear on the TOEFL CBT exam.

Qualitative	Comparative	Superlative	Distributive	Quantitative
colorful	faster than	the fastest	both	less admired
rapid	smaller than	the smallest	each	many
severe	greater than	the greatest	every	fifteenth
slender	longer than	the longest	another	some
evident	lower than	the lowest	other	few
complex	larger than	the largest	used	
capable	more abundant	the most abundant	distributive	

You will encounter "adjectival" questions as both sentence completion and error identification questions in the Structure section of the TOEFL CBT. For sentence completion questions, you must be able to click on the adjective that best completes the sentence.

Click on the correct answer in this typical adjectival question found in the Structure section of the TOEFL CBT.

_____ the root and the foliage of the red beet are safe for consumption.

- ○ While
- ○ Both
- ○ Either
- ○ Though

ETS tries to make adjectival questions confusing by adding in a few conjunctions and other parts of speech. In this case, "while" and "though" create dependent clauses that lack main verbs. The conjunction "either" must be paired with "or," not "and."

For error identification questions, ETS will replace the adjective with either an adverb or a noun.

Click on the error in this typical adjectival question found in the Structure section of the TOEFL CBT.

John Quincy Adams, <u>like</u> his father President John Adams, was intelligent, strong-willed, <u>energetically</u>, and totally <u>dedicated to</u> serving <u>his</u> country.

Remember, many of the error identification questions contain lists of adjectives separated by commas. If one of the words in this list is underlined, make sure it parallels with the other listed words. In this case, "intelligent," "strong-willed," and "dedicated" are all adjectives. However, "energetically" is an adverb. It should also be an adjective: "energetic."

Click on the error in this typical adjectival question found in the Structure section of the TOEFL CBT.

> <u>Much</u> like movies, <u>radio</u> could not have
> been developed <u>without</u> the remarkable and
> <u>technology</u> advances of the times.

Remember, adjectives modify nouns. Nouns *cannot* modify nouns. In this sentence, the noun "technology" is modifying the noun "advances." It should be the adjective "technological."

On the TOEFL CBT, ETS will also test your basic knowledge of adjectives by placing a noun *in front of* an adjective, or an adverb *after* an adjective. Take a look at this type of question commonly found in the Structure section of the TOEFL CBT.

> Under <u>current</u> tax laws, couples who
> have more than one child <u>receive</u> a
> <u>reduction significant</u> in <u>their</u> income tax.

Remember, adjectives must precede the nouns that they modify. In this sentence, the adjective "significant" must come before the noun "reduction."

PRACTICE!

The following exercises contain the sort of adjective questions most frequently found in the Structure section of the TOEFL CBT. Click on (in this case circle) the one word or phrase that best completes the sentence, or the one underlined word or phrase that must be changed for the sentence to be correct.

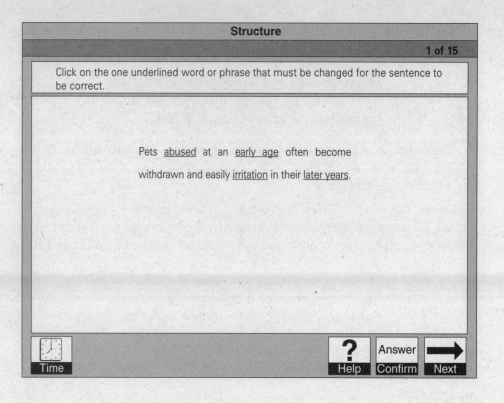

Click on the one underlined word or phrase that must be changed for the sentence to be correct.

Pets <u>abused</u> at an <u>early age</u> often become withdrawn and easily <u>irritation</u> in their <u>later years</u>.

Time | Help | Answer Confirm | Next

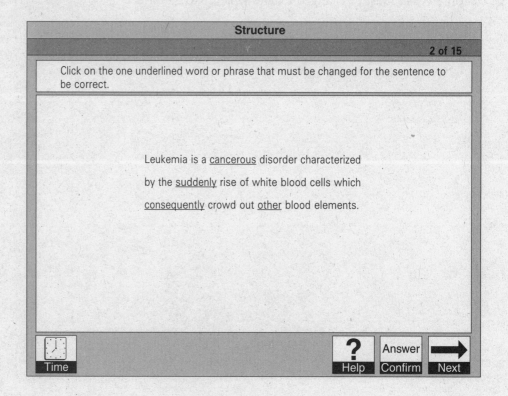

Click on the one underlined word or phrase that must be changed for the sentence to be correct.

Leukemia is a <u>cancerous</u> disorder characterized by the <u>suddenly</u> rise of white blood cells which <u>consequently</u> crowd out <u>other</u> blood elements.

Time | Help | Answer Confirm | Next

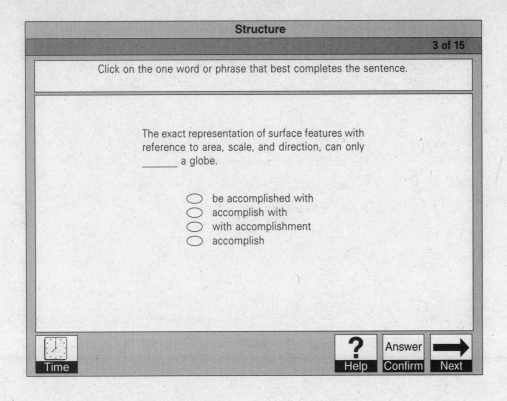

Click on the one word or phrase that best completes the sentence.

The exact representation of surface features with reference to area, scale, and direction, can only _____ a globe.

- ○ be accomplished with
- ○ accomplish with
- ○ with accomplishment
- ○ accomplish

Time | ? Help | Answer Confirm | → Next

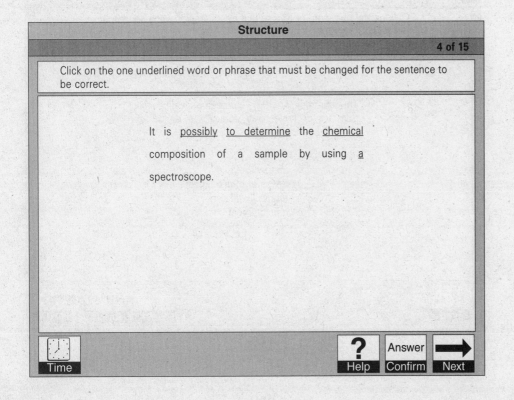

Click on the one underlined word or phrase that must be changed for the sentence to be correct.

It is <u>possibly</u> <u>to determine</u> the <u>chemical</u> composition of a sample by using <u>a</u> spectroscope.

Time | ? Help | Answer Confirm | → Next

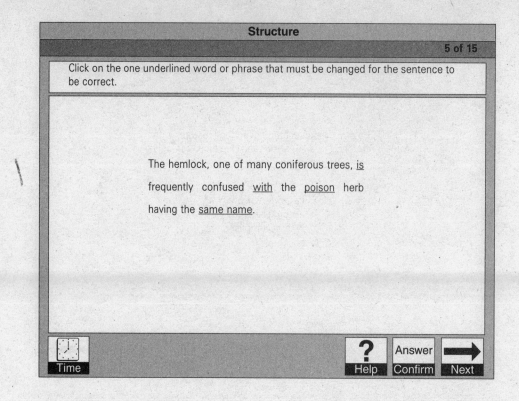

Click on the one underlined word or phrase that must be changed for the sentence to be correct.

The hemlock, one of many coniferous trees, <u>is</u> frequently confused <u>with</u> the <u>poison</u> herb having the <u>same name</u>.

Time   Help   Answer Confirm   Next

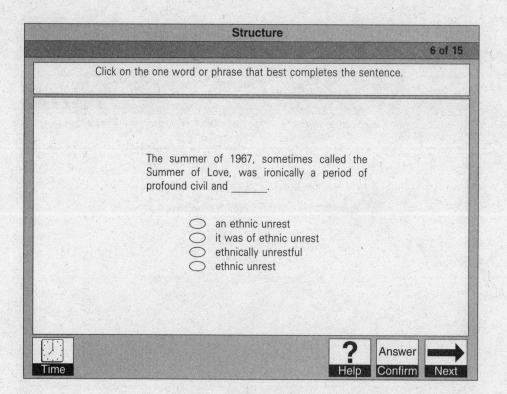

Click on the one word or phrase that best completes the sentence.

The summer of 1967, sometimes called the Summer of Love, was ironically a period of profound civil and _____.

○ an ethnic unrest
○ it was of ethnic unrest
○ ethnically unrestful
○ ethnic unrest

Time   Help   Answer Confirm   Next

Click on the one underlined word or phrase that must be changed for the sentence to be correct.

The <u>recently</u> epidemic of church fires in southern communities <u>is</u> a <u>painful reminder</u> of the <u>violent</u> civil rights battles of the 60's.

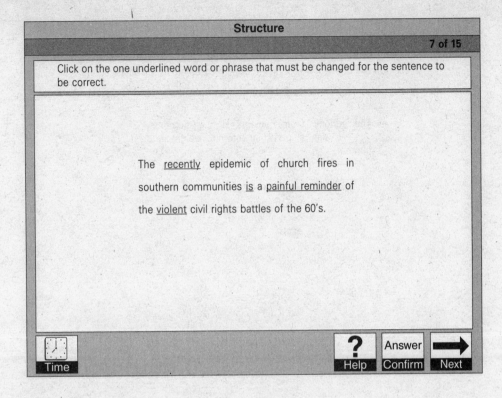

Time

?
Help

Answer
Confirm

Next

Click on the one word or phrase that best completes the sentence.

During the 1950's, Chinese and North American ginseng became so popular among herbalists that _____ species were almost exterminated.

◯ both
◯ the both
◯ and both
◯ both of

Time

?
Help

Answer
Confirm

Next

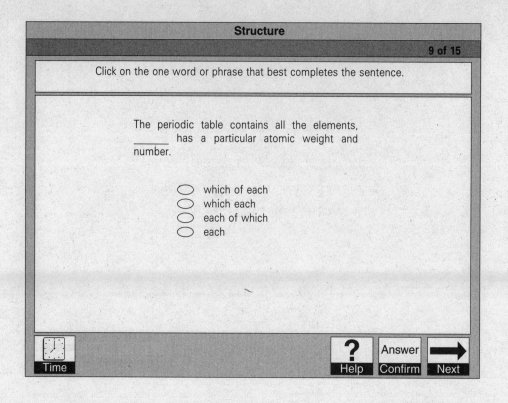

Click on the one word or phrase that best completes the sentence.

The periodic table contains all the elements, _____ has a particular atomic weight and number.

- ○ which of each
- ○ which each
- ○ each of which
- ○ each

Time   Help   Answer Confirm   Next

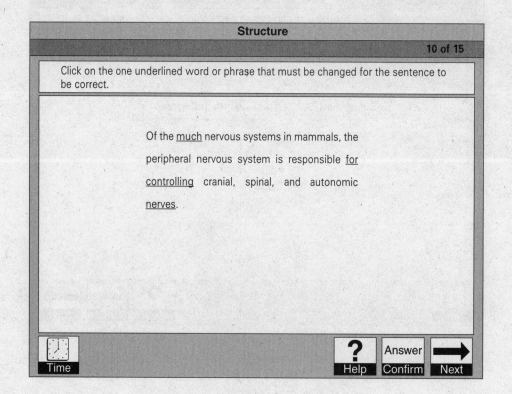

Click on the one underlined word or phrase that must be changed for the sentence to be correct.

Of the <u>much</u> nervous systems in mammals, the peripheral nervous system is responsible <u>for</u> <u>controlling</u> cranial, spinal, and autonomic <u>nerves</u>.

Time   Help   Answer Confirm   Next

Click on the one underlined word or phrase that must be changed for the sentence to be correct.

Martina Navratilova has won <u>more</u> consecutive

<u>professional</u> tennis titles than any <u>another</u>

<u>player</u>.

Time Help Answer Confirm Next

Click on the one word or phrase that best completes the sentence.

Airplanes that used to take more than half a day
to cross the Atlantic are now _____ to make
the crossing in several hours.

 ◯ faster than
 ◯ fast enough
 ◯ so fast
 ◯ faster

Time Help Answer Confirm Next

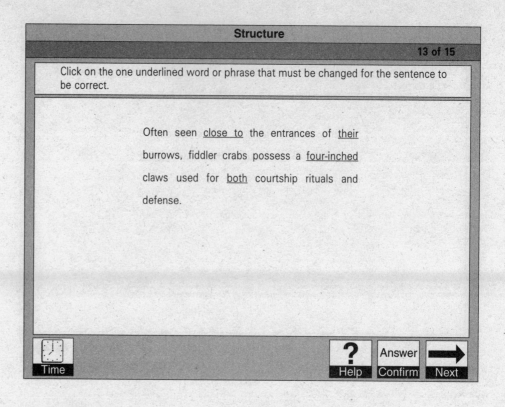

Click on the one underlined word or phrase that must be changed for the sentence to be correct.

Often seen <u>close to</u> the entrances of <u>their</u> burrows, fiddler crabs possess a <u>four-inched</u> claws used for <u>both</u> courtship rituals and defense.

Time   Help   Answer Confirm   Next

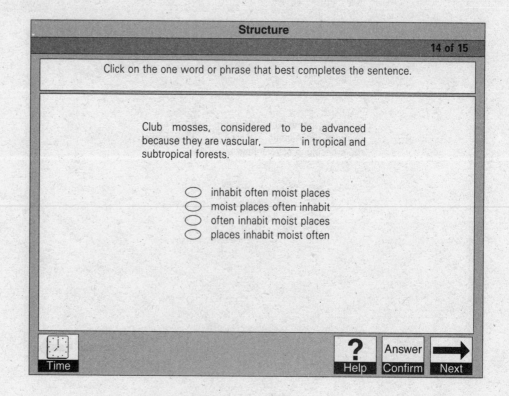

Click on the one word or phrase that best completes the sentence.

Club mosses, considered to be advanced because they are vascular, _____ in tropical and subtropical forests.

○ inhabit often moist places
○ moist places often inhabit
○ often inhabit moist places
○ places inhabit moist often

Time   Help   Answer Confirm   Next

Click on the one underlined word or phrase that must be changed for the sentence to be correct.

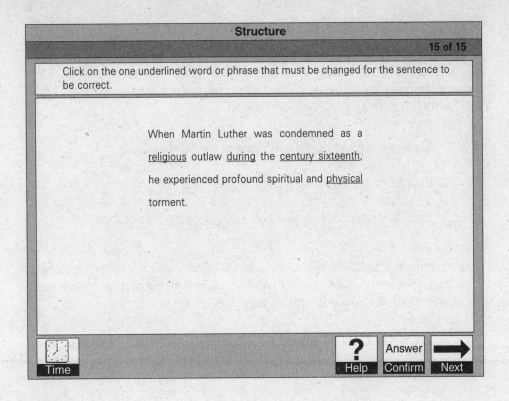

When Martin Luther was condemned as a religious outlaw <u>during</u> the <u>century sixteenth</u>, he experienced profound spiritual and <u>physical</u> torment.

Time

? Help

Answer Confirm

→ Next

Adverbs

Simply, adverbs modify verbs, adjectives, or other adverbs. Adverbs *never* modify nouns. They report *how, when, where, how often,* or *how much.* Most adverbs in English end in -ly, but not all. Look at the following typical TOEFL CBT sentence with all the modifiers labeled.

> Most of the <u>hastily</u> <u>built</u> platforms of the subway are <u>so</u>
>   adv.   adj.   adv.
> <u>incredibly</u> <u>decrepit</u> that warning signs were <u>finally</u>
>   adv.   adj.   adv.
> <u>hung</u> to protect riders from <u>potentially</u> <u>dangerous</u> situations.
> verb   adv.   adj.

Paying attention to the word order will drastically increase your chances of clicking on the best possible answer. Always make sure the parts of speech come in the right order. Look at the following chart.

Word #1	Word #2	Word #3	Word #1	Word #2	Word #3
Adverb	Verb		quickly	ran	
Adverb	Adverb	Verb	very	quickly	ran
Adverb	Adjective		very	pretty	
Adverb	Adverb	Adjective	still	very	pretty

Here are the types of adverbs that frequently appear on the TOEFL CBT exam:

Manner	Time	Frequency	Degree
dramatically	still	rarely	so
typically	today	seldom	very
thoroughly	soon	occasionally	hardly
intentionally	now	frequently	rather
originally	yet	never	instead

You will encounter a few adverbial questions in the sentence completion questions, but mainly they will be tested in error identification questions. Look at a typical adverbial question found in the Structure section of the TOEFL CBT.

> _____ a national catastrophe such as an earthquake, tornado, or flood destroys property, insurance companies require that all policyholders complete the necessary forms.
>
> ○ Being
> ○ Whenever
> ○ Are
> ○ When can

ETS tries to make adverbial questions confusing by adding in gerunds, verbs, and other parts of speech. In this sentence, "whenever" answers the question, *"When* do insurance companies require that all policy holders complete the necessary forms?" The other answer choices fail to do so.

For error identification questions, ETS will replace the adverb with either an adjective or a noun. Look at some typical adverbial questions found in the Structure section of the TOEFL CBT.

The claim that humans only use ten
percent of their intellectual capacity has
never been scientific confirmed.

Remember, adverbs usually precede the verbs they modify. In this sentence, the adjective "scientific" has been incorrectly substituted for the adverb "scientifically." Look at another typical adverbial question found in the Structure section of the TOEFL CBT.

Emile Zola's surprise accusation of the
French military following the scandalous
Dreyfus Affair ultimate resulted in the
pardon of the unfairly accused Dreyfus.

Remember, adverbs must modify verbs or adjectives. Adjectives can **NOT** modify verbs. In this sentence the main verb "resulted" is being modified by a adjective. It should be the adverb "ultimately."

On the TOEFL CBT, ETS will also test your basic knowledge of adverbs by replacing an adverb for another adverb. Look at this type of question found on the TOEFL CBT.

During the civil rights movement of the
1960's, Martin Luther King Jr. proved that
one could accomplish more with pacifistic
measures instead than violence.

The adverb "instead" has been incorrectly substituted for the adverb "rather." The fixed pattern is "rather than" and "instead of." Remember, you never have to correct the answer on the TOEFL CBT; you simply must recognize that it is incorrect.

PRACTICE!

The following exercises contain adverbial questions most frequently found in the Structure section of the TOEFL CBT. Click on (in this case circle) the one word or phrase that best completes the sentence, or the one underlined word or phrase that must be changed for the sentence to be correct.

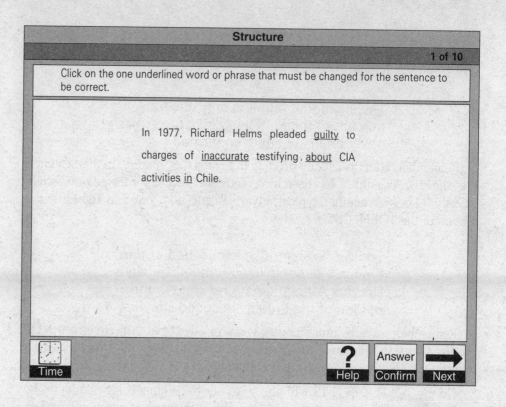

Click on the one underlined word or phrase that must be changed for the sentence to be correct.

In 1977, Richard Helms pleaded <u>guilty</u> to charges of <u>inaccurate</u> testifying, <u>about</u> CIA activities <u>in</u> Chile.

Time Help Answer Confirm Next

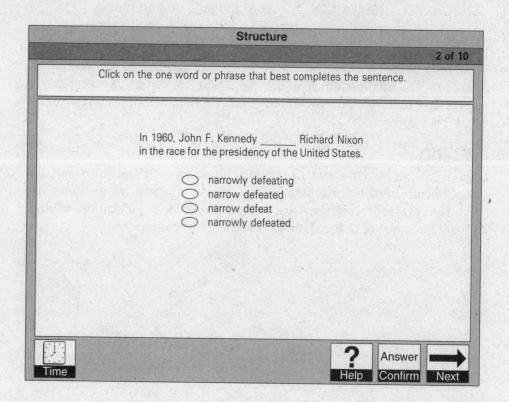

Click on the one word or phrase that best completes the sentence.

In 1960, John F. Kennedy _____ Richard Nixon in the race for the presidency of the United States.

○ narrowly defeating
○ narrow defeated
○ narrow defeat
○ narrowly defeated

Time Help Answer Confirm Next

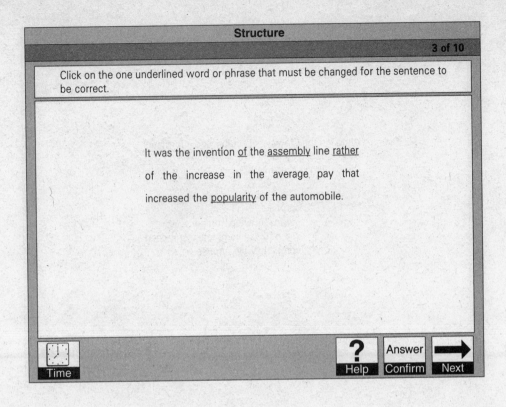

Click on the one underlined word or phrase that must be changed for the sentence to be correct.

It was the invention of the assembly line rather
of the increase in the average pay that
increased the popularity of the automobile.

Time ? Help Answer Confirm Next

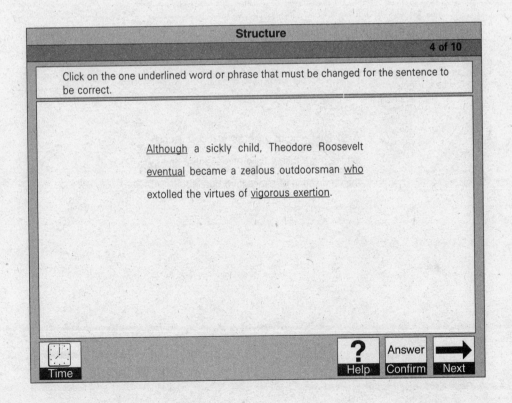

Click on the one underlined word or phrase that must be changed for the sentence to be correct.

Although a sickly child, Theodore Roosevelt
eventual became a zealous outdoorsman who
extolled the virtues of vigorous exertion.

Time ? Help Answer Confirm Next

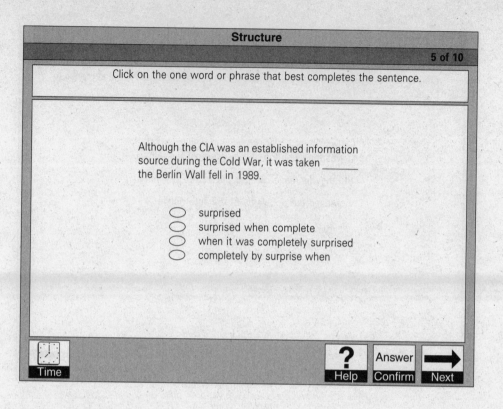

Click on the one word or phrase that best completes the sentence.

Although the CIA was an established information source during the Cold War, it was taken _____ the Berlin Wall fell in 1989.

○ surprised
○ surprised when complete
○ when it was completely surprised
○ completely by surprise when

Time   Help   Answer Confirm   Next

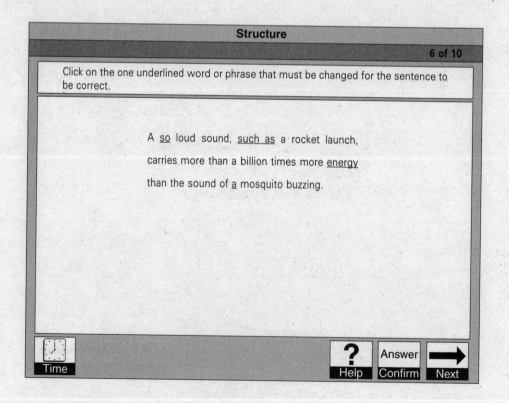

Click on the one underlined word or phrase that must be changed for the sentence to be correct.

A <u>so</u> loud sound, <u>such as</u> a rocket launch,

carries more than a billion times more <u>energy</u>

than the sound of <u>a</u> mosquito buzzing.

Time   Help   Answer Confirm   Next

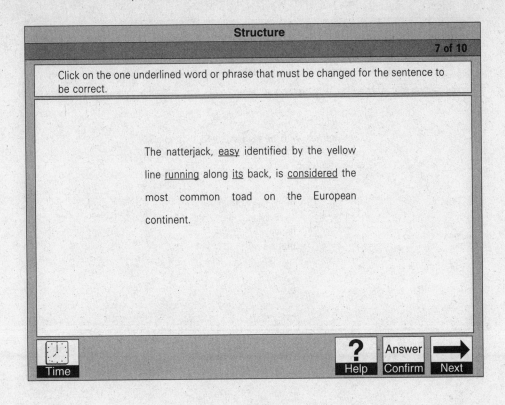

Click on the one underlined word or phrase that must be changed for the sentence to be correct.

The natterjack, <u>easy</u> identified by the yellow line <u>running</u> along <u>its</u> back, is <u>considered</u> the most common toad on the European continent.

Time   Help   Answer Confirm   Next

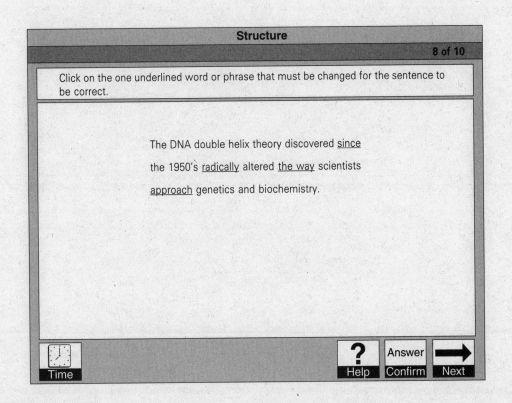

Click on the one underlined word or phrase that must be changed for the sentence to be correct.

The DNA double helix theory discovered <u>since</u> the 1950's <u>radically</u> altered <u>the way</u> scientists <u>approach</u> genetics and biochemistry.

Time   Help   Answer Confirm   Next

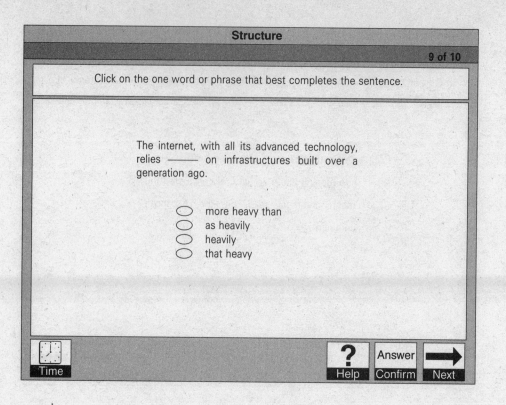

Click on the one word or phrase that best completes the sentence.

The internet, with all its advanced technology, relies ——— on infrastructures built over a generation ago.

- ○ more heavy than
- ○ as heavily
- ○ heavily
- ○ that heavy

Time | Help | Answer Confirm | Next

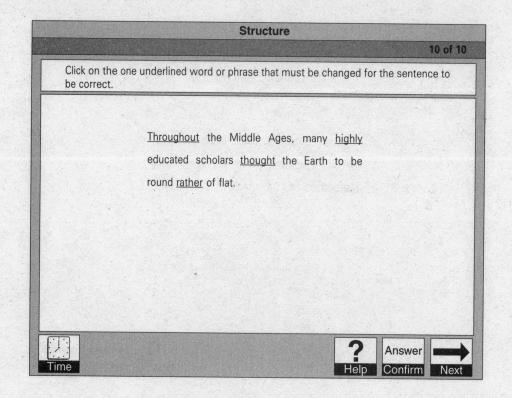

Click on the one underlined word or phrase that must be changed for the sentence to be correct.

Throughout the Middle Ages, many highly educated scholars thought the Earth to be round rather of flat.

Time | Help | Answer Confirm | Next

SUBORDINATION

In the English language, subordination (also known as modifying clauses) is used to combine two or more sentences into one sentence. The subordinate clause usually contains a relative pronoun, and must appear immediately after the words it modifies. Look at the following three sentences.

> Some types of rice are grown for their large kernels.
>
> The kernels have a high protein content.
>
> The high protein content reduces malnutrition in many third-world countries.

Although these three sentences are grammatically correct, they are repetitive and a little awkward to read. By using subordination, the three sentences can become one.

> Some types of rice are grown for their large kernels, **which** have a high protein content **that** reduces malnutrition in many third world countries.

Notice how the relative pronouns connect the clauses to that which they are modifying. Look at the list of the relative pronouns ETS uses on the TOEFL CBT:

who	that	when
whose	where	which

On the TOEFL CBT, one way that ETS tests your basic knowledge of subordination is by substituting one relative pronoun for another. Look at a typical TOEFL CBT example:

> Some types of rice are grown for their large kernels, who have a high protein content that reduces malnutrition in many third world countries.

In this sentence, the subordination is providing more specific information about "kernels." Since the word "kernels" is not a person, the relative pronoun cannot be "who." The relative pronoun "who" has been incorrectly substituted for "which." Don't worry about the difference between "that" and "which." This point is *never* tested on the TOEFL CBT.

ETS never tests the difference between "that" and "which."

- **RULE #1**—The relative pronoun that you use in subordination depends on what you are modifying. If the relative pronoun is
  who, the subordination must modify a person.
  whose, the subordination must indicate possession.

that, the subordination must modify a thing by defining it, and answering the question, "which one?"

which, the subordination must modify a thing by providing more specific information.

where, the subordination must modify a place.

when, the subordination must refer to a time.

- **RULE #2**—Every subordinate clause *must* have a subject and verb. If the relative pronoun serves as the subject, no additional subject is needed. In the following example, the entire modifier is in bold:

> The Statue of Liberty, **which** **was given** **to the United States from France**,
>   Sub.   Verb   Preposition
> still greets many new immigrants to the United States every year.

On the TOEFL CBT, ETS will insert another pronoun into the sentence, or omit part of the verb. Look at the example again.

> The Statue of Liberty, <u>which it was</u> given to the United States <u>from</u> France, <u>still</u> greets <u>many</u> new immigrants to the United States every year.

OR

> The Statue of Liberty, <u>which given</u> to the United States <u>from</u> France, <u>still</u> greets <u>many</u> new immigrants to the United States every year.

In the first sentence, the pronoun "it" unnecessarily repeats the relative pronoun "which." In the second example, the auxiliary verb "was" is omitted. Look for these subordination question patterns on the TOEFL CBT.

PRACTICE!

The following exercises contain the sort of subordination questions most frequently found in the Structure section of the TOEFL CBT. Click on (in this case circle) the one word or phrase that best completes the sentence, or the one underlined word or phrase that must be changed for the sentence to be correct.

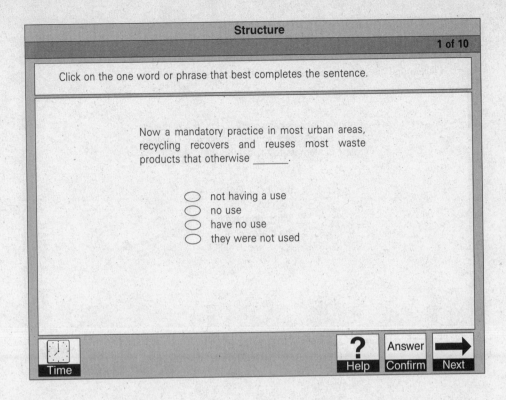

Click on the one word or phrase that best completes the sentence.

Now a mandatory practice in most urban areas, recycling recovers and reuses most waste products that otherwise _____.

- ○ not having a use
- ○ no use
- ○ have no use
- ○ they were not used

Time   Help   Answer Confirm   Next

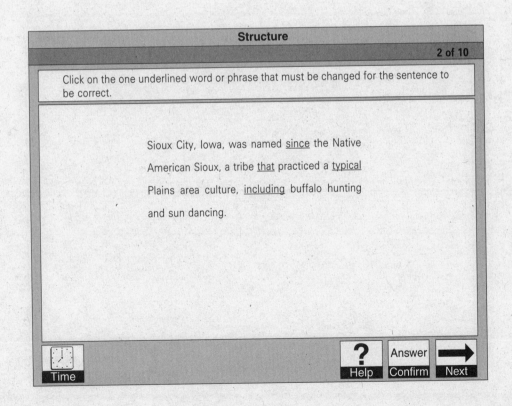

Click on the one underlined word or phrase that must be changed for the sentence to be correct.

Sioux City, Iowa, was named <u>since</u> the Native

American Sioux, a tribe <u>that</u> practiced a <u>typical</u>

Plains area culture, <u>including</u> buffalo hunting

and sun dancing.

Time   Help   Answer Confirm   Next

Structure

3 of 10

Click on the one word or phrase that best completes the sentence.

Robert Duncan's paintings, _______ the Midwest as a serene and settled landscape, inspired many Easterners to relocate to the West.

- ◯ they portrayed
- ◯ portrays
- ◯ which portrayed
- ◯ the portrayal of

Time | Help | Answer Confirm | Next

Structure

4 of 10

Click on the one underlined word or phrase that must be changed for the sentence to be correct.

Since the 1960's, population and development have steadily increased along the Amazon River, all of which it is easily accessible to ships.

Time | Help | Answer Confirm | Next

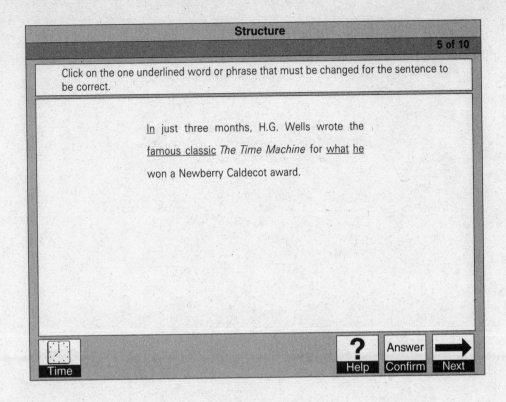

Click on the one underlined word or phrase that must be changed for the sentence to be correct.

<u>In</u> just three months, H.G. Wells wrote the <u>famous classic</u> *The Time Machine* for <u>what</u> <u>he</u> won a Newberry Caldecot award.

Time | Help ? | Answer Confirm | Next →

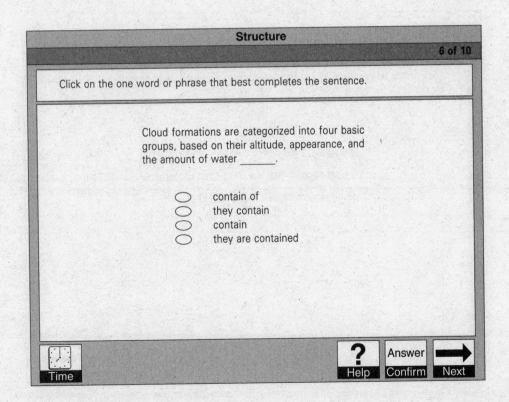

Click on the one word or phrase that best completes the sentence.

Cloud formations are categorized into four basic groups, based on their altitude, appearance, and the amount of water _____.

- ◯ contain of
- ◯ they contain
- ◯ contain
- ◯ they are contained

Time | Help ? | Answer Confirm | Next →

Structure

7 of 10

Click on the one word or phrase that best completes the sentence.

While living in the White House, Eleanor Roosevelt was harshly criticized by those who later _______ her humanitarian efforts.

- ○ they praised
- ○ praised
- ○ were praised
- ○ praising

Time | Help | Answer Confirm | Next

Structure

8 of 10

Click on the one underlined word or phrase that must be changed for the sentence to be correct.

There was great concern in the 1950's when it was discovered that the paint used on certainly dining sets contained radioactive uranium.

Time | Help | Answer Confirm | Next

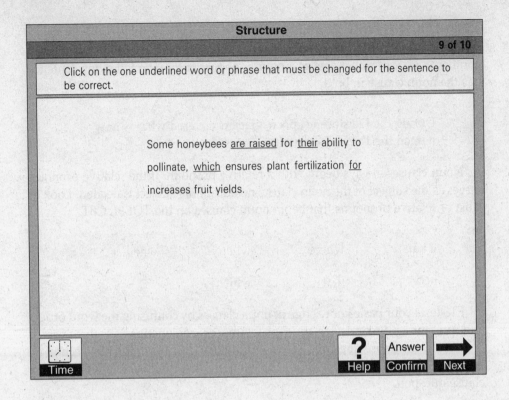

Click on the one underlined word or phrase that must be changed for the sentence to be correct.

Some honeybees <u>are raised</u> for <u>their</u> ability to pollinate, <u>which</u> ensures plant fertilization <u>for</u> increases fruit yields.

Time | Help | Answer Confirm | Next

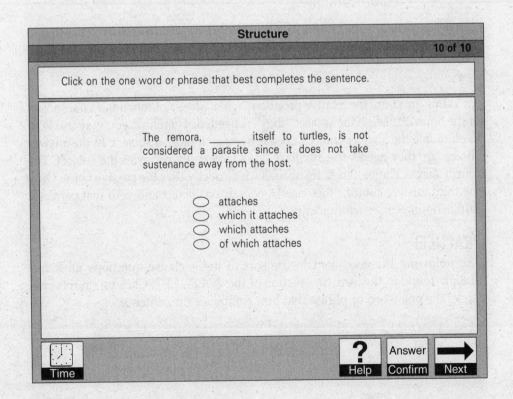

Click on the one word or phrase that best completes the sentence.

The remora, _____ itself to turtles, is not considered a parasite since it does not take sustenance away from the host.

- ◯ attaches
- ◯ which it attaches
- ◯ which attaches
- ◯ of which attaches

Time | Help | Answer Confirm | Next

Noun Clauses

A noun clause is a special type of subordinate clause that does not modify another noun, but rather acts as a noun independently. The following sentence has the noun clause in bold.

> During the Pleistocene epoch, glaciers covered **what is now named the Rocky Mountains.**

Noun clauses always begin with a relative pronoun. If the relative pronoun serves as the subject of the noun clause, no additional subject is needed. Look at a list of relative pronouns that begin noun clauses on the TOEFL CBT.

what	where	when	whether
how	that	which	

ETS tests your basic knowledge of noun clauses by confusing the word order, and presenting incorrect relative pronouns or conjunctions in the answer choices. Noun clause questions are tested in the sentence completion section of the TOEFL CBT. Look at the following example of a typical TOEFL CBT noun clause question.

According to some scientists, the goal of technology is to provide the masses with what _____ to comfortably live a self-sufficient life.

- ○ do they need
- ○ needs
- ○ they need
- ○ they are needed

In this question, the relative pronoun "what" does not function as the subject of the noun clause, so the subject "they" is needed. Therefore, you may use POE to eliminate the answer choice "needs" because it lacks a subject. In the answer choice "do they need," the auxiliary "do" incorrectly precedes the subject. The fourth answer choice, "they are needed," incorrectly uses the passive voice. Only the third answer choice, "they need," contains a subject and verb that correctly fulfills noun clause requirements.

PRACTICE!

The following exercises contain the sort of **noun clause** questions most frequently found in the Structure section of the TOEFL CBT. Click on (in this case circle) the one word or phrase that best completes the sentence.

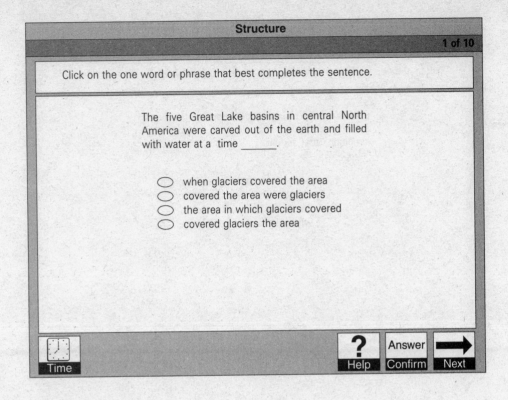

Click on the one word or phrase that best completes the sentence.

The five Great Lake basins in central North America were carved out of the earth and filled with water at a time _____.

- ○ when glaciers covered the area
- ○ covered the area were glaciers
- ○ the area in which glaciers covered
- ○ covered glaciers the area

Time · Help · Answer Confirm · Next

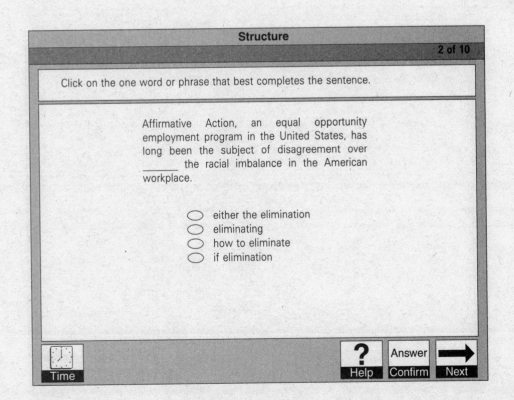

Click on the one word or phrase that best completes the sentence.

Affirmative Action, an equal opportunity employment program in the United States, has long been the subject of disagreement over _____ the racial imbalance in the American workplace.

- ○ either the elimination
- ○ eliminating
- ○ how to eliminate
- ○ if elimination

Time · Help · Answer Confirm · Next

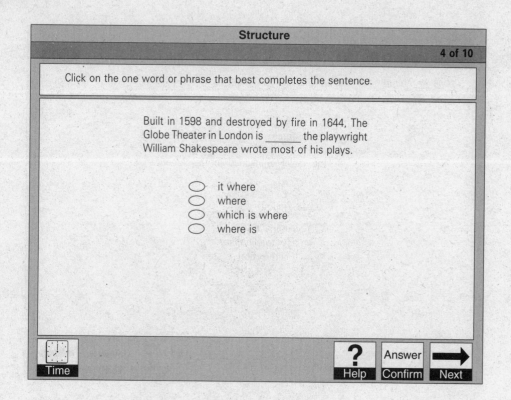

Click on the one word or phrase that best completes the sentence.

People hoping to see unidentified flying objects are often fooled by unusual atmospheric conditions that appear _____.

- ○ on the horizon which clouds form
- ○ do clouds form on the horizon
- ○ clouds forming on the horizon
- ○ when clouds form on the horizon

Time | ? Help | Answer Confirm | → Next

Click on the one word or phrase that best completes the sentence.

Built in 1598 and destroyed by fire in 1644, The Globe Theater in London is _____ the playwright William Shakespeare wrote most of his plays.

- ○ it where
- ○ where
- ○ which is where
- ○ where is

Time | ? Help | Answer Confirm | → Next

Structure

5 of 10

Click on the one word or phrase that best completes the sentence.

Just inside the outer layer of the earth's atmosphere ______ needed to protect it from foreign substances.

- ◯ are the elements
- ◯ where the elements are
- ◯ the elements are
- ◯ which are the elements

Time | Help | Answer Confirm | Next

Structure

6 of 10

Click on the one word or phrase that best completes the sentence.

Essentially, a hologram is a three-dimensional, projected image of ______ to be a real object.

- ◯ what is perceived
- ◯ to perceive what
- ◯ that perceiving
- ◯ which perceiving

Time | Help | Answer Confirm | Next

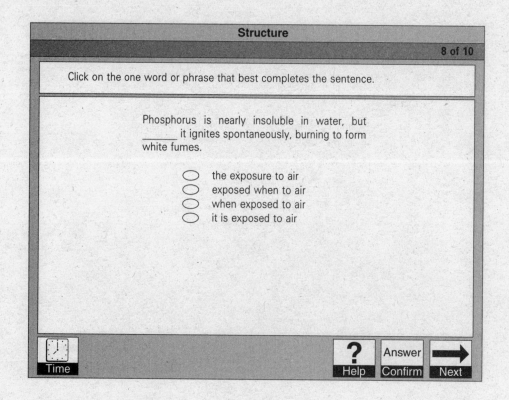

Click on the one word or phrase that best completes the sentence.

One of the first Native American tribes to live in _____ was the Apache, who are known principally for their fierce fighting qualities and matriarchal organization.

- ○ this is Arizona now
- ○ Arizona is now
- ○ what is now Arizona
- ○ is now Arizona

Time   Help   Answer Confirm   Next

Click on the one word or phrase that best completes the sentence.

Phosphorus is nearly insoluble in water, but _____ it ignites spontaneously, burning to form white fumes.

- ○ the exposure to air
- ○ exposed when to air
- ○ when exposed to air
- ○ it is exposed to air

Time   Help   Answer Confirm   Next

Click on the one word or phrase that best completes the sentence.

Human survival rates in serious motor vehicle accidents depend mostly on _____ or passengers are wearing their seatbelts.

- ◯ the driver
- ◯ either the driver
- ◯ whether the driver
- ◯ that the driver

Time Help Answer Confirm Next

Click on the one word or phrase that best completes the sentence.

According to developers, the purpose of virtual reality software is to provide the users with what _____ to explore otherwise unattainable environments.

- ◯ they want
- ◯ do they want
- ◯ so they want
- ◯ they are wanted

Time Help Answer Confirm Next

PASSIVE AND ACTIVE MODIFIERS

In addition to functioning as verbs, verbs can also act as other parts of speech. Two parts of speech that use a verb form are passive and active modifiers (also called verbal modifiers). Passive modifiers take the past participial form of the verb, that is, the "third" verb form. For example, *given, taken, chosen, compared, known, provided, unparalleled,* and *located* are verbs in the participial form. Active modifiers are verbs that take the present participial form, the *-ing* ending. For example, *beginning, making, using, including,* and *maintaining* can all act as active modifiers.

In the subordination section, you learned that subordination is used to combine several sentences into one. Passive and active modifiers are used for the same reason. Look at the two following sentences:

> The National Institute of Technology was established in 1901.
>
> The National Institute of Technology dedicates its services to strengthening and advancing the application of science for national interest.

Although these two sentences are grammatically correct, they are repetitive and a little awkward to read. By using a passive modifier, the two sentences can become one. The passive modifier in the following sentence is in bold.

> **Established** in 1901, the National Institute of Technology dedicates its services to strengthening and advancing the application of science for national interest.

Passive modifiers are used to replace passive clauses and must immediately precede or follow the word they are modifying. Regardless of the main tense of the sentence, the passive modifier is always the past participle.

Active modifiers work the exact same way as passive modifiers, except they take the *-ing* form of the verb. They are also used to combine more than one sentence into one. Look at the two following sentences:

> After it hatches, the caterpillar experiences several stages of metamorphosis.
>
> The metamorphosis begins with a pupa.

Although these two sentences are grammatically correct, they are repetitive and a little awkward to read. By using an active modifier, the two sentences can become one. The active modifier in the following sentence is in bold.

> After it hatches, the caterpillar experiences several stages of metamorphosis, **beginning** with a pupa.

Active modifiers are used to replace active clauses and must immediately precede or follow the word they are modifying. Regardless of the main tense of the sentence, the active modifier always takes the *-ing* ending.

On the error identification questions of the TOEFL CBT, ETS will test your basic knowledge of passive and active modifiers by simply substituting one for the other. Look at a typical passive/active modifier question found on the Structure section of the TOEFL CBT.

> <u>Establishing</u> in 1901, the National Institute of Technology dedicates <u>its</u> services to <u>strengthening and advancing</u> the application of science <u>for</u> national interest.

To solve these types of questions, identify what the passive/active modifier is modifying and ask a question. For example, in this sentence, "The National Institute of Technology" is being modified. Simply ask the question, "Can the National Institute of Technology be establishing?" No. An institute *cannot* establish anything, but it *can* be established by someone.

Look at another typical passive/active modifier question found on the Structure section of the TOEFL CBT.

> After it hatches, the caterpillar experiences several stages of metamorphosis, _____ with a pupa.
>
> ○ began
> ○ is begun
> ○ beginning
> ○ begin

In this sentence, use POE on the answer choices that function as main verbs or change the tense of the sentence ("begin", "is begun", "began"). The "stages of metamorphosis" is active because it can begin with something. Therefore the best answer to select is "beginning."

PRACTICE!

The following exercises contain passive/active questions most frequently found in the Structure section of the TOEFL CBT. Click on (in this case circle) the one word or phrase that best completes the sentence, or the one underlined word or phrase that must be changed for the sentence to be correct.

Click on the one word or phrase that best completes the sentence.

With time, the thickness of human eyelashes decreases, _____ them less likely to protect the eye from dust and disease.

○ make
○ which they make
○ and is making
○ making

Time   Help Answer   Next
              Confirm

Click on the one word or phrase that best completes the sentence.

The Native American group _____ as the Cherokee Nation established their own constitution and elected their own leaders.

○ known
○ were known
○ the unknown
○ are unknown

Time   Help Answer   Next
              Confirm

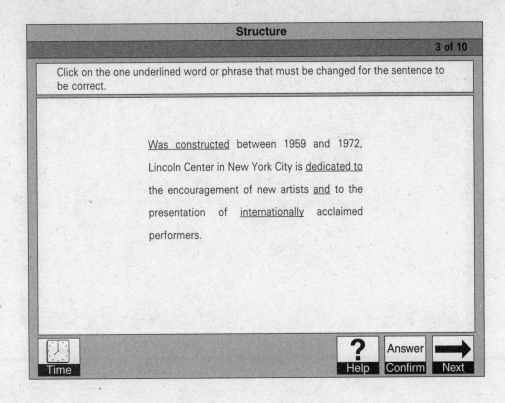

Click on the one underlined word or phrase that must be changed for the sentence to be correct.

<u>Was constructed</u> between 1959 and 1972, Lincoln Center in New York City is <u>dedicated to</u> the encouragement of new artists <u>and</u> to the presentation of <u>internationally</u> acclaimed performers.

Time

? Help | Answer Confirm | → Next

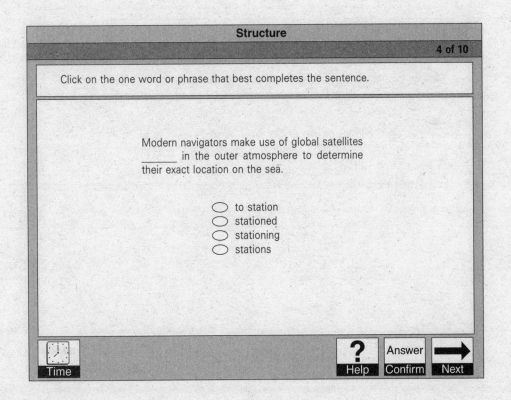

Click on the one word or phrase that best completes the sentence.

Modern navigators make use of global satellites _____ in the outer atmosphere to determine their exact location on the sea.

- ◯ to station
- ◯ stationed
- ◯ stationing
- ◯ stations

Time

? Help | Answer Confirm | → Next

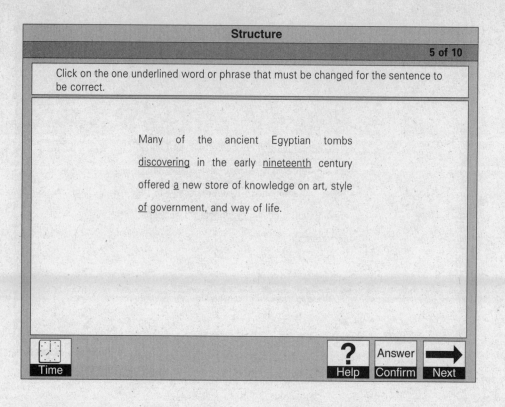

Click on the one underlined word or phrase that must be changed for the sentence to be correct.

Many of the ancient Egyptian tombs <u>discovering</u> in the early <u>nineteenth</u> century offered <u>a</u> new store of knowledge on art, style <u>of</u> government, and way of life.

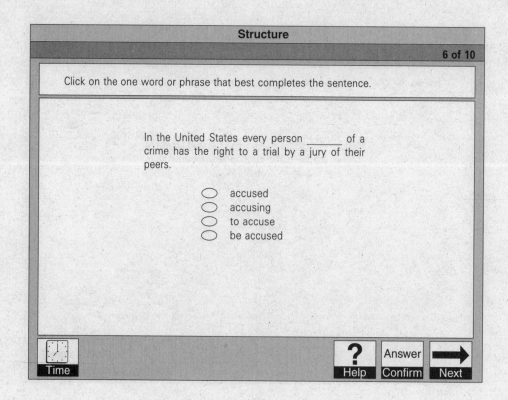

Click on the one word or phrase that best completes the sentence.

In the United States every person _____ of a crime has the right to a trial by a jury of their peers.

◯ accused
◯ accusing
◯ to accuse
◯ be accused

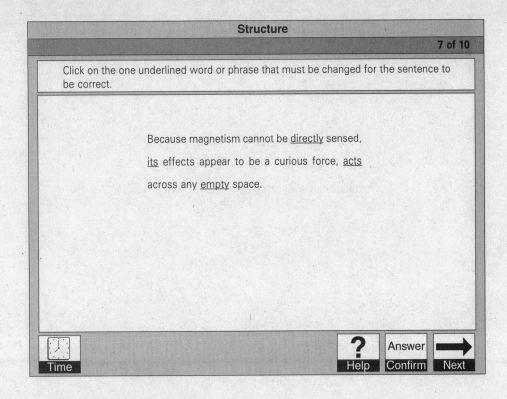

Click on the one underlined word or phrase that must be changed for the sentence to be correct.

Because magnetism cannot be <u>directly</u> sensed,

<u>its</u> effects appear to be a curious force, <u>acts</u>

across any <u>empty</u> space.

Time ? Help Answer Confirm Next

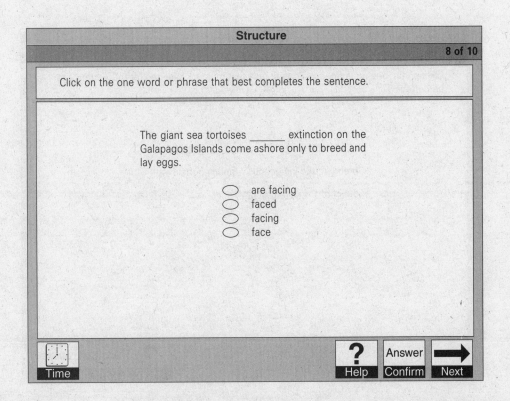

Click on the one word or phrase that best completes the sentence.

The giant sea tortoises _____ extinction on the Galapagos Islands come ashore only to breed and lay eggs.

- ⬭ are facing
- ⬭ faced
- ⬭ facing
- ⬭ face

Time ? Help Answer Confirm Next

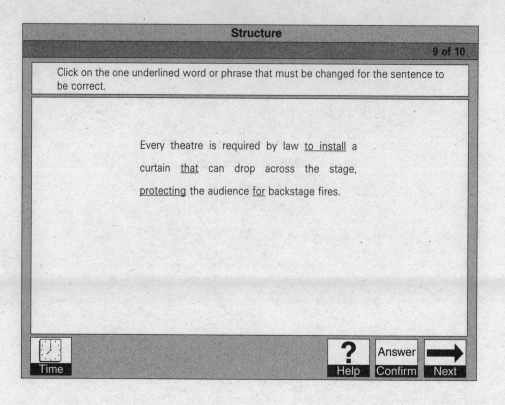

Click on the one underlined word or phrase that must be changed for the sentence to be correct.

Every theatre is required by law <u>to install</u> a curtain <u>that</u> can drop across the stage, <u>protecting</u> the audience <u>for</u> backstage fires.

Time   Help   Answer Confirm   Next

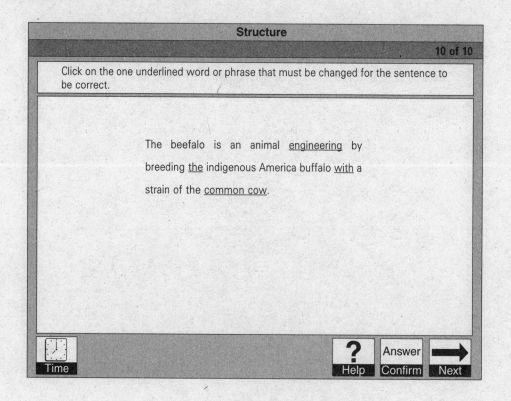

Click on the one underlined word or phrase that must be changed for the sentence to be correct.

The beefalo is an animal <u>engineering</u> by breeding <u>the</u> indigenous America buffalo <u>with</u> a strain of the <u>common cow</u>.

Time   Help   Answer Confirm   Next

GERUNDS AND INFINITIVES

When the *-ing* ending is added to a verb, making it function as a *noun*, it is called a "gerund." A gerund represents the performance of the verb in noun form. To clarify what a gerund is, compare the *-ing* ending with the *-er* ending. If you add the *-er* ending to any verb—for example, *swimmer*, *runner*, *teacher*, and so forth—the verb expresses the performer of the verb. Likewise, adding the *-ing* form to any verb—for example, *swimming*, *running*, *teaching*, and so forth—the verb expresses the performance of the verb. Like a noun, a gerund can function as a subject, object, and complement. For example:

> Since its invention in 1834, refrigeration has greatly improved the **buying** and **selling** of food products.

On the TOEFL CBT, ETS tests your basic knowledge of gerunds that either follow verb/preposition combinations or adjective/preposition combinations. Identify the error in this typical TOEFL CBT question.

> <u>Some</u> politicians complain <u>about</u> border guards' <u>inability</u> to prevent people from illegally <u>cross</u> the Texan-Mexican border.

In this example, the gerund in the fixed phrase "to prevent someone from *doing something*" has been replaced with the infinitive. The sentence should read:

> <u>Some</u> politicians complain <u>about</u> border guards' <u>inability</u> to prevent people from illegally <u>crossing</u> the Texan-Mexican border.

The following is a common list of fixed adjectival and verbal phrases followed by a gerund that frequently appear on the TOEFL CBT. Try to memorize a few each day. Learning these fixed expressions will not only improve your TOEFL CBT Structure score, but they can also be used in the Writing section of the TOEFL CBT, and improve your level of conversational English.

Adjectival and Verbal Phrases Followed by a Gerund

1. to object to doing something
2. to prevent/stop someone from doing something
3. to be responsible for doing something
4. to punish someone for doing something
5. to be capable of doing something
6. to be interested in doing something
7. to be known for doing something
8. to believe in doing something
9. to be committed to doing something
10. to forgive someone for something
11. to participate/take part in doing something
12. to admit/confess to doing something
13. to accuse someone of doing something
14. to succeed in doing something
15. to be excited about doing something
16. to keep/prohibit someone from doing something
17. to accuse someone of doing something
18. to blame someone for doing something
19. to consist of doing something
20. to be guilty of doing something

On the TOEFL CBT, ETS will also test your ability to recognize if a gerund or an infinitive comes after another verb. Look at the following TOEFL CBT sentence.

> As minister of justice, Nicolas Avellaneda worked _____ the failing banks of Argentina reform into respectable financial institutions.
>
> ○ help
> ○ for helping
> ○ to help
> ○ the help that

In English, when one verb follows another, it must take *either* the gerund or the infinitive form. There is no rule as to why some verbs take a gerund and others take an infinitive. The following is a reference list of verbs followed by either gerunds or infinitives that frequently appear on the TOEFL CBT. Try to memorize a few each day. Learning these verb patterns will not only improve your TOEFL CBT Structure score, but also help in the Writing section of the TOEFL CBT and improve your level of conversational English.

Verbs Followed by Infinitives	Verbs Followed by Gerunds
1. continue	1. mention
2. appear	2. postpone
3. consent	3. resist
4. pretend	4. tolerate
5. hesitate	5. consider
6. promise	6. delay
7. appear	7. keep
8. claim	8. enjoy
9. begin	9. mind
10. work	10. practice
11. threaten	11. risk
12. manage	12. finish
13. expect	13. recall
14. beg	14. avoid
15. refuse	15. anticipate

On the TOEFL CBT, ETS tests your basic knowledge of infinitives that follow verb/noun combinations. Identify the error in this typical TOEFL CBT question.

> <u>Composers</u> of the late twentieth century heavily rely <u>on</u> computers and specialized software <u>to helping</u> <u>write</u> their scores.

In this example the infinitive in the fixed phrase "to rely on something <u>to do</u> something" has been replaced with the gerund. The sentence should read:

> <u>Composers</u> of the late twentieth century
> heavily rely <u>on</u> computers and specialized
> software <u>to help</u> <u>write</u> their scores.

The following is a common list of fixed verb/noun phrases followed by an infinitive that frequently appear on the TOEFL CBT. Try to memorize a few each day. Learning these fixed expressions will not only improve your TOEFL CBT Structure score, but they can also be used in the Writing section of the TOEFL CBT, and improve your level of conversational English.

Verb/Noun Phrases Followed by Infinitives

1. to persuade someone to do something
2. to make it possible to do something
3. to enable someone to do something
4. to lead someone to do something
5. to rely on something/someone to do something
6. to equip someone to do something
7. to permit someone to do something
8. to cause someone to do something
9. to encourage someone to do something
10. to convince someone to do something
11. to need someone to do something
12. to remind someone to do something
13. to challenge someone to do something
14. to allow someone to do something
15. to expect someone to do something

PRACTICE!

The following exercises contain passive/active questions most frequently found in the Structure section of the TOEFL CBT. Click on (in this case circle) the one word or phrase that best completes the sentence, or the one underlined word or phrase that must be changed for the sentence to be correct.

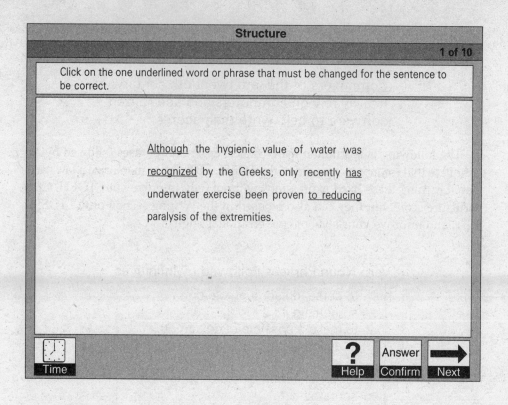

Click on the one underlined word or phrase that must be changed for the sentence to be correct.

<u>Although</u> the hygienic value of water was <u>recognized</u> by the Greeks, only recently <u>has</u> underwater exercise been proven <u>to reducing</u> paralysis of the extremities.

Time   Help   Answer Confirm   Next

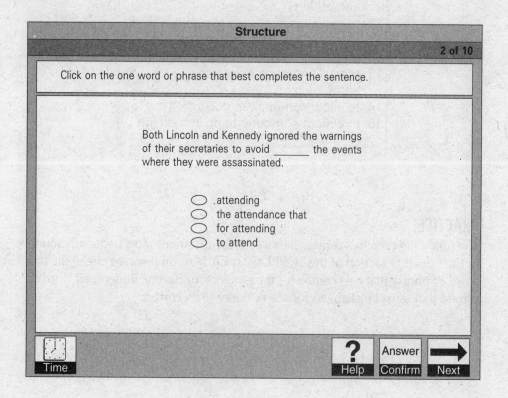

Click on the one word or phrase that best completes the sentence.

Both Lincoln and Kennedy ignored the warnings of their secretaries to avoid _____ the events where they were assassinated.

- ○ attending
- ○ the attendance that
- ○ for attending
- ○ to attend

Time   Help   Answer Confirm   Next

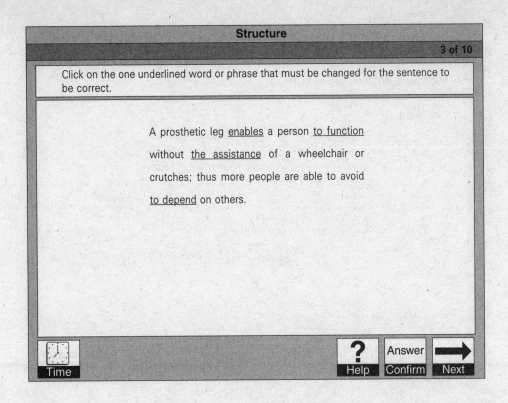

Click on the one underlined word or phrase that must be changed for the sentence to be correct.

A prosthetic leg <u>enables</u> a person <u>to function</u> without <u>the assistance</u> of a wheelchair or crutches; thus more people are able to avoid <u>to depend</u> on others.

?
Help

Answer
Confirm

→
Next

Time

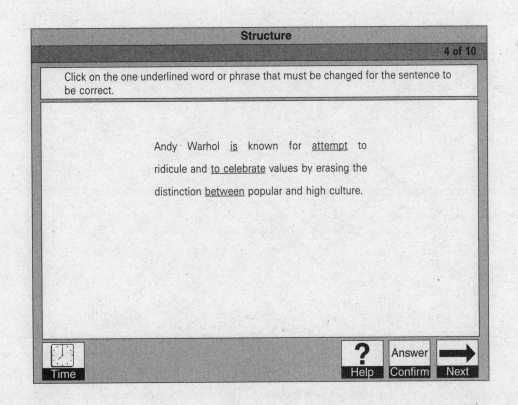

Click on the one underlined word or phrase that must be changed for the sentence to be correct.

Andy Warhol <u>is</u> known for <u>attempt</u> to ridicule and <u>to celebrate</u> values by erasing the distinction <u>between</u> popular and high culture.

?
Help

Answer
Confirm

→
Next

Time

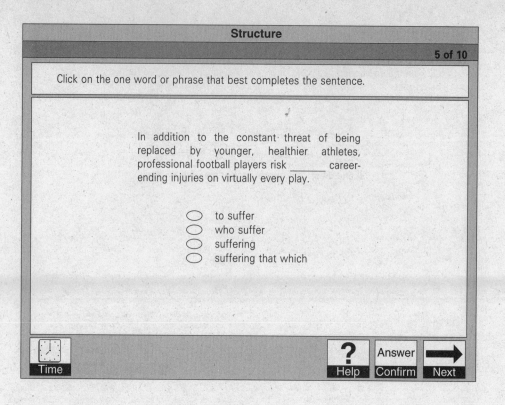

Click on the one word or phrase that best completes the sentence.

In addition to the constant threat of being replaced by younger, healthier athletes, professional football players risk _____ career-ending injuries on virtually every play.

- ⬭ to suffer
- ⬭ who suffer
- ⬭ suffering
- ⬭ suffering that which

Time   Help   Answer Confirm   Next

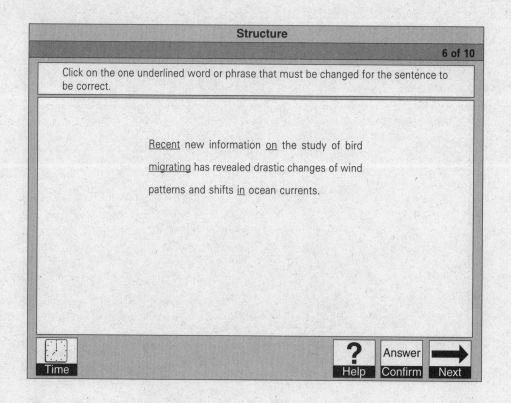

Click on the one underlined word or phrase that must be changed for the sentence to be correct.

Recent new information on the study of bird

migrating has revealed drastic changes of wind

patterns and shifts in ocean currents.

Time   Help   Answer Confirm   Next

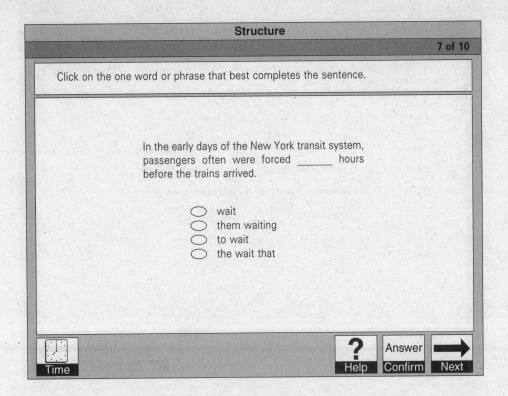

Click on the one word or phrase that best completes the sentence.

In the early days of the New York transit system, passengers often were forced _____ hours before the trains arrived.

○ wait
○ them waiting
○ to wait
○ the wait that

Time   Help Answer Next
              Confirm

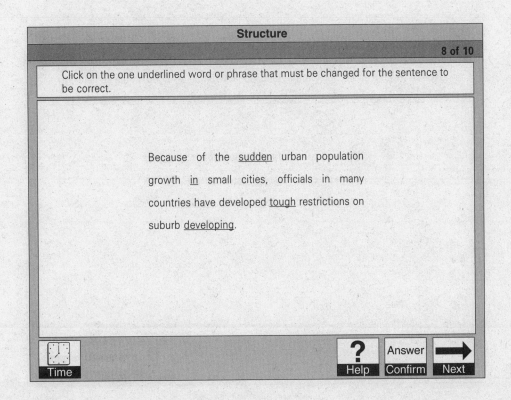

Click on the one underlined word or phrase that must be changed for the sentence to be correct.

Because of the <u>sudden</u> urban population growth <u>in</u> small cities, officials in many countries have developed <u>tough</u> restrictions on suburb <u>developing</u>.

Time   Help Answer Next
              Confirm

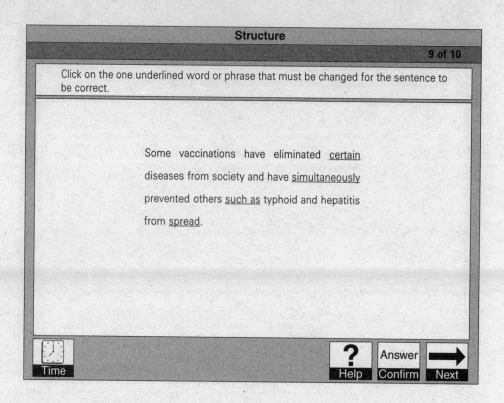

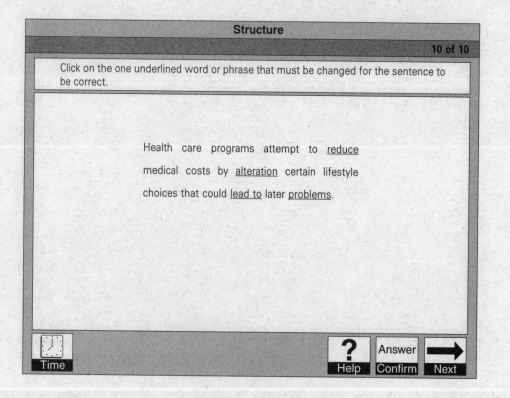

PREPOSITIONS

In the Structure section of the TOEFL CBT, ETS will test your basic knowledge of prepositions. You can expect 3 to 5 preposition questions per test. Preposition questions are some of the most difficult questions you will encounter on the TOEFL CBT. Prepositions are illogical and are inconsistent *from* one situation *to* another. Fortunately, your POE techniques will be extremely beneficial. Simply, if all other answer choices seem correct, and a preposition is underlined, chances are good that it will be the best answer choice.

Prepositions are only tested in error identification questions.

Prepositions that follow adjectives must be followed by an object, noun, or pronoun. Look at a typical TOEFL CBT preposition question:

> Doris Lessing has been <u>recognized</u> <u>from</u> her skill <u>as a</u> short-story writer and as <u>a</u> writer of nonfiction.

In the above example, ETS has substituted the incorrect preposition "from" for the correct preposition "for." ETS will test your knowledge of prepositions that follow adjectives. Following is a list of prepositions that ETS has used on recent exams. Try to memorize a few each day.

If a preposition is omitted, the words on either side are underlined.

Prepositions

1. to be jealous of	16. to be associated with
2. to be characterized by	17. to believe in
	18. to be committed to
3. to be dedicated to	19. to be concerned about
4. to differ in	20. to be guilty of
5. to benefit from	21. to be distinguished from
6. to be given to	
7. to be known for	22. to escape from
8. to serve as	23. to be excited about
9. to be rich with	24. to be furnished with
10. to be related to	25. to be interested in
11. to be on account of	26. to be prepared for
12. to depend on	27. to recover from
13. to be accused of	28. to take advantage of
14. to be acquainted with	29. to be worried about
	30. to participate in
15. to protect from	

PRACTICE!

The following exercises contain the sort of prepositional phrase questions most frequently found in the Structure section of the TOEFL CBT. Click on (in this case circle) the one underlined word or phrase that must be changed for the sentence to be correct.

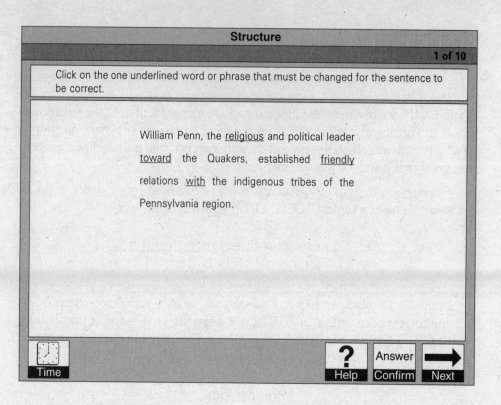

Click on the one underlined word or phrase that must be changed for the sentence to be correct.

William Penn, the <u>religious</u> and political leader <u>toward</u> the Quakers, established <u>friendly</u> relations <u>with</u> the indigenous tribes of the Pennsylvania region.

Time

? Help

Answer Confirm

Next

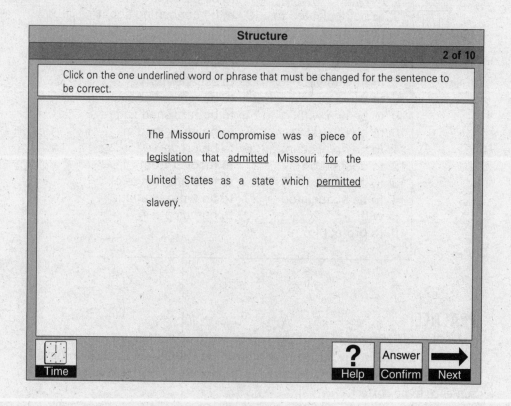

Click on the one underlined word or phrase that must be changed for the sentence to be correct.

The Missouri Compromise was a piece of <u>legislation</u> that <u>admitted</u> Missouri <u>for</u> the United States as a state which <u>permitted</u> slavery.

Time

? Help

Answer Confirm

Next

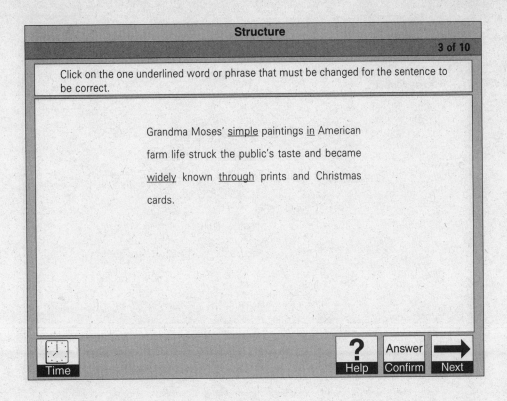

Click on the one underlined word or phrase that must be changed for the sentence to be correct.

Grandma Moses' <u>simple</u> paintings <u>in</u> American farm life struck the public's taste and became <u>widely</u> known <u>through</u> prints and Christmas cards.

Time | **?** Help | Answer Confirm | → Next

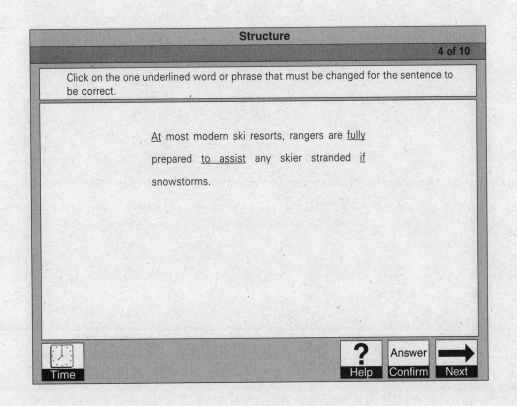

Click on the one underlined word or phrase that must be changed for the sentence to be correct.

<u>At</u> most modern ski resorts, rangers are <u>fully</u> prepared <u>to assist</u> any skier stranded <u>if</u> snowstorms.

Time | **?** Help | Answer Confirm | → Next

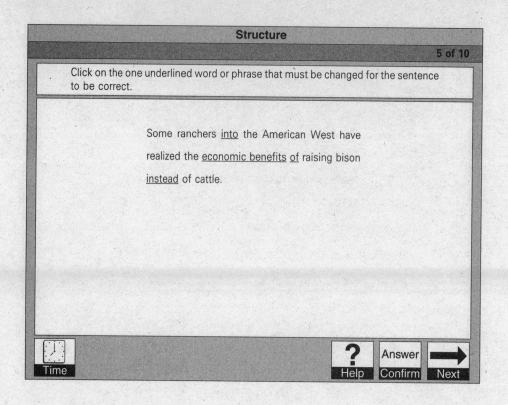

Click on the one underlined word or phrase that must be changed for the sentence to be correct.

Some ranchers <u>into</u> the American West have realized the <u>economic benefits</u> <u>of</u> raising bison <u>instead</u> of cattle.

Time   Help   Answer Confirm   Next

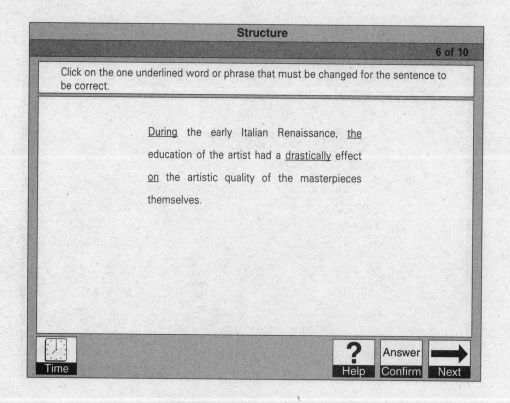

Click on the one underlined word or phrase that must be changed for the sentence to be correct.

<u>During</u> the early Italian Renaissance, <u>the</u> education of the artist had a <u>drastically</u> effect <u>on</u> the artistic quality of the masterpieces themselves.

Time   Help   Answer Confirm   Next

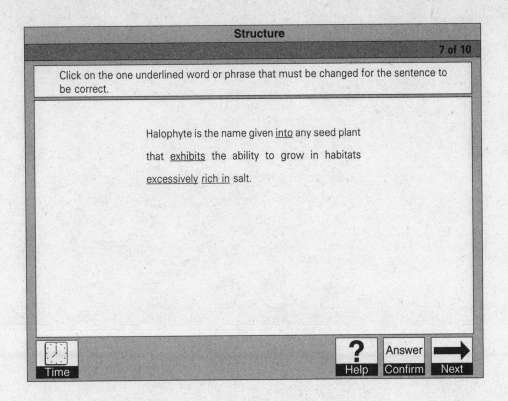

Click on the one underlined word or phrase that must be changed for the sentence to be correct.

Halophyte is the name given <u>into</u> any seed plant

that <u>exhibits</u> the ability to grow in habitats

<u>excessively</u> <u>rich in</u> salt.

Time   ? Help   Answer Confirm   Next

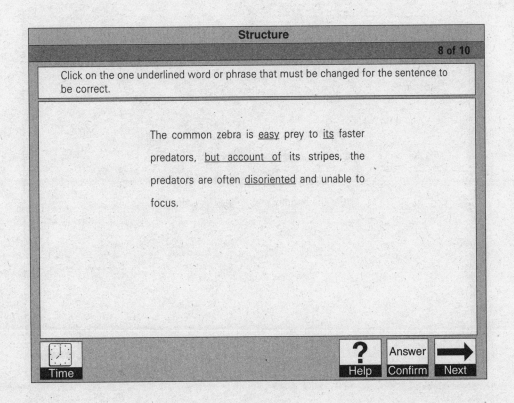

Click on the one underlined word or phrase that must be changed for the sentence to be correct.

The common zebra is <u>easy</u> prey to <u>its</u> faster

predators, <u>but account of</u> its stripes, the

predators are often <u>disoriented</u> and unable to

focus.

Time   ? Help   Answer Confirm   Next

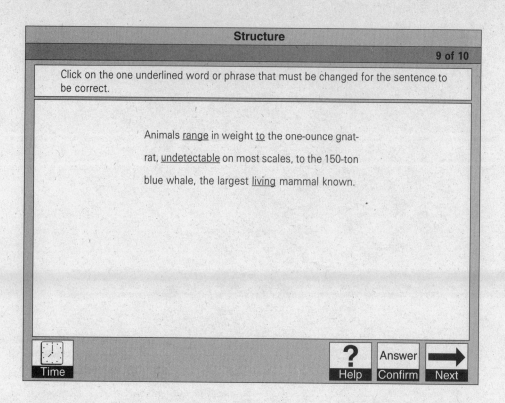

Click on the one underlined word or phrase that must be changed for the sentence to be correct.

Animals <u>range</u> in weight <u>to</u> the one-ounce gnat-rat, <u>undetectable</u> on most scales, to the 150-ton blue whale, the largest <u>living</u> mammal known.

Time   Help   Answer Confirm   Next

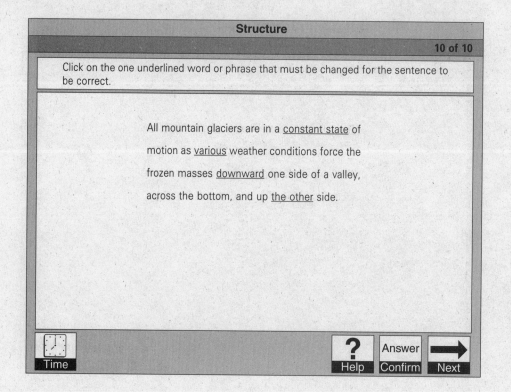

Click on the one underlined word or phrase that must be changed for the sentence to be correct.

All mountain glaciers are in a <u>constant state</u> of motion as <u>various</u> weather conditions force the frozen masses <u>downward</u> one side of a valley, across the bottom, and up <u>the other</u> side.

Time   Help   Answer Confirm   Next

Conjunctions

Conjunctions express a relationship between ideas. They connect different types of words and phrases: nouns with nouns, verbs with verbs, modifiers with modifiers, phrases with phrases, or clauses with clauses. On the TOEFL CBT, both conjunctions and conjunction patterns will be tested in both sentence completion and error identification question types.

There are two basic types of conjunctions; those that show *agreement* between ideas, and those that show *disagreement* between ideas. Conjunctions that show agreement give additional information that agrees with or further explains the idea in the main sentence. For example:

> Benjamin Franklin was a successful inventor **as well as** a politician and statesman.

In the above sentence, the conjunction "as well as" provides additional information that agrees with what is already stated or implied in the main sentence. Conjunctions that show disagreement between ideas contrast the idea in the main sentence. For example:

> **Although** petroleum is refined into industrial products such as plastic and synthetic fiber, it is primarily prized for its ability to combust.

In the above sentence, the conjunction "although" contradicts the idea that is stated or implied in the main sentence. Both types of conjunctions are tested in the TOEFL CBT. The following is a common list of conjunctions that show agreement and disagreement between ideas. Try to incorporate them into your vocabulary by practicing a few each day. Learning these conjunctions will not only improve your TOEFL CBT Structure score, but can also help in the Writing section of the TOEFL CBT, and improve your level of conversational English.

Agreement	Disagreement
such as	but
as well as	however
because	despite
also	although
in addition to	in spite of
as	whereas

On the TOEFL CBT, ETS usually tests your basic knowledge of conjunctions in the sentence completion type of question. ETS will try to confuse you by including articles, adverbs, and other parts of speech with conjunctions in the answer choices. Look at the following example.

_____ the consumption of tobacco has dramatically decreased, smoking continues to be a widespread and costly health problem.

   ○ Despite
   ○ Although
   ○ Whereas
   ○ Neither

In this example, the main sentence states that "smoking continues to be a widespread and costly health problem." However, the dependent clause states that the consumption of tobacco has dramatically decreased. The disagreement of ideas between the main sentence and the dependent clause requires a conjunction of disagreement. The first answer choice, "Despite," can't begin a modifying phrase that contains a verb. The conjunction "Whereas" can't show contrast between the same subject. The conjunction "Neither" must be paired with "nor." Only the answer choice "Although" successfully competes conjunction requirements.

ETS also tests your basic knowledge of conjunction patterns. Conjunction patterns are fixed expressions that need to include all the words in the pattern in order to be correct. Look at several types of conjunction patterns typically found on the TOEFL CBT.

• either . . . . or	Paleontology, which deals with prehistoric life forms, can be treated as **either** a part of geology **or** biology.
• neither . . . . nor	Virus particles can **neither** function as a living cell **nor** survive for extended periods of time outside a host.
• both . . . . and	**Both** earthquakes **and** volcanoes require specific geological conditions.
• not only . . . . but also	In order to ensure ample food supplies, **not only** do some species of fish attack intruders in their hunting territories, **but** they **also** kill their own offspring.
• such as	Early types of gunpowder were created with **such** materials **as** sulfur, saltpeter, and carbon in the form of charcoal.

Remember, when the negative "not only" acts as the subject, the auxiliary must immediately follow.

PRACTICE!

The following exercises contain the sort of conjunction questions most frequently found in the Structure section of the TOEFL CBT. Click on (in this case circle) the one word or phrase that best completes the sentence, or the one underlined word or phrase that must be changed for the sentence to be correct.

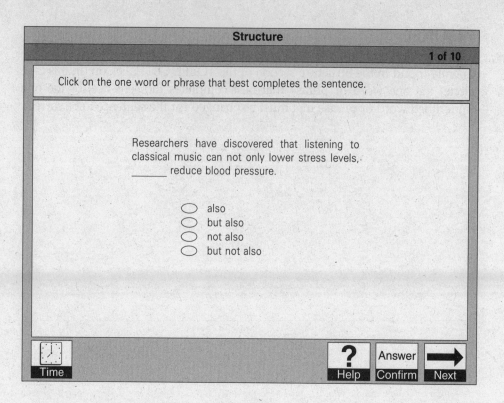

Click on the one word or phrase that best completes the sentence.

Researchers have discovered that listening to classical music can not only lower stress levels, _____ reduce blood pressure.

○ also
○ but also
○ not also
○ but not also

Time   Help   Answer Confirm   Next

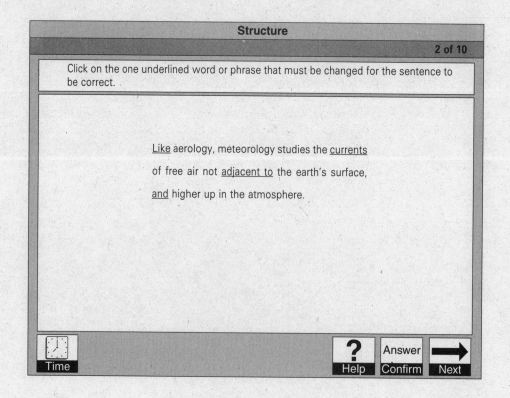

Click on the one underlined word or phrase that must be changed for the sentence to be correct.

<u>Like</u> aerology, meteorology studies the <u>currents</u>

of free air not <u>adjacent to</u> the earth's surface,

<u>and</u> higher up in the atmosphere.

Time   Help   Answer Confirm   Next

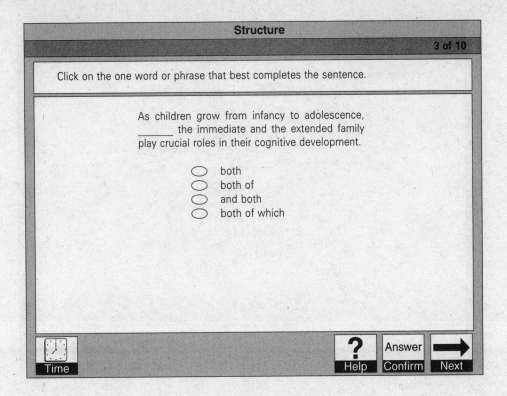

Click on the one word or phrase that best completes the sentence.

As children grow from infancy to adolescence, _____ the immediate and the extended family play crucial roles in their cognitive development.

- ○ both
- ○ both of
- ○ and both
- ○ both of which

Time Help Answer Confirm Next

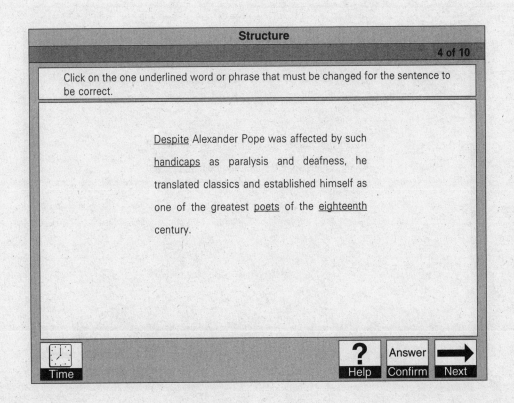

Click on the one underlined word or phrase that must be changed for the sentence to be correct.

Despite Alexander Pope was affected by such handicaps as paralysis and deafness, he translated classics and established himself as one of the greatest poets of the eighteenth century.

Time Help Answer Confirm Next

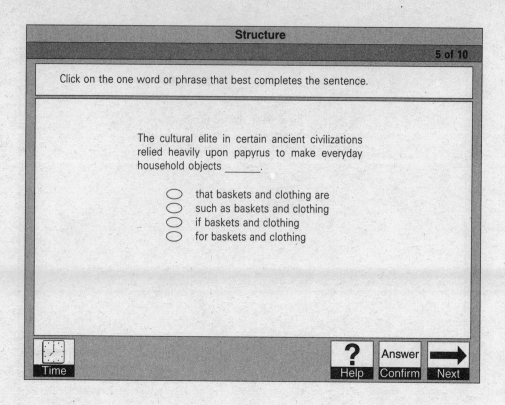

Click on the one word or phrase that best completes the sentence.

The cultural elite in certain ancient civilizations relied heavily upon papyrus to make everyday household objects _____.

○ that baskets and clothing are
○ such as baskets and clothing
○ if baskets and clothing
○ for baskets and clothing

Time   Help   Answer Confirm   Next

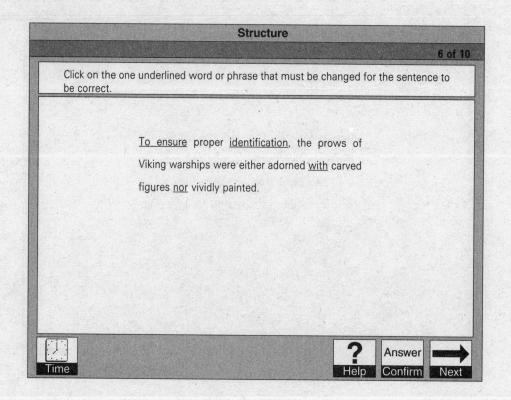

Click on the one underlined word or phrase that must be changed for the sentence to be correct.

To ensure proper identification, the prows of Viking warships were either adorned with carved figures nor vividly painted.

Time   Help   Answer Confirm   Next

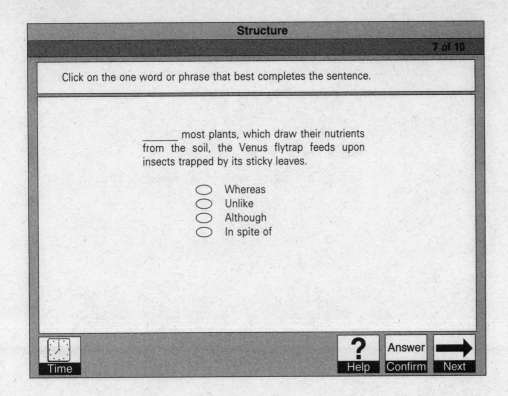

Click on the one word or phrase that best completes the sentence.

_____ most plants, which draw their nutrients from the soil, the Venus flytrap feeds upon insects trapped by its sticky leaves.

○ Whereas
○ Unlike
○ Although
○ In spite of

Time   Help   Answer Confirm   Next

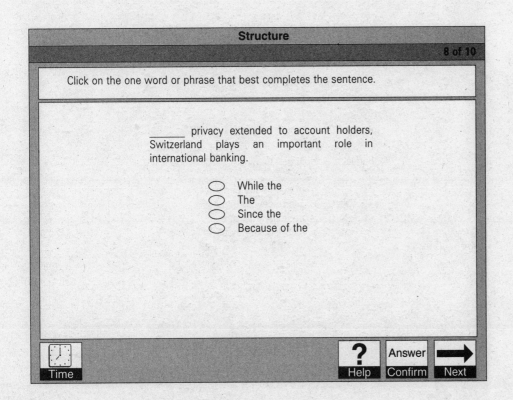

Click on the one word or phrase that best completes the sentence.

_____ privacy extended to account holders, Switzerland plays an important role in international banking.

○ While the
○ The
○ Since the
○ Because of the

Time   Help   Answer Confirm   Next

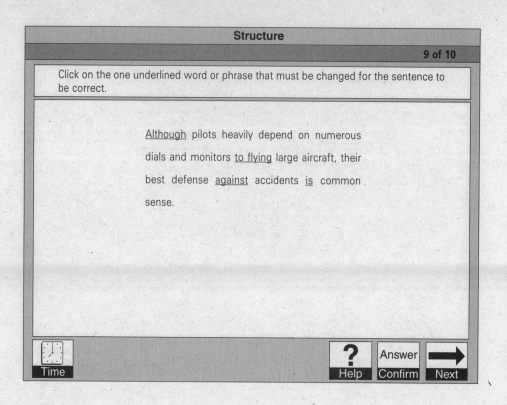

Click on the one underlined word or phrase that must be changed for the sentence to be correct.

<u>Although</u> pilots heavily depend on numerous dials and monitors <u>to flying</u> large aircraft, their best defense <u>against</u> accidents <u>is</u> common sense.

Time | Help | Answer Confirm | Next

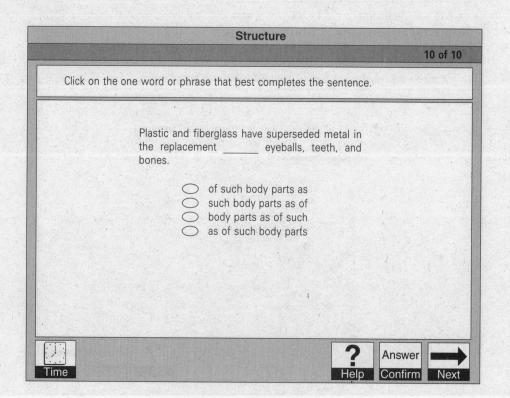

Click on the one word or phrase that best completes the sentence.

Plastic and fiberglass have superseded metal in the replacement _____ eyeballs, teeth, and bones.

○ of such body parts as
○ such body parts as of
○ body parts as of such
○ as of such body parts

Time | Help | Answer Confirm | Next

COMPARISONS AND SUPERLATIVES

Comparative adjectives compare the qualities of two nouns. If the adjective has only one syllable, the comparative form of the adjective is usually created by adding -er to the end of the adjective, and must be followed by "than." If the adjective has two syllables or more, the comparative form of the adjective is usually created by the preceding adverbs "more" or "less," and must also be followed by "than." There are exceptions to this "syllable" rule, but ETS will not test them.

Superlative adjectives show that a noun has a particular quality in the highest degree. If the adjective has less than two syllables, the superlative form of the adjective is usually created by adding -est to the end of the adjective. If the adjective has two syllables or more, the superlative form of the adjective is usually created by the preceding adverbs "most" or "least." There are exceptions to this "syllable" rule, but ETS will not test them.

Look at a list of adjectives in the comparative and superlative form.

low	lower	the lowest
abundant	more abundant	the most abundant
large	larger	the largest
terrible	less terrible	the least terrible
great	greater	the greatest
expensive	more expensive	the most expensive
long	longer	the longest
beautiful	less beautiful	the least beautiful

The adverbs "more," "less," "most," and "least" can never modify adjectives that end with -er, and -est. Look at a typical comparison/superlative question that frequently appears on the TOEFL CBT.

> Even though all rabbits are known to breed prolifically, the snowshoe rabbit actually has _____ than the cottontail does.
>
> ○ the longer the gestation period
> ○ its longer gestation period
> ○ the gestation period is longer
> ○ a longer gestation period

In this sentence, the first answer choice "the longer the gestation period" is part of a fixed comparative expression that needs another comparison to be complete. For example, "The bigger apartment, the higher the rent." The second answer choice "its longer gestation period" incorrectly adds a possessive pronoun. The third answer choice "the gestation period is longer" creates an independent sentence. Only the fourth answer choice "a longer gestation period" completes the grammatical requirements for a correct comparative structure.

PRACTICE!

The following exercises contain the sort of comparison and superlative questions most frequently found in the Structure section of the TOEFL CBT. Click on (in this case circle) the one word or phrase that best completes the sentence, or the one underlined word or phrase that must be changed for the sentence to be correct.

Structure

1 of 10

Click on the one word or phrase that best completes the sentence.

Microwaves that once took up entire kitchen counters are now ______ to fit conveniently under cabinets and on cupboard shelves.

- ○ so tiny
- ○ as tiny as
- ○ tiny enough
- ○ tinier than

Time | Help | Answer Confirm | Next

Structure

2 of 10

Click on the one word or phrase that best completes the sentence.

Although headache pain is ______ back pain, both can interfere with ordinary daily activities.

- ○ more effectively controlled than
- ○ the effect is more than controlled
- ○ more than effectively controlled
- ○ controlled more than effectively

Time | Help | Answer Confirm | Next

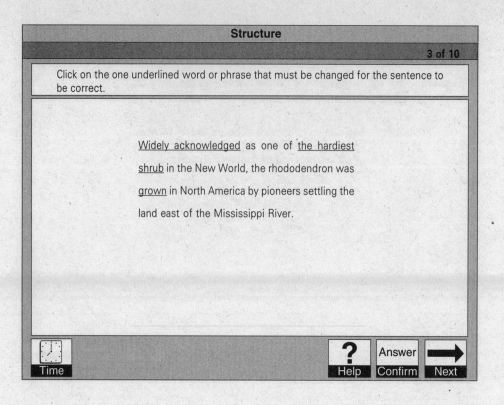

Click on the one underlined word or phrase that must be changed for the sentence to be correct.

Widely acknowledged as one of the hardiest shrub in the New World, the rhododendron was grown in North America by pioneers settling the land east of the Mississippi River.

Time | Help | Answer Confirm | Next

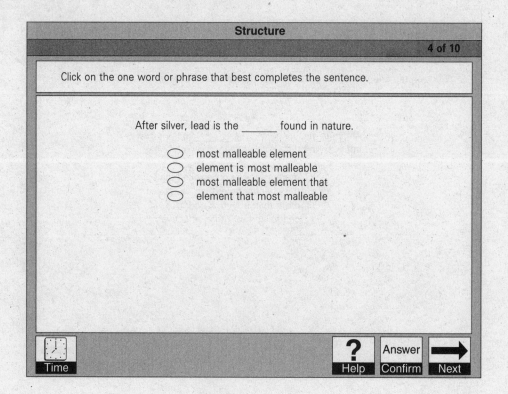

Click on the one word or phrase that best completes the sentence.

After silver, lead is the _____ found in nature.

- ○ most malleable element
- ○ element is most malleable
- ○ most malleable element that
- ○ element that most malleable

Time | Help | Answer Confirm | Next

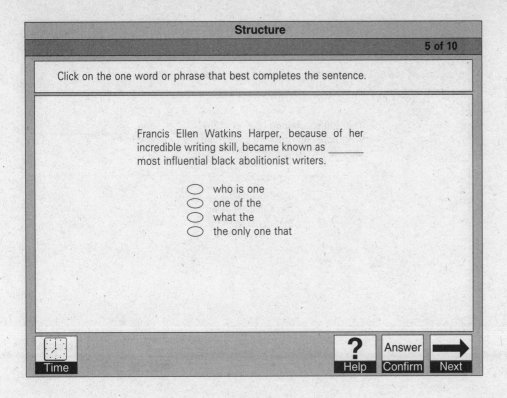

Click on the one word or phrase that best completes the sentence.

Francis Ellen Watkins Harper, because of her incredible writing skill, became known as _____ most influential black abolitionist writers.

- ⬭ who is one
- ⬭ one of the
- ⬭ what the
- ⬭ the only one that

Time | ? Help | Answer Confirm | ➡ Next

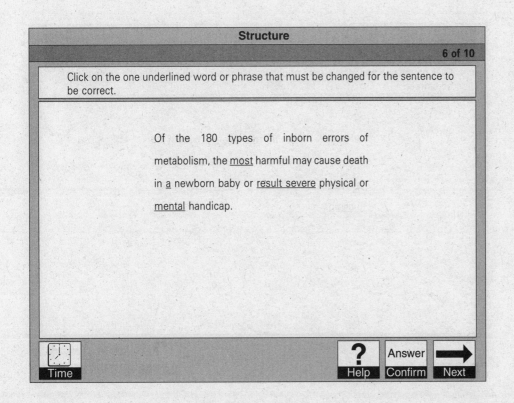

Click on the one underlined word or phrase that must be changed for the sentence to be correct.

Of the 180 types of inborn errors of metabolism, the <u>most</u> harmful may cause death in <u>a</u> newborn baby or <u>result severe</u> physical or <u>mental</u> handicap.

Time | ? Help | Answer Confirm | ➡ Next

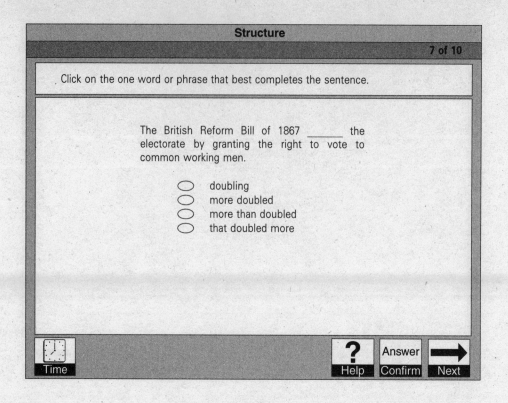

Click on the one word or phrase that best completes the sentence.

The British Reform Bill of 1867 _____ the electorate by granting the right to vote to common working men.

- ⬭ doubling
- ⬭ more doubled
- ⬭ more than doubled
- ⬭ that doubled more

Time   Help   Answer Confirm   Next

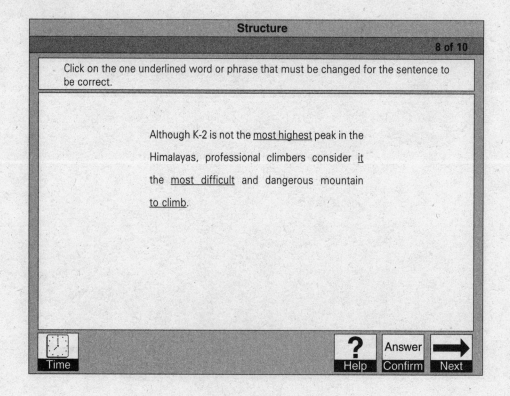

Click on the one underlined word or phrase that must be changed for the sentence to be correct.

Although K-2 is not the <u>most highest</u> peak in the Himalayas, professional climbers consider <u>it</u> the <u>most difficult</u> and dangerous mountain <u>to climb</u>.

Time   Help   Answer Confirm   Next

Click on the one word or phrase that best completes the sentence.

The soybean, a plant native to China and Japan, has become _____ in the United States farming community.

○ one of the most popular crops
○ as one of most popular crops
○ only of the most popular crops
○ one popular crops most are in

Time   ? Help   Answer Confirm   → Next

Click on the one word or phrase that best completes the sentence.

Dehydration occurs when _____ through perspiration or diarrhea than is replaced by fluid intake.

○ more water it is lost
○ losing more water
○ the loss of more water
○ more water is lost

Time   ? Help   Answer Confirm   → Next

ANSWER KEYS

Subjects

1. There are
2. The most significant program
3. The scientific study
4. playwright Oscar Wilde distinguished
5. are diseases diagnosed
6. to discover
7. Many professional athletes gain
8. an earthworm bores
9. It is not easy
10. Drug addiction is
11. it was
12. hunting was probably the quickest
13. Collecting nectar
14. biofeedback programs help patients
15. they have

Verbs

1. dates back
2. incubate
3. produces
4. prescribes
5. is named
6. synthesize
7. have no
8. container
9. receive
10. disinfection

Nouns

1. versatile
2. The discover
3. much
4. their
5. first gained national prominence
6. from bacteria
7. infectious
8. a greater range
9. live
10. structural

Singular and Plural Nouns

1. collection
2. area
3. symptom
4. site
5. type
6. formation
7. foot
8. Chameleon
9. whales
10. theory

Articles

1. a
2. an
3. a
4. a
5. A
6. is important
7. The archaeology
8. After beginning
9. for
10. many a miles

Pronouns

1. him
2. artist
3. those
4. them
5. its
6. shield surface
7. its
8. of own
9. those
10. whose

Appositives

1. a French landscape painter
2. the
3. a more adaptable animal
4. the cultivation of
5. microscopic parasites

Modifiers/Adjectives

1. irritation
2. suddenly
3. be accomplished with
4. possibly
5. poison
6. ethnic unrest
7. recently
8. both
9. each of which
10. much
11. another
12. fast enough
13. four-inched
14. often inhabit moist places
15. century sixteenth

Modifiers/Adverbs

1. inaccurate
2. narrowly defeated
3. rather
4. eventual
5. completely by surprise when
6. so
7. easy
8. approach
9. heavily
10. rather

Subordination

1. have no use
2. since
3. which portrayed
4. which it
5. what
6. they contain
7. praised
8. certainly
9. for
10. which attaches

Noun Clauses

1. when glaciers covered the area
2. how to eliminate
3. when clouds form on the horizon
4. where
5. are the elements
6. what is perceived
7. what is now Arizona
8. when exposed to air
9. whether the driver
10. they want

Passive and Active Modifiers

1. making
2. known
3. Was constructed
4. stationed
5. discovering
6. accused
7. acts
8. facing
9. for
10. engineering

Gerunds and Infinitives

1. to reducing
2. attending
3. to depend
4. attempt
5. suffering
6. migrating
7. to wait
8. developing
9. spread
10. alteration

Prepositions

1. toward
2. for
3. in
4. if
5. into
6. drastically
7. into
8. but account of
9. to
10. downward

Conjunctions

1. but also
2. and
3. both
4. Despite
5. such as baskets and clothing
6. nor
7. Unlike
8. Because of the
9. to flying
10. of such body parts as

Comparisons and Superlatives

1. tiny enough
2. more effectively controlled than
3. shrub
4. most malleable element
5. one of the
6. result severe
7. more than doubled
8. most highest
9. one of the most popular crops
10. more water is lost

PART ◆ IV

Reading

6
Reading

THE BASICS

Only the Listening and Structure sections are computer adaptive.

After the 10-minute break given after the Structure section, you should feel well rested and completely relaxed. The TOEFL CBT Reading section will require all of your remaining brainpower. Luckily, this section is *not* computer adaptive, meaning the difficulty of a question is not based on how you answered the previous question. Therefore, you will be able to focus on the easier questions and skip the more time-consuming questions, saving them for last. The Reading section contains four or five passages, each 250 to 350 words in length. Each passage is followed by 10 to 13 questions, for a total of approximately 44 to 60 questions. The passages will appear on the left side of the screen and the questions on the right side of the screen, one at a time. The computer screen looks something like this:

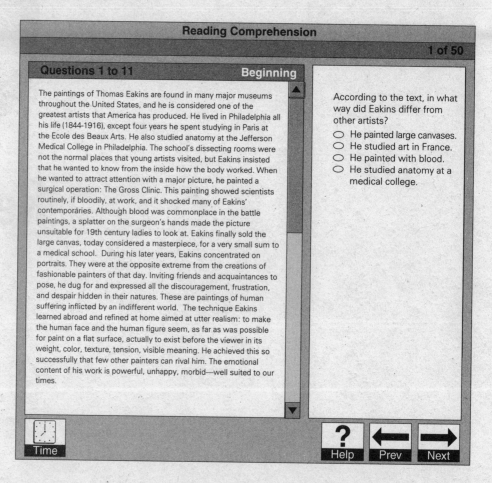

You have 70 to 90 minutes to complete this section. Seventy to 90 minutes seems like a long time, but you will be surprised by how quickly it passes. Fortunately, The Princeton Review has developed several time-saving techniques to help you work as efficiently as possible and make the most of your brainpower and time.

THE TUTORIAL

The mandatory tutorial begins by explaining once again how to scroll—that is, how you can see more of the reading passage that isn't on the screen. If you feel comfortable with line scrolling, speed line scrolling, and page scrolling, don't waste your brainpower! Move through them as quickly as possible. If you think you need extra work on this technique, by all means, review.

Move through the tutorials as quickly as possible.

Next, the tutorial explains the icons you need to know in order to move from one question to another. In the lower left-hand corner of the computer screen, you will see two icons, "Next" and "Prev." Simply click on the "Next" icon to jump to the next question. Click on the "Prev" icon to jump to the previous question. If at any time you need help, click on the "Help" icon located to the left on the "Prev" icon. However, time is running while you are in "Help." Fortunately, you will not need to click on "Help" after completing this book. Find the icons in the diagram below.

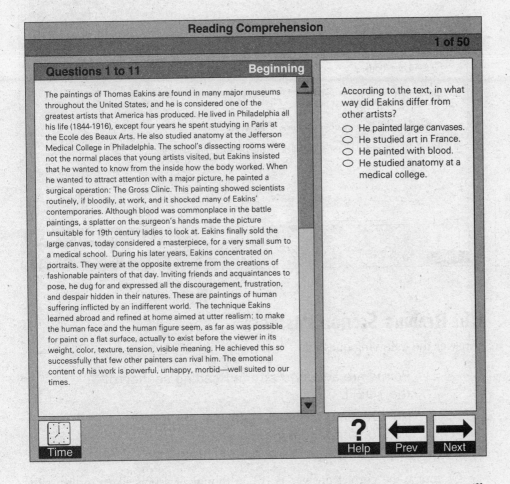

At this point, ETS familiarizes you with the type of questions you will encounter on the Reading section:

- ◆ Select one of four choices (just like the paper-and-pencil format)
- ◆ Click on a word, phrase, or sentence
- ◆ Add a sentence

Once again, work through this section as quickly as possible. You will have already learned how to handle these question types by the time you finish this chapter.

When you are finished with the tutorial, the TOEFL CBT Reading section finally begins. The first thing you can do to save yourself some time and brainpower on this section is learning the directions. As you can see, reading these directions can waste a lot of time! Read them once, before the test, and learn them. A short sample passage and a couple of examples might follow the directions. *Don't read them!* Get straight to work!

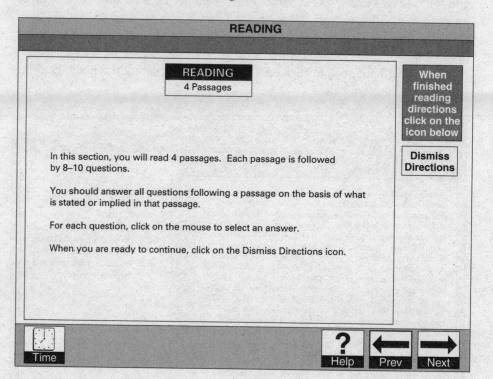

You should immediately click on the "Dismiss Directions" icon and begin working on the Reading section.

THE READING SECTION PASSAGES

Answer the following question:

Points are awarded on the Reading section of the TOEFL CBT for

(A)   reading the passage carefully and understanding every word
(B)   answering the questions correctly

Of course the correct answer is (B). Although it seems like a pretty silly question, most test takers approach the Reading section as if they get points just for reading and understanding the passage. When you take the TOEFL CBT, you can bet that a lot of the other students in the room will waste most of their allotted time reading and rereading the passages, trying to comprehend every word. In fact, ETS will inform you on the computer screen to read the entire passage before clicking on the "Proceed" icon. *Don't read the passage!*

If you try to read the entire passage as ETS suggests, you will *not* be able to finish the test.

TOEFL CBT reading passages are about science, humanities, and social studies, but they differ from the reading you do in school and for pleasure. They contain *no* information that you want to remember for your career or lifestyle. They only contain the answers to the questions ETS asks you.

TOEFL CBT reading material is carefully edited by ETS personnel, who make sure that all of the reading passages are:

1. *Boring* and difficult to concentrate on. ETS wants boring passages; it is much easier to understand an interesting passage.

2. *Dense,* contain many unimportant details. The answers to the questions are hidden among all the complicated details and perplexing vocabulary. This makes the answers extremely difficult to find.

3. *Poorly constructed,* lack transitional phrases that make passages clear and easy to understand. This interrupts the flow of the passage and confuses the reader.

Each TOEFL CBT passage can be up to 350 words long. ETS makes sure you don't have enough time to read all of the passages *and* answer all the questions. Believe it or not, even native English speakers find it extremely tough to complete all the passages and comprehend all of the new vocabulary and details. You don't receive any points for reading the passage; you only get points for correctly answering the question.

Saving Time = 1-1-1-L

Students who want to score as many points as possible use the proven time saving technique **1-1-1-L**. Instead of reading the entire passage, you should only read:

1— the first sentence of the **first** paragraph.

1— the first sentence of the **second** paragraph.

1— the first sentence of **each remaining** paragraph.

L— the last sentence of the **final** paragraph.

Let's try it. Practice the above 1-1-1-L concept with the following example. Read the first sentence of each paragraph, and the last sentence of the last paragraph.

During the TOEFL CBT, you will have to scroll down to read the first sentences of the final few paragraphs.

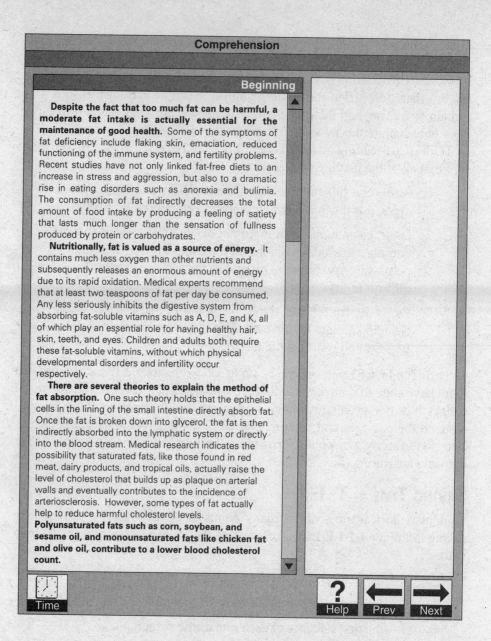

Beginning

Despite the fact that too much fat can be harmful, a moderate fat intake is actually essential for the maintenance of good health. Some of the symptoms of fat deficiency include flaking skin, emaciation, reduced functioning of the immune system, and fertility problems. Recent studies have not only linked fat-free diets to an increase in stress and aggression, but also to a dramatic rise in eating disorders such as anorexia and bulimia. The consumption of fat indirectly decreases the total amount of food intake by producing a feeling of satiety that lasts much longer than the sensation of fullness produced by protein or carbohydrates.

Nutritionally, fat is valued as a source of energy. It contains much less oxygen than other nutrients and subsequently releases an enormous amount of energy due to its rapid oxidation. Medical experts recommend that at least two teaspoons of fat per day be consumed. Any less seriously inhibits the digestive system from absorbing fat-soluble vitamins such as A, D, E, and K, all of which play an essential role for having healthy hair, skin, teeth, and eyes. Children and adults both require these fat-soluble vitamins, without which physical developmental disorders and infertility occur respectively.

There are several theories to explain the method of fat absorption. One such theory holds that the epithelial cells in the lining of the small intestine directly absorb fat. Once the fat is broken down into glycerol, the fat is then indirectly absorbed into the lymphatic system or directly into the blood stream. Medical research indicates the possibility that saturated fats, like those found in red meat, dairy products, and tropical oils, actually raise the level of cholesterol that builds up as plaque on arterial walls and eventually contributes to the incidence of arteriosclerosis. However, some types of fat actually help to reduce harmful cholesterol levels. **Polyunsaturated fats such as corn, soybean, and sesame oil, and monounsaturated fats like chicken fat and olive oil, contribute to a lower blood cholesterol count.**

Time | Help | Prev | Next

Congratulations! You just saved yourself approximately 5 minutes of valuable time. Remember, the TOEFL CBT passages are filled with so many poorly constructed sentences, unnecessary details, and strange vocabulary that most of them are incomprehensible. Don't waste time reading the passage. You do not receive any points for reading the passage. You only get points for answering the questions.

After using the "1-1-1-L" technique, you should have some idea as to what the main idea of the passage is about. Go back to the previous bold sentences in the passage and circle the words that keep reappearing in the sentences you just read.

Drill 1

1. What subject keeps reoccurring in the sentences? _____

2. How many times does it appear?_____

3. What do you think the main topic of the passage is? _____

Identifying the main topic of the passage not only helps you focus on what the questions are most likely going to be about, but it also better prepares you to click on the correct answers. In addition, as you answer the questions, you will gradually learn more and more about the topic of the passage. The key is to indirectly read the passage as you are hunting for the answers to the questions.

> You indirectly read the passage as you answer the questions!

THE QUESTIONS!

Now that you have some idea of what the passage is about, it is time to tackle the questions. You want to approach the questions efficiently. The most important thing you want to remember is that *all questions are created equal*! Each question is worth *one* point. You get just as many points for answering an easy question as you do a difficult one. Therefore, the precious time that you have is best spent working on the easier questions. Difficult questions are harder, and take much more time. *Reminder:* The Reading section is *linear*. This means that the questions do not disappear forever once you have answered them. You can skip the hard questions and return to answer them later.

Answer the easy questions first!

The first crucial step you need to take is to learn how to distinguish the easy questions from the hard ones.

There are three types of questions in Reading section:

Easy Questions: We'll call these questions "first-pass questions."

Medium Questions: We'll call these questions "second-pass questions."

Difficult Questions: We'll call these questions "third-pass questions."

Here, "pass" means to systematically work through or pass through the passage or text. As the various question types are introduced, we'll tell you which ones to do the first time you pass through the text, the second time you pass through the text, and the third time you pass through the text.

There are basically nine (yes, nine) different types of questions in the TOEFL CBT Reading section. By labeling each TOEFL CBT question as first-pass (easy), second-pass (medium), or third-pass (difficult), you will be able to work more confidently and the correct answers will be easier to anticipate. Study the diagram below to see the different question types.

First-Pass Questions	Second-Pass Questions	Third-Pass Questions
Vocabulary Questions	Main Idea Questions	Infer/Imply Questions
Reference Questions	Conclusion Questions	Except/Not Questions
Detail Questions	Click on Sentence Questions	Black Square Questions

Categorizing all the different questions make them less threatening. You will now be able to make some sense out of all the confusion. We will introduce, explain, and teach you specific strategy for each question type.

CHRONOLOGICAL ORDER

An essential strategy for the TOEFL CBT is chronological order. ETS arranges all the questions in the order in which they appear in the text. Always remember where you found the answer to the previous question to help you locate the next question. In other words, the answer to question 5 will be found in the text after the line where you found the answer to question 4. This time-saving strategy will drastically reduce the time you spend searching for the answer to the questions, and give you more time to click on the correct answer.

PACING

THE PASSAGES

Pacing is crucial when you are taking the TOEFL CBT. You want to avoid going too fast or too slow. ETS arranges the passages in a loose order of progressive difficulty. The writing, the vocabulary, and the syntax of the questions and answers tend to be more complex in the *last* passage than in the *first*. Due to this progression, it is logical to start at the beginning of the Reading section, answer the easy questions first, and save the more difficult questions for later.

There is no penalty for guessing!

Begin with the first passage, and answer the first-pass questions first, the second pass questions second, and then the third-pass questions third. Then continue to the second, third, and fourth passages and do the same thing. If at any time a question seems too difficult and is taking too much time, you can either skip it and come back at the very end of the test, or use POE, guess, and go on. But remember, *you have to pick an answer for every question*.

If you try to answer the questions in the order ETS gives them, you will <u>NOT</u> be able to finish the test

The information you learn from the passage as you answer the first-pass questions will make it easier to answer the second-pass questions. Likewise, the information you learn from the passage as you answer the first- and second-pass questions will make it easier to answer the third-pass questions.

It will take a lot of mouse clicking to become familiar with skipping some questions, and answering others. However, with practice, it will get easier.

EASY ─────────────▶ MEDIUM ─────────────▶ DIFFICULT

Passage 1	Passage 2	Passage 3	Passage 4
STEP ONE	STEP ONE	STEP ONE	STEP ONE
1-1-1-L	1-1-1-L	1-1-1-L	1-1-1-L
STEP TWO	STEP TWO	STEP TWO	STEP TWO
1st pass questions	1st pass questions	1st pass questions	1st pass questions
STEP THREE	STEP THREE	STEP THREE	STEP THREE
2nd pass questions	2nd pass questions	2nd pass questions	2nd pass questions
STEP FOUR	STEP FOUR	STEP FOUR	STEP FOUR
3rd pass questions	3rd pass questions	3rd pass questions	3rd pass questions
STEP FIVE	STEP FIVE	STEP FIVE	STEP FIVE
Go to the next passage	Go to the next passage	Go to the next passage	Check work

Answer the first pass questions in the order in which they come!

(Note: There may be as many as five passages. If so, just keep following this technique.)

FIRST-PASS QUESTIONS

- *Vocabulary in context (VIC) questions*: ask you for the meaning of a specific word in the passage.

- *Reference questions:* ask you what a specific pronoun or noun in the passage refers to.

- *Detail questions:* ask for a specific piece of information found in the passage.

First-pass questions are considered the easiest questions on the TOEFL CBT. They are easy to locate and take the least amount of time to answer. More than half of the questions on the TOEFL CBT will be first-pass. Immediately after using the 1-1-1-L technique, make your best effort to answer all the following first-pass questions in the order in which they come.

Vocabulary in Context

For VIC questions, you want to select the best synonym for a specific word or phrase in the passage. In other words, a VIC question is about the *definition* of a word. Look at an example:

Look for other vocabulary words in the surrounding sentences that function as clues.

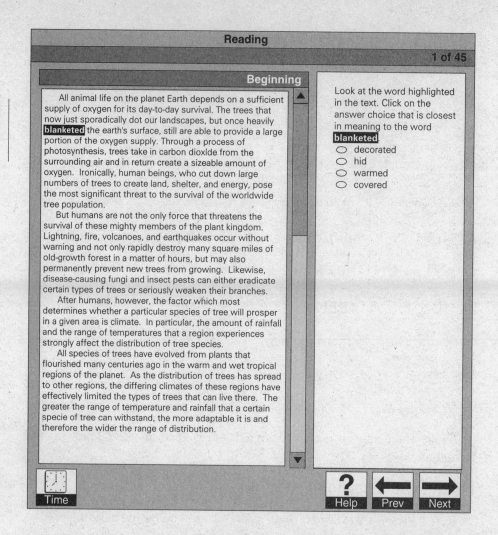

Beginning

All animal life on the planet Earth depends on a sufficient supply of oxygen for its day-to-day survival. The trees that now just sporadically dot our landscapes, but once heavily **blanketed** the earth's surface, still are able to provide a large portion of the oxygen supply. Through a process of photosynthesis, trees take in carbon dioxide from the surrounding air and in return create a sizeable amount of oxygen. Ironically, human beings, who cut down large numbers of trees to create land, shelter, and energy, pose the most significant threat to the survival of the worldwide tree population.

But humans are not the only force that threatens the survival of these mighty members of the plant kingdom. Lightning, fire, volcanoes, and earthquakes occur without warning and not only rapidly destroy many square miles of old-growth forest in a matter of hours, but may also permanently prevent new trees from growing. Likewise, disease-causing fungi and insect pests can either eradicate certain types of trees or seriously weaken their branches.

After humans, however, the factor which most determines whether a particular species of tree will prosper in a given area is climate. In particular, the amount of rainfall and the range of temperatures that a region experiences strongly affect the distribution of tree species.

All species of trees have evolved from plants that flourished many centuries ago in the warm and wet tropical regions of the planet. As the distribution of trees has spread to other regions, the differing climates of these regions have effectively limited the types of trees that can live there. The greater the range of temperature and rainfall that a certain specie of tree can withstand, the more adaptable it is and therefore the wider the range of distribution.

Look at the word highlighted in the text. Click on the answer choice that is closest in meaning to the word **blanketed**.

○ decorated
○ hid
○ warmed
○ covered

Time

Help   Prev   Next

Whenever you see a vocabulary in context question, you'll need to read *two* sentences: the one in which the word is contained, and the one that comes before it. Quickly focusing on other vocabulary within the two sentences will help you to determine the tone of the sentences. Understanding the tone will help you to comprehend the context. ETS will try to trick you by giving the literal definition of the word in the answer choices. You might need to look for a second sense of the word. Here, you might know that the noun "blanket" is what you put on your bed. However, as a verb, it might have a different meaning. Focus on the other vocabulary words to help you avoid ETS's tricks and traps. In this example, focus on the vocabulary "sufficient" and "heavily." These words indicate a sense of adequacy and quantity. Also, the words "sporadically dot" in the same sentence give a sense of the opposite meaning to the words "heavily blanketed." Be sure to keep all these helpful vocabulary words in mind as you approach VIC questions.

One helpful way to eliminate incorrect answer choices in VIC questions is to use a technique called "positive/negative." First, look at the word being tested. To determine if it is a positive word or a negative word, ask yourself if it conveys a positive or a negative sense. If the word being tested conveys a positive sense, you can eliminate all negative words from the answer choices. On the other hand, if the word conveys a negative sense, you can eliminate all positive words from the answer choices. You might be able to eliminate one or even two answer choices just by determining if the VIC word is either positive or negative. In this example, you may consider the VIC word "blanketed" as positive since it does not give off any negative connotations. Be sure to keep this in mind as you read the four answer choices.

In this case, the VIC word is a verb. Find the subject and the object of the sentence in which the VIC word is contained, and mentally make a sentence. Eliminate as many distracting modifiers as possible. For example:

- The trees heavily *blanketed* the earth's surface.

Now replace the VIC word with the 4 given answer choices, and form a question.

- Did the trees heavily *decorate* the earth's surface? No. The word "decorate" doesn't give you any connection with trees providing oxygen. Use your common sense and eliminate this answer choice.

- Did the trees heavily *hide* the earth's surface? No. This doesn't make sense. Trees don't serve to hide the earth. Also, the word "hide" conveys a negative sense. Remember, you have already determined that "blanketed" is a positive word: therefore you can eliminate negative answer choices. Use your common sense and eliminate this answer choice.

- Did the trees heavily *warm* the earth's surface? No. Watch out for ETS's tricks and traps. A blanket on your bed will warm you, but in this example, the word "warm" has no connection to the trees providing oxygen. Use your common sense and eliminate this answer choice.

- Did the trees heavily *cover* the earth's surface? Yes. This answer choice is not only complemented by the other vocabulary words "sufficient" and "heavily," but it also is the opposite of "sporadically dot." It also makes the most sense to connect trees with providing oxygen.

Making questions in your own words helps you avoid the trap of being led astray by the answer choices. Chances are good that more than one answer choice will sound fine if you just go back and replace it into the sentence. ETS loves using this trap.

If the VIC word is familiar to you, simply click on the answer choice. However, *always* go back to the passage and plug your answer choice into the sentence. Double check that it makes sense. If you have never heard of the vocabulary word, either guess and go on, or skip it and make it a third pass question.

In summary of the VIC strategy:

Step 1: Read the sentence in which the VIC word is contained as well as the sentence before, to determine the tone of the sentences.

Step 2: Mentally make a sentence with the VIC word, eliminating as many distracting modifiers as possible.

Step 3: Ask yourself questions, replacing the VIC word with the other answer choices to see which one makes the most sense.

Step 4: Use POE (process of elimination) to determine the incorrect answer choices and click on the best possible answer choice.

Vocabulary in Context (Part 2)

In the TOEFL CBT, ETS has come up with another method of testing VIC words. On the left side of the computer screen, you will see several sentences in bold text with the VIC word being tested highlighted. On the right side of the screen you will see a question similar to the following:

Look at the word **greedy** in the passage. Click on the word or phrase in the bold text that has the same meaning.

Rather than clicking on the four answer choices that ETS has provided, you now must click on the word that "greedy" is synonymous (the same) or antonymous (the opposite) to in the bold text. Be careful! There are many answer choices in these types of questions. ETS calls these words "distractors." Look at the following example.

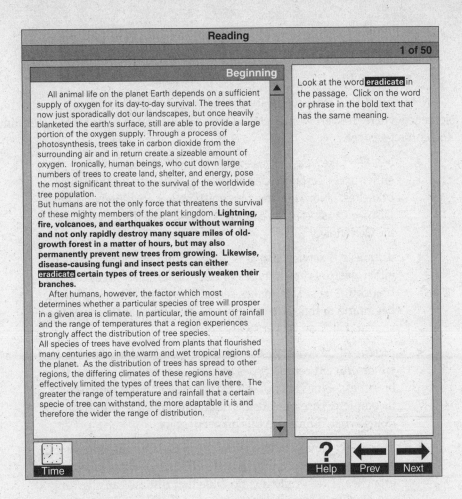

Beginning

All animal life on the planet Earth depends on a sufficient supply of oxygen for its day-to-day survival. The trees that now just sporadically dot our landscapes, but once heavily blanketed the earth's surface, still are able to provide a large portion of the oxygen supply. Through a process of photosynthesis, trees take in carbon dioxide from the surrounding air and in return create a sizeable amount of oxygen. Ironically, human beings, who cut down large numbers of trees to create land, shelter, and energy, pose the most significant threat to the survival of the worldwide tree population.

But humans are not the only force that threatens the survival of these mighty members of the plant kingdom. **Lightning, fire, volcanoes, and earthquakes occur without warning and not only rapidly destroy many square miles of old-growth forest in a matter of hours, but may also permanently prevent new trees from growing. Likewise, disease-causing fungi and insect pests can either eradicate certain types of trees or seriously weaken their branches.**

After humans, however, the factor which most determines whether a particular species of tree will prosper in a given area is climate. In particular, the amount of rainfall and the range of temperatures that a region experiences strongly affect the distribution of tree species.

All species of trees have evolved from plants that flourished many centuries ago in the warm and wet tropical regions of the planet. As the distribution of trees has spread to other regions, the differing climates of these regions have effectively limited the types of trees that can live there. The greater the range of temperature and rainfall that a certain specie of tree can withstand, the more adaptable it is and therefore the wider the range of distribution.

Look at the word **eradicate** in the passage. Click on the word or phrase in the bold text that has the same meaning.

Time   ? Help   ← Prev   → Next

The strategies for this type of VIC question are similar to those for the first type of VIC question. First of all, since the answer is in the bold text, read the sentences that appear in bold and locate the VIC word. As in the previous VIC strategy, look for other vocabulary words to determine the tone of the sentences. In order to find the synonym of the VIC, you first need to know the meaning of the word being tested. If you don't know the definition of the VIC word, try to determine it from the context of the sentences. In this case, you know that "disease" does something to "entire populations of trees." Therefore, the word "eradicate" must mean something bad.

Next, identify which part of speech the VIC word is. In this case, "eradicate" is a verb. In the bold text, search for all the words that are verbs and eliminate all other distractors, such as nouns, adjectives, conjunctions, prepositions, articles, or adverbs. The word you want to click on will be the same part of speech. Also, eliminate words that repeat themselves in the bolded sentences. These techniques will increase your chances of clicking on the correct answer. In this example, how many other verbs do you find?

The other verbs are:

- occur
- prevent
- destroy
- weaken

Now insert the other verbs (*prevent*, *destroy*, *occur*, and *weaken*) into the sentence where the verb being tested (*eradicate*) is located in order to determine the correct answer.

- *occur*—"Likewise, disease-causing fungi and insect pests can either **occur** certain types of trees or seriously weaken their branches." No. This answer choice makes absolutely no sense. Disease-causing fungi cannot "occur" a tree. Eliminate this answer choice.

- *destroy*—"Likewise, disease-causing fungi and insect pests can either **destroy** certain types of trees or seriously weaken their branches." Yes. This makes sense! The word "likewise" at the beginning of the sentence gives us the clue that these verbs are similar. Click on this answer choice.

- *prevent*—"Likewise, disease-causing fungi and insect pests can either **prevent** certain types of trees or seriously weaken their branches." No. This doesn't make sense and the sentence is incomplete. Disease-causing fungi prevents the trees from doing what? Eliminate this answer choice.

You will encounter 2 or 3 of these question types in the Reading section.

- *weaken*—"Likewise, disease-causing fungi and insect pests can either **weaken** certain types of trees or seriously weaken their branches." No. While it is possible that disease-causing fungi can weaken trees, you know from the "either...or" structure that the verbs must have different meanings. Eliminate this answer choice.

In summary of the VIC (Part 2) strategy:

Step 1: Read the bold sentences in which the VIC word is contained and determine the tone of the sentences.

Step 2: Eliminate all "distractors" and focus on those words that are the same part of speech. Never click on articles, conjunctions, prepositions, etc.

Step 3: Insert the VIC word into the sentence to see which answer choice makes the most sense.

Step 4: Use POE (process of elimination) to determine the incorrect answer choices and click on the best possible answer choice located in the bold text.

Remember: If you *know* the VIC word being tested, quickly click on its synonym. However, *always* go to the passage and plug your answer choice into the sentence just to make sure. If you *don't know* the VIC word being tested, try to determine the meaning from the passage. If you simply can't determine the meaning, plug it into the same part of speech (adjective for adjective, noun for noun, and verb for verb) anyway. This might give you some extra help. Always use POE on as many answer choices as possible in order to better your chances of clicking on the correct answer. If you have never heard of the vocabulary word, either guess and go on or skip it and make it a third-pass question.

For reference questions, the answer is in the bold text.

If the question is looking for the antonym rather than the synonym, simply follow the same steps as above. Just keep in mind that an antonym means you are looking for the opposite meaning.

Reference Questions

In the TOEFL CBT, reference questions ask you to determine what a pronoun or noun refers to. On the left side of the computer screen, you will see several sentences in bold text with the VIC reference word being tested highlighted. On the right side of the screen you will see a question similar to the following:

> Look at the word **one** in the passage. Click on the word or phrase in the bold text that this word refers to.

Using your mouse, click on the noun in the bold text that the VIC reference word is synonymous to. Although you have more than just four choices, the answer is in the bold text. Reference questions are easy to spot. Simply look for the questions that use the word "refer." Look at the following example:

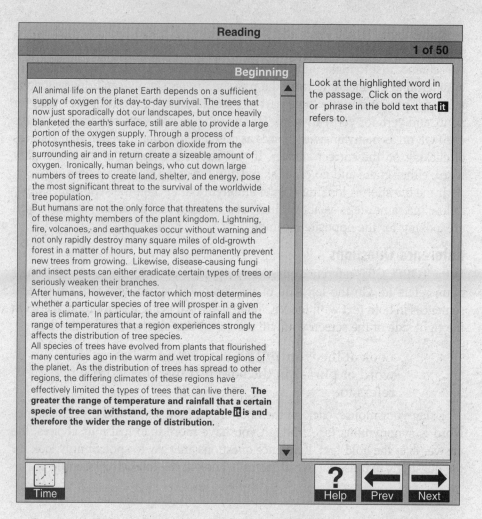

Beginning

All animal life on the planet Earth depends on a sufficient supply of oxygen for its day-to-day survival. The trees that now just sporadically dot our landscapes, but once heavily blanketed the earth's surface, still are able to provide a large portion of the oxygen supply. Through a process of photosynthesis, trees take in carbon dioxide from the surrounding air and in return create a sizeable amount of oxygen. Ironically, human beings, who cut down large numbers of trees to create land, shelter, and energy, pose the most significant threat to the survival of the worldwide tree population.

But humans are not the only force that threatens the survival of these mighty members of the plant kingdom. Lightning, fire, volcanoes, and earthquakes occur without warning and not only rapidly destroy many square miles of old-growth forest in a matter of hours, but may also permanently prevent new trees from growing. Likewise, disease-causing fungi and insect pests can either eradicate certain types of trees or seriously weaken their branches.

After humans, however, the factor which most determines whether a particular species of tree will prosper in a given area is climate. In particular, the amount of rainfall and the range of temperatures that a region experiences strongly affects the distribution of tree species.

All species of trees have evolved from plants that flourished many centuries ago in the warm and wet tropical regions of the planet. As the distribution of trees has spread to other regions, the differing climates of these regions have effectively limited the types of trees that can live there. **The greater the range of temperature and rainfall that a certain specie of tree can withstand, the more adaptable it is and therefore the wider the range of distribution.**

Look at the highlighted word in the passage. Click on the word or phrase in the bold text that **it** refers to.

Time | Help | Prev | Next

To answer VIC reference questions, first read the sentences in bold and find the pronoun or noun being tested. Determine if the VIC reference word is plural or singular. In this case, "it" is singular. Search for other singular nouns in the bold text. How many do you find?

The other singular nouns are:

- range of temperature
- rainfall
- specie of tree
- range of distribution

There are four possibilities. Mentally cross out the pronoun and plug the other singular nouns into the sentence to see if the sentence makes sense.

- "The greater the range of temperature and rainfall that a certain specie of tree can withstand, the more adaptable *the range of temperature* is and therefore the wider the range of distribution." No. This doesn't make sense. "The range of temperature" cannot adapt. Eliminate this answer choice.

- "The greater the range of temperature and rainfall that a certain specie of tree can withstand, the more adaptable *rainfall* is and therefore the wider the range of distribution." No. This doesn't make sense. "Rainfall" cannot adapt. Eliminate this answer choice.

- "The greater the range of temperature and rainfall that a certain specie of tree can withstand, the more adaptable *the specie of tree* is and therefore the wider the range of distribution." Yes. A "specie of tree" is adaptable and can be distributed. Click on this answer choice.

- "The greater the range of temperature and rainfall that a certain specie of tree can withstand, the more adaptable *the range of distribution* is and therefore the wider the range of distribution." No. Eliminate any answer choice that illogically repeats itself.

VIC questions and reference questions should take you no more than 30 seconds to do. As you practice, you will get faster! If the questions take longer than one minute, guess and go on, or save them for the third pass.

In summary of the VIC reference question strategy:

Step 1: Locate the pronoun in the bold passage and determine if it refers to a singular or plural noun.

Step 2: Locate the other singular or plural nouns in the bold text.

Step 3: Mentally cross out the pronoun and replace it with the other possible noun choices and read the complete sentence. Does the noun correctly replace the pronoun?

Step 4: Using POE, eliminate answer choices that don't make sense or aren't consistent with the surrounding sentences and click on the best possible answer choice.

Detail Questions

Detail questions ask you for specific facts contained in the passage. You'll need to read the question to see what information is required, then go to the passage to find it. There are at least two detail questions for each passage. Although detail questions are phrased in various ways, the strategy to finding the answer is the same: Use chronological order and "lead words."

Lead Words

The best way to find the answers to detail questions is by using "lead words" together with chronological order. The lead word is the most specific word or phrase in the question. It tells you what the question is about, which in turn tells you where to look in the passage. Lead words are often nouns or noun phrases, and tend to be mentioned only once in the passage. Once you locate the lead word, simply scan the passage in order to locate it. The answer to the question is near the location of the lead word.

Some hints for identifying lead words:

1. It's all right to be looking for more than one word, but more than three words are too many.

2. Words with capital letters, numbers, and abbreviations are particularly easy to spot in a passage (for example, 1776, Warren G. Harding, UNICEF, and so forth).

A pronoun must agree in number and gender with the noun to which it refers.

3. If the question itself doesn't have any lead words, check out the answers. They might contain words or numbers that contain great lead words.

The information you need usually appears within a few lines of the lead. After you have found the information you need, click on the answer choice that best paraphrases the information. A paraphrase is simply a restatement of the information in other words.

In summary of the detail question strategy.

Step 1: Read the question and identify the lead word.

Step 2: Using chronological order, look for the lead word in the passage.

Step 3: Once the lead word has been located, read the sentence in which it is contained.

Step 4: If you've found the answer to the question, click on the answer choice that is closest to the answer you found in the passage.

Step 5: If you haven't found the information in the text, and you think you might have chosen a poor lead, go ahead and choose a different one. However, if you think you have chosen a good lead, the question is probably very difficult. Save it for the third pass, or guess and go on.

Drill 2

Directions: Circle the lead words in the sample questions below.

1. According to the passage, vitamin C can be found in . . .

2. Why was Rosa Parks arrested in 1955?

3. The "wings" of the manta ray are used for . . .

4. The Democratic Party is mentioned as an example of a bipartisan group that . . .

5. According to the passage, why was Karl XII of Sweden considered not typical of Swedish kings?

6. As described in the passage, the function of the legislative branch of the United States government is . . .

7. Why are snapping turtles in danger of becoming extinct?

8. Which of the following is most likely to cause a sudden climatic change?

Drill 3

Use all the strategies you have learned so far to answer the first-pass questions about the passage. Click on (in this case circle) the best answer.

Questions 1 to 8

Beginning

Without regular supplies of some hormones, the human capacity to behave would be seriously impaired. The absence of others would cause immediate death. The most abundant hormones act to modify moods and affect actions. The most **minute** amounts of hormones can suppress appetite, alter aggressive or submissive attitudes, and change reproductive and parental behavior. Early in life, hormones accelerate the development of bodily form and may even define an individual's personality characteristics. Later in life, the changing hormonal outputs of some endocrine glands and the body's changing sensitivity to them bolster immunity and hasten the aging phenomena.

Up to the beginning of the present century, communication within the body and the consequent integration of behavior were considered the primary province of the nervous system. The emergence of endocrinology as a separate discipline can be traced to the experiments of Dr. William Bayliss and Dr. Ernest Starling on the hormone secretin, which is secreted from cells in the intestinal walls when food enters the stomach. It then travels through the bloodstream and stimulates the pancreas to liberate digestive fluid. By stimulating these special stomach cells to secrete hormones that in turn regulate distant target organs and tissues, Bayliss and Starling demonstrated that chemical integration could occur without the participation of the nervous system.

The term hormone was first used with reference to secretin. Starling derived the term from the Greek word hormon, meaning to excite or set in motion. The term endocrine was introduced shortly thereafter. Endocrine is used to refer to glands that secrete products directly into the bloodstream such as the pancreas, thyroid, and pituitary glands. Because the lack of any one of them may cause serious disorders, many hormones are now produced synthetically and used in treatment where a deficiency exists. Insects also have a unique hormone ecdysone. Much like steroids stimulate muscle formation in humans, ecdysone strengthens the exoskeleton of insects while they metamorphose into the adult stage. Plants rely on a variety of hormones such as auxin, gibberellin, and cytokinin that assist in flower, tuber, bulb, and bud formation. Ethylene, a synthetic hormone used by horticulturists, is believed to accelerate the ripening of fruit.

Look at the word highlighted in the text. Click on the answer choice that is closest in meaning to the word **minute**.

- beneficial
- tiny
- predetermined
- short

Next

Prev

Help

Time

Look at the word **hasten** in the passage. Click on the word or phrase in the bold text that this word refers to.

Beginning

Questions 1 to 8

Without regular supplies of some hormones, the human capacity to behave would be seriously impaired. The absence of others would cause immediate death. The most abundant hormones act to modify moods and affect actions. The most minute amounts of hormones can suppress appetite, alter aggressive or submissive attitudes, and change reproductive and parental behavior. **Early in life, hormones accelerate the development of bodily form and may even define an individual's personality characteristics. Later in life, the changing hormonal outputs of some endocrine glands and the body's changing sensitivity to them bolster immunity and** hasten **the aging phenomena.**

Up to the beginning of the present century, communication within the body and the consequent integration of behavior were considered the primary province of the nervous system. The emergence of endocrinology as a separate discipline can be traced to the experiments of Dr. William Bayliss and Dr. Ernest Starling on the hormone secretin, which is secreted from cells in the intestinal walls when food enters the stomach. It then travels through the bloodstream and stimulates the pancreas to liberate digestive fluid. By stimulating these special stomach cells to secrete hormones that in turn regulate distant target organs and tissues, Bayliss and Starling demonstrated that chemical integration could occur without the participation of the nervous system.

The term hormone was first used with reference to secretin. Starling derived the term from the Greek word hormon, meaning to excite or set in motion. The term endocrine was introduced shortly thereafter. Endocrine is used to refer to glands that secrete products directly into the bloodstream such as the pancreas, thyroid, and pituitary glands. Because the lack of any one of them may cause serious disorders, many hormones are now produced synthetically and used in treatment where a deficiency exists. Insects also have a unique hormone ecdysone. Much like steroids stimulate muscle formation in humans, ecdysone strengthens the exoskeleton of insects while they metamorphose into the adult stage. Plants rely on a variety of hormones such as auxin, gibberellin, and cytokinin that assist in flower, tuber, bulb, and bud formation. Ethylene, a synthetic hormone used by horticulturists, is believed to accelerate the ripening of fruit.

Time

Next

Prev

Help

Time

Questions 1 to 8

Beginning

Without regular supplies of some hormones, the human capacity to behave would be seriously impaired. The absence of others would cause immediate death. The most abundant hormones act to modify moods and affect actions. The most minute amounts of hormones can suppress appetite, alter aggressive or submissive attitudes, and change reproductive and parental behavior. Early in life, hormones accelerate the development of bodily form and may even define an individual's personality characteristics. Later in life, the changing hormonal outputs of some endocrine glands and the body's changing sensitivity to them bolster immunity and hasten the aging phenomena.

Up to the beginning of the present century, communication within the body and the consequent integration of behavior were considered the primary province of the nervous system. The emergence of endocrinology as a separate discipline can be traced to the experiments of Dr. William Bayliss and Dr. Ernest Starling on the hormone secretin, which is secreted from cells in the intestinal walls when food enters the stomach. It then travels through the bloodstream and stimulates the pancreas to liberate digestive fluid. By stimulating these special stomach cells to secrete hormones that in turn regulate distant target organs and tissues, Bayliss and Starling demonstrated that chemical integration could occur without the participation of the nervous system.

The term hormone was first used with reference to secretin. Starling derived the term from the Greek word hormon, meaning to excite or set in motion. The term endocrine was introduced shortly thereafter. Endocrine is used to refer to glands that secrete products directly into the bloodstream such as the pancreas, thyroid, and pituitary glands. Because the lack of any one of them may cause serious disorders, many hormones are now produced synthetically and used in treatment where a deficiency exists. Insects also have a unique hormone ecdysone. Much like steroids stimulate muscle formation in humans, ecdysone strengthens the exoskeleton of insects while they metamorphose into the adult stage. Plants rely on a variety of hormones such as auxin, gibberellin, and cytokinin that assist in flower, tuber, bulb, and bud formation. Ethylene, a synthetic hormone used by horticulturists, is believed to accelerate the ripening of fruit.

According to the passage, which of the following was believed prior to the experiments led by Dr. Bayliss and Dr. Starling?

○ Bodily behavior was controlled exclusively by the nervous system.

○ The endocrine glands stimulated chemical integration

○ Intestinal glands regulated hormones

○ Endocrinology was limited to stimulating the aging phenomena

Look at the highlighted word in the passage. Click on the word or phrase in the bold text that **it** refers to.

Questions 1 to 8

Beginning

Without regular supplies of some hormones, the human capacity to behave would be seriously impaired. The absence of others would cause immediate death. The most abundant hormones act to modify moods and affect actions. The most minute amounts of hormones can suppress appetite, alter aggressive or submissive attitudes, and change reproductive and parental behavior. Early in life, hormones accelerate the development of bodily form and may even define an individual's personality characteristics. Later in life, the changing hormonal outputs of some endocrine glands and the body's changing sensitivity to them bolster immunity and hasten the aging phenomena.

Up to the beginning of the present century, communication within the body and the consequent integration of behavior were considered the primary province of the nervous system. **The emergence of endocrinology as a separate discipline can be traced to the experiments of Dr. William Bayliss and Dr. Ernest Starling on the hormone secretin, which is secreted from cells in the intestinal walls when food enters the stomach. It then travels through the bloodstream and stimulates the pancreas to liberate digestive fluid.** By stimulating these special stomach cells to secrete hormones that in turn regulate distant target organs and tissues, Bayliss and Starling demonstrated that chemical integration could occur without the participation of the nervous system.

The term hormone was first used with reference to secretin. Starling derived the term from the Greek word *hormon*, meaning to excite or set in motion. The term endocrine was introduced shortly thereafter. Endocrine is used to refer to glands that secrete products directly into the bloodstream such as the pancreas, thyroid, and pituitary glands. Because the lack of any one of them may cause serious disorders, many hormones are now produced synthetically and used in treatment where a deficiency exists. Insects also have a unique hormone ecdysone. Much like steroids stimulate muscle formation in humans, ecdysone strengthens the exoskeleton of insects while they metamorphose into the adult stage. Plants rely on a variety of hormones such as auxin, gibberellin, and cytokinin that assist in flower, tuber, bulb, and bud formation. Ethylene, a synthetic hormone used by horticulturists, is believed to accelerate the ripening of fruit.

Time

Help   Prev   Next

Questions 1 to 8

Without regular supplies of some hormones, the human capacity to behave would be seriously impaired. The absence of others would cause immediate death. The most abundant hormones act to modify moods and affect actions. The most minute amounts of hormones can suppress appetite, alter aggressive or submissive attitudes, and change reproductive and parental behavior. Early in life, hormones accelerate the development of bodily form and may even define an individual's personality characteristics. Later in life, the changing hormonal outputs of some endocrine glands and the body's changing sensitivity to them bolster immunity and hasten the aging phenomena.

Up to the beginning of the present century, communication within the body and the consequent integration of behavior were considered the primary province of the nervous system. The emergence of endocrinology as a separate discipline can be traced to the experiments of Dr. William Bayliss and Dr. Ernest Starling on the hormone secretin, which is secreted from cells in the intestinal walls when food enters the stomach. It then travels through the bloodstream and stimulates the pancreas to liberate digestive fluid. By stimulating these special stomach cells to secrete hormones that in turn regulate distant target organs and tissues, Bayliss and Starling demonstrated that chemical integration could occur without the participation of the nervous system.

The term hormone was first used with reference to secretin. Starling derived the term from the Greek word hormon, meaning to excite or set in motion. The term endocrine was introduced shortly thereafter. Endocrine is used to refer to glands that secrete products directly into the bloodstream such as the pancreas, thyroid, and pituitary glands. Because the lack of any one of them may cause serious disorders, many hormones are now produced synthetically and used in treatment where a deficiency exists. Insects also have a unique hormone ecdysone. Much like steroids stimulate muscle formation in humans, ecdysone strengthens the exoskeleton of insects while they metamorphose into the adult stage. Plants rely on a variety of hormones such as auxin, gibberellin, and cytokinin that assist in flower, tuber, bulb, and bud formation. Ethylene, a synthetic hormone used by horticulturists, is believed to accelerate the ripening of fruit.

What could Bayliss and Starling conclude after their experiments on hormone secretion?

○ Hormones can be digested.

○ Certain hormones are dangerous to organs and tissues.

○ Only the stomach can secrete hormones.

○ Chemical integration is not entirely dependent on the nervous system.

Help

Prev

Next

Time

Next

Prev

Help

? Help

Time

Questions 1 to 8

Beginning

Without regular supplies of some hormones, the human capacity to behave would be seriously impaired. The absence of others would cause immediate death. The most abundant hormones act to modify moods and affect actions. The most minute amounts of hormones can suppress appetite, alter aggressive or submissive attitudes, and change reproductive and parental behavior. Early in life, hormones accelerate the development of bodily form and may even define an individual's personality characteristics. Later in life, the changing hormonal outputs of some endocrine glands and the body's changing sensitivity to them bolster immunity and hasten the aging phenomena.

Up to the beginning of the present century, communication within the body and the consequent integration of behavior were considered the primary province of the nervous system. The emergence of endocrinology as a separate discipline can be traced to the experiments of Dr. William Bayliss and Dr. Ernest Starling on the hormone secretin, which is secreted from cells in the intestinal walls when food enters the stomach. It then travels through the bloodstream and stimulates the pancreas to liberate digestive fluid. By stimulating these special stomach cells to secrete hormones that in turn regulate distant target organs and tissues, Bayliss and Starling demonstrated that chemical integration could occur without the participation of the nervous system.

The term hormone was first used with reference to secretin. Starling derived the term from the Greek word hormon, meaning to excite or set in motion. The term endocrine was introduced shortly thereafter. Endocrine is used to refer to glands that secrete products directly into the bloodstream such as the pancreas, thyroid, and pituitary glands. Because the lack of any one of them may cause serious disorders, many hormones are now produced synthetically and used in treatment where a deficiency exists. Insects also have a unique hormone ecdysone. Much like steroids stimulate muscle formation in humans, ecdysone strengthens the exoskeleton of insects while they metamorphose into the adult stage. Plants rely on a variety of hormones such as auxin, gibberellin, and cytokinin that assist in flower, tuber, bulb, and bud formation. Ethylene, a synthetic hormone used by horticulturists, is believed to accelerate the ripening of fruit.

Look at the word highlighted in the text. Click on the answer choice that is closest in meaning to the word lack.

○ abuse
○ excess
○ injury
○ absence

Next

Prev

Help

Questions 1 to 8

Beginning

Without regular supplies of some hormones, the human capacity to behave would be seriously impaired. The absence of others would cause immediate death. The most abundant hormones act to modify moods and affect actions. The most minute amounts of hormones can suppress appetite, alter aggressive or submissive attitudes, and change reproductive and parental behavior. Early in life, hormones accelerate the development of bodily form and may even define an individual's personality characteristics. Later in life, the changing hormonal outputs of some endocrine glands and the body's changing sensitivity to them bolster immunity and hasten the aging phenomena.

Up to the beginning of the present century, communication within the body and the consequent integration of behavior were considered the primary province of the nervous system. The emergence of endocrinology as a separate discipline can be traced to the experiments of Dr. William Bayliss and Dr. Ernest Starling on the hormone secretin, which is secreted from cells in the intestinal walls when food enters the stomach. It then travels through the bloodstream and stimulates the pancreas to liberate digestive fluid. By stimulating these special stomach cells to secrete hormones that in turn regulate distant target organs and tissues, Bayliss and Starling demonstrated that chemical integration could occur without the participation of the nervous system.

The term hormone was first used with reference to secretin. Starling derived the term from the Greek word hormon, meaning to excite or set in motion. The term endocrine was introduced shortly thereafter. Endocrine is used to refer to glands that secrete products directly into the bloodstream such as the pancreas, thyroid, and pituitary glands. Because the lack of any one of them may cause serious disorders, many hormones are now produced synthetically and used in treatment where a deficiency exists. Insects also have a unique hormone ecdysone. Much like steroids stimulate muscle formation in humans, ecdysone strengthens the exoskeleton of insects while they metamorphose into the adult stage. Plants rely on a variety of hormones such as auxin, gibberellin, and cytokinin that assist in flower, tuber, bulb, and bud formation. Ethylene, a synthetic hormone used by horticulturists, is believed to accelerate the ripening of fruit.

Time

The author mentions ecdysone as a hormone that

○ helps insects harden their outer shells

○ inhibits the immune system

○ desensitizes insects' sense of smell

○ camouflages certain insects from predators

Questions 1 to 8

Beginning

Without regular supplies of some hormones, the human capacity to behave would be seriously impaired. The absence of others would cause immediate death. The most abundant hormones act to modify moods and affect actions. The most minute amounts of hormones can suppress appetite, alter aggressive or submissive attitudes, and change reproductive and parental behavior. Early in life, hormones accelerate the development of bodily form and may even define an individual's personality characteristics. Later in life, the changing hormonal outputs of some endocrine glands and the body's changing sensitivity to them bolster immunity and hasten the aging phenomena.

Up to the beginning of the present century, communication within the body and the consequent integration of behavior were considered the primary province of the nervous system. The emergence of endocrinology as a separate discipline can be traced to the experiments of Dr. William Bayliss and Dr. Ernest Starling on the hormone secretin, which is secreted from cells in the intestinal walls when food enters the stomach. It then travels through the bloodstream and stimulates the pancreas to liberate digestive fluid. By stimulating these special stomach cells to secrete hormones that in turn regulate distant target organs and tissues, Bayliss and Starling demonstrated that chemical integration could occur without the participation of the nervous system.

The term hormone was first used with reference to secretin. Starling derived the term from the Greek word hormon, meaning to excite or set in motion. The term endocrine was introduced shortly thereafter. Endocrine is used to refer to glands that secrete products directly into the bloodstream such as the pancreas, thyroid, and pituitary glands. Because the lack of any one of them may cause serious disorders, many hormones are now produced synthetically and used in treatment where a deficiency exists. Insects also have a unique hormone ecdysone. Much like steroids stimulate muscle formation in humans, ecdysone strengthens the exoskeleton of insects while they metamorphose into the adult stage. Plants rely on a variety of hormones such as auxin, gibberellin, and cytokinin that assist in flower, tuber, bulb, and bud formation. Ethylene, a synthetic hormone used by horticulturists, is believed to accelerate the ripening of fruit.

Which of the following is affected by the hormone ethylene?

- ○ Correcting digestive disorders
- ○ Bud and flower formation
- ○ Insect metamorphosis
- ○ Ripening fruits

Help   Prev   Next

SECOND-PASS QUESTIONS

While you were answering the first-pass questions, you indirectly read the passage. You actually take in more information than you might think! Use that information to answer the second-pass questions.

Use the information from first pass questions to answer the second pass questions.

- *Main idea questions* ask you for the topic of either the entire passage or a specific paragraph.

- *Conclusion questions* ask you to select the statement that best summarizes the author's opinion.

- *Click on sentence questions* ask you click on the sentence that answers a detail question.

Main Idea Questions

Main idea questions almost always appear *first*! This is a trap that ETS uses to force you to read the entire passage. If you answer this question first, not only will you lose an incredible amount of time reading and rereading the passage, but you will also most likely answer incorrectly! Skip this question for the second pass. Think about this: After using the 1-1-1-L technique, and after answering all of the first-pass questions (VIC, VIC reference, and detail questions), you will know what the main idea of the passage or paragraph is about.

The way to find the main topic of any passage is to ask yourself one simple question:

Which answer choice is repeated in the first-pass questions?

Whatever topic the detail questions and answers have in common is the main idea! Main idea questions are phrased as follows:

Which of the following statements best expresses the main idea of the passage?

What does the passage mainly discuss?

With which of the following subjects is the passage mainly concerned?

Which of the following assumptions about _____ is expressed in the passage?

What is the main topic of the passage?

Which of the following questions does the author answer in the first paragraph?

What is the main point of the first paragraph?

When answering main idea questions, bear in mind that the answer shouldn't introduce anything new.

In summary of the main idea question strategy:

Step 1: Quickly 1-1-1-L the passage again (if necessary).

Step 2: Consider what you learned from the first-pass questions and eliminate answer choices that introduce a new topic.

Step 3: Eliminate answer choices that seem too specific.

Step 4: Click on the answer choice mentioned in the majority of the first-pass questions.

Conclusion Questions

Conclusion questions almost always appear *last*! The strategy for conclusion questions is the same as main idea questions. After answering all the first-pass questions (VIC, VIC reference, and detail questions), you will know enough about the passage to click on the conclusion the author most likely agrees with.

The way to find the conclusion of any passage is to ask yourself one simple question:

Which answer choice is referred to in the first-pass questions?

Click on the answer choice that best paraphrases the information in the detail questions.

Conclusion questions are phrased as followed:

With which of the following conclusions would the author most likely agree?

The passage supports which of the following generalizations?

Which of the following statements is supported by the passage?

When answering conclusion questions, bear in mind that the answer shouldn't introduce anything new.

In summary of the conclusion question strategy:

Step 1: Quickly 1-1-1-L the passage again (if necessary).

Step 2: Consider what you learned from the first-pass questions and eliminate answer choices that introduce a new topic.

Step 3: Eliminate answer choices that seem too specific.

Step 4: Select the answer choice mentioned in the majority of the first-pass questions.

CLICK ON SENTENCE QUESTIONS

In the TOEFL CBT, ETS has developed a new type of question called click on sentence questions. Like detail questions, click on sentence questions ask you for specific facts contained in the passage. There is at least one click on sentence question for each passage. Unlike detail questions, the paragraph in which the answer is located is indicated with arrows. Therefore *no* hunting or lead words are necessary. The passage will be located on the left side of the screen. On the right side you will see a question similar to the following:

Click on the sentence in paragraph 4 that explains why the electron microscope has become a necessity for laboratories.

The paragraph in which the answer is contained has a minimum of four sentences. First, read the question to see what information is required to correctly answer the question. Then, quickly read the sentences and click on the one that best answers the question asked. For example:

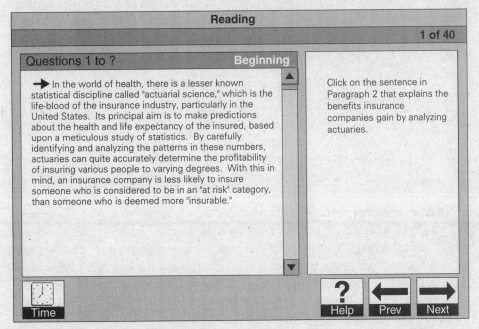

As you read the four sentences in Paragraph 2, be sure to ask yourself this question: "Does the information in this sentence explain the benefits insurance companies gain by analyzing actuaries?" In this case, sentence three best answers the question.

In summary of the click on sentence question strategy:

Step 1: Read the question closely and identify the information needed.

Step 2: Read the sentences in the paragraph indicated and eliminate those answer choices that do *not* answer the question.

Step 3: Click on the sentence that best answers the question.

THIRD-PASS QUESTIONS

Third-pass questions should be left until last, because they almost always use paraphrases and synonyms. They take longer to answer and can't be answered by reading only one or two sentences.

- Except/not questions ask you for the information *not* found in the passage.

- Infer/imply questions ask for information based on what is indirectly stated or implied.

Use the information from first and second pass questions to answer the third pass questions.

+ Black square questions ask you to insert a sentence into the passage.

Except/Not Questions

Except/not questions are the easiest of the third-pass questions, but they can require a lot of time. The correct answer to except/not questions is the choice that *does not* answer the question. In other words, the right answer is the one that is *not* mentioned! You will encounter at least four except/not questions on the TOEFL CBT. To identify except/not questions, simply look for the words *EXCEPT* or *NOT* in the question. For example:

> All of the following are mentioned as predators
> of the gadfly EXCEPT
>
> ○   birds
> ○   spiders
> ○   squirrels
> ○   frogs

To answer except/not questions, use chronology to narrow down the area of text you need to search. Also, work backwards! Use the answer choices as lead words to find where they appear in the passage. Usually, the three answers are located together. If the answers are spread throughout the passage, chronology will not be helpful. In either case, the fourth answer will *not* be mentioned in the passage and will be the answer you need to click on.

In summary of the except/not question strategy:

Step 1: Using chronology and the answer choices as lead words, locate the information in the text.

Step 2: Click on the answer choice *not* mentioned in the text.

Infer/Imply Questions

Infer/imply questions are difficult to answer and if you are having trouble, you should spend minimal time on them. They contain the words "infer," "imply," and "suggest," and request information not directly stated in the passage. Read the following infer question types:

> It can be inferred from the passage that . . .
>
> The author implies that . . .
>
> The passage suggests that . . .
>
> Based on the information in the passage, what
> can be inferred about . . .

"Inferred" and "implied" both refer to information that must be true, but is not actually written in the passage. To answer infer/imply questions, concentrate on what the passage says! Avoid being distracted by what could *possibly* be true. The answers to infer/imply questions are paraphrases of the facts in the text. Ask yourself this question: "Does the answer choice paraphrase the details found in the passage?" If not, you can eliminate that answer.

For infer/imply questions, eliminate any answer choice that:

1. is not directly supported by the passage. Your answer choice must be in the form of a paraphrase.

2. repeats information word for word from the passage. Any answer choice that contains too many words from the passage is probably a trap.

3. introduces new material. Since you have already answered first- and second-pass questions, you should have a pretty good idea regarding the main idea of the passage.

4. contains "extreme" words (words and phrases such as "always," "completely," "rarely," and so forth).

5. violates common sense. Get rid of the ridiculous, the illogical, and the just plain crazy.

Practice the above concepts with the following example.

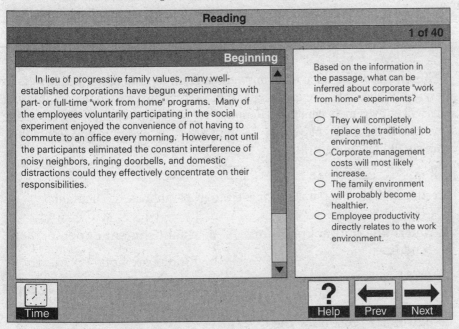

- ◆ The first choice, "They will completely replace the traditional job environment," contains the extreme word "completely." Think about it! Eventually, will *everyone* work at home? No, this is illogical. Eliminate this answer choice.

- ◆ The subject of the second choice, "Corporate management costs will most likely increase," isn't mentioned at all in the passage. Eliminate all answer choices that introduce new subject matter.

- ◆ The third answer choice, "The family environment will probably become healthier," could be true, but it is *not* a paraphrase of the facts. Eliminate this answer choice.

- Only the fourth answer choice, "Employee productivity directly relates to the work environment," correctly paraphrases the statement, "However, not until the participants eliminated the constant interference . . . could they effectively concentrate on their responsibilities." Click on this answer choice.

Since infer/imply questions are third-pass questions, check your time. If time allows, spend a little more time finding the correct answer. However, if you have less than 5 or 10 minutes, work quickly.

In summary of the infer/imply question strategy:

Step 1: Using chronological order and lead words, locate the information that the question refers to. The information will be located within a few lines of the lead.

Step 2: Eliminate any answer choice that is not a paraphrase, quotes material, contradicts the main idea of the passage, includes "extreme" words, or simply violates common sense.

Step 3: Click on the answer choice that best paraphrases the text and answers the question being asked.

ETS likes to make the correct answers difficult to find. Since the answers to infer/imply questions are always paraphrased, improving your paraphrasing skills will be extremely beneficial. Reminder: A paraphrase simply expresses the same idea with different words. To improve your paraphrasing techniques, complete the following drill.

Drill 4
Directions: Match the phrase on the left to its paraphrase on the right.

1. determine optimal planting schedules
2. due to comprehensive adjustments
3. a primary reason for the victory
4. improvise a solution
5. introduction of a representative form of government
6. keep topsoil in place
7. a chronic shortage of
8. various emotional responses
9. roughly at the same time
10. a more conservative style

a. establishment of democracy
b. hinder erosion
c. find a new way to solve the problem
d. find the best time to sow seeds
e. almost simultaneously
f. because of drastic changes in
g. a more traditional approach
h. a major cause of its success
i. experience of different feelings
j. in dire need of

Black Square Questions

In the TOEFL CBT test, ETS introduces a new question type we call black square questions. In the passage on the left side of the computer screen, anywhere from 4 to 10 black boxes will appear. On the right side of the screen, a sentence will appear followed by the question, "Where would the sentence best fit in the passage? Click on the square ■ to add the sentence to the passage." When you point and click the mouse on a black square, the designated sentence will magically appear in place of it. If you click on another black square, the sentence will reappear there.

Because every black square is considered a possible answer choice, this question should be the very *last* you attempt to answer. As you approach this question type, remember the strategy for detail questions. Read the sentence you are required to insert, and select a lead word. Then, starting from the top of the text, quickly scan the text around the black squares for the lead word you have chosen. Once you have located the lead word, click on the black square to insert the sentence.

Read the sentences both before and after the sentence you just inserted. The sentence right before should contain information that introduces your new sentence. The following sentence should include information that continues the idea in your new sentence. If all three sentences flow with the text, you have correctly answered the question.

Look at the following example.

> Answer black square
> questions last.

Reading

Beginning

All animal life on the planet Earth depends on a sufficient supply of oxygen for its day-to-day survival. ■ The trees that now just sporadically dot our landscapes, but once heavily blanketed the earth's surface, still are able to provide a large portion of the oxygen supply. Through a process of photosynthesis, trees take in carbon dioxide from the surrounding air and in return create a sizeable amount of oxygen. ■ Ironically, human beings, who cut down large numbers of trees to create land, shelter, and energy, pose the most significant threat to the survival of the world-wide tree population. ■

But humans are not the only force that threatens the survival of these mighty members of the plant kingdom. ■ Lightning, fire, volcanoes, and earthquakes, occur without warning and not only rapidly destroy many square miles of old-growth forest in a matter of hours, but may also permanently prevent new trees from growing. Likewise, disease-causing fungi and insect pests can either eradicate certain types of trees or seriously weaken their branches.

After humans, however, the factor which most determines whether a particular species of tree will prosper in a given area is climate. ■ In particular, the amount of rainfall and the range of temperatures that a region experiences strongly affects the distribution of tree species.

All species of trees have evolved from plants that flourished many centuries ago in the warm and wet tropical regions of the planet. ■ As the distribution of trees has spread to other regions, the differing climates of these regions have effectively limited the types of trees that can live there. The greater the range of temperature and rainfall that a certain specie of tree can withstand, the more adaptable it is and therefore the wider the range of distribution. ■

The following sentence can be added to the passage.

Trees also face many natural dangers.

Where would it best fit in the passage? Click on the square ■ to add the sentence to the passage.

Time | ? Help | ← Prev | → Next

Read the sentence and select the lead word. Avoid the words that frequently appear in the text. The phrase "natural dangers" contains great lead words. Scan the text for "natural dangers," or for a paraphrase of it. In paragraph 2 you see a list of natural disasters: lightning, fire, volcanoes, and earthquakes. Click on the square in front of these natural disasters to insert the sentence. Reminder: Always read the sentence on either side of the inserted sentence to check for subject flow.

In summary of black square questions:

Step 1: Read the sentence that appears on the right side of your screen and select an appropriate lead word.

Step 2: From the top of the passage, scan the sentences around the black squares to locate your lead word.

Step 3: Click on the black square either before or after the sentence that contains the lead word.

Step 4: Read the sentences that precede and follow your answer to check for logical placement.

Drill 5

Use all the strategies you have learned to answer the following questions. Click on (in this case circle) the best answer.

Help   Prev   Next

With which of the following topics is the author primarily concerned?

○ The increasing costs of daguerreotype development

○ The relation between daguerreotypes and modern-day photography

○ The effects photographic chemicals have on picture quality

○ The complicated process of daguerreotype development

Beginning

Questions 1 to 8

Although only a small portion of professional photographers have had any practical knowledge of daguerreotypes, they are nevertheless one of the most influential and notable inventions of the nineteenth century. Predecessors to photographs, daguerreotypes were perfected and subsequently popularized by Daguerre during the 1830's. The complicated process of development made use of copper plates upon which several thin coats of silver were applied. The faint layers so sensitized the plates that when exposed to natural light, various images gradually appeared. Unfortunately, prior to actually viewing the impressions, a sequence of complex procedures had to be strictly followed.

The final picture quality of daguerreotypes completely depended on the careful preparation of the plates, and great attention was placed on keeping the working area spotless. After being fastened to wooden blocks, the daguerreotypes were fastened to wooden blocks where they were thoroughly scoured with alcohol and squares of soft flannel. Since even one speck of dust would easily create a groove deep enough in the malleable plate surfaces to render the daguerreotypes worthless, they required extensive polishing until completely smooth.

Once the copper plates were buffed, they were relocated to a darkroom in order to be first soaked in trays and then in enclosed boxes filled with iodine and bromine respectively. Now that the plates were rendered sensitive to light by the thin layer of bromo-iodine on their surfaces, they were inserted into specialized holders and placed in cameras for exposure. Factors such as the quality of the lenses, natural sunlight, and subject matter all greatly influenced the exposure time required. Only through trial and error would daguerreotypists learn the correct amount of time essential for the likeness of the subject matter to be identically reproduced on the copper plates.

After what the daguerreotypists thought to be an adequate exposure time, the plates were taken to yet another darkroom. There they were alternately dipped in iron containers of heated mercury and immersed in vats of freezing water. The mercury vapors adhered the images to the plates and subsequently developed the pictures, whereas the water limited any possibility of the plates breaking up. The daguerreotypists meticulously applied hydrosulphite-soda to the plate surfaces to dissolve any remaining bromo-iodine not previously exposed to light. Finally, a thin solution of heated gold and chlorine was meticulously brushed over the plates. The gold served to accent the black and white hues in the final picture, and the chlorine brightened the finish. The daguerreotypes were then ready for display.

Time

Next

Prev

Help

Look at the highlighted word in the passage. Click on the word or phrase in the bold text that **layers** refers to.

Questions 1 to 8

◄ Beginning

Although only a small portion of professional photographers have had any practical knowledge of daguerreotypes, they are nevertheless one of the most influential and notable inventions of the nineteenth century. Predecessors to photographs, daguerreotypes were perfected and subsequently popularized by Daguerre during the 1830's. **The complicated process of development made use of copper plates upon which several thin coats of silver were applied. The faint layers so sensitized the plates that when exposed to natural light, various images gradually appeared.** Unfortunately, prior to actually viewing the impressions, a sequence of complex procedures had to be strictly followed.

The final picture quality of daguerreotypes completely depended on the careful preparation of the plates, and great attention was placed on keeping the working area spotless. After being fastened to wooden blocks, the daguerreotypes were fastened to wooden blocks where they were thoroughly scoured with alcohol and squares of soft flannel. Since even one speck of dust would easily create a groove deep enough in the malleable plate surfaces to render the daguerreotypes worthless, they required extensive polishing until completely smooth.

Once the copper plates were buffed, they were relocated to a darkroom in order to be first soaked in trays and then in enclosed boxes filled with iodine and bromine respectively. Now that the plates were rendered sensitive to light by the thin layer of bromo-iodine on their surfaces, they were inserted into specialized holders and placed in cameras for exposure. Factors such as the quality of the lenses, natural sunlight, and subject matter all greatly influenced the exposure time required. Only through trial and error would daguerreotypists learn the correct amount of time essential for the likeness of the subject matter to be identically reproduced on the copper plates.

After what the daguerreotypists thought to be an adequate exposure time, the plates were taken to yet another darkroom. There they were alternately dipped in iron containers of heated mercury and immersed in vats of freezing water. The mercury vapors adhered the images to the plates and subsequently developed the pictures, whereas the water limited any possibility of the plates breaking up. The daguerreotypists meticulously applied hydrosulphite-soda to the plate surfaces to dissolve any remaining bromo-iodine not previously exposed to light. Finally, a thin solution of heated gold and chlorine was meticulously brushed over the plates. The gold served to accent the black and white hues in the final picture, and the chlorine brightened the finish. The daguerreotypes were then ready for display.

►

Time

Next

Prev

Help

Look at the word highlighted in the text. Click on the word that **they** refers to.

Beginning

Questions 1 to 8

Although only a small portion of professional photographers have had any practical knowledge of daguerreotypes, they are nevertheless one of the most influential and notable inventions of the nineteenth century. Predecessors to photographs, daguerreotypes were perfected and subsequently popularized by Daguerre during the 1830's. The complicated process of development made use of copper plates upon which several thin coats of silver were applied. The faint layers so sensitized the plates that when exposed to natural light, various images gradually appeared. Unfortunately, prior to actually viewing the impressions, a sequence of complex procedures had to be strictly followed.

The final picture quality of daguerreotypes completely depended on the careful preparation of the plates, and great attention was placed on keeping the working area spotless. After being fastened to wooden blocks, the daguerreotypes were fastened to wooden blocks where they were thoroughly scoured with alcohol and squares of soft flannel. **Since even one speck of dust would easily create a groove deep enough in the malleable plate surfaces to render the daguerreotypes worthless, they required extensive polishing until completely smooth.**

Once the copper plates were buffed, they were relocated to a darkroom in order to be first soaked in trays and then in enclosed boxes filled with iodine and bromine respectively. Now that the plates were rendered sensitive to light by the thin layer of bromo-iodine on their surfaces, they were inserted into specialized holders and placed in cameras for exposure. Factors such as the quality of the lenses, natural sunlight, and subject matter all greatly influenced the exposure time required. Only through trial and error would daguerreotypists learn the correct amount of time essential for the likeness of the subject matter to be identically reproduced on the copper plates.

After what the daguerreotypists thought to be an adequate exposure time, the plates were taken to yet another darkroom. There they were alternately dipped in iron containers of heated mercury and immersed in vats of freezing water. The mercury vapors adhered the images to the plates and subsequently developed the pictures, whereas the water limited any possibility of the plates breaking up. The daguerreotypists meticulously applied hydrosulphite-soda to the plate surfaces to dissolve any remaining bromo-iodine not previously exposed to light. Finally, a thin solution of heated gold and chlorine was meticulously brushed over the plates. The gold served to accent the black and white hues in the final picture, and the chlorine brightened the finish. The daguerreotypes were then ready for display.

Time

Look at the highlighted word in the text. Click on the following answer choice that is closest in meaning to the word malleable.

○ soft
○ unusual
○ persistent
○ flat

Help   Prev   Next

Questions 1 to 8

Beginning

Although only a small portion of professional photographers have had any practical knowledge of daguerreotypes, they are nevertheless one of the most influential and notable inventions of the nineteenth century. Predecessors to photographs, daguerreotypes were perfected and subsequently popularized by Daguerre during the 1830's. The complicated process of development made use of copper plates upon which several thin coats of silver were applied. The faint layers so sensitized the plates that when exposed to natural light, various images gradually appeared. Unfortunately, prior to actually viewing the impressions, a sequence of complex procedures had to be strictly followed.

The final picture quality of daguerreotypes completely depended on the careful preparation of the plates, and great attention was placed on keeping the working area spotless. After being fastened to wooden blocks, the daguerreotypes were fastened to wooden blocks where they were thoroughly scoured with alcohol and squares of soft flannel. Since even one speck of dust would easily create a groove deep enough in the malleable plate surfaces to render the daguerreotypes worthless, they required extensive polishing until completely smooth.

Once the copper plates were buffed, they were relocated to a darkroom in order to be first soaked in trays and then in enclosed boxes filled with iodine and bromine respectively. Now that the plates were rendered sensitive to light by the thin layer of bromo-iodine on their surfaces, they were inserted into specialized holders and placed in cameras for exposure. Factors such as the quality of the lenses, natural sunlight, and subject matter all greatly influenced the exposure time required. Only through trial and error would daguerreotypists learn the correct amount of time essential for the likeness of the subject matter to be identically reproduced on the copper plates.

After what the daguerreotypists thought to be an adequate exposure time, the plates were taken to yet another darkroom. There they were alternately dipped in iron containers of heated mercury and immersed in vats of freezing water. The mercury vapors adhered the images to the plates and subsequently developed the pictures, whereas the water limited any possibility of the plates breaking up. The daguerreotypists meticulously applied hydrosulphite-soda to the plate surfaces to dissolve any remaining bromo-iodine not previously exposed to light. Finally, a thin solution of heated gold and chlorine was meticulously brushed over the plates. The gold served to accent the black and white hues in the final picture, and the chlorine brightened the finish. The daguerreotypes were then ready for display.

Time

Next

Prev

Help

According to the passage, what were the copper plates first soaked in?

○ boxes
○ bromine
○ alcohol
○ iodine

Questions 1 to 8

Beginning

Although only a small portion of professional photographers have had any practical knowledge of daguerreotypes, they are nevertheless one of the most influential and notable inventions of the nineteenth century. Predecessors to photographs, daguerreotypes were perfected and subsequently popularized by Daguerre during the 1830's. The complicated process of development made use of copper plates upon which several thin coats of silver were applied. The faint layers so sensitized the plates that when exposed to natural light, various images gradually appeared. Unfortunately, prior to actually viewing the impressions, a sequence of complex procedures had to be strictly followed.

The final picture quality of daguerreotypes completely depended on the careful preparation of the plates, and great attention was placed on keeping the working area spotless. After being fastened to wooden blocks, the daguerreotypes were fastened to wooden blocks where they were thoroughly scoured with alcohol and squares of soft flannel. Since even one speck of dust would easily create a groove deep enough in the malleable plate surfaces to render the daguerreotypes worthless, they required extensive polishing until completely smooth.

Once the copper plates were buffed, they were relocated to a darkroom in order to be first soaked in trays and then in enclosed boxes filled with iodine and bromine respectively. Now that the plates were rendered sensitive to light by the thin layer of bromo-iodine on their surfaces, they were inserted into specialized holders and placed in cameras for exposure. Factors such as the quality of the lenses, natural sunlight, and subject matter all greatly influenced the exposure time required. Only through trial and error would daguerreotypists learn the correct amount of time essential for the likeness of the subject matter to be identically reproduced on the copper plates.

After what the daguerreotypists thought to be an adequate exposure time, the plates were taken to yet another darkroom. There they were alternately dipped in iron containers of heated mercury and immersed in vats of freezing water. The mercury vapors adhered the images to the plates and subsequently developed the pictures, whereas the water limited any possibility of the plates breaking up. The daguerreotypists meticulously applied hydrosulphite-soda to the plate surfaces to dissolve any remaining bromo-iodine not previously exposed to light. Finally, a thin solution of heated gold and chlorine was meticulously brushed over the plates. The gold served to accent the black and white hues in the final picture, and the chlorine brightened the finish. The daguerreotypes were then ready for display.

Time

Questions 1 to 8

Although only a small portion of professional photographers have had any practical knowledge of daguerreotypes, they are nevertheless one of the most influential and notable inventions of the nineteenth century. Predecessors to photographs, daguerreotypes were perfected and subsequently popularized by Daguerre during the 1830's. The complicated process of development made use of copper plates upon which several thin coats of silver were applied. The faint layers so sensitized the plates that when exposed to natural light, various images gradually appeared. Unfortunately, prior to actually viewing the impressions, a sequence of complex procedures had to be strictly followed.

The final picture quality of daguerreotypes completely depended on the careful preparation of the plates, and great attention was placed on keeping the working area spotless. After being fastened to wooden blocks, the daguerreotypes were fastened to wooden blocks where they were thoroughly scoured with alcohol and squares of soft flannel. Since even one speck of dust would easily create a groove deep enough in the malleable plate surfaces to render the daguerreotypes worthless, they required extensive polishing until completely smooth.

Once the copper plates were buffed, they were relocated to a darkroom in order to be first soaked in trays and then in enclosed boxes filled with iodine and bromine respectively. Now that the plates were rendered sensitive to light by the thin layer of bromo-iodine on their surfaces, they were inserted into specialized holders and placed in cameras for exposure. Factors such as the quality of the lenses, natural sunlight, and subject matter all greatly influenced the exposure time required. Only through trial and error would daguerreotypists learn the correct amount of time essential for the likeness of the subject matter to be identically reproduced on the copper plates.

 After what the daguerreotypists thought to be an adequate exposure time, the plates were taken to yet another darkroom. There they were alternately dipped in iron containers of heated mercury and immersed in vats of freezing water. The mercury vapors adhered the images to the plates and subsequently developed the pictures, whereas the water limited any possibility of the plates breaking up. The daguerreotypists meticulously applied hydrosulphite-soda to the plate surfaces to dissolve any remaining bromo-iodine not previously exposed to light. Finally, a thin solution of heated gold and chlorine was meticulously brushed over the plates. The gold served to accent the black and white hues in the final picture, and the chlorine brightened the finish. The daguerreotypes were then ready for display.

Click on the sentence in Paragraph 4 that tells how the daguerreotypists kept the plates from disintegrating. Paragraph 4 is marked with an arrow ( ).

Questions 1 to 8

▲ Beginning

Although only a small portion of professional photographers have had any practical knowledge of daguerreotypes, they are nevertheless one of the most influential and notable inventions of the nineteenth century. Predecessors to photographs, daguerreotypes were perfected and subsequently popularized by Daguerre during the 1830's. The complicated process of development made use of copper plates upon which several thin coats of silver were applied. The faint layers so sensitized the plates that when exposed to natural light, various images gradually appeared. Unfortunately, prior to actually viewing the impressions, a sequence of complex procedures had to be strictly followed.

The final picture quality of daguerreotypes completely depended on the careful preparation of the plates., and great attention was placed on keeping the working area spotless. After being fastened to wooden blocks, the daguerreotypes were fastened to wooden blocks where they were thoroughly scoured with alcohol and squares of soft flannel. Since even one speck of dust would easily create a groove deep enough in the malleable plate surfaces to render the daguerreotypes worthless, they required extensive polishing until completely smooth.

Once the copper plates were buffed, they were relocated to a darkroom in order to be first soaked in trays and then in enclosed boxes filled with iodine and bromine respectively. Now that the plates were rendered sensitive to light by the thin layer of bromo-iodine on their surfaces, they were inserted into specialized holders and placed in cameras for exposure. Factors such as the quality of the lenses, natural sunlight, and subject matter all greatly influenced the exposure time required. Only through trial and error would daguerreotypists learn the correct amount of time essential for the likeness of the subject matter to be identically reproduced on the copper plates.

After what the daguerreotypists thought to be an adequate exposure time, the plates were taken to yet another darkroom. There they were alternately dipped in iron containers of heated mercury and immersed in vats of freezing water. The mercury vapors adhered the images to the plates and subsequently developed the pictures, whereas the water limited any possibility of the plates breaking up. The daguerreotypists meticulously applied hydrosulphite-soda to the plate surfaces to dissolve any remaining bromo-iodine not previously exposed to light. Finally, a thin solution of heated gold and chlorine was meticulously brushed over the plates. The gold served to accent the black and white hues in the final picture, and the chlorine brightened the finish. The daguerreotypes were then ready for display.

▶

It can be inferred from the text that all of the following influence final picture quality of daguerreotype EXCEPT

◯ cleanliness
◯ weather
◯ lens quality
◯ daguerreotypists' education

Help

Prev

Next

Time

Next

Prev

Help

Time

Beginning

Questions 1 to 8

Although only a small portion of professional photographers have had any practical knowledge of daguerreotypes, they are nevertheless one of the most influential and notable inventions of the nineteenth century. ■Predecessors to photographs, daguerreotypes were perfected and subsequently popularized by Daguerre during the 1830's. The complicated process of development made use of copper plates upon which several thin coats of silver were applied. The faint layers so sensitized the plates that when exposed to natural light, various images gradually appeared. ■Unfortunately, prior to actually viewing the impressions, a sequence of complex procedures had to be strictly followed.

The final picture quality of daguerreotypes completely depended on the careful preparation of the plates, and great attention was placed on keeping the working area spotless. ■After being fastened to wooden blocks, the daguerreotypes were fastened to wooden blocks where they were thoroughly scoured with alcohol and squares of soft flannel. Since even one speck of dust would easily create a groove deep enough in the malleable plate surfaces to render the daguerreotypes worthless, they required extensive polishing until completely smooth. ■

Once the copper plates were buffed, they were relocated to a darkroom in order to be first soaked in trays and then in enclosed boxes filled with iodine and bromine respectively. Now that the plates were rendered sensitive to light by the thin layer of bromo-iodine on their surfaces, they were inserted into specialized holders and placed in cameras for exposure. Factors such as the quality of the lenses, natural sunlight, and subject matter all greatly influenced the exposure time required. ■Only through trial and error would daguerreotypists learn the correct amount of time essential for the likeness of the subject matter to be identically reproduced on the copper plates.

After what the daguerreotypists thought to be an adequate exposure time, the plates were taken to yet another darkroom. ■There they were alternately dipped in iron containers of heated mercury and immersed in vats of freezing water. The mercury vapors adhered the images to the plates and subsequently developed the pictures, whereas the water limited any possibility of the plates breaking up. ■The daguerreotypists meticulously applied hydrosulphite-soda to the plate surfaces to dissolve any remaining bromo-iodine not previously exposed to light. Finally, a thin solution of heated gold and chlorine was meticulously brushed over the plates. The gold served to accent the black and white hues in the final picture, and the chlorine brightened the finish. ■The daguerreotypes were then ready for display.

The following sentence can be added to the passage.

Without these two chemicals, the final pictures would appear flat and dull.

Where would it best fit in the passage? Click on the square to add the sentence to the passage.

SUMMARY OF READING SECTION STRATEGY

Passage Strategy

- Move through the tutorial as quickly as possible.

- 1-1-1-L the passage. Don't read the entire text! This is crucial.

- Answer the first-pass questions first, the second-pass questions next, and the third-pass questions last in passage 1, then go to passage 2 and do the same thing until the last passage. (See diagram on page 290.)

- Keep your eye on the time.

- Never get stuck on one question.

- Use process of elimination (POE) and common sense to reduce answer choice possibility.

- Answer every question! If you absolutely can't find the answer, *guess!*

Question Strategy

First-Pass Questions

1. **VIC**—Replace the VIC word with the other answer choices to see which one makes the most sense.

2. **Reference**—Plug each answer choice back into the sentence and see if the sentence makes sense. Remember, pronouns must agree in number and gender with the nouns they replace.

3. **Detail**—Use chronological order and lead words to find the information.

Second-Pass Questions

1. **Main Idea**—Consider what is mentioned in the first pass questions.

2. **Conclusion**—Select the answer choice mentioned in the majority of the first pass questions.

3. **Click on Sentence**—Read sentences indicated and POE the answer choices that fail to answer the question.

Third-Pass Questions

1. **Except/Not**—Using chronology and the answer choices as lead words, locate the information in the text. Click on the answer *not* mentioned.

2. **Infer/Imply**—Using chronology and lead words, locate the information that the question refers to. Click on the answer choice that best paraphrases the text.

3. **Black Square**—Use lead words to locate the correct black square.

Helpful Hints

1. Memorize the different question types and whether they are first-, second-, or third-pass questions.

2. Have confidence! Familiarize yourself with a computer and a mouse *before* taking the TOEFL CBT. You want to "fast forward" through these tutorials.

3. The first-, second-, and third-pass questions are not fixed. It depends on what you feel. If you see a third-pass question that seems easy, go ahead and click on the correct answer. If you see a first-pass question that seems difficult, go ahead and skip it. Use the method to your advantage!

4. Avoid reading the entire passage: Use 1-1-1-L. If you don't, you will *not* be able to finish!

ANSWER KEYS

Drill 1

1. fat
2. 8 times
3. fat

Drill 2

1. vitamin C
2. Rosa Parks or 1955
3. wings (Because the passage is probably about manta rays, those words will appear many times in the passage, and thus are not good choices for lead words.)
4. bipartisan
5. Karl XII
6. legislative branch
7. snapping turtles (or, if the passage is about snapping turtles, try *extinct*)
8. sudden climatic change

Drill 3

1. tiny
2. accelerate
3. Bodily behavior was controlled exclusively by the nervous system.
4. secretin
5. Chemical integration is not entirely dependent on the nervous system.
6. absence
7. helps insects harden their outer shells
8. ripening fruits

Drill 4

1. d
2. f
3. h
4. c
5. a
6. b
7. j
8. i
9. e
10. g

Drill 5

1. The complicated process of daguerreotype development
2. coats
3. Daguerreotypes
4. soft
5. iodine
6. The mercury vapors adhered the images to the plates and subsequently developed the pictures, whereas the water limited any possibility of the plates breaking up.
7. Daguerrotypists' education
8. The last black square

PART V

Writing

7
Writing

THE BASICS

Formerly known as the Test of Written English (TWE), the Writing section of the TOEFL CBT consists of a *mandatory* essay you must write based on a simple topic given to you by ETS. It is the last section of the TOEFL CBT, and you are given 30 minutes to complete it.

If possible, you should type your essay.

Since the essay asks for your opinion and the topics are very general, you do *not* need any specialized knowledge to write the essay. On the day of the exam, you have the option of either *writing* the essay by hand, or *typing* the essay into the computer. If you choose to write your essay, the test proctor will give you several sheets of scratch paper and an official test booklet in which to write your final essay. If you choose to type your essay, you will also receive several sheets of scratch paper, and the computer will then lead you through a tutorial for the Writing section.

SHOULD I WRITE OR TYPE MY ESSAY?

If you are at all familiar with a standard keyboard and have some basic knowledge about word processing, you should absolutely choose the option to type your essay. Typing your essay will *drastically* improve your score in two essential ways. First, you will be able to cut, paste, and move sentences around, which will no doubt improve the organization and content of your essay. In addition, typing your paper will look a hundred times neater than if you write it, and neatness is taken into consideration when your essay is graded.

If you are unfamiliar with a keyboard, have never typed before, or have no knowledge about a basic word processing program, then of course it would be to your benefit to write your essay by hand. Your final score will be lower, however, due to content and the neatness factor. Keep in mind that if your ultimate goal is to go to a university or college, it will be to your advantage to be proficient in both typing and word processing. In other words, if you are computer illiterate and want to attend an American university, take a computer class and learn the basics, or have a friend explain word processing to you and then practice, practice, and practice some more!

THE TUTORIAL

ETS begins the Writing section of the TOEFL CBT with a tutorial. It teaches you how to highlight, cut and paste, and undo text. ETS also informs you how to move around the text using the page up, page down, home, end, and arrow keys. If you are familiar with any word processing program, you will have no problem completing this tutorial. Move through it as quickly as possible. If you are *not* familiar with a word processing program, or are unable to type on a standard keyboard, don't waste your time and energy trying to learn 10 minutes before the Writing section. It is impossible to learn how to type or become comfortable with word processing in that short amount of time. You want to spend your 30 minutes composing your essay, not familiarizing yourself with cutting and pasting. The tutorial will teach you basic skills, but it will not teach you speed or efficient typing. If this is your situation, you should handwrite your essay.

SCORING

According to ETS, your essay will be separately scored and evaluated by two "qualified" readers. (How ETS defines "qualified" remains a mystery.) If the ratings given by the "qualified" readers differ by more than one point, a third "qualified" reader will be called in to make a final grading decision. In any event, your essay could receive a score (from excellent to poor) of 6.0, 5.5, 5.0, 4.5, 4.0, 3.5, 3.0, 2.5, 2.0, 1.5, or 1. If you choose *not* to write your essay, or if you write in your native language, or you type a profanity directed at ETS, you will receive a big, fat 0. We recommend that you *not* choose any of these last three options due to the fact that your Writing section score is combined with your Grammar section score for a final Structure score. In other words:

> **1/2 Grammar section score + 1/2 Writing section score =**
> **Final Structure score.**

Look at the following TOEFL CBT scoring guide that the "qualified" readers refer to. Any essay that is scored a:

6—**effectively** addresses the essay, is **well** organized and developed, **clearly** uses support, and **effectively** demonstrates a variety of vocabulary and sentence structure.

5—**generally** addresses the essay, is **generally** well organized and developed, **generally** uses support, and demonstrates **some** variety of vocabulary and sentence structure.

4—**adequately** addresses the essay topic, is **adequately** organized and developed, **adequately** uses support, and **adequately** demonstrates a variety of vocabulary and sentence structure, either of which may contain **occasional** errors.

3—**inadequately** addresses the essay topic, is **inadequately** organized and developed, **inadequately** uses support, and contains **inappropriate** vocabulary and sentence structure, either of which contain **many** errors.

2—is seriously **disorganized** and **underdeveloped**, contains **little** detail and support, and demonstrates **serious problems** with vocabulary and sentence structure.

1—is incoherent, **underdeveloped**, contains **no** detail and support, and contains **severe** and **consistent errors**.

DIRECTIONS

Learn the directions before you take the real TOEFL CBT!

After you begin the TOEFL CBT Writing section, the directions appear on the screen. The clock is running, so dismiss the directions immediately to see the essay topic.

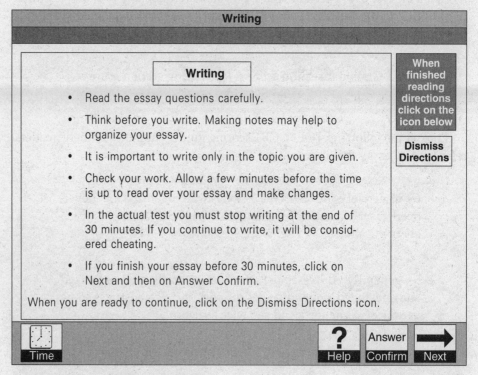

Writing

Writing

- Read the essay questions carefully.

- Think before you write. Making notes may help to organize your essay.

- It is important to write only in the topic you are given.

- Check your work. Allow a few minutes before the time is up to read over your essay and make changes.

- In the actual test you must stop writing at the end of 30 minutes. If you continue to write, it will be considered cheating.

- If you finish your essay before 30 minutes, click on Next and then on Answer Confirm.

When you are ready to continue, click on the Dismiss Directions icon.

When finished reading directions click on the icon below

Dismiss Directions

Time | ? Help | Answer Confirm | Next

WRITING THE ESSAY

Each language has it own stylistic rules for writing an essay. English is no different. To maximize your score, you should follow American English rules for writing a successful essay. ETS holds that the writing section gives you the "opportunity to demonstrate your ability to write in English." They also state that "this includes the ability to generate and organize ideas, to support those ideas with examples or evidence, and to compose in standard written English a response to an assigned topic." That's a lot to accomplish in 30 minutes. In fact, it seems impossible to complete. However, The Princeton Review has developed effective and efficient techniques to help you crack the Writing Section on the TOEFL CBT.

APPEARANCE

Graders spend less than two minutes reading your essay; you must pay attention to its appearance!

Keep in mind that your essay is read and graded in less than two minutes. The first thing readers do is glance at the layout of your essay on the page. What they see at first glance is what sticks in their minds the most. For that reason you need to pay close attention to how your essay looks.

Tips for an attractive essay:

- **Write neatly**. If you decide to write your essay rather than type it, you must write neatly. Nothing will make a "qualified" reader less happy than handwriting that's difficult to decipher. It's better to have a mediocre, legible essay than one that's brilliant but hard to read.

- **Length**. Make sure the essay is at least 200 words. If your essay is too short, regardless of the quality of what you write, the reader will start off by thinking, "This person couldn't come up with 200 words in English."

- **Indentation**. If you choose to type your essay, keep in mind that the tab key will not work during the Writing section of the TOEFL CBT. Therefore, you must manually hit the space bar 5 times to indent your paragraphs. For handwritten essays, indents at the beginning of each paragraph make your essay look structured and well planned.

BODY

Now you need to keep in mind what the essay reader is looking for in terms of content. Most importantly, the reader does **not** care *what* you say, but *how* you say it. In other words, the reader isn't wondering if your examples, details, and evidence are true or false, he only looks for complete English sentences that support your opinion. Feel free to be as creative as you want! Personal examples and stories do *not* have to be true; they can be completely made up and invented. Nothing needs to be true! Nor does the reader care if you actually agree or disagree with the essay topic questions! He is only examining your sentence structure, grammar, vocabulary, and (most importantly) whether you support your points with specific examples.

> The reader does not care *what* you say, just *how* you say it.

Look at the following tips to help construct a great essay:

- **Short and simple**. The longer your sentences, the more likely it is that they contain some kind of error. No sentence should exceed two lines in length.

- **Tense and Person**. Decide if you want to write in the past or present tense. Write in the first person ("I"). This makes the essay more personal to the reader.

- **Grammar**. Use grammatical structures you are comfortable with. If you're not sure whether a sentence structure you'd like to use is okay in English, don't use it. You can probably do just as well by splitting that sentence into two sentences.

- **Vocabulary**. Only use words and phrases you know. Being overly ambitious with your vocabulary will only lead to improper usage. A few advanced vocabulary words or idioms are a fantastic way to spruce up your essay; just make sure you know what they mean.

- **Spelling**. If you're not sure of the spelling of a word, don't use it. You can probably think of a great synonym to replace it. Words from your native language might have the same meaning as English words, but the spelling could be different. The computer you will use on the TOEFL CBT Writing section will *not* have a spell check function.

- **Punctuation**. Make sure that all sentences have periods at the end and that all lists are separated by commas. Avoid trying to use colons, semicolons, or other advanced forms of punctuation unless you're sure of their correct usage.

- **Repetition**. Avoid repeating yourself. As you read your essay, any adjective or verb that appears more than once or twice should be replaced by a synonym.

PACING

In the Writing section of the TOEFL CBT, you have 30 minutes to read the essay topic and write an essay. In order to complete the Writing section, break it down into the following 5 minute intervals:

Minutes **1–5**: Read the essay topic, choose a side, and write the outline on the provided scratch paper.

Minutes **6–10**: Write the *introduction* paragraph.

Minutes **11–15**: Write the *first support* paragraph.

Minutes **16–20**: Write the *second support* paragraph

Minutes **21–25**: Write the *conclusion* paragraph.

Minutes **26–30**: Reread your essay and make any final corrections.

Keep an eye on the clock to allow only 5 minutes for each section. Try not to fall behind. Four mediocre paragraphs will score higher than two well-developed ones. Do *not* continue after your 30 minutes is up. Any students caught writing after the official 30 minutes is over will forfeit their entire TOEFL CBT exam and *no* refund will be made.

1. The Essay Question

There is no "right" or "wrong" answer to a Writing topic!

First, you must read and understand the essay question. Essay questions are very general, and cover a wide range of topics including sports, pollution, technology, or entertainment. They will *not* include topics on current political events, historical figures, or any details or facts. The questions do *not* require any specific knowledge. The following are some typical essay questions found on the Writing section of the TOEFL CBT.

> Your university has enough money to build either a new sports stadium or a new library. Which project should your university build: a sports stadium or a library? Use specific reasons and examples to support your opinion.

Do you agree or disagree with the following statement? Sometimes it is acceptable to tell a lie. Use specific reasons and details to support your answer.

Some people are perfectionists. Others do only what is necessary to complete their responsibilities. Compare these two attitudes. Which attitude do you agree with? Support your choice with specific examples.

For a complete list of TOEFL CBT essay topics, see page 35 of the official ETS TOEFL CBT bulletin.

2. Choosing Your Side

All TOEFL CBT essay questions ask for your *opinion*, so you must choose a side. The first thing you must do is decide which opinion you would like to support, or whether you agree or disagree with the statement. Once you have chosen a side, do *not* change. There is *no* right correct side to choose, and ETS does *not* care which side you choose. Therefore, pick the one you're most comfortable with; more importantly, pick the side that appears the easiest to support.

3. Outlining the Essay

The first 5 minutes (or less if possible) should be spent quickly preparing a rough outline. ETS will *not* see this outline, so it doesn't matter how neat it is. Outlines help you organize your thoughts and prepare you for efficient writing. Think of it this way: If you were driving your car to a new and unfamiliar place, would you leave your house without a map? No, you wouldn't. If you did, you would waste time just driving around trying to find your destination. The same idea applies for the TOEFL CBT Writing section. Your essay needs to be focused, concise, and well organized. An outline provides the map necessary for a well-written essay. It will help you organize your thoughts, keeping you from aimlessly wandering around.

An outline must include the following **four** essential paragraphs.

Paragraph I: <u>Introduction</u>: The initial presentation of the essay and your *opinion statement* (whether you agree or disagree with the essay question).

Paragraph II: <u>Support #1</u>: Reasons, details, and examples to support your opinion statement.

Paragraph III: <u>Support #2</u>: Reasons, details, and examples to *further* support your opinion statement.

Paragraph IV: <u>Conclusion</u>: The *restatement* of your opinion statement, plus a brief *summary* of the essay.

Each above listed point is just *one* paragraph, which consists of 4 to 6 sentences each, so you have to write a minimum of 16 to 24 sentences in 20 minutes. (Remember, the first 5 minutes are spent writing an outline and the last 5 are spent checking over the essay). This amounts to approximately one sentence per minute. This is possible to accomplish! Breaking the TOEFL CBT essay down and thinking about it in this way makes it seem much more feasible to complete.

Ask the test proctors for paper.

Step 1: First, focus on writing the opinion statement. This is your opinion about the essay question and is the backbone of your essay.

Step 2: Next, think of a sentence that supports your opinion statement and have one personal example or specific detail to illustrate it.

Step 3: Next, think of another sentence that supports your opinion statement, and have another personal example or specific detail to illustrate it. If you ever have trouble thinking of a personal example or specific detail, *make it up!*

Step 4: Finally, summarize and restate your opinion statement for the conclusion.

Look at an example outline.

Topic: Some people believe that everyone should have the opportunity to attend a college or university. Others suggest that university education be reserved for the smartest and best high school students. Which belief do you agree with? Use specific reasons and details to explain your answer.

For the topic above, your outline might look something like this:

Paragraph I: <u>Introduction</u>: Education should be for everyone, not just for those individuals who are naturally smart.

Paragraph II: <u>Support #1</u>: Few students mentally develop at the same rates.

   A) Specific detail: A poor high school student becomes the top university graduate.

Paragraph III: <u>Support #2</u>: Academic institutions are for more than just memorizing facts and data.

   A) Personal experience: Being elected to the student government.

Paragraph IV: <u>Conclusion</u>: Every student should be able to decide for herself whether or not she wants more education.

Don't worry about using complete sentences for your outline. No one will ever see your outline. Its purpose is to keep your essay directed and focused as you write. Make sure to limit yourself to 5 (or fewer) minutes to write your outline. If you need more time than that, your plans for your essay are too ambitious. Now that you have written your outline, the next 20 minutes will be spent filling in the details with complete sentences in order to complete your essay. Remember, your essay only needs to have about 16 to 24 sentences.

Now that you have seen an example of how to write an outline, try writing some on your own. Remember that ETS will never see your outline.

Drill 1

Spend the first 5 minutes writing the outline.

Directions: Read the essay topics and write outlines. Follow the guidelines for writing outlines. Give yourself 5 minutes to complete each outline.

Topic 1:   Certain high schools require that students study foreign languages. Other schools let students study whatever subjects they like. Which of these two policies do you think a school should adopt? Give specific reasons and examples to support your opinion.

I   Introduction:

_____

II   Support #1:

_____

A) Specific detail:

_____

III   Support #2:

_____

A) Personal experience:

_____

IV   Conclusion:

_____

Topic 2:   There are many types of pollution in this world. Pick one type of pollution and tell what you have done to try to reduce it. Be sure to use specific examples and details in your answer.

I   Introduction:

_____

II   Support #1:

_____

   A) Specific detail:

_____

III   Support #2:

_____

   A) Personal experience:

_____

IV   Conclusion:

_____

Topic 3:   In the past decades, computers have had a tremendous effect on our society. Some experts state that people are relying upon computers too much. Others believe we should rely on computers even more. Which of these two statements do you agree with? Give specific reasons and examples to support your opinion.

I   Introduction:

_____

II   Support #1:

_____

   A) Specific detail:

_____

III   Support #2:

_____

   A) Personal experience:

_____

IV   Conclusion:

_____

4. Writing the Essay

Once you have finished practicing writing outlines, the next step is expanding them into essay form. Look at the standard English essay diagram for writing a composition:

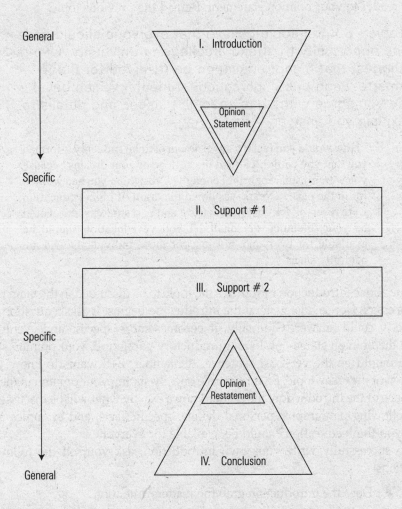

With a few adjustments, your outline will fit neatly within this standard English essay diagram. Begin with the introduction.

The Introduction

The introduction is the first interaction the "qualified" readers have with your essay. Therefore, it has to grab the readers' attention and prepare them for what is to follow. The introduction can be anywhere from 3 to 4 sentences in length. It begins with a general statement and gradually becomes more specific as it leads your reader to your opinion statement. Reread the previous topic.

> Topic: Some people believe that everyone should have the opportunity to attend a college or university. Others suggest that higher education be reserved for the smartest and best high school students. Which belief do you agree with? Use specific reasons and details to explain you answer.

> How would you feel if a government official suddenly informed you that you couldn't attend the college of your dreams because you weren't smart or bright enough? Everything you had worked for in the past 12 years was down the drain. If higher education were reserved for only the smartest and best students, this would be your dilemma. Personally, I believe education should be available for everyone, not just for those individuals who are naturally smart.

The above introduction introduces the topic to be discussed in the main body of the essay. Notice how general the introduction begins. It asks a question that anybody could answer. Gradually, it becomes more specific and eventually gives the opinion statement. In an introductory paragraph, your opinion statement should be the very *last* sentence. Remember, ETS wants to know your opinion of the essay topic. Be sure to give one. By stating your opinion in the last sentence of the introduction, the reader knows exactly what will be discussed in the following paragraphs: personal details, specific facts, and examples as to why you think education should be available for everyone.

The last sentence of your introduction should be your opinion statement

To successfully write your own introduction, ask yourself the following questions:

- Does the introduction grab the readers' attention?

- Does it begin with a general statement and gradually become more specific?

- Is my opinion statement located in the last sentence of the introduction?

Now that you have seen an example of how to write an introduction, try writing some on your own. Remember, ETS doesn't care *what* you write, they only care *how* you write it.

Drill 2

Directions: Reread the following topics and write *introductions* for each. Follow the guidelines for writing introductions. Give yourself 5 minutes to write each introduction. You may refer to your outlines that you have already written.

Topic 1:   Certain high schools require that students study foreign languages. Other schools let students study whatever subjects they like. Which of these two policies do you think a school should adopt? Give specific reasons and examples to support your opinion.

_____

_____

_____

_____

_____

_____

Topic 2:   There are many types of pollution in this world. Pick one type of pollution and tell what you have done to try to reduce it. Be sure to use specific examples and details in your answer.

_____

_____

_____

_____

_____

_____

_____

_____

Topic 3:   In the past decades, computers have had a tremendous affect on our society. Some experts state that people are relying upon computers too much. Others believe we should rely on computers even more. Which of these two statements do you agree with? Give specific reasons and examples to support your opinion.

_____

_____

_____

_____

_____

_____

_____

The Support

All the TOEFL CBT essay topics have *one* thing in common. They all ask for specific details and examples to support your opinion. If you write a terrific essay with a lot of hard vocabulary and grammatical structures, yet you fail to mention any specific details or examples, your final score will be limited. The paragraph following the introduction must give the first reason that supports your opinion statement. The third paragraph must give an additional reason that supports your opinion statement. In both paragraphs, specific examples must follow. In your basic essay, opinions without specific support mean *nothing*.

Look at an example. Reread the previous topic, and the introduction.

Topic 4:   Some people believe that everyone should have the opportunity to attend a college or university. Others suggest that higher education be reserved for the smartest and best high school students. Which belief do you agree with? Use specific reasons and details to explain you answer.

> How would you feel if a government official suddenly informed you that you couldn't attend the college of your dreams because you weren't smart or bright enough? Everything you had worked for in the past 12 years was down the drain. If higher education were reserved for only the smartest and best students, this would be your dilemma. Personally, I believe education should be available for everyone, not just for those individuals who are naturally smart.

Generally speaking, few students mentally develop at the same rate. Some high school students might reach their intellectual peak at 17, while others might reach it at 21. To be honest, I was a mediocre high-school student at best. I seldom applied myself, and quite frankly, was bored with the dull high-school subjects such as mathematics, science, and history. However, once I was accepted into the university, I could select my own classes such as theatre production, videotape editing, and graphic design. Not only did my grades hit A level, but I also grew excited about what I was studying. In fact, I graduated in the top 10 students of my class.

I also believe that academic institutions are for more than just memorizing facts and data. It is possible to interact with other cultures, learn how to manage your stress, and become involved in various organizations. I was elected president of my freshman class. In addition to completing my studies, I also organized fund raising events, led class activities, and spoke publicly. To my surprise, these experiences were much more rewarding and valuable than my classes were.

Notice that the first sentence in paragraphs two and three above repeat the general sentences from the outline. Now all you need to do is fill in the specific details. The two support paragraphs must back up your opinion statement by providing personal details, specific facts, and examples. Remember, the personal details, specific facts, and examples do *not* need to be true. They only have to support your opinion statement. In the above case, none of the facts are true, yet the argument sounds convincing.

To successfully write your own support paragraphs, ask yourself the following questions:

- Is the general sentence from the outline the first sentence of my paragraph?

- Do the paragraphs contain personal details, specific facts, and examples?

- Do the personal details, specific facts, and examples support my opinion statement?

Now that you have seen an example of how to write support paragraphs, try writing some on your own. Remember, ETS doesn't care *what* you write, they only care *how* you write it.

Drill 3:

Directions: Reread the following topics and write two *support paragraphs* for each. Follow the guidelines for writing support paragraphs. Give yourself *10 minutes* to write both paragraphs. You may refer to your outlines and introduction you have already written.

Topic 1:   Certain high schools require that students study foreign languages. Other schools let students study whatever subjects they like. Which of these two policies do you think a school should adopt? Give specific reasons and examples to support your opinion.

_____

_____

_____

_____

_____

_____

_____

_____

_____

_____

_____

_____

_____

_____

Topic 2: There are many types of pollution in this world. Pick one type of pollution and tell what you have done to try to reduce it. Be sure to use specific examples and details in your answer.

_____

_____

_____

_____

_____

_____

_____

_____

_____

_____

_____

_____

_____

Topic 3:   In the past decades, computers have had a tremendous affect on our society. Some experts state that people are relying upon computers too much. Others believe we should rely on computers even more. Which of these two statements do you agree with? Give specific reasons and examples to support your opinion.

_____

_____

_____

_____

_____

_____

_____

_____

_____

_____

_____

_____

_____

_____

_____

_____

The Conclusion

The conclusion is the last opportunity to demonstrate to the ETS "qualified" readers that you can compose an essay in response to a general topic. While the introduction begins with a general tone and develops a specific opinion statement, the conclusion is the opposite. It begins with a specific statement, working its way toward a more general close to the essay. The very first sentence should be the *opinion restatement*. In other words, summarize your original opinion statement. Do *not* simply repeat it word for word. It needs to be rewritten to convey the same message. The opinion restatement has already been written in the outline. Simply return to the outline and make it the first sentence. The next 3 to 4 sentences should summarize the points you have mentioned in the support paragraphs.

Look at an example. Reread the previous essay topic, the introduction, and the main support paragraphs

Topic: Some people believe that everyone should have the opportunity to attend a college or university. Others suggest that higher education be reserved for the smartest and best high school students. Which belief do you agree with? Use specific reasons and details to explain you answer.

How would you feel if a government official suddenly informed you that you couldn't attend the college of your dreams because you weren't smart or bright enough? Everything you had worked for in the past 12 years would be down the drain. If higher education were reserved for only the smartest and best students, this would be your dilemma. Personally, I believe education should be available for everyone, not just for those individuals who are naturally smart.

Generally speaking, few students mentally develop at the same rate. Some high school students might reach their intellectual peak at 17, while others might reach it at 21. To be honest, I was a mediocre high-school student at best. I seldom applied myself, and quite frankly, was completely bored with the dull high-school subjects such as mathematics, science, and history. However, once I was accepted into the university, I could easily select my own classes such as theatre production, videotape editing, and graphic design. Not only did my grades hit A level, but I also grew excited about what I was studying. In fact, I graduated in the top 10 students of my class.

I also believe that academic institutions are for more than just memorizing facts and data. It is possible to personally interact with other cultures, learn how to better manage your stress, and become involved in various organizations. I was president of my class. In addition to completing my studies, I also organized fund raising events, led class activities, and spoke publicly. To my surprise, these experiences were much more rewarding and valuable than my classes were.

> In conclusion, every student should be able to decide for himself whether he desires more education or not. As one who wasn't academically strong in high school, I improved my grades in college and even surpassed my classmates. I also developed important skills outside of the classroom. Given all this, one could say that I am living proof why a student must have control over his own educational destiny.

Notice that the first sentence of the conclusion repeats the opinion restatement from the outline. All that is then needed are 2 or 3 more sentences to summarize the points in the two middle support passages. Try to end the conclusion with a strong statement declaring why you believe the way you do about the essay topic. Convince the ETS "qualified" readers that you are confident in your assertions. A strong argument equals a strong score. A weak argument equals a weak score.

To successfully write your own conclusion, ask yourself the following questions:

- Does the conclusion begin with the opinion restatement and gradually become more general?

- Does the conclusion summarize the details of the two middle supporting paragraphs?

- Does the conclusion end with a strong statement?

Now that you have seen an example of how to write a conclusion, try writing some on your own. Again, ETS doesn't care *what* you write, they only care *how* you write it.

Drill 4

Directions: Reread the following topics and write **conclusions** for each. Follow the guidelines for writing conclusions. Give yourself 5 minutes to write each conclusion. You may refer to the outlines, introductions, and main support paragraphs that you have already written.

Topic 1: Certain high schools require that students study foreign languages. Other schools let students study whatever subjects they like. Which of these two policies do you think a school should adopt? Give specific reasons and examples to support your opinion.

_____

_____

_____

_____

_____

_____

_____

_____

Topic 2:   There are many types of pollution in this
world. Pick one type of pollution and tell what you have
done to try to reduce it. Be sure to use specific
examples and details in your answer.

_____

_____

_____

_____

_____

_____

Topic 3:   In the past decades, computers have had a
tremendous affect on our society. Some experts state
that people are relying upon computers too much.
Others believe we should rely on computers even more.
Which of these two statements do you agree with? Give
specific reasons and examples to support your opinion.

_____

_____

_____

_____

_____

_____

_____

5. Checking Your Work

The last five minutes of the Written section of the TOEFL CBT should be spent rereading your essay to check for mistakes. Since many of you will be typing your essay, any errors can be corrected with a few simple clicks of the mouse. This is yet one more reason why you should type the essay rather than hand-write it. Look over our checklist to help find the most common essay errors.

Grammar

- ◆ Do the subject and verb agree in each sentence?
- ◆ Do the pronouns agree with what they refer to?
- ◆ Do you vary your sentence structure?

Spelling

- ◆ Are the plural words in the plural form?
- ◆ Have you confused your native language's spelling with the English spelling?

Punctuation

- ◆ Is there a period at the end of every sentence?
- ◆ Do commas separate items in a list?
- ◆ Does each sentence begin with a capital letter?
- ◆ Are proper names capitalized?

Diction (word choice)

- ◆ Are the nouns, adjectives, and adverbs in the correct form?
- ◆ Are your prepositions correct?
- ◆ Do any sentences begin with the word "and"? If so, eliminate and rewrite.

Making a Good Essay Better

Although you will become a better writer as you compose more essays, there are some basic tricks that can initially help you improve your essay.

Easy Verbs and Adjectives

Too often, students will continually repeat the same verbs and adjective over and over. In order to impress your ETS "qualified" reader and raise your score, try to replace such verbs as go, take, make, walk, tell, see, is, am, are, was, were, etc. with more descriptive words and phrases such as attend, run, grab, create, hurry, inform, and observe, to name just a few. Adjectives such as big, little, fast, fat, fun, ugly, beautiful can also be replaced by more descriptive adjectives such as enormous, minute, speedy, obese, exciting, hideous, gorgeous, etc. The English language is full of descriptive vocabulary. Use as many as possible.

Modifiers

A modifier is any word that gives additional information to another word. Every verb and adjective can be modified by an adverb. Likewise, every noun can be modified by an adjective. A boring *subject + verb + object* sentence can be made more exciting by adding some modifiers.

Linking Words

Linking words help essays flow. They connect each paragraph and sentence with the next one. Ideas blend together and make the essay more cohesive. Some common linking words that should be practiced are:

as far as I'm concerned	however
in my opinion	for the most part
to be honest	for instance
to my surprise	for example
fortunately	what's more
unfortunately	furthermore
personally	on the contrary
I believe	nevertheless
definitely	moreover
by all means	in addition
apparently	in conclusion
perhaps	in fact
clearly	in that case
frankly	lastly
honestly	moreover
generally speaking	on the contrary
at first	on the whole
finally	even though

Keep these linking words in mind while writing your essay as well as while checking it. Paragraphs and sentences that flow together will absolutely increase your score.

For example, take a sentence from the example essay on higher education.

I was president of my class.

To make this sentence more interesting, first change the verb.

I was selected as president of my class.

Now add some modifiers

I was randomly selected as president of my freshman class.

Now add some linking words

Fortunately, I was randomly selected as president of my freshman class.

The original sentence has drastically improved. It has become longer, more developed, more interesting and informative, and much more "essay" friendly.

Drill 5

Directions: Practice changing verbs, adding modifiers, and adding linking words to the following sentences. Because there is no one correct answer, practice rewriting each sentence using different verbs, modifiers, and linking words.

It is important to concentrate while studying.

_____

_____

_____

_____

_____

_____

The professor went to the cafeteria, but it was closed.

_____

_____

_____

_____

_____

_____

Some of the classed were cancelled, but the student went anyway.

_____

_____

_____

_____

_____

_____

A computer is a tool that helps students improve their grades.

_____

_____

_____

_____

_____

_____

Supervisors get their employees by putting advertisements in the newspaper.

_____

_____

_____

_____

_____

_____

In order to go to college, a student must take a special exam.

_____

_____

_____

_____

_____

Two people share a room on most college campuses.

_____

_____

_____

_____

_____

New students have many problems when they go to college.

_____

_____

_____

_____

_____

TOEFL CBT Practice Topics

Directions: For the following topics, use what you have learned to demonstrate your ability to write in English. Give yourself 30 minutes to complete each essay. If possible, practice on a computer. If you don't have access to a computer, write legibly by hand on the lines provided.

Essay Topic #1

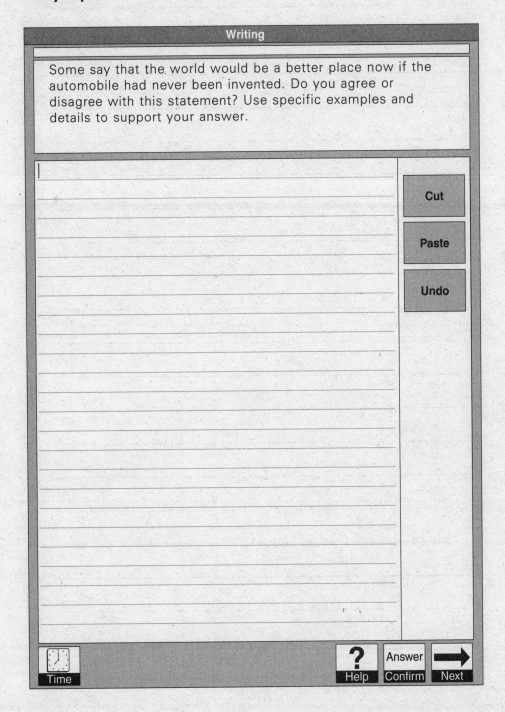

Essay Topic #2

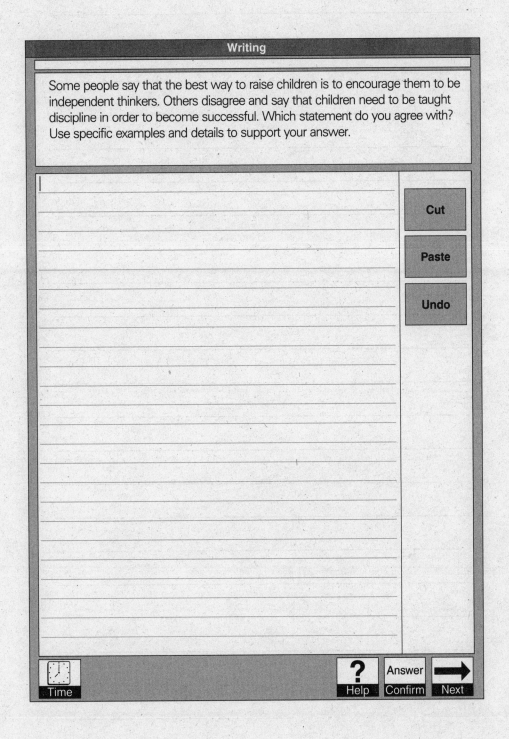

Writing

Some people say that the best way to raise children is to encourage them to be independent thinkers. Others disagree and say that children need to be taught discipline in order to become successful. Which statement do you agree with? Use specific examples and details to support your answer.

Cut

Paste

Undo

Time

? Help

Answer Confirm

→ Next

Essay Topic #3

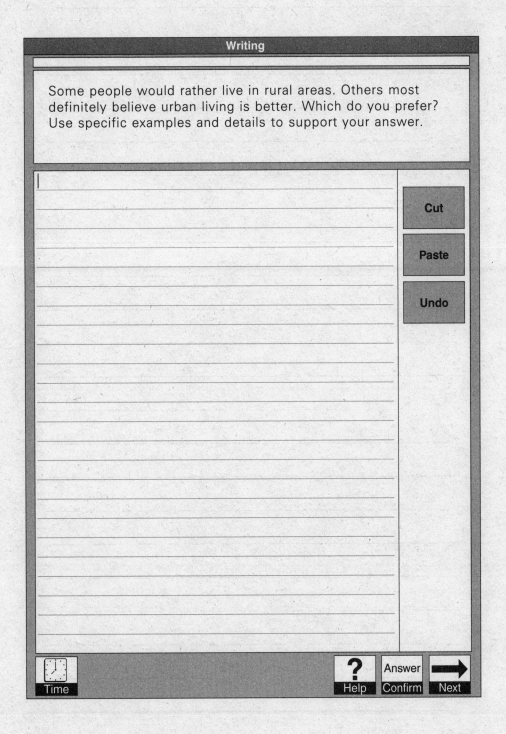

Essay Topic #4

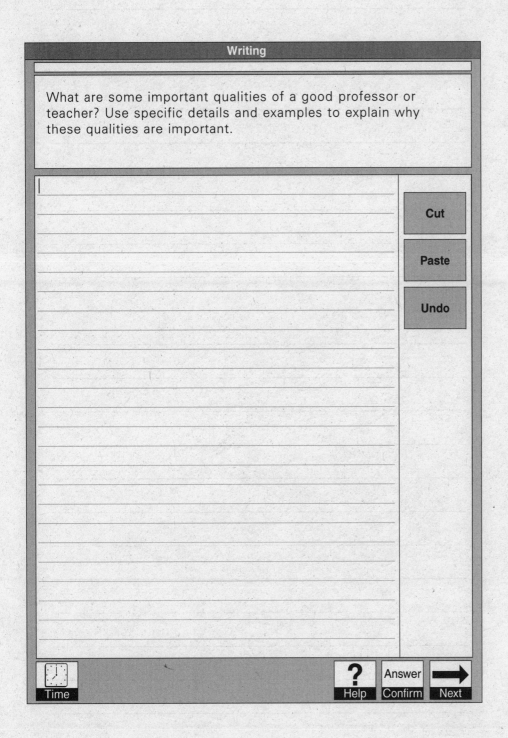

Essay Topic #5

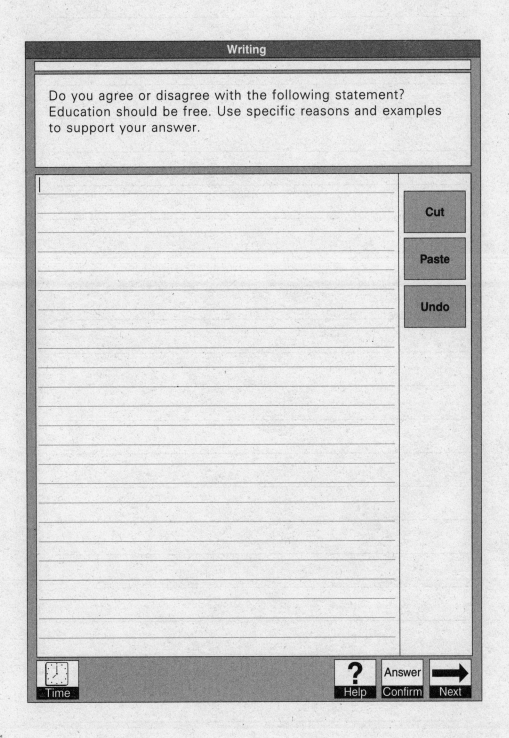

Writing

Do you agree or disagree with the following statement?
Education should be free. Use specific reasons and examples
to support your answer.

Cut

Paste

Undo

Time

? Help

Answer Confirm

Next

PART ◆ VI

Getting Ready to Take the Test

HOW TO TAKE THE PRINCETON REVIEW TOEFL CBT DIAGNOSTIC

You should take the diagnostic exam that comes with this book once you have finished reading the techniques, completing the drills and exercises, and learning the vocabulary. Make sure to review all of the test-taking tips in this book before you sit down to take the test.

When taking the diagnostic exam, your goal should be to approximate actual test conditions as closely as possible. Because the diagnostic exam is a paper version of the TOEFL CBT, it is impossible for you to point and click a mouse. Therefore, use a pen or pencil to circle the correct answer. To help better prepare yourself, practice clicking on the "Next" and "Answer Confirm" icons by circling them with your pen or pencil. Remember, once you click on the "Answer Confirm" icon, you will never see that question again. Therefore, answer the questions in the order they appear, and do NOT change an answer once you have circled the "Answer Confirm" icon. To take The Princeton Review diagnostic test, you will need:

- A quiet room
- A compact-disc player (preferably a Walkman or CD player that requires headphones)
- A pen or a pencil
- A watch
- Approximately three hours and fifteen minutes of uninterrupted time.

When you are ready to begin, remember the following:

1. Adjust the volume on your compact-disc player before the actual questions begin.

2. Use only the amount of time actually allotted for each section.

3. Take the entire test in one sitting.

4. Circle your answer choices (since you will be unable to "click" on them as on the actual TOEFL CBT). Remember to also circle the "Next" and "Answer Confirm" icons in the Listening and Structure sections.

5. Do not score the test until you have read the next couple of pages and until you have at least an hour to spend examining your results.

EVALUATING YOUR PERFORMANCE

Use the answer key that appears after the test to determine your score. Make sure to correct and study your performance carefully. Try to do it within twenty-four hours of taking the test, or you'll have a hard time remembering why you chose one answer over another. When looking at your performance on the diagnostic, don't just settle for counting up the number of wrong and right answers and looking up the vocabulary words you didn't know. Pay special attention to all of the following:

1. "STUPID" MISTAKES

We use the term *stupid mistakes* to refer to the mistakes you make on questions you *know* you should have been able to answer correctly. In other words, if the correct answer seems obvious now and you can't understand why you chose the answer you did, and you find yourself saying, "Wow, that was really stupid of me," you've run across a "stupid" mistake.

Interestingly enough, you'll find that "stupid" mistakes usually aren't stupid at all; they're more often due to simple *carelessness*, and they usually happen for one of two reasons:

> **Reason 1:** *Impatience.* "Haste makes waste," the saying in English goes—you probably have a similar saying in your native language. You'll probably find that you got some questions wrong because you didn't bother to read through all of the answer choices before choosing your answer.

> **Reason 2:** *Misunderstanding the question.* Sometimes even native speakers have to read a question two or three times before understanding what the question is actually asking. Why should *you* expect understand everything the first time you read it? Many students get questions wrong just because they are answering the wrong question.

Once you figure out the real cause for any "stupid" mistakes, you know what you need to pay particular attention to the next time you take a test.

2. "LUCKY" GUESSES

Sometimes the only thing more surprising than mysterious wrong answers (such as the stupid mistakes discussed above) are all those questions you answer correctly and are not sure *why*. Most students tend to attribute these right answers to plain, old-fashioned good luck. That may be true for some of them. After all, if you guess on four questions, the odds are you will get one of them right and the other three wrong. However, that probably doesn't explain all of the questions you answer correctly, even though you didn't think you knew the answer. Chances are you were using the test-taking strategies from this book without even realizing it, the most important of which is POE.

The best way to recognize questions on which you used POE effectively is to look for questions you answered correctly to which you did not "know" the answer. For these questions try to remember the reasons you chose the answers you did, and the next time you take a test, you can use those reasons to help you answer even more questions.

3. Other "Wrong" Answers

Some wrong answers are due to carelessness, but some can be attributed to information you just didn't know or remember. When you look over your test, make sure that the wrong answer you chose isn't one you could have eliminated using POE. Did you pick a silly answer in the Listening section just because you missed the statement? Did you choose an answer with poor syntax in the Grammar section? Try to discover if you could have eliminated an answer or two before guessing.

4. Pacing Problems

To determine if you had problems with time, ask yourself the following questions:

- Were you unable to finish any of the sections?

If so, then you probably spent too much time answering one question. ETS gives you plenty of time on the TOEFL CBT, but don't linger over questions. Choose and move on.

- Did you run out of time before getting to the last passage on the Reading section?

If so, you may have spent too much time on a couple of questions. Remember, don't get bogged down on any one question! Skip the third-pass questions, and save them for last. Use chronology to find the information you need and use POE to eliminate any answer choices.

WHAT SHOULD YOU DO NOW?

If you have some time before you are scheduled to take the actual TOEFL CBT, you can use the results of your diagnostic test to help decide if you need any additional preparation. You can order a CD-ROM from ETS with a form provided in the TOEFL CBT Bulletin. Just make sure you leave plenty of time for the materials to arrive.

We do not recommend any test materials published by anyone other than ETS. Many of the examples in non-ETS publications contain problems that are poorly written or that just don't appear on real TOEFL CBT exams, leading you to waste time studying things that won't help you on the test. Try to schedule your use of the materials so that you have a full-length TOEFL CBT exam (either ours or ETS's) to take sometime in the week before the test.

THE WEEK BEFORE THE TEST

Here's a list of *dos* and *don'ts* for the week before the test:

- *Don't* try to learn any new material the week before the TOEFL CBT. You can't learn much vocabulary or grammar in that amount of time. You're better off practicing the test-taking tips.

- *Do* make sure you know exactly how to get to your test center. You don't want to be late, or feel rushed to get there. Getting lost is one way to really hurt your self-confidence on a day when you need to remain calm and in control. Take a practice trip to the test site so you can see how long it takes.

- *Don't* study at all on the day before the test. The most helpful thing you can do is relax; at most, maybe see a movie or watch television, in English if you can, and go to sleep early.

- *Do* make sure you have read, well in advance, everything that you need to take with you to the test.

By the time the actual test day rolls around, you won't be worrying about any minor details, and you'll be able to focus completely on the test.

THE DAY OF THE TEST

Wake up a little earlier than you have to. Give yourself time to eat a light breakfast and try to make time to do some "warm-up" questions of each type. Then make sure you have the following items with you before you leave for the test:

- Identification: Check your TOEFL CBT Bulletin for a list of acceptable forms of identification.

- Your confirmation number.

- Names of institutions to which you want your scores to be sent.

- A TOEFL CBT Voucher, if you have one.

- A positive attitude.

When you're finished, go home and forget about the TOEFL CBT. It takes about 15 days for your scores to arrive. (Remember, your 30-minute essay needs grading!) You can wait with confidence because you've mastered a skill that won't help you anywhere else in your life, the skill of taking the TOEFL CBT. Won't it be nice to forget it?

PART ◆ VII

The Princeton Review
TOEFL CBT Diagnostic
Exam

Listening

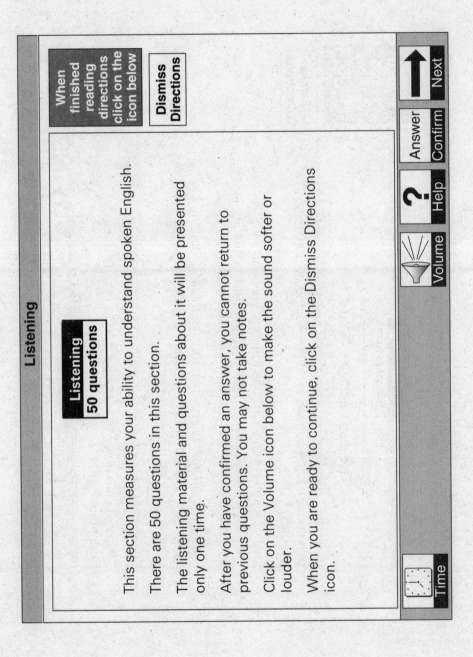

Listening
50 questions

This section measures your ability to understand spoken English.

There are 50 questions in this section.

The listening material and questions about it will be presented only one time.

After you have confirmed an answer, you cannot return to previous questions. You may not take notes.

Click on the Volume icon below to make the sound softer or louder.

When you are ready to continue, click on the Dismiss Directions icon.

When finished reading directions click on the icon below

Dismiss Directions

Volume   Help   Confirm   Next
Answer

Time

You may only take 60 minutes to answer the following 50 questions. Do not take more than 60 minutes to complete this section.

Listening

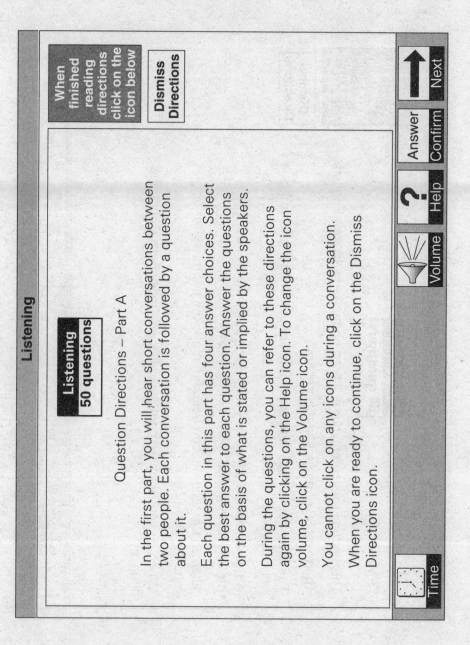

Listening

**Listening
50 questions**

Question Directions – Part A

In the first part, you will hear short conversations between two people. Each conversation is followed by a question about it.

Each question in this part has four answer choices. Select the best answer to each question. Answer the questions on the basis of what is stated or implied by the speakers.

During the questions, you can refer to these directions again by clicking on the Help icon. To change the icon volume, click on the Volume icon.

You cannot click on any icons during a conversation.

When you are ready to continue, click on the Dismiss Directions icon.

When finished reading directions click on the icon below

**Dismiss
Directions**

Volume

? Help

Answer Confirm

↑ Next

Time

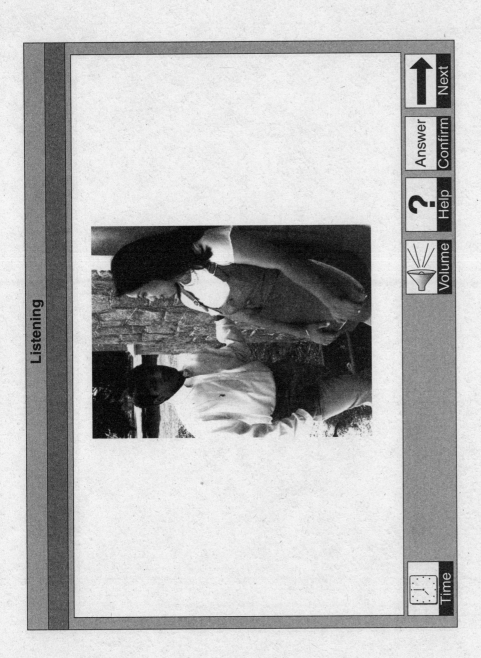

Listening

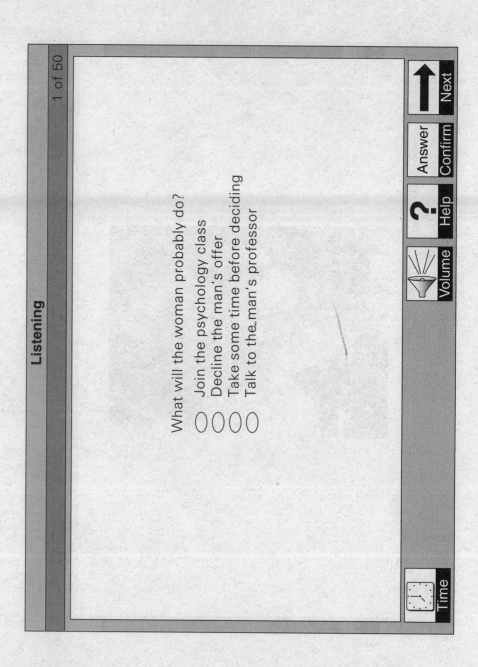

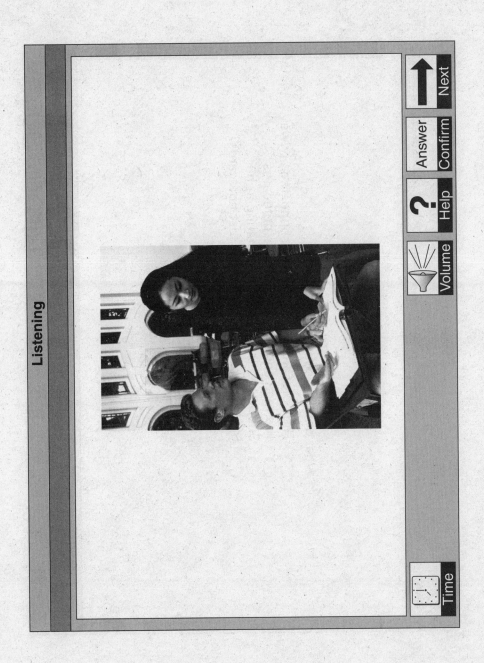

Listening

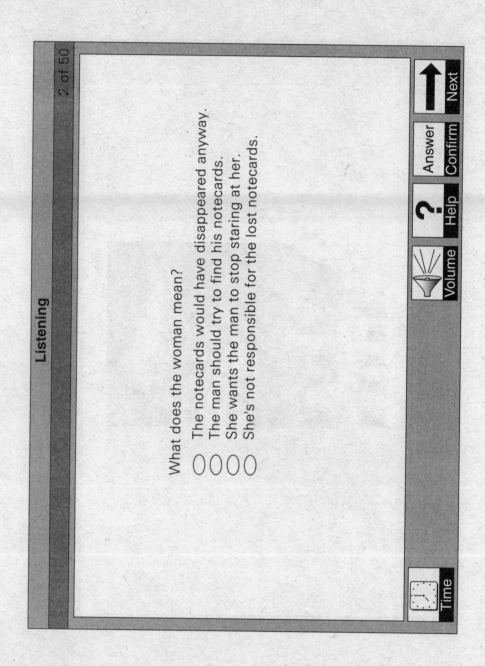

What does the woman mean?

○ The notecards would have disappeared anyway.
○ The man should try to find his notecards.
○ She wants the man to stop staring at her.
○ She's not responsible for the lost notecards.

Volume   Help   Answer Confirm   Next

Time

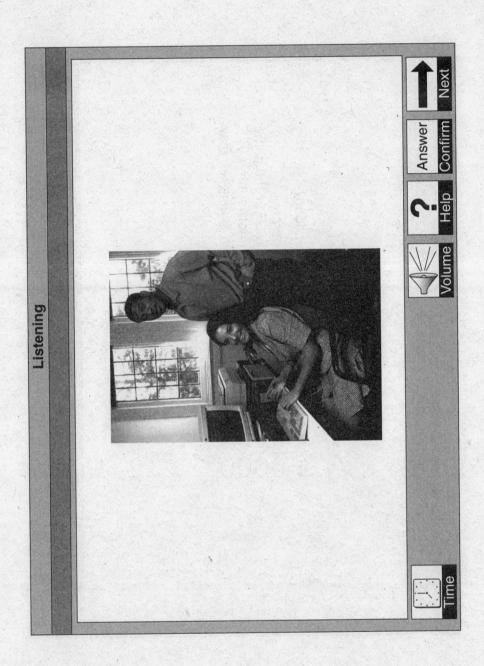

Listening

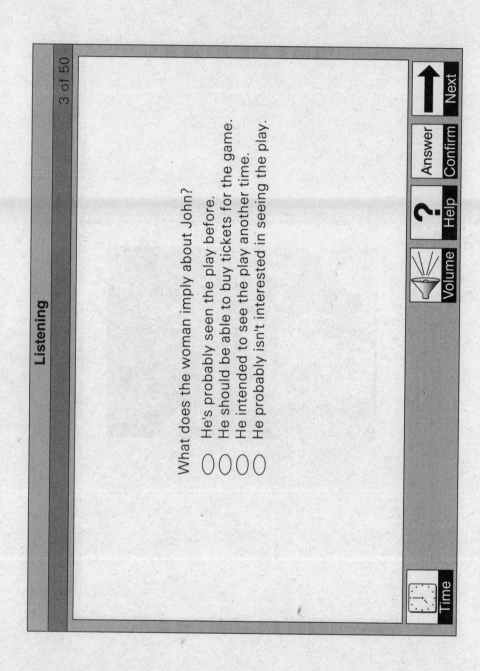

What does the woman imply about John?

He's probably seen the play before.
He should be able to buy tickets for the game.
He intended to see the play another time.
He probably isn't interested in seeing the play.

○ ○ ○ ○

Volume   Help   Answer   Next
          ?   Confirm

Time

Listening

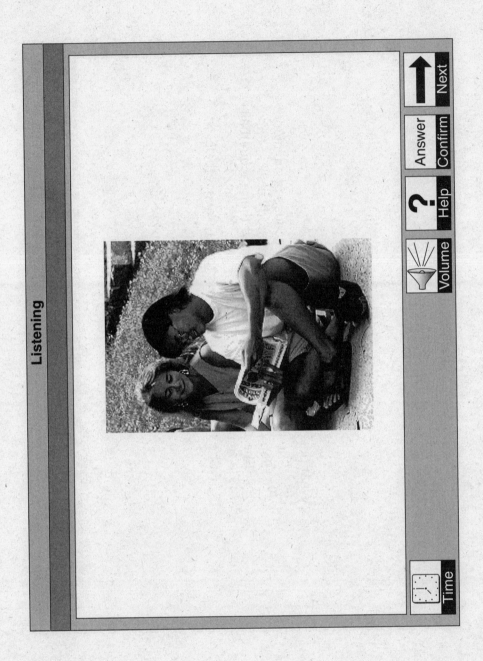

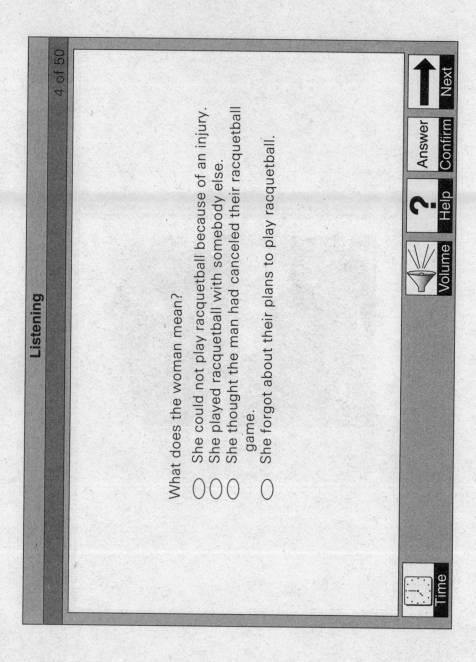

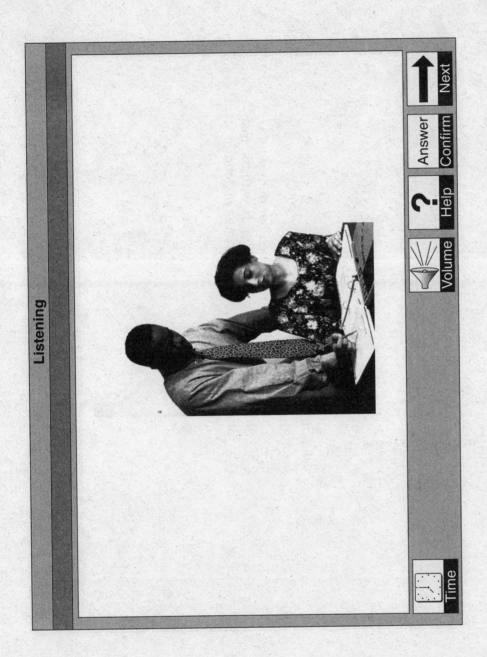

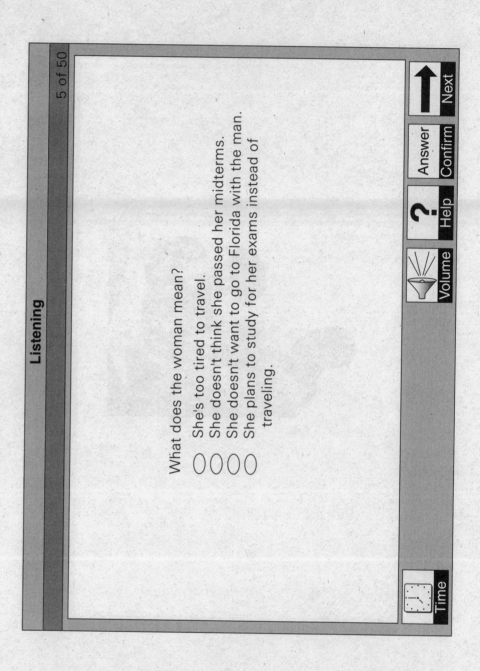

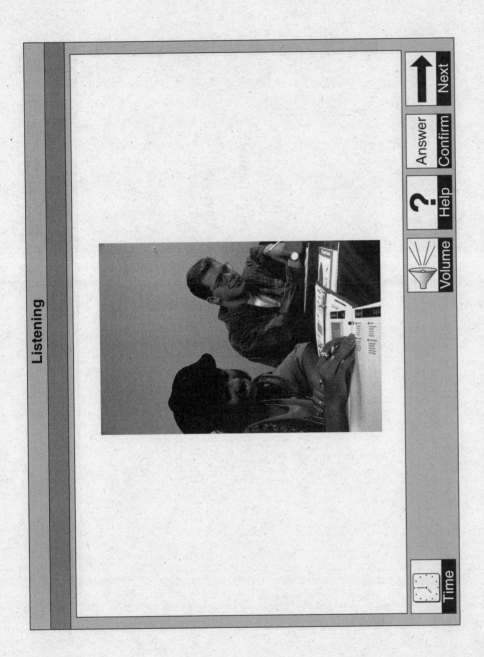

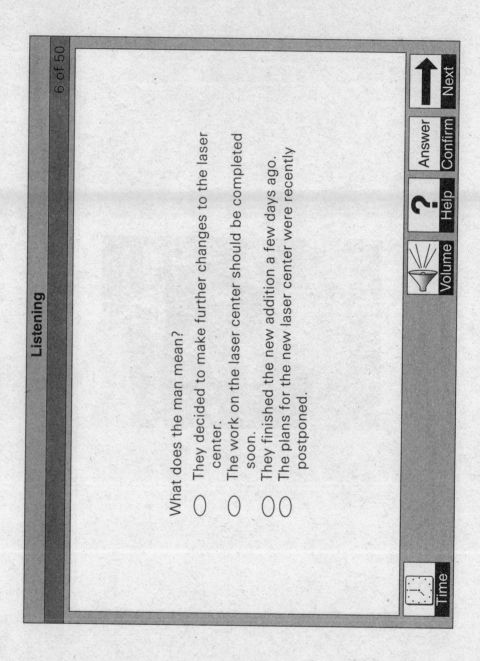

What does the man mean?

○ They decided to make further changes to the laser center.

○ The work on the laser center should be completed soon.

○ They finished the new addition a few days ago.

○ The plans for the new laser center were recently postponed.

Volume   Help   Answer   Confirm   Next

Time

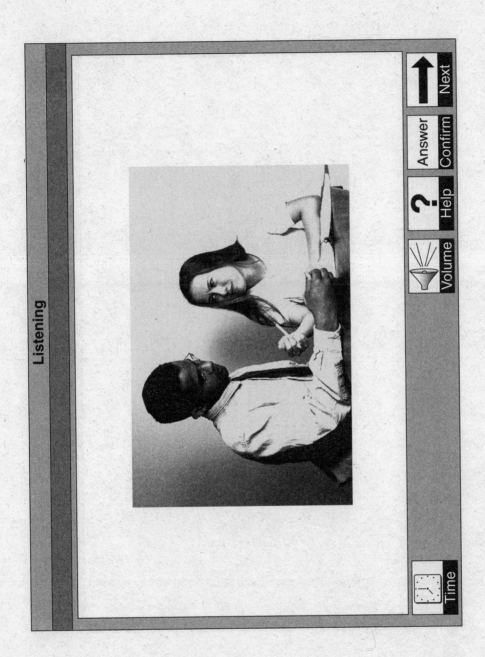

Listening

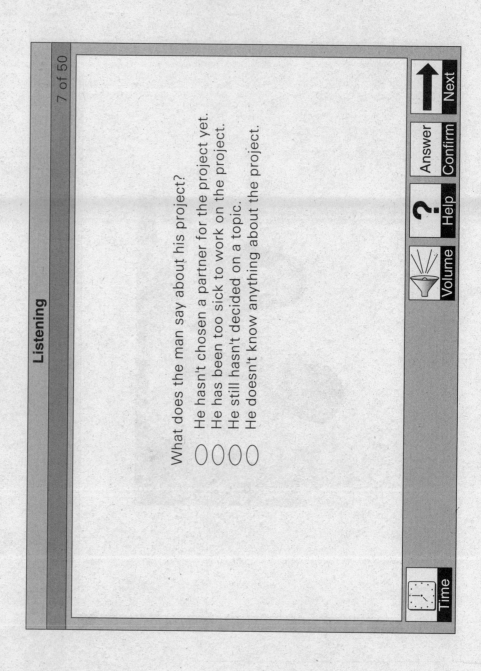

What does the man say about his project?

He hasn't chosen a partner for the project yet.
He has been too sick to work on the project.
He still hasn't decided on a topic.
He doesn't know anything about the project.

○ ○ ○ ○

Volume   Help   Answer / Confirm   Next

Time

Listening

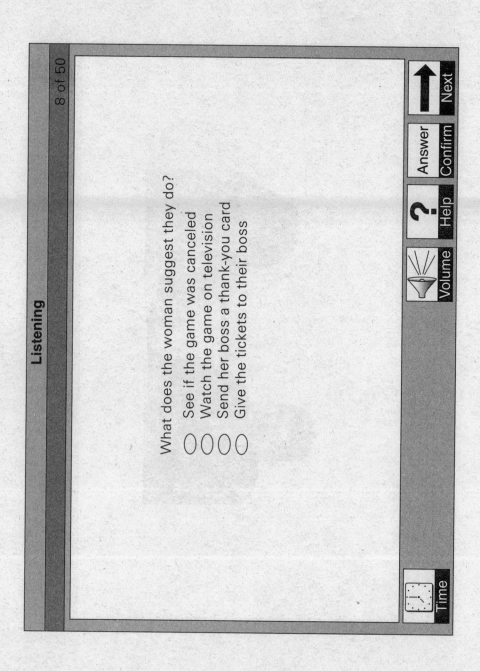

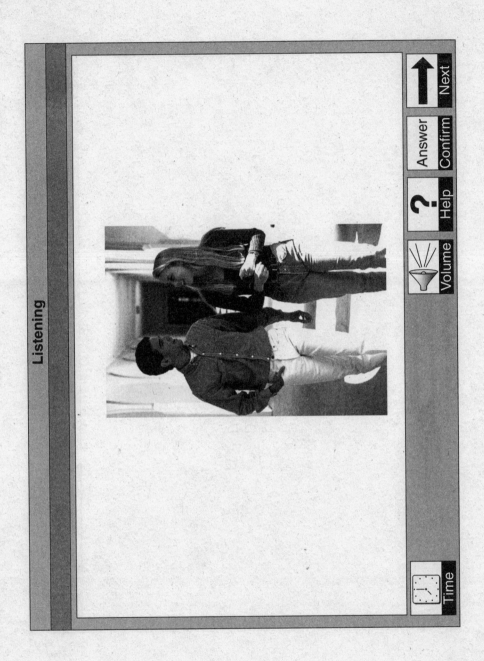

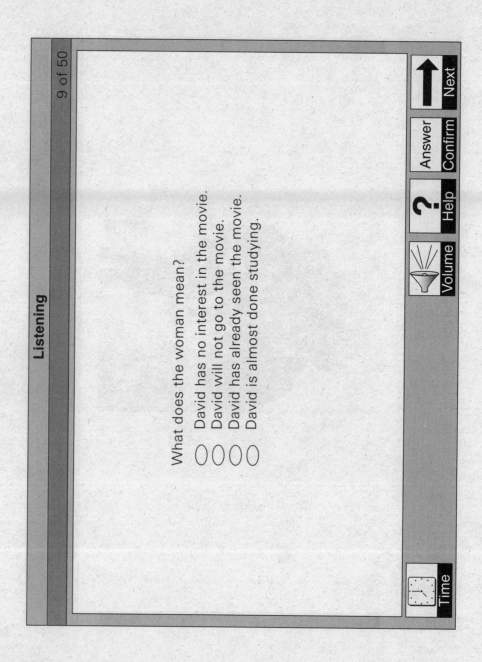

Listening

9 of 50

What does the woman mean?

○ David has no interest in the movie.
○ David will not go to the movie.
○ David has already seen the movie.
○ David is almost done studying.

Volume   Help   Answer   Next
         ?   Confirm
Time

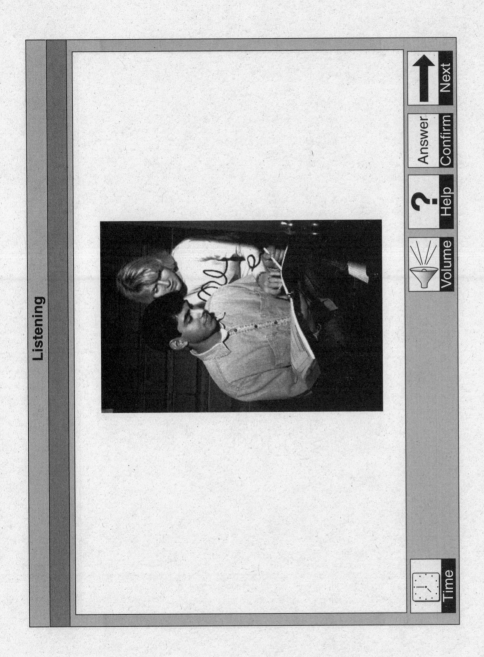

Listening

What does the man mean?

○ He would prefer to take a taxi.
○ The bus rates were recently raised.
○ The bus frequently comes late.
○ Taxis are cheaper than buses.

Volume   Help   Answer Confirm   Next

Time

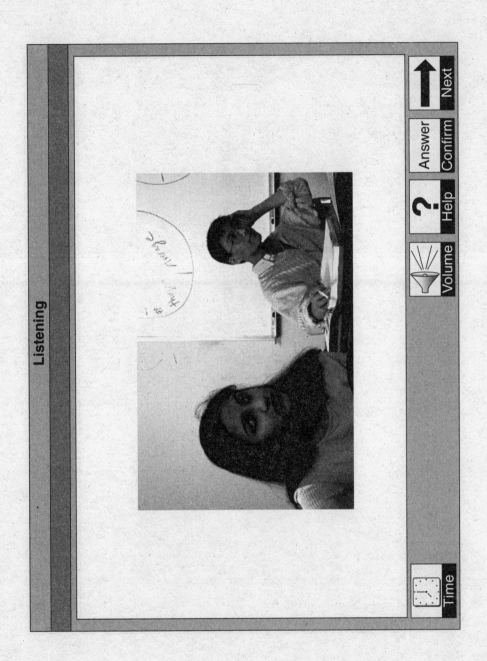

Listening

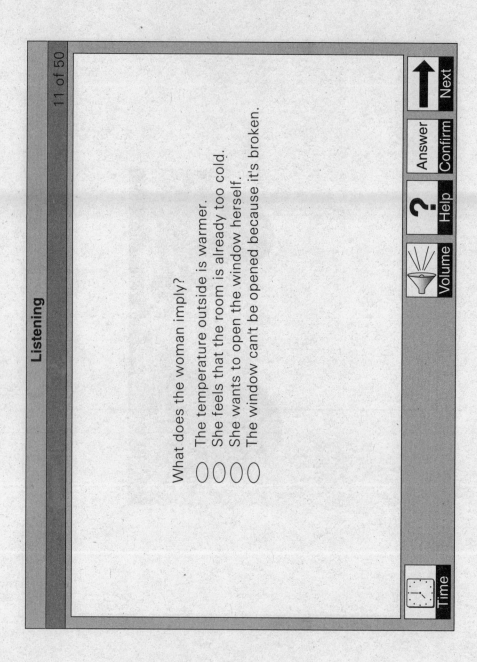

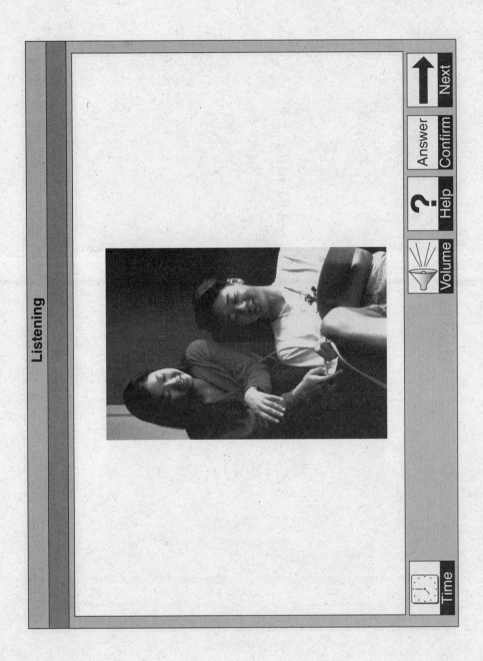

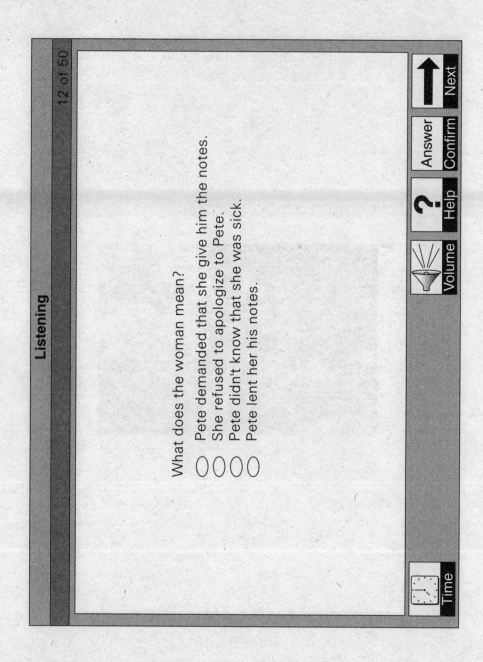

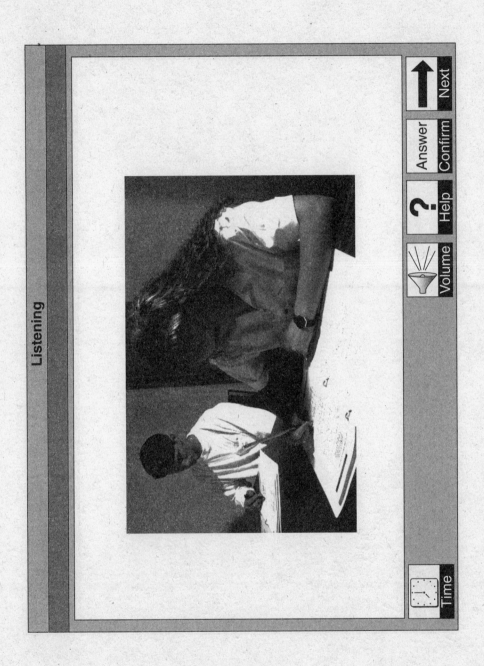

Listening

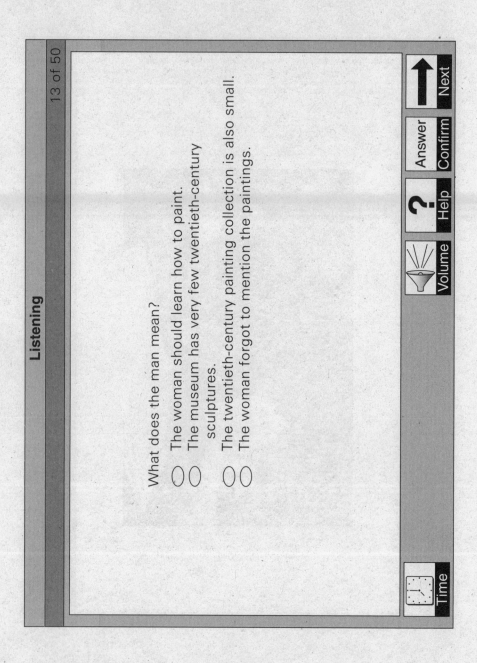

What does the man mean?

- The woman should learn how to paint.
- The museum has very few twentieth-century sculptures.
- The twentieth-century painting collection is also small.
- The woman forgot to mention the paintings.

Volume Help Answer Confirm Next

Time

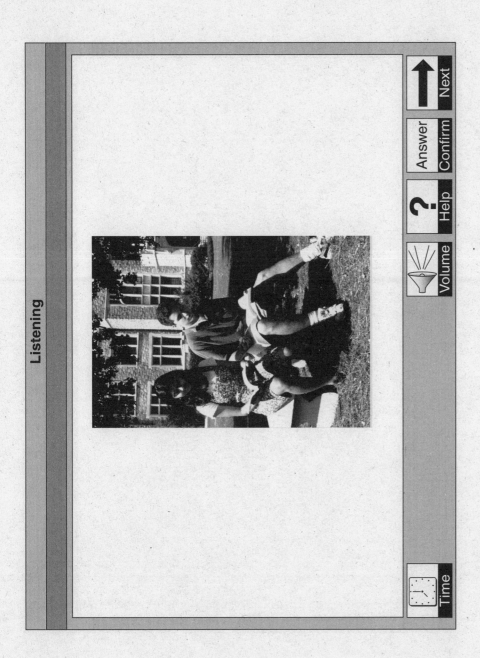

Listening

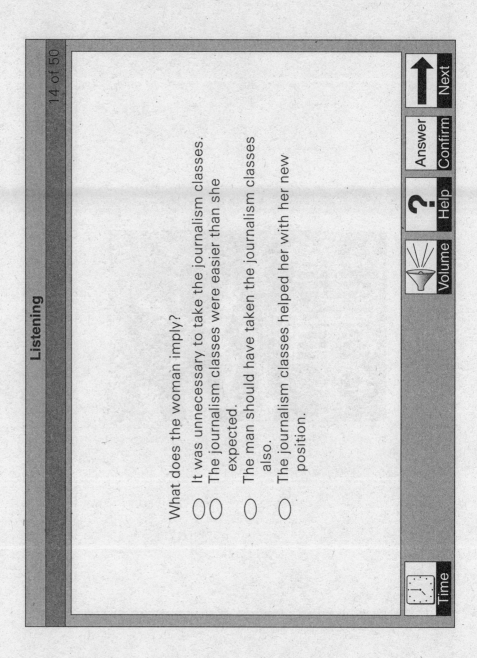

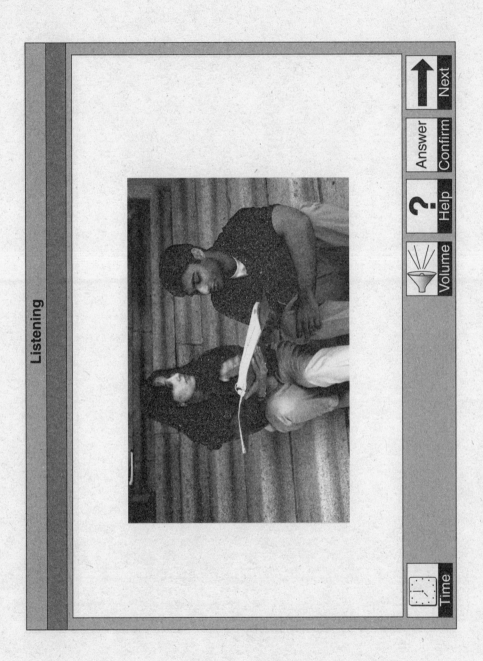

Listening

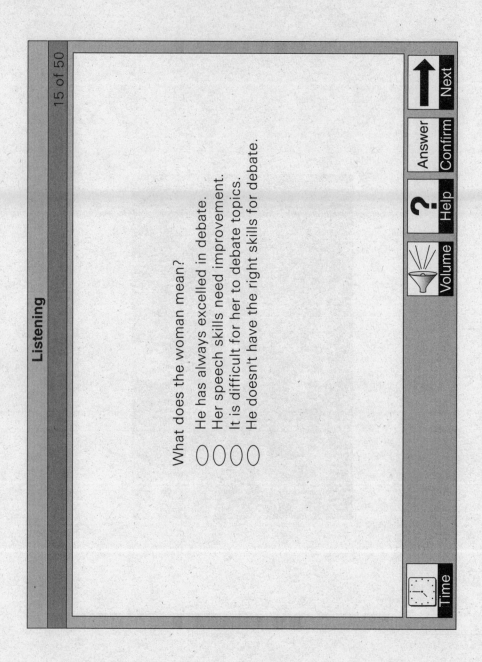

Listening

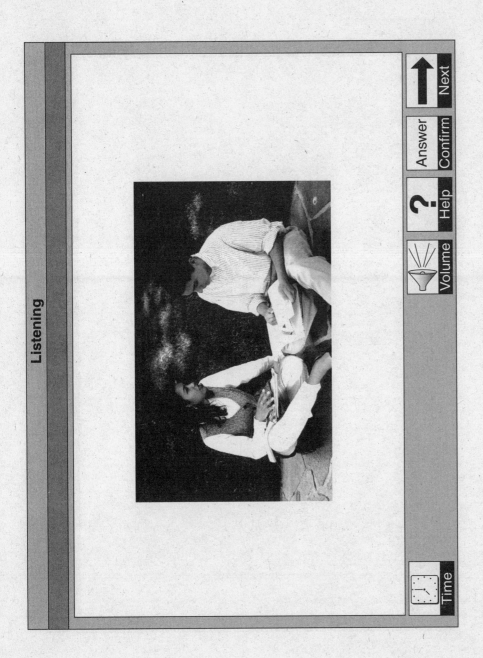

Listening

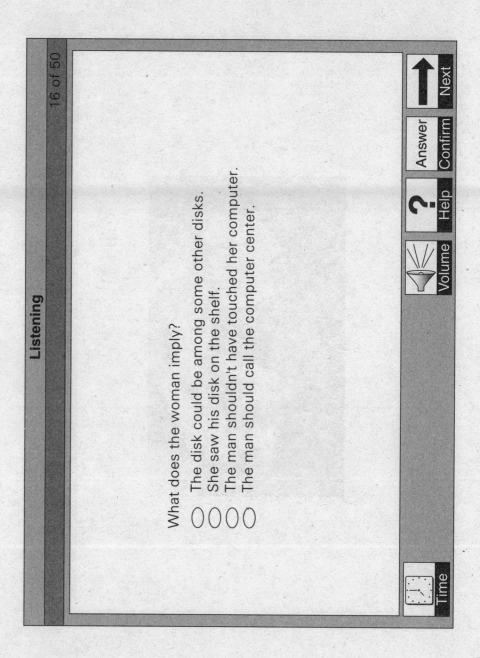

What does the woman imply?

○ The disk could be among some other disks.
○ She saw his disk on the shelf.
○ The man shouldn't have touched her computer.
○ The man should call the computer center.

Volume Help Answer Confirm Next

Time

Listening

Question Directions – Part B

In this part, there are several talks and conversations. Each talk or conversation is followed by several questions.

The conversations and talks are about a variety of topics. You do not need special knowledge of the topics to answer the questions correctly. Rather, you should answer each question on the basis of what is stated or implied by the speakers in the conversation or talk.

During the questions, you can refer to these directions again by clicking on the Help icon. To change the volume, click on the Volume icon.

You cannot click on any icons during a talk or conversation.

When you are ready to continue, click on the Dismiss Directions icon.

When finished reading directions click on the icon below

Dismiss Directions

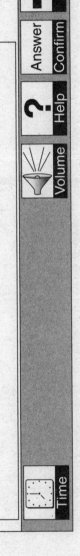

Time

Volume

? Help

Answer Confirm

Next

Listening

Listening

Business

Volume | Help | Answer Confirm | Next

Time

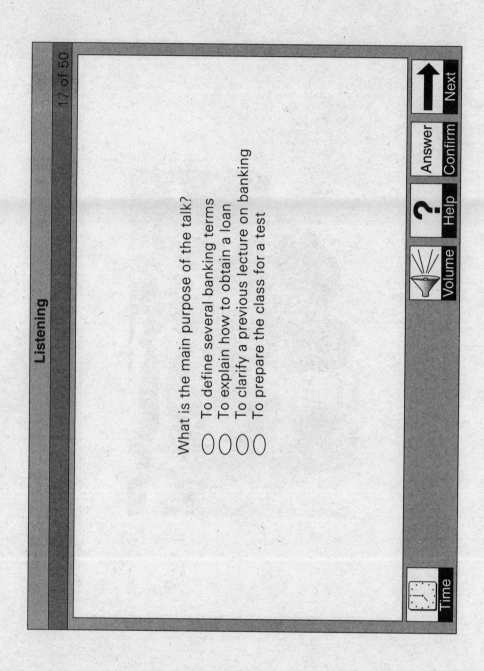

Listening

17 of 50

What is the main purpose of the talk?

○ To define several banking terms
○ To explain how to obtain a loan
○ To clarify a previous lecture on banking
○ To prepare the class for a test

Volume   Help   Answer   Next
                  Confirm

Time

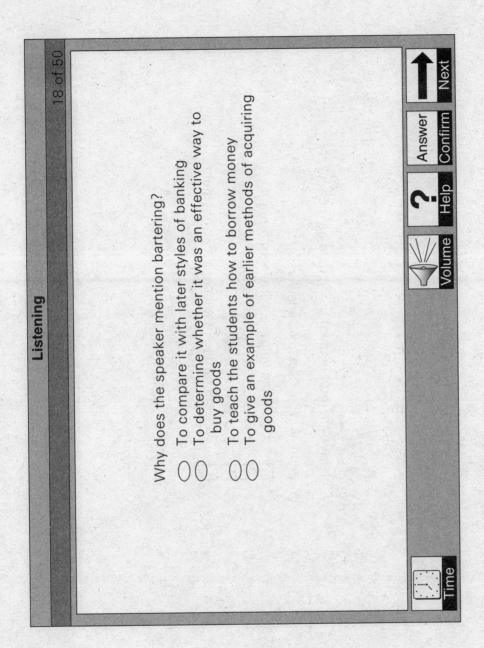

Why does the speaker mention bartering?

To compare it with later styles of banking
To determine whether it was an effective way to
buy goods
To teach the students how to borrow money
To give an example of earlier methods of acquiring
goods

Volume

? Help

Answer Confirm

Next

Time

Listening

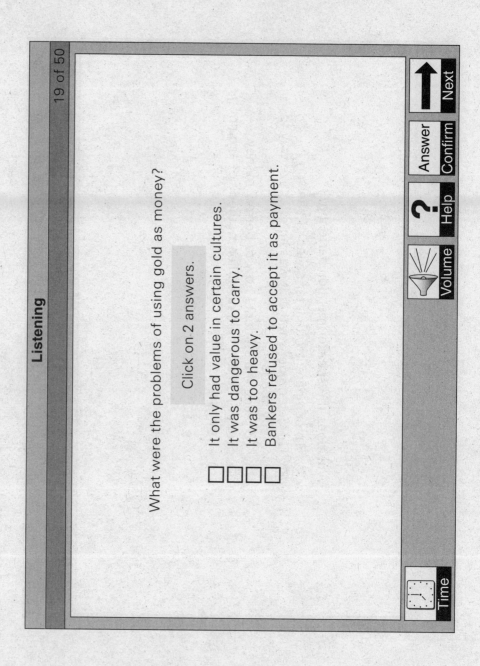

What were the problems of using gold as money?

Click on 2 answers.

It only had value in certain cultures.
It was dangerous to carry.
It was too heavy.
Bankers refused to accept it as payment.

☐ ☐ ☐ ☐

Volume   Help   Answer Confirm   Next

Time

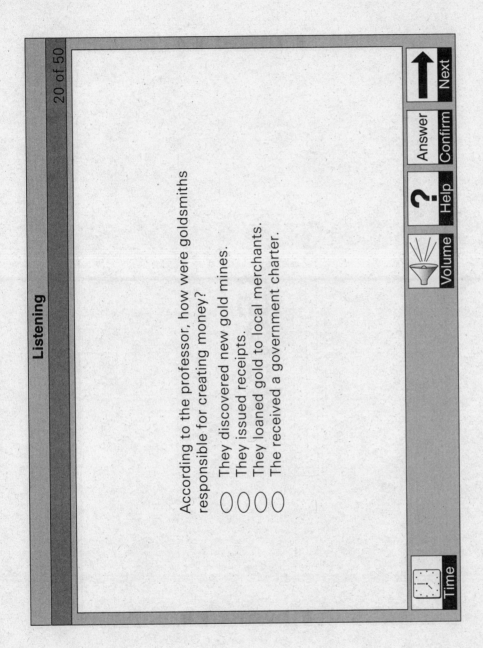

According to the professor, how were goldsmiths responsible for creating money?

○ They discovered new gold mines.
○ They issued receipts.
○ They loaned gold to local merchants.
○ The received a government charter.

Volume

? Help

Answer
Confirm

↑ Next

Time

Listening

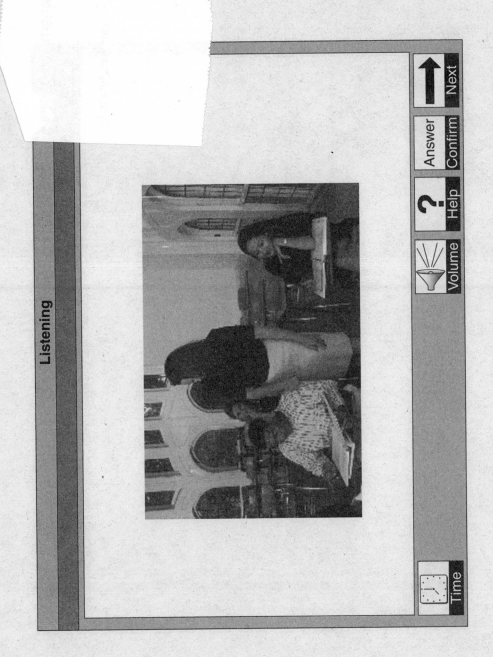

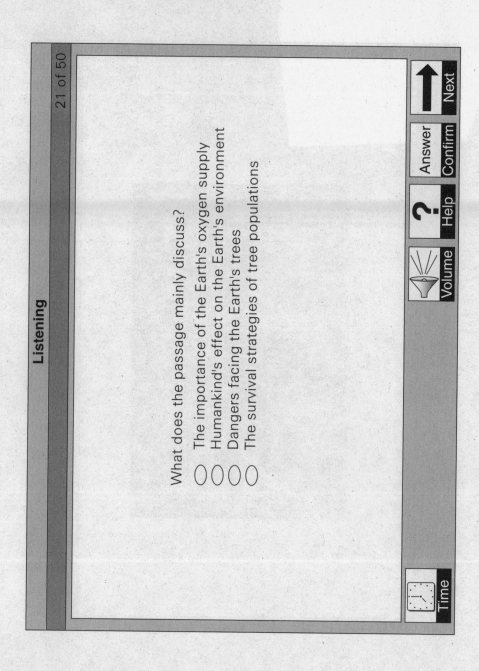

What does the passage mainly discuss?

○ The importance of the Earth's oxygen supply
○ Humankind's effect on the Earth's environment
○ Dangers facing the Earth's trees
○ The survival strategies of tree populations

Volume | Help | Answer | Next
| ? | Confirm |

Time

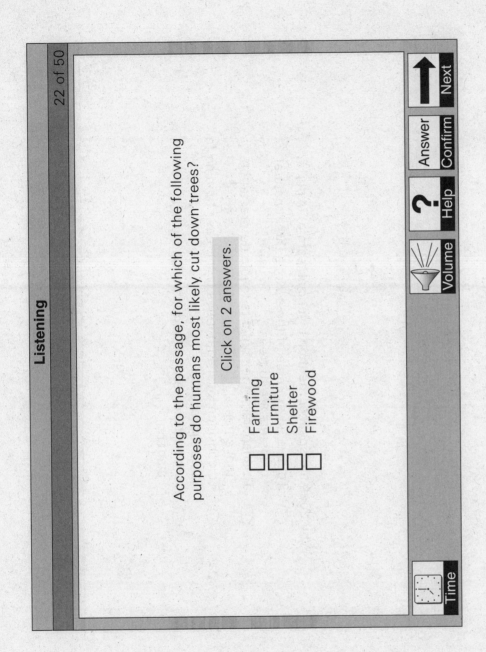

Listening

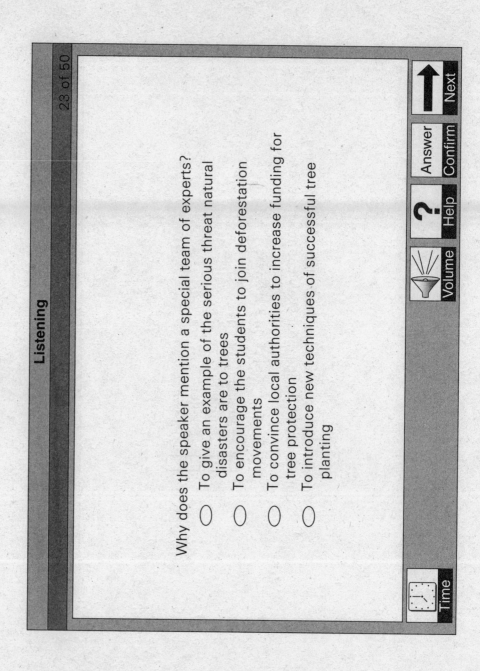

23 of 50

Why does the speaker mention a special team of experts?

○ To give an example of the serious threat natural disasters are to trees

○ To encourage the students to join deforestation movements

○ To convince local authorities to increase funding for tree protection

○ To introduce new techniques of successful tree planting

Volume   Help   Answer Confirm   Next

Time

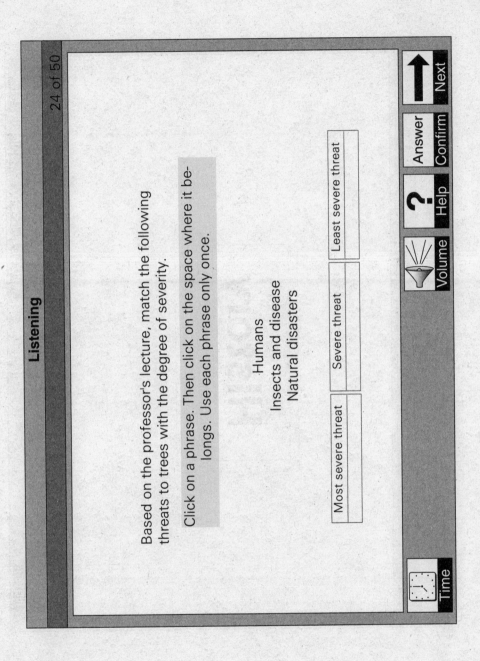

Listening

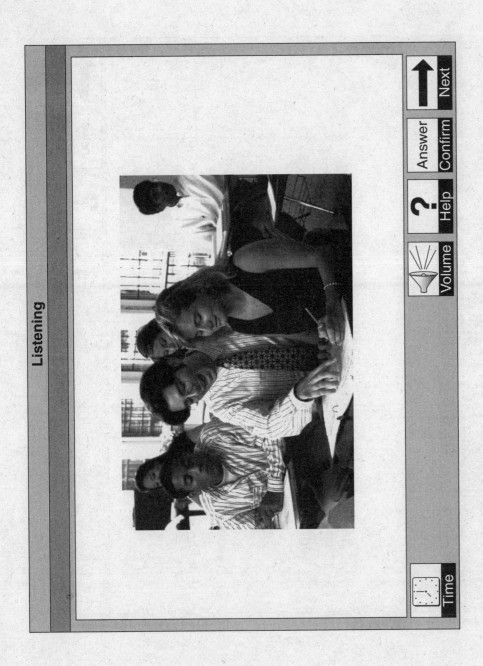

Listening

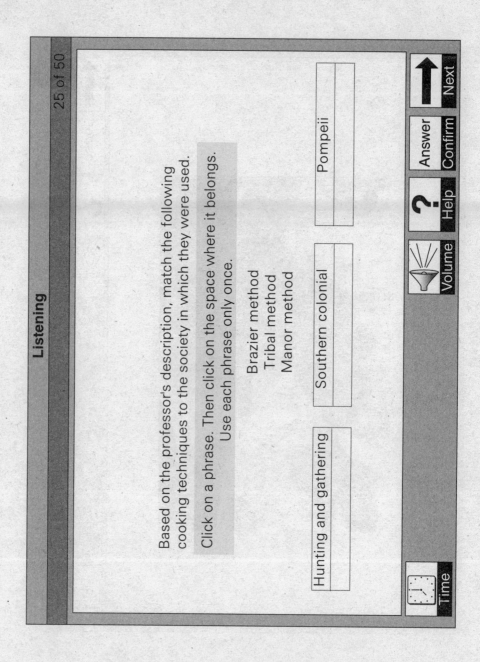

Based on the professor's description, match the following cooking techniques to the society in which they were used.

Click on a phrase. Then click on the space where it belongs. Use each phrase only once.

Brazier method
Tribal method
Manor method

Hunting and gathering

Southern colonial

Pompeii

Volume   Help   Answer
          Confirm   Next

Time

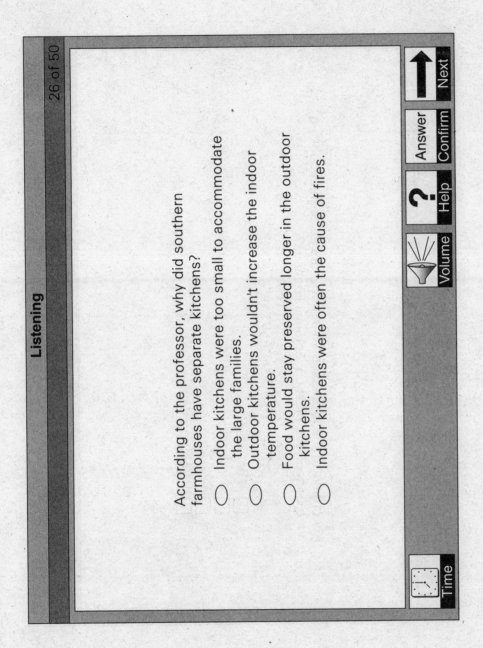

According to the professor, why did southern farmhouses have separate kitchens?

○ Indoor kitchens were too small to accommodate the large families.

○ Outdoor kitchens wouldn't increase the indoor temperature.

○ Food would stay preserved longer in the outdoor kitchens.

○ Indoor kitchens were often the cause of fires.

Volume   Help   Answer

?

Confirm   Next

Time

Listening

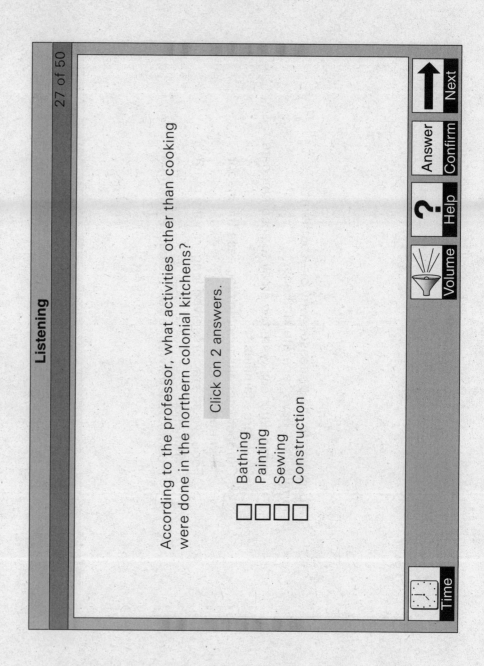

According to the professor, what activities other than cooking were done in the northern colonial kitchens?

Click on 2 answers.

☐ Bathing
☐ Painting
☐ Sewing
☐ Construction

Volume | Help | Answer Confirm | Next

Time

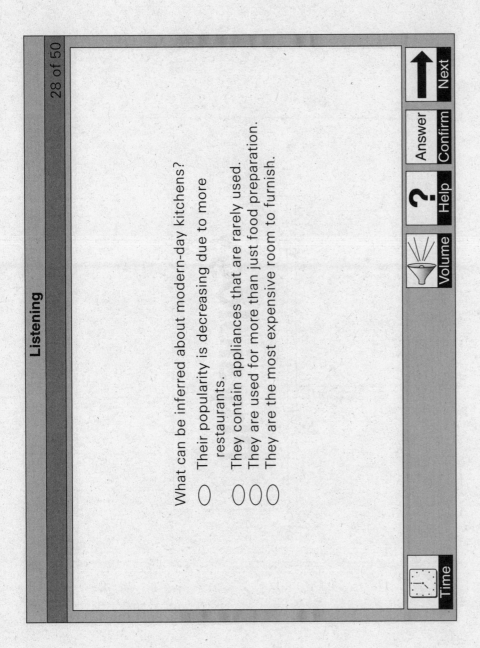

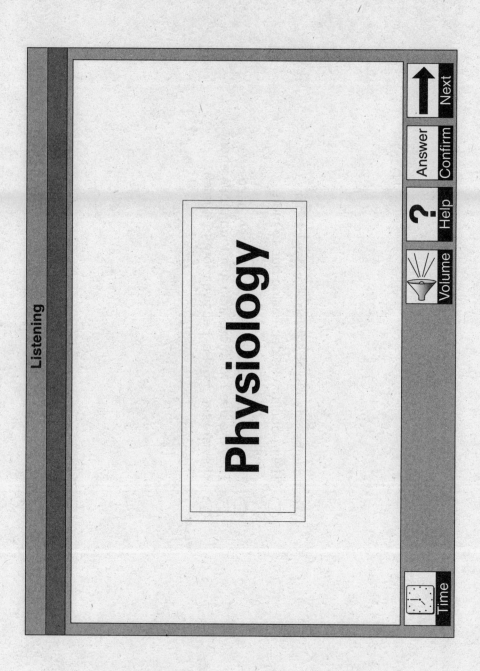

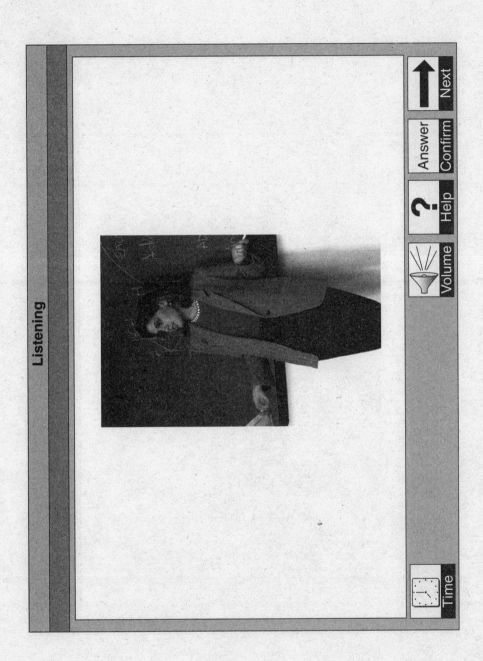

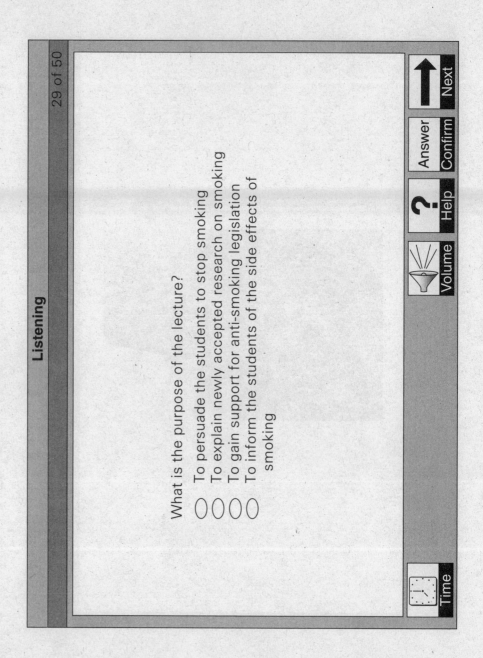

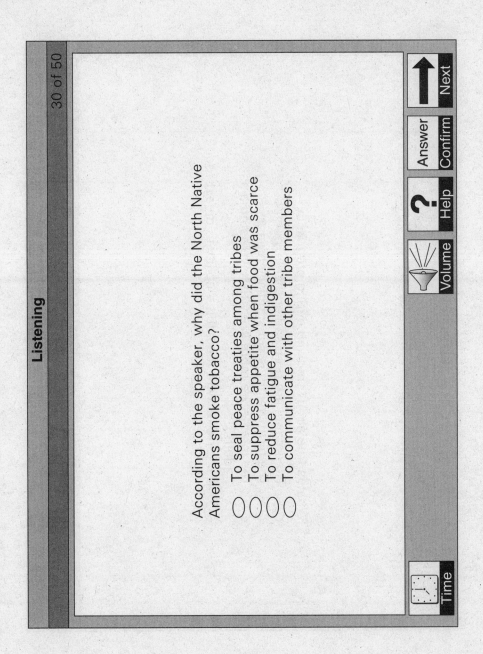

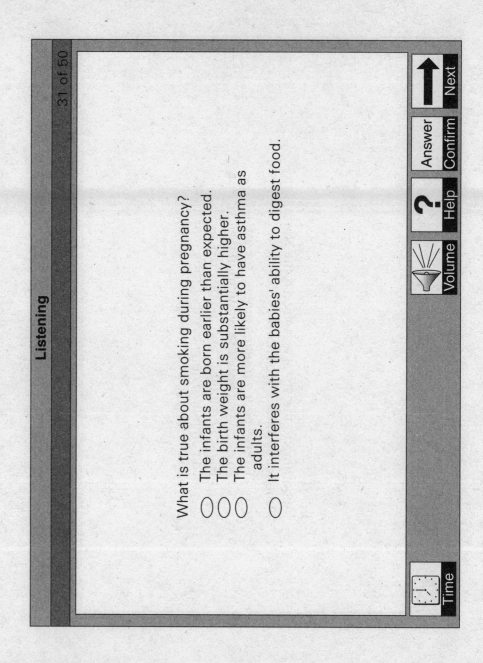

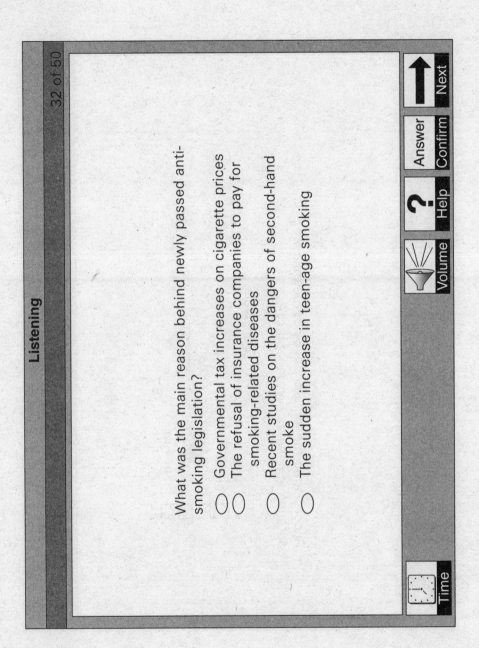

What was the main reason behind newly passed anti-smoking legislation?

○ Governmental tax increases on cigarette prices
○ The refusal of insurance companies to pay for smoking-related diseases
○ Recent studies on the dangers of second-hand smoke
○ The sudden increase in teen-age smoking

Volume   Help   Answer   Next
           ?   Confirm

Time

Listening

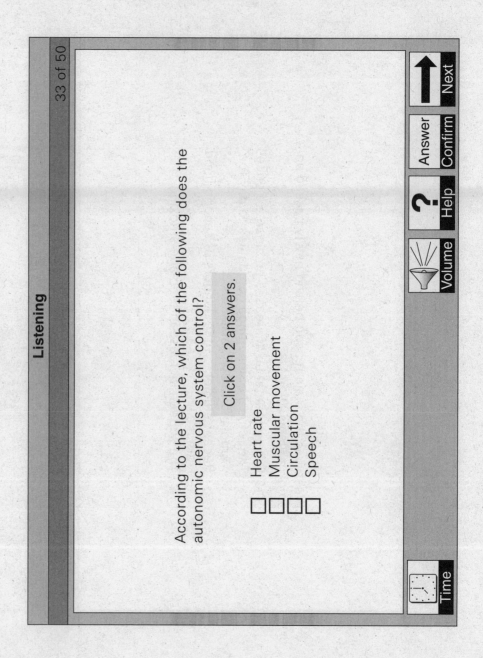

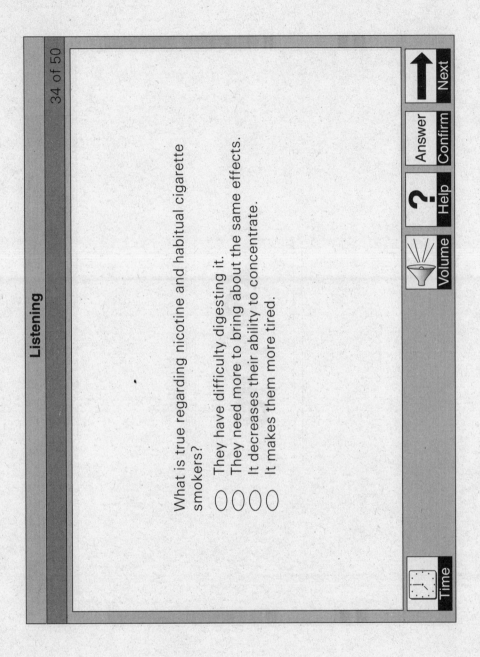

What is true regarding nicotine and habitual cigarette smokers?

○ ○ ○ ○ They have difficulty digesting it.
They need more to bring about the same effects.
It decreases their ability to concentrate.
It makes them more tired.

Volume

? Help

Answer Confirm

↑ Next

Time

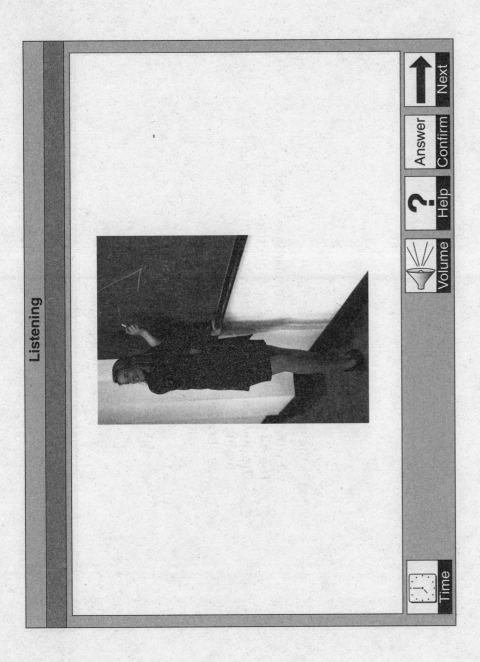

Listening

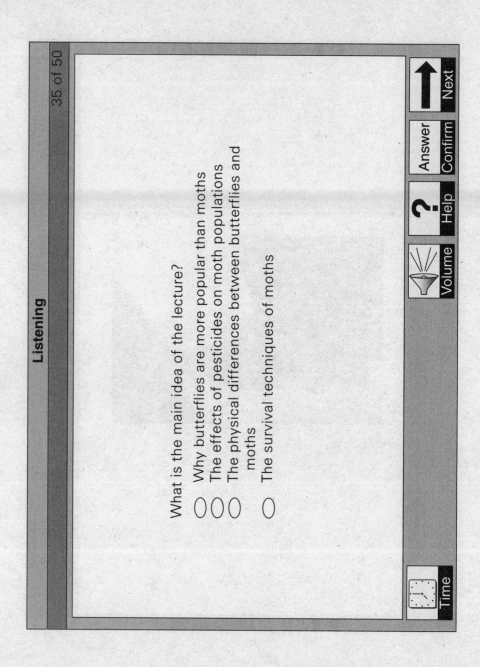

What is the main idea of the lecture?

○ Why butterflies are more popular than moths
○ The effects of pesticides on moth populations
○ The physical differences between butterflies and
  moths
○ The survival techniques of moths

Volume   Help   Answer   Next
                  Confirm

Time

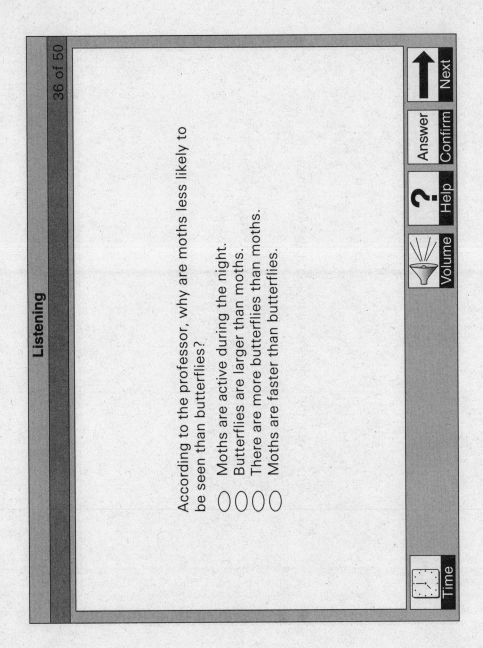

According to the professor, why are moths less likely to be seen than butterflies?

○ Moths are active during the night.
○ Butterflies are larger than moths.
○ There are more butterflies than moths.
○ Moths are faster than butterflies.

Volume   Help   Answer
                  Confirm   Next

Time

Listening

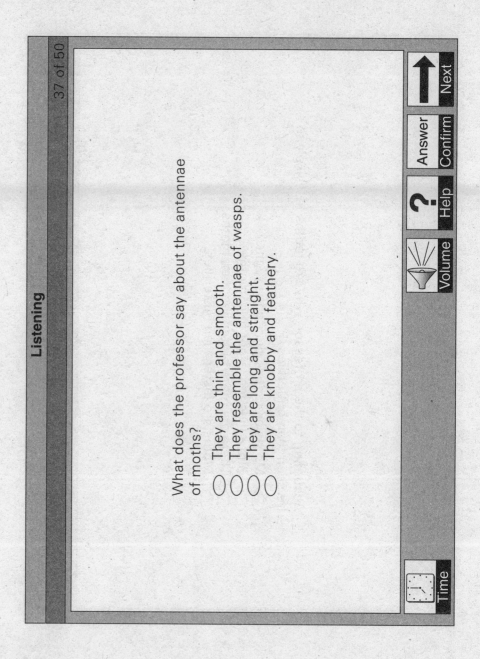

What does the professor say about the antennae of moths?

○ They are thin and smooth.
○ They resemble the antennae of wasps.
○ They are long and straight.
○ They are knobby and feathery.

Volume   Help   Answer   Next
                  Confirm

Time

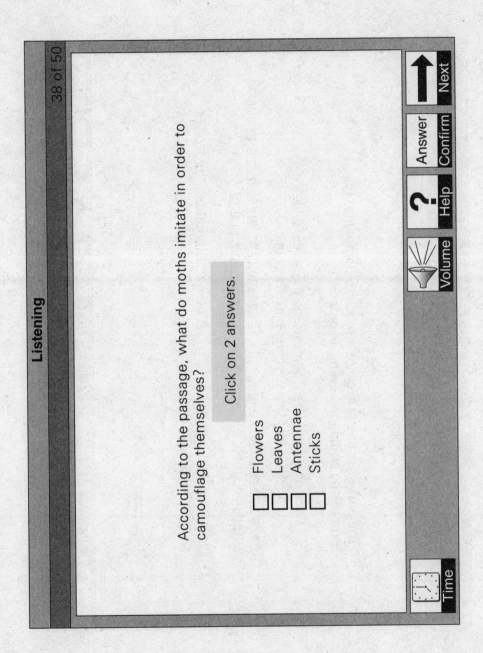

According to the passage, what do moths imitate in order to camouflage themselves?

Click on 2 answers.

☐ Flowers
☐ Leaves
☐ Antennae
☐ Sticks

Time

Volume

Help

Answer Confirm

Next

Listening

The professor briefly explains a process. Summarize the process by putting the events in order.

Click on a sentence. Then click on the space where it belongs. Use each sentence only once.

The larvae release a highly offensive smell.

Thousands of larvae begin to wiggle and squirm.

The caterpillars weave a communal silk tent.

A predator threatens the larvae.

1

2

3

4

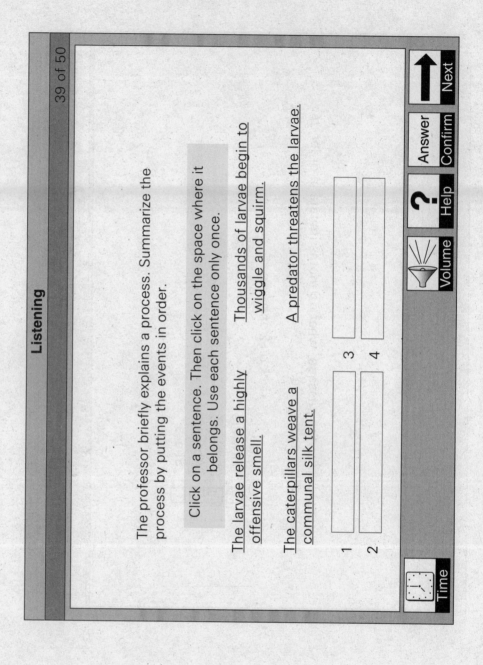

Time   Volume   Help   Answer Confirm   Next

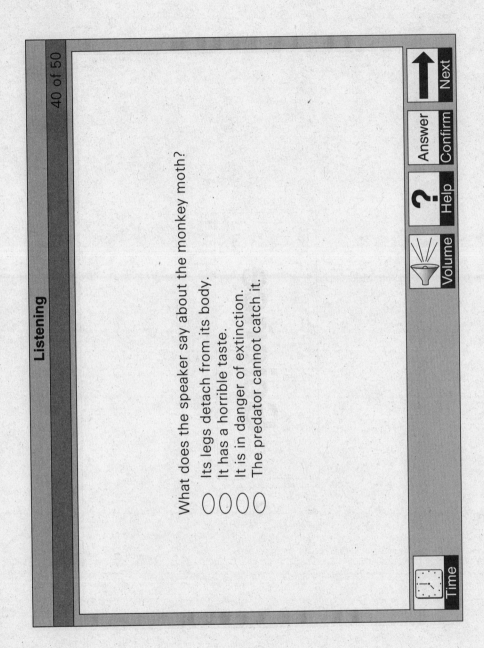

What does the speaker say about the monkey moth?

○ Its legs detach from its body.
○ It has a horrible taste.
○ It is in danger of extinction.
○ The predator cannot catch it.

Volume   Help   Answer
                  Confirm   Next

Time

Listening

Listening

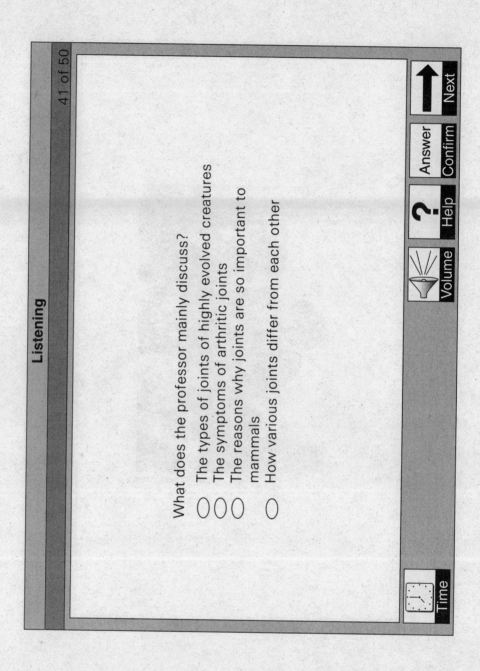

What does the professor mainly discuss?

○ The types of joints of highly evolved creatures
○ The symptoms of arthritic joints
○ The reasons why joints are so important to mammals
○ How various joints differ from each other

Volume   Help   Answer   Next
               ?   Confirm

Time

Based on the professor's description, classify the following types of joints.

Click on a phrase. Then click on the space where it belongs. Use each phrase only once.

Ball and socket joint
Hinge joint
Pivot joint

Neck		Shoulder		Elbow

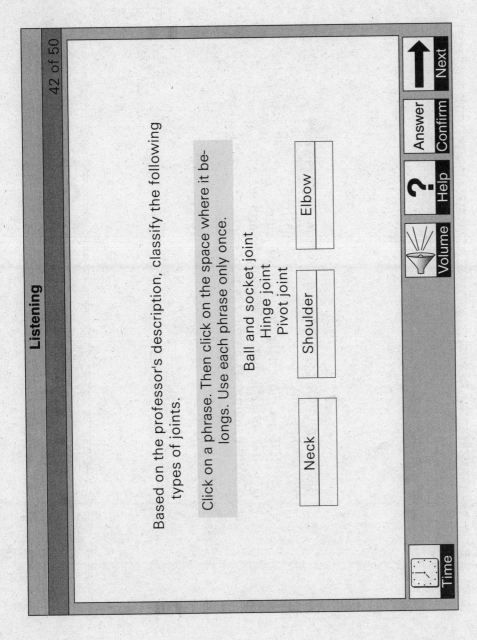

Time   Volume   Help   Answer Confirm   Next

Listening

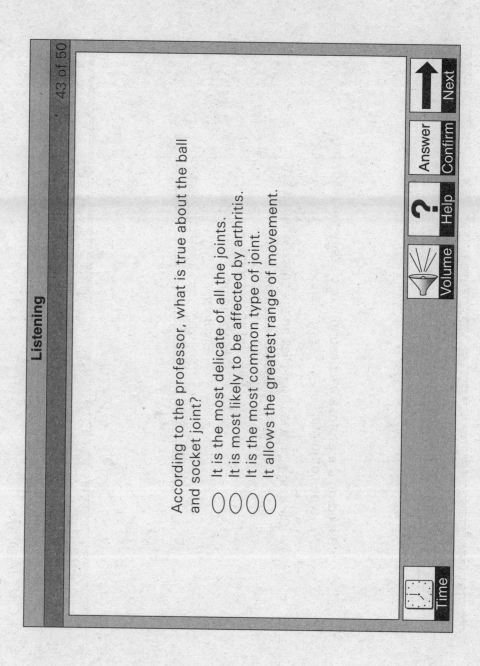

According to the professor, what is true about the ball and socket joint?

○ It is the most delicate of all the joints.
○ It is most likely to be affected by arthritis.
○ It is the most common type of joint.
○ It allows the greatest range of movement.

Volume   Help   Answer Confirm   Next

Time

44 of 50

What type of joint is typically characteristic of more evolved creatures?

○ Hinge
○ Ball and socket
○ Pivot
○ Immovable

Volume
Help
Answer
Confirm
Next

Time

Listening

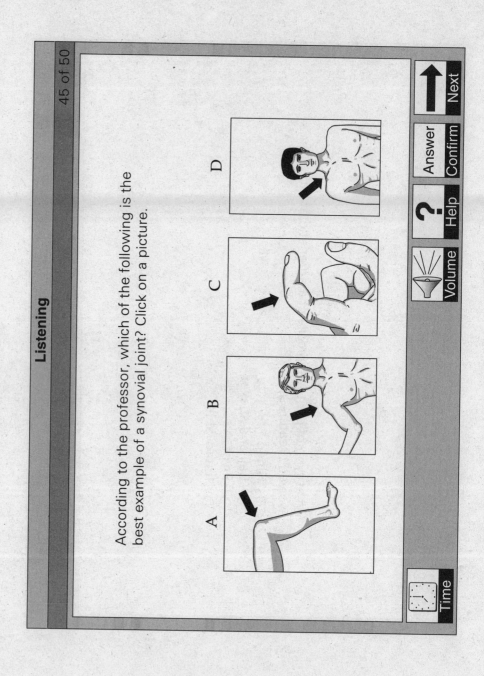

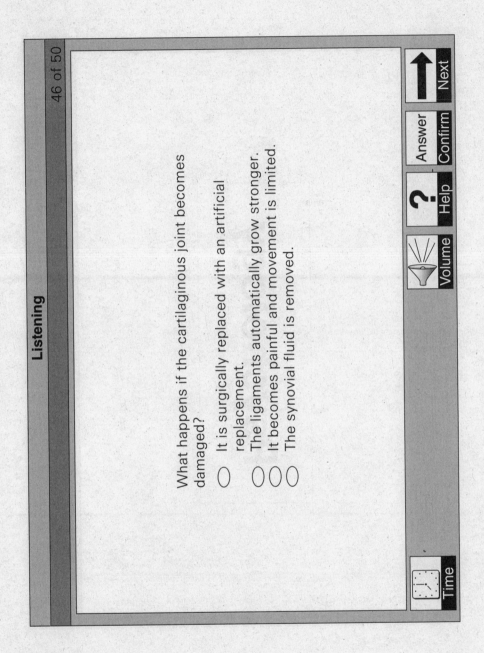

What happens if the cartilaginous joint becomes damaged?

- It is surgically replaced with an artificial replacement.
- The ligaments automatically grow stronger.
- It becomes painful and movement is limited.
- The synovial fluid is removed.

Next
Answer
Confirm
?
Help
Volume
Time

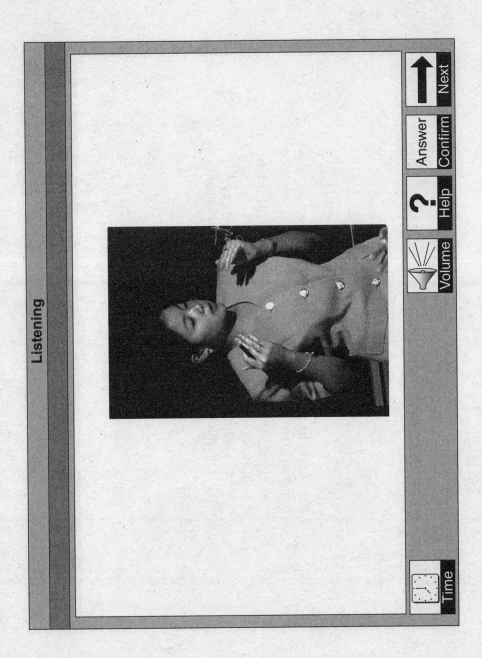

Listening

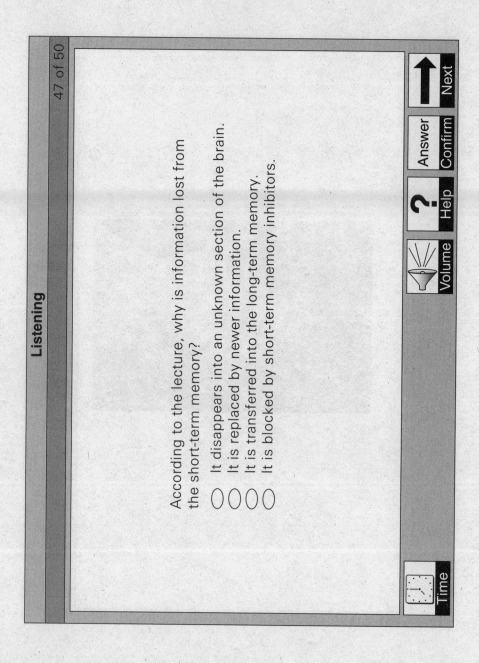

Listening

47 of 50

According to the lecture, why is information lost from the short-term memory?

○ It disappears into an unknown section of the brain.
○ It is replaced by newer information.
○ It is transferred into the long-term memory.
○ It is blocked by short-term memory inhibitors.

Volume   Help   Answer   ↑
                   Confirm   Next

Time

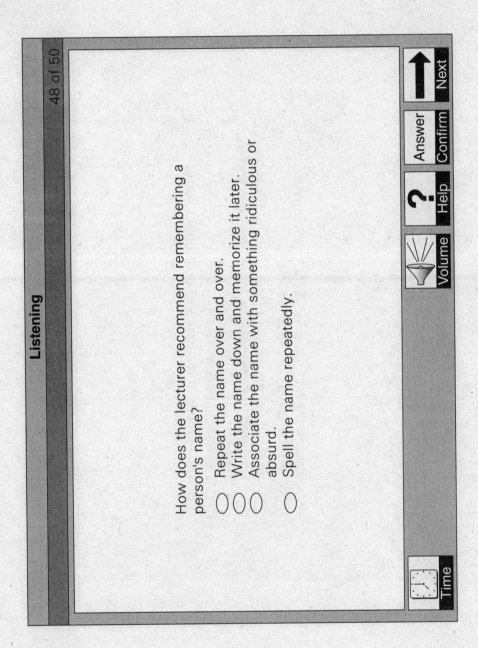

How does the lecturer recommend remembering a person's name?

○ Repeat the name over and over.

○ Write the name down and memorize it later.

○ Associate the name with something ridiculous or absurd.

○ Spell the name repeatedly.

Volume   Help   Answer
                  Confirm

Next

Time

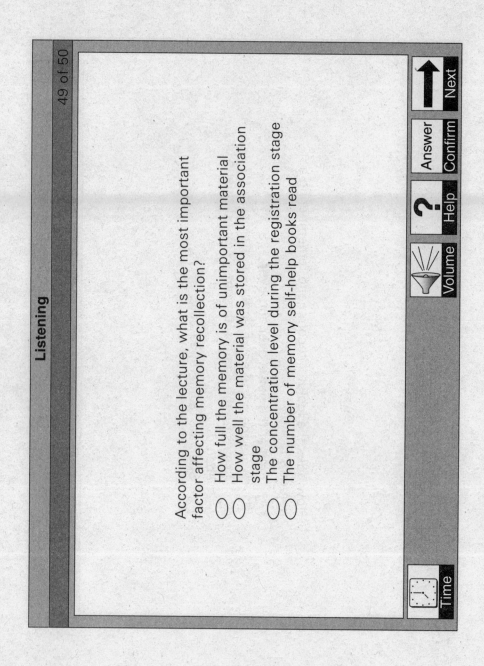

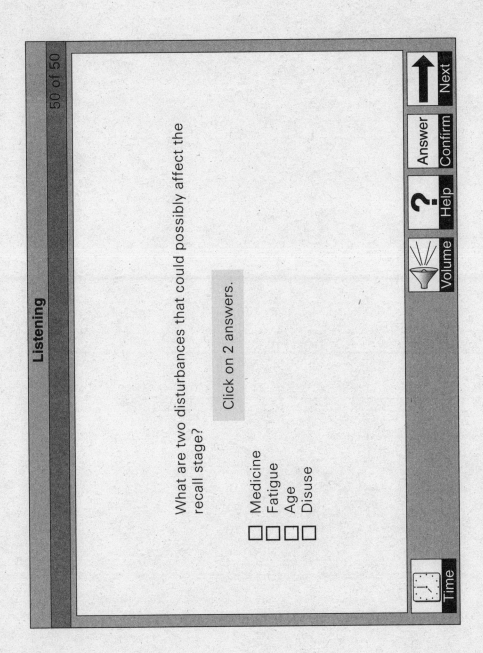

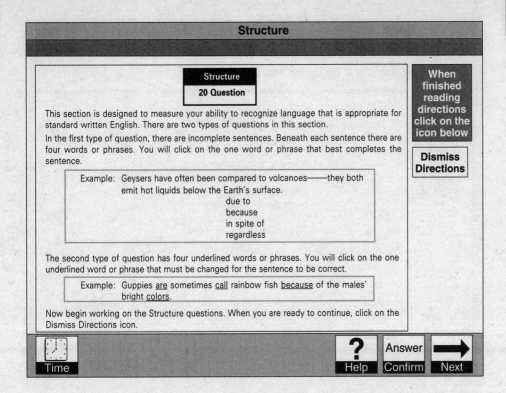

Structure

Structure

20 Question

This section is designed to measure your ability to recognize language that is appropriate for standard written English. There are two types of questions in this section.

In the first type of question, there are incomplete sentences. Beneath each sentence there are four words or phrases. You will click on the one word or phrase that best completes the sentence.

> Example: Geysers have often been compared to volcanoes——they both emit hot liquids below the Earth's surface.
>> due to
>> because
>> in spite of
>> regardless

The second type of question has four underlined words or phrases. You will click on the one underlined word or phrase that must be changed for the sentence to be correct.

> Example: Guppies <u>are</u> sometimes <u>call</u> rainbow fish <u>because</u> of the males' bright <u>colors</u>.

Now begin working on the Structure questions. When you are ready to continue, click on the Dismiss Directions icon.

When finished reading directions click on the icon below

Dismiss Directions

Time | ? Help | Answer Confirm | → Next

You may only take 16 minutes to answer the folowing 20 questions.
Do not take more than 16 minutes to complete this section.

Structure

Click on the word or phrase that best completes the sentence.

After hydrogen, oxygen is the _____ in the atmosphere of the Earth.

- ⬭ element is most plentiful
- ⬭ most plentiful element that
- ⬭ element that most plentiful
- ⬭ most plentiful element

Time   ?   Answer   ➡
Help   Confirm   Next

Click on the word or phrase that best completes the sentence.

Born in 1961, Diana, the princess of Wales, <u>founded a number of</u> non-profit <u>organization</u> before <u>losing</u> her life on a well-traveled expressway in Paris, France.

Time   ?   Answer   ➡
Help   Confirm   Next

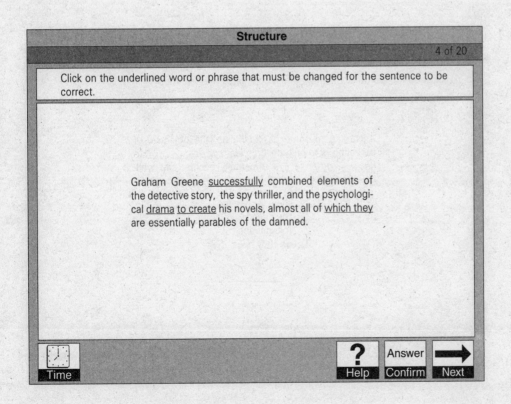

Click on the word or phrase that best completes the sentence.

Aluminum's extreme malleability, durability, and conductivity make _____ for high-tension electrical power transmission.

○ it useful
○ it a useful
○ it is of useful
○ it uses

Time

? Help

Answer Confirm

→ Next

Structure

4 of 20

Click on the underlined word or phrase that must be changed for the sentence to be correct.

Graham Greene <u>successfully</u> combined elements of the detective story, the spy thriller, and the psychological <u>drama</u> <u>to create</u> his novels, almost all of <u>which they</u> are essentially parables of the damned.

Time

? Help

Answer Confirm

→ Next

Structure

Click on the underlined word or phrase that must be changed for the sentence to be correct.

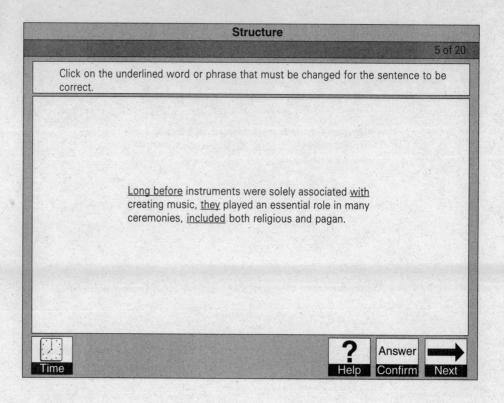

Long before instruments were solely associated with creating music, they played an essential role in many ceremonies, included both religious and pagan.

Click on the word or phrase that best completes the sentence.

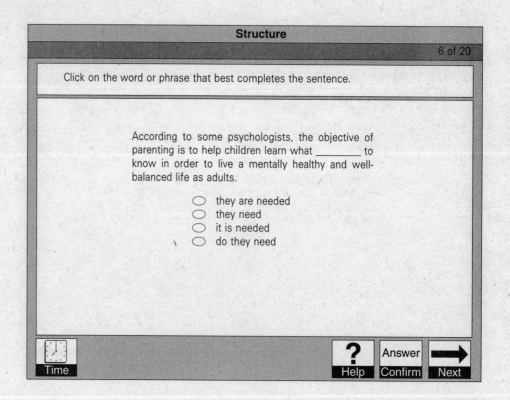

According to some psychologists, the objective of parenting is to help children learn what _____ to know in order to live a mentally healthy and well-balanced life as adults.

- ○ they are needed
- ○ they need
- ○ it is needed
- ○ do they need

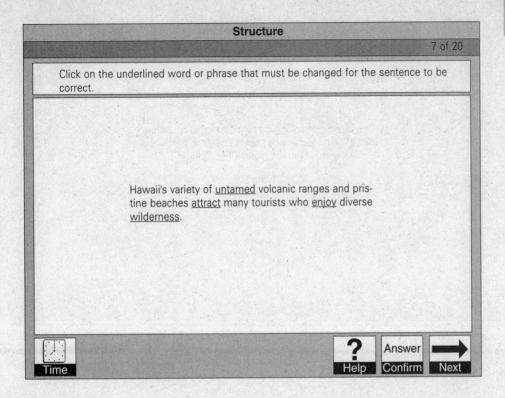

Click on the underlined word or phrase that must be changed for the sentence to be correct.

Hawaii's variety of <u>untamed</u> volcanic ranges and pristine beaches <u>attract</u> many tourists who <u>enjoy</u> diverse <u>wilderness</u>.

? Help   Answer Confirm   → Next

Time

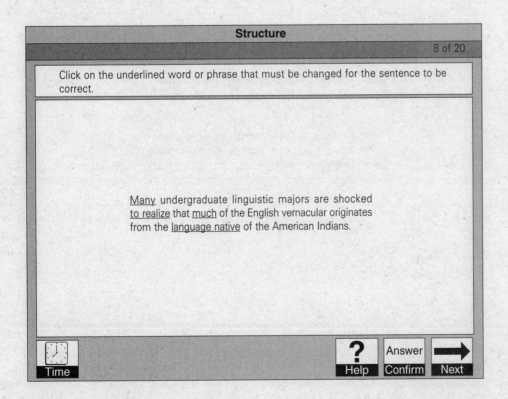

Click on the underlined word or phrase that must be changed for the sentence to be correct.

<u>Many</u> undergraduate linguistic majors are shocked <u>to realize</u> that <u>much</u> of the English vernacular originates from the <u>language native</u> of the American Indians.

? Help   Answer Confirm   → Next

Time

Structure

Click on the word or phrase that best completes the sentence.

One of the principles held by modern-day educators is that a math teacher need not tell student _____ about solving complex mathematical equations.

- ○ that going
- ○ to go how
- ○ which going
- ○ how to go

Time   Help   Answer Confirm   Next

Click on the word or phrase that best completes the sentence.

Historically, the knife is perhaps the earliest form of a weapon, _____ its availability varied depending on the geographical area.

- ○ whereas
- ○ despite
- ○ although
- ○ unlike

Time   Help   Answer Confirm   Next

Click on the underlined word or phrase that must be changed for the sentence to be correct.

The common white potato <u>closely</u> <u>resembles</u> a fruit, <u>but account</u> of several botanical features <u>it</u> is considered a part of the vegetable family.

Time   ? Help   Answer Confirm   Next

Click on the word or phrase that best completes the sentence.

With age, veins and arteries lose their elasticity and ability to quickly transport blood throughout the body, _____ them less efficient.

○ and to make
○ makes
○ which it makes
○ thereby making

Time   ? Help   Answer Confirm   Next

Structure

Click on the underlined word or phrase that must be changed for the sentence to be correct.

Electricity, at first considered a luxury seventy years <u>ago</u>, is now viewed as a <u>necessary</u> to human survival and <u>plays</u> an essential role <u>in</u> modern-day progress.

Time   ?   Answer   →
       Help Confirm   Next

Click on the underlined word or phrase that must be changed for the sentence to be correct.

Despite <u>overgrazing</u> and land <u>reduction</u>, <u>ranch</u> in the western United States has survived due to <u>scientifically</u> controlled irrigation farming.

Time   ?   Answer   →
       Help Confirm   Next

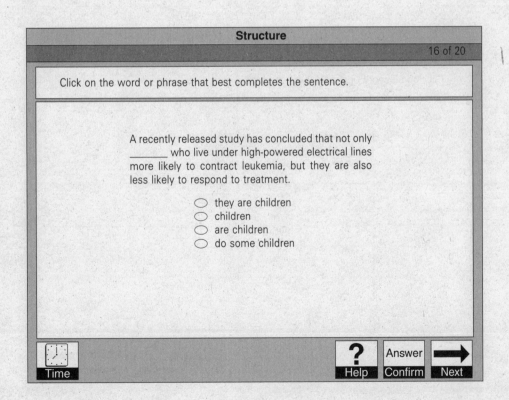

Click on the word or phrase that best completes the sentence.

_____ 500 artificial satellites orbiting the earth, and although they were all initially designed for communication, only 75 percent are actually functioning.

- ○ About
- ○ There are about
- ○ If there are about
- ○ It is about

Time Help Answer Confirm Next

Click on the word or phrase that best completes the sentence.

A recently released study has concluded that not only _____ who live under high-powered electrical lines more likely to contract leukemia, but they are also less likely to respond to treatment.

- ○ they are children
- ○ children
- ○ are children
- ○ do some children

Time Help Answer Confirm Next

Structure

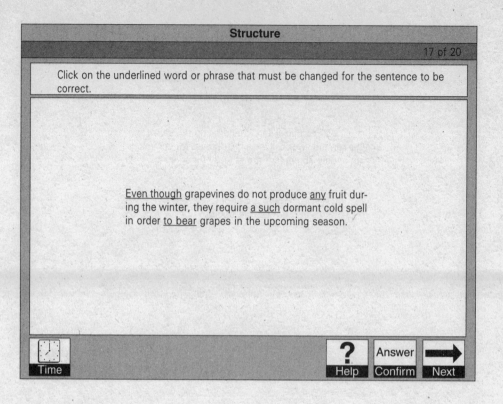

Click on the underlined word or phrase that must be changed for the sentence to be correct.

Even though grapevines do not produce any fruit during the winter, they require a such dormant cold spell in order to bear grapes in the upcoming season.

Time   Help   Answer Confirm   Next

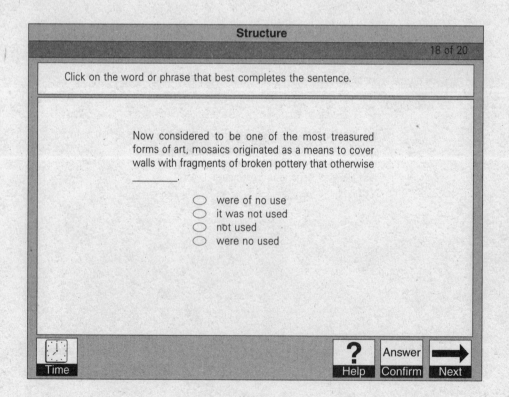

Click on the word or phrase that best completes the sentence.

Now considered to be one of the most treasured forms of art, mosaics originated as a means to cover walls with fragments of broken pottery that otherwise _____.

- ○ were of no use
- ○ it was not used
- ○ not used
- ○ were no used

Time   Help   Answer Confirm   Next

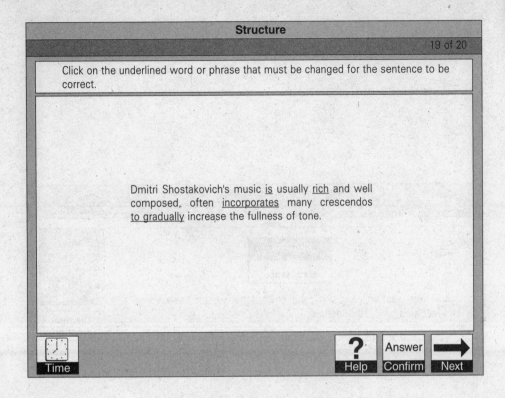

Click on the underlined word or phrase that must be changed for the sentence to be correct.

Dmitri Shostakovich's music <u>is</u> usually <u>rich</u> and well composed, often <u>incorporates</u> many crescendos <u>to gradually</u> increase the fullness of tone.

Time   Help   Answer Confirm   Next

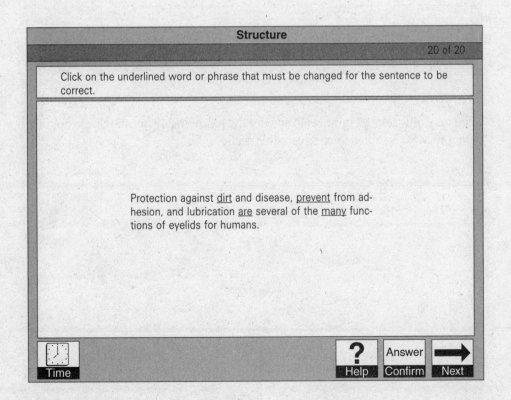

Click on the underlined word or phrase that must be changed for the sentence to be correct.

Protection against <u>dirt</u> and disease, <u>prevent</u> from adhesion, and lubrication <u>are</u> several of the <u>many</u> functions of eyelids for humans.

Time   Help   Answer Confirm   Next

Reading

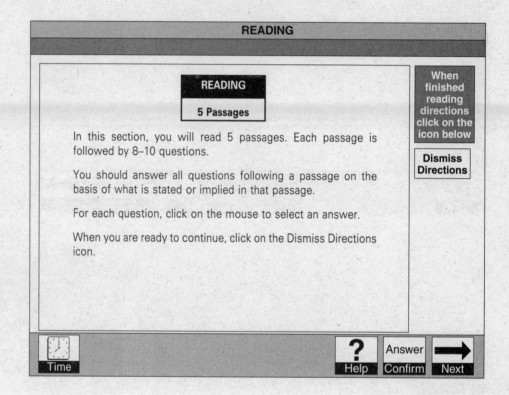

You may only take 90 minutes to answer the following 49 questions. Do not take more than 90 minutes to complete this section.

Reading — Practice Questions & Review

When finished reading the passage, click on the icon below

Early studies of anatomy were hampered by the authorities' disapproval of dissections, and by the lack of refrigeration. By the 1500's in Europe the collected knowledge about the human body had been codified and was the exclusive domain of the Doctors of Physick, a group of scholars who went to great lengths to prevent medical information from spreading. To this end, the Doctors stored their knowledge in obscure languages such as Greek, Latin, and Arabic. The Doctors, by not allowing the works of anatomy to be translated into common tongues, remained invincible to intellectual assaults by laymen. Not only did Doctors of Physick refuse to supplement the bodily lore they learned at the university with practical observations, but they also charged ludicrous amounts to treat their patients.

The doctors generally prescribed two different treatments for disease, blood lettings for those with physical disorders, and point-branding for those in need of psychiatric care. The treatments involved using leeches and needles respectively, and often caused patients to end up worse off than they were prior to treatment. Given these conditions, the common people opted to patronize the village apothecary, who was typically a local grocer selling ineffectual herbal remedies.

Protected by an imposing guild system, the citadel of medicine was finally cracked by Paracelsus, a rogue physician of the sixteenth century. Paracelsus was a self-taught medicine man who instructed his own students at the University of Basal in a local dialect instead of Latin, and actually burned copies of books on the traditional principles of medicine. Teaching only from his own experience as a doctor who had treated hundreds of patients, he enraged his fellow professors by freely disseminating the safeguarded wisdom of his profession among the common man. This not only violated the Hippocratic oath, in which the Doctor of Physick swore to guard his professional knowledge, but it also eventually proved detrimental to Paracelsus' career.

In 1528, Paracelsus was thrown out from the University, but the damage to medical tradition had already been done. The works of Paracelsus were published after his death, and among other things they completely altered the European notion of disease, overturning the then-popular opinion that disease was caused by unbalanced "humors" within a patient's body. But this was just the beginning of the far-reaching impact Paracelsus had on Western medicine.

Proceed

Time

? Help

← Prev

→ Next

Beginning

Early studies of anatomy were hampered by the authorities' disapproval of dissections, and by the lack of refrigeration. By the 1500's in Europe the collected knowledge about the human body had been codified and was the exclusive domain of the Doctors of Physick, a group of scholars who went to great lengths to prevent medical information from spreading. To this end, the Doctors stored their knowledge in obscure languages such as Greek, Latin, and Arabic. The Doctors, by not allowing the works of anatomy to be translated into common tongues, remained invincible to intellectual assaults by laymen. Not only did Doctors of Physick refuse to supplement the bodily lore they learned at the university with practical observations, but they also charged ludicrous amounts to treat their patients.

The doctors generally prescribed two different treatments for disease, blood lettings for those with physical disorders, and point-branding for those in need of psychiatric care. The treatments involved using leeches and needles respectively, and often caused patients to end up worse off than they were prior to treatment. Given these conditions, the common people opted to patronize the village apothecary, who was typically a local grocer selling ineffectual herbal remedies.

Protected by an imposing guild system, the citadel of medicine was finally cracked by Paracelsus, a rogue physician of the sixteenth century. Paracelsus was a self-taught medicine man who instructed his own students at the University of Basal in a local dialect instead of Latin, and actually burned copies of books on the traditional principles of medicine. Teaching only from his own experience as a doctor who had treated hundreds of patients, he enraged his fellow professors by freely disseminating the safeguarded wisdom of his profession among the common man. This not only violated the Hippocratic oath, in which the Doctor of Physick swore to guard his professional knowledge, but it also eventually proved detrimental to Paracelsus' career.

In 1528, Paracelsus was thrown out from the University, but the damage to medical tradition had already been done. The works of Paracelsus were published after his death, and among other things they completely altered the European notion of disease, overturning the then-popular opinion that disease was caused by unbalanced "humors" within a patient's body. But this was just the beginning of the far-reaching impact Paracelsus had on Western medicine.

What is the main topic?
- ◯ The overthrow of established medical tradition
- ◯ The ethical questions encountered by ancient doctors
- ◯ The archaic notion of bodily humors
- ◯ The university system in the sixteenth century

Time

Help

Prev

Next

Reading

Beginning

Early studies of anatomy were hampered by the authorities' disapproval of dissections, and by the lack of refrigeration. By the 1500's in Europe the collected knowledge about the human body had been codified and was the exclusive domain of the Doctors of Physick, a group of scholars who went to great lengths to prevent medical information from spreading. To this end, the Doctors stored their knowledge in obscure languages such as Greek, Latin, and Arabic. The Doctors, by not allowing the works of anatomy to be translated into common tongues, remained invincible to intellectual assaults by laymen. Not only did Doctors of Physick refuse to supplement the bodily lore they learned at the university with practical observations, but they also charged ludicrous amounts to treat their patients.

The doctors generally prescribed two different treatments for disease, blood lettings for those with physical disorders, and point-branding for those in need of psychiatric care. The treatments involved using leeches and needles respectively, and often caused patients to end up worse off than they were prior to treatment. Given these conditions, the common people opted to patronize the village apothecary, who was typically a local grocer selling ineffectual herbal remedies.

Protected by an imposing guild system, the citadel of medicine was finally cracked by Paracelsus, a rogue physician of the sixteenth century. Paracelsus was a self-taught medicine man who instructed his own students at the University of Basal in a local dialect instead of Latin, and actually burned copies of books on the traditional principles of medicine. Teaching only from his own experience as a doctor who had treated hundreds of patients, he enraged his fellow professors by freely disseminating the safeguarded wisdom of his profession among the common man. This not only violated the Hippocratic oath, in which the Doctor of Physick swore to guard his professional knowledge, but it also eventually proved detrimental to Paracelsus' career.

In 1528, Paracelsus was thrown out from the University, but the damage to medical tradition had already been done. The works of Paracelsus were published after his death, and among other things they completely altered the European notion of disease, overturning the then-popular opinion that disease was caused by unbalanced "humors" within a patient's body. But this was just the beginning of the far-reaching impact Paracelsus had on Western medicine.

Look at the highlighted word in the passage. Click on the word or phrase in the **bold** text that is closest in meaning to hamper.

Time

Help

Prev

Next

Beginning

Early studies of anatomy were hampered by the authorities' disapproval of dissections, and by the lack of refrigeration. By the 1500's in Europe the collected knowledge about the human body had been codified and was the exclusive domain of the Doctors of Physick, a group of scholars who went to great lengths to prevent medical information from spreading. To this end, the Doctors stored their knowledge in obscure languages such as Greek, Latin, and Arabic. The Doctors, by not allowing the works of anatomy to be translated into common tongues, remained invincible to intellectual assaults by laymen. Not only did Doctors of Physick refuse to supplement the bodily lore they learned at the university with practical observations, but they also charged ludicrous amounts to treat their patients.

The doctors generally prescribed two different treatments for disease, blood lettings for those with physical disorders, and point-branding for those in need of psychiatric care. The treatments involved using leeches and needles respectively, and often caused patients to end up worse off than they were prior to treatment. Given these conditions, the common people opted to patronize the village apothecary, who was typically a local grocer selling ineffectual herbal remedies.

Protected by an imposing guild system, the citadel of medicine was finally cracked by Paracelsus, a rogue physician of the sixteenth century. Paracelsus was a self-taught medicine man who instructed his own students at the University of Basal in a local dialect instead of Latin, and actually burned copies of books on the traditional principles of medicine. Teaching only from his own experience as a doctor who had treated hundreds of patients, he enraged his fellow professors by freely disseminating the safeguarded wisdom of his profession among the common man. This not only violated the Hippocratic oath, in which the Doctor of Physick swore to guard his professional knowledge, but it also eventually proved detrimental to Paracelsus' career.

In 1528, Paracelsus was thrown out from the University, but the damage to medical tradition had already been done. The works of Paracelsus were published after his death, and among other things they completely altered the European notion of disease, overturning the then-popular opinion that disease was caused by unbalanced "humors" within a patient's body. But this was just the beginning of the far-reaching impact Paracelsus had on Western medicine.

According to the passages, why did the doctors use languages such as Greek, Latin, and Arabic?
- They were languages spoken by the laymen.
- They allowed the doctors to publish documents.
- They were the languages Socrates spoke.
- They kept the common people from understanding medicine.

Time

Help

Prev   Next

Reading

Beginning

Early studies of anatomy were hampered by the authorities' disapproval of dissections, and by the lack of refrigeration. By the 1500's in Europe the collected knowledge about the human body had been codified and was the exclusive domain of the Doctors of Physick, a group of scholars who went to great lengths to prevent medical information from spreading. To this end, the Doctors stored their knowledge in obscure languages such as Greek, Latin, and Arabic. The Doctors, by not allowing the works of anatomy to be translated into common tongues, remained invincible to intellectual assaults by laymen. Not only did Doctors of Physick refuse to supplement the bodily lore they learned at the university with practical observations, but they also charged **ludicrous** amounts to treat their patients.

The doctors generally prescribed two different treatments for disease, blood lettings for those with physical disorders, and point-branding for those in need of psychiatric care. The treatments involved using leeches and needles respectively, and often caused patients to end up worse off than they were prior to treatment. Given these conditions, the common people opted to patronize the village apothecary, who was typically a local grocer selling ineffectual herbal remedies.

Protected by an imposing guild system, the citadel of medicine was finally cracked by Paracelsus, a rogue physician of the sixteenth century. Paracelsus was a self-taught medicine man who instructed his own students at the University of Basal in a local dialect instead of Latin, and actually burned copies of books on the traditional principles of medicine. Teaching only from his own experience as a doctor who had treated hundreds of patients, he enraged his fellow professors by freely disseminating the safeguarded wisdom of his profession among the common man. This not only violated the Hippocratic oath, in which the Doctor of Physick swore to guard his professional knowledge, but it also eventually proved detrimental to Paracelsus' career.

In 1528, Paracelsus was thrown out from the University, but the damage to medical tradition had already been done. The works of Paracelsus were published after his death, and among other things they completely altered the European notion of disease, overturning the then-popular opinion that disease was caused by unbalanced "humors" within a patient's body. But this was just the beginning of the far-reaching impact Paracelsus had on Western medicine.

Look at the highlighted word in the text. Click on the answer choice that is closest in meaning to the word **ludicrous**.

○ practical
○ dangerous
○ sharp
○ ridiculous

Time

? Help

← Prev

→ Next

Beginning

Early studies of anatomy were hampered by the authorities' disapproval of dissections, and by the lack of refrigeration. By the 1500's in Europe the collected knowledge about the human body had been codified and was the exclusive domain of the Doctors of Physick, a group of scholars who went to great lengths to prevent medical information from spreading. To this end, the Doctors stored their knowledge in obscure languages such as Greek, Latin, and Arabic. The Doctors, by not allowing the works of anatomy to be translated into common tongues, remained invincible to intellectual assaults by laymen. Not only did Doctors of Physick refuse to supplement the bodily lore they learned at the university with practical observations, but they also charged ludicrous amounts to treat their patients.

The doctors generally prescribed two different treatments for disease, blood lettings for those with physical disorders, and point-branding for those in need of psychiatric care. The treatments involved using leeches and needles respectively, and often caused patients to end up worse off than they were prior to treatment. Given these conditions, the common people opted to patronize the village apothecary, who was typically a local grocer selling ineffectual herbal remedies.

Protected by an imposing guild system, the citadel of medicine was finally cracked by Paracelsus, a rogue physician of the sixteenth century. Paracelsus was a self-taught medicine man who instructed his own students at the University of Basal in a local dialect instead of Latin, and actually burned copies of books on the traditional principles of medicine. Teaching only from his own experience as a doctor who had treated hundreds of patients, he enraged his fellow professors by freely disseminating the safeguarded wisdom of his profession among the common man. This not only violated the Hippocratic oath, in which the Doctor of Physick swore to guard his professional knowledge, but it also eventually proved detrimental to Paracelsus' career.

In 1528, Paracelsus was thrown out from the University, but the damage to medical tradition had already been done. The works of Paracelsus were published after his death, and among other things they completely altered the European notion of disease, overturning the then-popular opinion that disease was caused by unbalanced "humors" within a patient's body. But this was just the beginning of the far-reaching impact Paracelsus had on Western medicine.

According to the text, which of the following were used by doctors to treat those with mental disorders?
- ○ leeches
- ○ needles
- ○ blood letting
- ○ herbal remedies

Time

Help

Prev

Next

Reading

Beginning

Early studies of anatomy were hampered by the authorities' disapproval of dissections, and by the lack of refrigeration. By the 1500's in Europe the collected knowledge about the human body had been codified and was the exclusive domain of the Doctors of Physick, a group of scholars who went to great lengths to prevent medical information from spreading. To this end, the Doctors stored their knowledge in obscure languages such as Greek, Latin, and Arabic. The Doctors, by not allowing the works of anatomy to be translated into common tongues, remained invincible to intellectual assaults by laymen. Not only did Doctors of Physick refuse to supplement the bodily lore they learned at the university with practical observations, but they also charged ludicrous amounts to treat their patients.

The doctors generally prescribed two different treatments for disease, blood lettings for those with physical disorders, and point-branding for those in need of psychiatric care. The treatments involved using leeches and needles respectively, and often caused patients to end up worse off than they were prior to treatment. Given these conditions, the common people opted to patronize the village apothecary, who was typically a local grocer selling ineffectual herbal remedies.

Protected by an imposing guild system, the citadel of medicine was finally cracked by Paracelsus, a rogue physician of the sixteenth century. Paracelsus was a self-taught medicine man who instructed his own students at the University of Basal in a local dialect instead of Latin, and actually burned copies of books on the traditional principles of medicine. Teaching only from his own experience as a doctor who had treated hundreds of patients, he enraged his fellow professors by freely disseminating the safeguarded wisdom of his profession among the common man. This not only violated the Hippocratic oath, in which the Doctor of Physick swore to guard his professional knowledge, but it also eventually proved detrimental to Paracelsus' career.

In 1528, Paracelsus was thrown out from the University, but the damage to medical tradition had already been done. The works of Paracelsus were published after his death, and among other things they completely altered the European notion of disease, overturning the then-popular opinion that disease was caused by unbalanced "humors" within a patient's body. But this was just the beginning of the far-reaching impact Paracelsus had on Western medicine.

It can be inferred from the passage that the Doctors of Physick
- ○ only worked with the upper class
- ○ performed dissections for ceremonial purposes
- ○ learned what they could from their everyday practice
- ○ often were of no help to their patients

Time

Help   Prev   Next

Reading

Beginning

Early studies of anatomy were hampered by the authorities' disapproval of dissections, and by the lack of refrigeration. By the 1500's in Europe the collected knowledge about the human body had been codified and was the exclusive domain of the Doctors of Physick, a group of scholars who went to great lengths to prevent medical information from spreading. To this end, the Doctors stored their knowledge in obscure languages such as Greek, Latin, and Arabic. The Doctors, by not allowing the works of anatomy to be translated into common tongues, remained invincible to intellectual assaults by laymen. Not only did Doctors of Physick refuse to supplement the bodily lore they learned at the university with practical observations, but they also charged ludicrous amounts to treat their patients.

The doctors generally prescribed two different treatments for disease, blood lettings for those with physical disorders, and point-branding for those in need of psychiatric care. The treatments involved using leeches and needles respectively, and often caused patients to end up worse off than they were prior to treatment. Given these conditions, the common people **opted** to patronize the village apothecary, who was typically a local grocer selling ineffectual herbal remedies.

Protected by an imposing guild system, the citadel of medicine was finally cracked by Paracelsus, a rogue physician of the sixteenth century. Paracelsus was a self-taught medicine man who instructed his own students at the University of Basal in a local dialect instead of Latin, and actually burned copies of books on the traditional principles of medicine. Teaching only from his own experience as a doctor who had treated hundreds of patients, he enraged his fellow professors by freely disseminating the safeguarded wisdom of his profession among the common man. This not only violated the Hippocratic oath, in which the Doctor of Physick swore to guard his professional knowledge, but it also eventually proved detrimental to Paracelsus' career.

In 1528, Paracelsus was thrown out from the University, but the damage to medical tradition had already been done. The works of Paracelsus were published after his death, and among other things they completely altered the European notion of disease, overturning the then-popular opinion that disease was caused by unbalanced "humors" within a patient's body. But this was just the beginning of the far-reaching impact Paracelsus had on Western medicine.

Look at the highlighted word in the text. Click on the answer choice that is closest in meaning to the word **opted**.

○ chose
○ loved
○ refused
○ planned

Time

Help Prev Next

Reading

Beginning

Early studies of anatomy were hampered by the authorities' disapproval of dissections, and by the lack of refrigeration. By the 1500's in Europe the collected knowledge about the human body had been codified and was the exclusive domain of the Doctors of Physick, a group of scholars who went to great lengths to prevent medical information from spreading. To this end, the Doctors stored their knowledge in obscure languages such as Greek, Latin, and Arabic. The Doctors, by not allowing the works of anatomy to be translated into common tongues, remained invincible to intellectual assaults by laymen. Not only did Doctors of Physick refuse to supplement the bodily lore they learned at the university with practical observations, but they also charged ludicrous amounts to treat their patients.

The doctors generally prescribed two different treatments for disease, blood lettings for those with physical disorders, and point-branding for those in need of psychiatric care. The treatments involved using leeches and needles respectively, and often caused patients to end up worse off than they were prior to treatment. Given these conditions, the common people opted to patronize the village apothecary, who was typically a local grocer selling ineffectual herbal remedies.

Protected by an imposing guild system, the citadel of medicine was finally cracked by Paracelsus, a rogue physician of the sixteenth century. Paracelsus was a self-taught medicine man who instructed his own students at the University of Basal in a local dialect instead of Latin, and actually burned copies of books on the traditional principles of medicine. Teaching only from his own experience as a doctor who had treated hundreds of patients, he enraged his fellow professors by freely disseminating the safeguarded wisdom of his profession among the common man. This not only violated the Hippocratic oath, in which the Doctor of Physick swore to guard his professional knowledge, but it also eventually proved detrimental to Paracelsus' career.

In 1528, Paracelsus was thrown out from the University, but the damage to medical tradition had already been done. The works of Paracelsus were published after his death, and among other things they completely altered the European notion of disease, overturning the then-popular opinion that disease was caused by unbalanced "humors" within a patient's body. But this was just the beginning of the far-reaching impact Paracelsus had on Western medicine.

According to the passage, what can be concluded about Paracelsus' medical education?
- ○ He graduated from the University of Basal.
- ○ He educated himself about medicine.
- ○ He was disliked by his university professors.
- ○ He kept his medical knowledge to himself.

Time

Help Prev Next

Beginning

Early studies of anatomy were hampered by the authorities' disapproval of dissections, and by the lack of refrigeration. By the 1500's in Europe the collected knowledge about the human body had been codified and was the exclusive domain of the Doctors of Physick, a group of scholars who went to great lengths to prevent medical information from spreading. To this end, the Doctors stored their knowledge in obscure languages such as Greek, Latin, and Arabic. The Doctors, by not allowing the works of anatomy to be translated into common tongues, remained invincible to intellectual assaults by laymen. Not only did Doctors of Physick refuse to supplement the bodily lore they learned at the university with practical observations, but they also charged ludicrous amounts to treat their patients.

The doctors generally prescribed two different treatments for disease, blood lettings for those with physical disorders, and point-branding for those in need of psychiatric care. The treatments involved using leeches and needles respectively, and often caused patients to end up worse off than they were prior to treatment. Given these conditions, the common people opted to patronize the village apothecary, who was typically a local grocer selling ineffectual herbal remedies.

Protected by an imposing guild system, the citadel of medicine was finally cracked by Paracelsus, a rogue physician of the sixteenth century. Paracelsus was a self-taught medicine man who instructed his own students at the University of Basal in a local dialect instead of Latin, and actually burned copies of books on the traditional principles of medicine. Teaching only from his own experience as a doctor who had treated hundreds of patients, he enraged his fellow professors by freely disseminating the safeguarded wisdom of his profession among the common man. This not only violated the Hippocratic oath, in which the Doctor of Physick swore to guard his professional knowledge, but it also eventually proved detrimental to Paracelsus' career.

In 1528, Paracelsus was thrown out from the University, but the damage to medical tradition had already been done. The works of Paracelsus were published after his death, and among other things they completely altered the European notion of disease, overturning the then-popular opinion that disease was caused by unbalanced "humors" within a patient's body. But this was just the beginning of the far-reaching impact Paracelsus had on Western medicine.

It can be inferred from the passage that the Hippocratic oath stated in part that

○ doctors would not question traditional medical knowledge

○ patients were not able to prosecute negligent doctors

○ doctors were not to share medical information with nonprofessionals

○ disease was caused by unbalanced humors

Time

 Help

 Prev

 Next

Reading

Beginning

Early studies of anatomy were hampered by the authorities' disapproval of dissections, and by the lack of refrigeration. By the 1500's in Europe the collected knowledge about the human body had been codified and was the exclusive domain of the Doctors of Physick, a group of scholars who went to great lengths to prevent medical information from spreading. To this end, the Doctors stored their knowledge in obscure languages such as Greek, Latin, and Arabic. The Doctors, by not allowing the works of anatomy to be translated into common tongues, remained invincible to intellectual assaults by laymen. Not only did Doctors of Physick refuse to supplement the bodily lore they learned at the university with practical observations, but they also charged ludicrous amounts to treat their patients.

The doctors generally prescribed two different treatments for disease, blood lettings for those with physical disorders, and point-branding for those in need of psychiatric care. The treatments involved using leeches and needles respectively, and often caused patients to end up worse off than they were prior to treatment. Given these conditions, the common people opted to patronize the village apothecary, who was typically a local grocer selling ineffectual herbal remedies.

Protected by an imposing guild system, the citadel of medicine was finally cracked by Paracelsus, a rogue physician of the sixteenth century. Paracelsus was a self-taught medicine man who instructed his own students at the University of Basal in a local dialect instead of Latin, and actually burned copies of books on the traditional principles of medicine. Teaching only from his own experience as a doctor who had treated hundreds of patients, he enraged his fellow professors by freely disseminating the safeguarded wisdom of his profession among the common man. This not only violated the Hippocratic oath, in which the Doctor of Physick swore to guard his professional knowledge, but it also eventually proved detrimental to Paracelsus' career.

In 1528, Paracelsus was **thrown out** from the University, but the damage to medical tradition had already been done. The works of Paracelsus were published after his death, and among other things they completely altered the European notion of disease, overturning the then-popular opinion that disease was caused .by unbalanced "humors" within a patient's body. But this was just the beginning of the far-reaching impact Paracelsus had on Western medicine.

Look at the highlighted word in the text. Click on the answer choice that is closest in meaning to the phrase **thrown out**.

- ○ graduated
- ○ dismissed
- ○ evicted
- ○ evacuated

Time

Help Prev Next

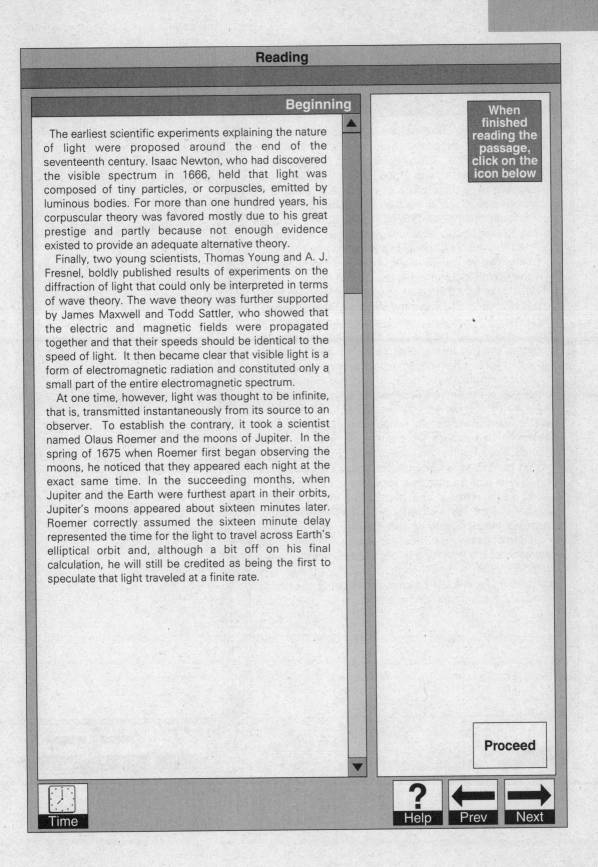

Reading

Beginning

When finished reading the passage, click on the icon below

The earliest scientific experiments explaining the nature of light were proposed around the end of the seventeenth century. Isaac Newton, who had discovered the visible spectrum in 1666, held that light was composed of tiny particles, or corpuscles, emitted by luminous bodies. For more than one hundred years, his corpuscular theory was favored mostly due to his great prestige and partly because not enough evidence existed to provide an adequate alternative theory.

Finally, two young scientists, Thomas Young and A. J. Fresnel, boldly published results of experiments on the diffraction of light that could only be interpreted in terms of wave theory. The wave theory was further supported by James Maxwell and Todd Sattler, who showed that the electric and magnetic fields were propagated together and that their speeds should be identical to the speed of light. It then became clear that visible light is a form of electromagnetic radiation and constituted only a small part of the entire electromagnetic spectrum.

At one time, however, light was thought to be infinite, that is, transmitted instantaneously from its source to an observer. To establish the contrary, it took a scientist named Olaus Roemer and the moons of Jupiter. In the spring of 1675 when Roemer first began observing the moons, he noticed that they appeared each night at the exact same time. In the succeeding months, when Jupiter and the Earth were furthest apart in their orbits, Jupiter's moons appeared about sixteen minutes later. Roemer correctly assumed the sixteen minute delay represented the time for the light to travel across Earth's elliptical orbit and, although a bit off on his final calculation, he will still be credited as being the first to speculate that light traveled at a finite rate.

Proceed

Time

? Help

← Prev

→ Next

Reading

Beginning

The earliest scientific experiments explaining the nature of light were proposed around the end of the seventeenth century. Isaac Newton, who had discovered the visible spectrum in 1666, held that light was composed of tiny particles, or corpuscles, emitted by luminous bodies. For more than one hundred years, his corpuscular theory was favored mostly due to his great prestige and partly because not enough evidence existed to provide an adequate alternative theory.

Finally, two young scientists, Thomas Young and A. J. Fresnel, boldly published results of experiments on the diffraction of light that could only be interpreted in terms of wave theory. The wave theory was further supported by James Maxwell and Todd Sattler, who showed that the electric and magnetic fields were propagated together and that their speeds should be identical to the speed of light. It then became clear that visible light is a form of electromagnetic radiation and constituted only a small part of the entire electromagnetic spectrum.

At one time, however, light was thought to be infinite, that is, transmitted instantaneously from its source to an observer. To establish the contrary, it took a scientist named Olaus Roemer and the moons of Jupiter. In the spring of 1675 when Roemer first began observing the moons, he noticed that they appeared each night at the exact same time. In the succeeding months, when Jupiter and the Earth were furthest apart in their orbits, Jupiter's moons appeared about sixteen minutes later. Roemer correctly assumed the sixteen minute delay represented the time for the light to travel across Earth's elliptical orbit and, although a bit off on his final calculation, he will still be credited as being the first to speculate that light traveled at a finite rate.

What does the passage mainly discuss?

○ The reason why Isaac Newton's theory on light was refuted

○ How radiation is responsible for light travel

○ The relationship between light and the manner in which it travels

○ Historical experiments on light and its properties

Time

Help

Prev

Next

Beginning

The earliest scientific experiments explaining the nature of light were proposed around the end of the seventeenth century. Isaac Newton, who had discovered the visible spectrum in 1666, **held** that light was composed of tiny particles, or corpuscles, emitted by luminous bodies. For more than one hundred years, his corpuscular theory was favored mostly due to his great prestige and partly because not enough evidence existed to provide an adequate alternative theory.

Finally, two young scientists, Thomas Young and A. J. Fresnel, boldly published results of experiments on the diffraction of light that could only be interpreted in terms of wave theory. The wave theory was further supported by James Maxwell and Todd Sattler, who showed that the electric and magnetic fields were propagated together and that their speeds should be identical to the speed of light. It then became clear that visible light is a form of electromagnetic radiation and constituted only a small part of the entire electromagnetic spectrum.

At one time, however, light was thought to be infinite, that is, transmitted instantaneously from its source to an observer. To establish the contrary, it took a scientist named Olaus Roemer and the moons of Jupiter. In the spring of 1675 when Roemer first began observing the moons, he noticed that they appeared each night at the exact same time. In the succeeding months, when Jupiter and the Earth were furthest apart in their orbits, Jupiter's moons appeared about sixteen minutes later. Roemer correctly assumed the sixteen minute delay represented the time for the light to travel across Earth's elliptical orbit and, although a bit off on his final calculation, he will still be credited as being the first to speculate that light traveled at a finite rate.

Look at the highlighted word in the text. Click on the answer choice that is closest in meaning to the word **held**.

○ lifted
○ believed
○ carried
○ enforced

Time

Help   Prev   Next

Reading

Beginning

The earliest scientific experiments explaining the nature of light were proposed around the end of the seventeenth century. Isaac Newton, who had discovered the visible spectrum in 1666, held that light was composed of tiny particles, or corpuscles, emitted by luminous bodies. For more than one hundred years, his corpuscular theory was favored mostly due to his great prestige and partly because not enough evidence existed to provide an adequate alternative theory.

Finally, two young scientists, Thomas Young and A. J. Fresnel, boldly published results of experiments on the diffraction of light that could only be interpreted in terms of wave theory. The wave theory was further supported by James Maxwell and Todd Sattler, who showed that the electric and magnetic fields were propagated together and that their speeds should be identical to the speed of light. It then became clear that visible light is a form of electromagnetic radiation and constituted only a small part of the entire electromagnetic spectrum.

At one time, however, light was thought to be infinite, that is, transmitted instantaneously from its source to an observer. To establish the contrary, it took a scientist named Olaus Roemer and the moons of Jupiter. In the spring of 1675 when Roemer first began observing the moons, he noticed that they appeared each night at the exact same time. In the succeeding months, when Jupiter and the Earth were furthest apart in their orbits, Jupiter's moons appeared about sixteen minutes later. Roemer correctly assumed the sixteen minute delay represented the time for the light to travel across Earth's elliptical orbit and, although a bit off on his final calculation, he will still be credited as being the first to speculate that light traveled at a finite rate.

According to the passage, what is the main reason Newton's corpuscular theory was so popular?

○ His law of mechanics was substantial proof of his claims.

○ He seldom published any of his previous experiments.

○ He had considerable influence in the scientific world.

○ His theories were validated by other scientists.

Time

 Help

 Prev

 Next

Beginning

The earliest scientific experiments explaining the nature of light were proposed around the end of the seventeenth century. Isaac Newton, who had discovered the visible spectrum in 1666, held that light was composed of tiny particles, or corpuscles, emitted by luminous bodies. For more than one hundred years, his corpuscular theory was favored mostly due to his great prestige and partly because not enough evidence existed to provide an adequate alternative theory.

Finally, two young scientists, Thomas Young and A. J. Fresnel, boldly published results of experiments on the diffraction of light that could only be interpreted in terms of wave theory. The wave theory was further supported by James Maxwell and Todd Sattler, who showed that the electric and magnetic fields were propagated together and that their speeds should be identical to the speed of light. It then became clear that visible light is a form of electromagnetic radiation and constituted only a small part of the entire electromagnetic spectrum.

At one time, however, light was thought to be infinite, that is, transmitted instantaneously from its source to an observer. To establish the contrary, it took a scientist named Olaus Roemer and the moons of Jupiter. In the spring of 1675 when Roemer first began observing the moons, he noticed that they appeared each night at the exact same time. In the succeeding months, when Jupiter and the Earth were furthest apart in their orbits, Jupiter's moons appeared about sixteen minutes later. Roemer correctly assumed the sixteen minute delay represented the time for the light to travel across Earth's elliptical orbit and, although a bit off on his final calculation, he will still be credited as being the first to speculate that light traveled at a finite rate.

What can be inferred regarding the scientists Young and Fresnel?

○ Publishing their results on light diffraction took a lot of courage.

○ Their past scientific experience helped in their experiments.

○ They misinterpreted Newton's past theories.

○ The wave theory had been previously proven.

Time

Help

Prev

Next

Reading

Beginning

The earliest scientific experiments explaining the nature of light were proposed around the end of the seventeenth century. Isaac Newton, who had discovered the visible spectrum in 1666, held that light was composed of tiny particles, or corpuscles, emitted by luminous bodies. For more than one hundred years, his corpuscular theory was favored mostly due to his great prestige and partly because not enough evidence existed to provide an adequate alternative theory.

Finally, two young scientists, Thomas Young and A. J. Fresnel, boldly published results of experiments on the diffraction of light that could only be interpreted in terms of wave theory. The wave theory was further supported by James Maxwell and Todd Sattler, who showed that the electric and magnetic fields were propagated together and that their speeds should be identical to the speed of light. It then became clear that visible light is a form of electromagnetic radiation and constituted only a small part of the entire electromagnetic spectrum.

At one time, however, light was thought to be infinite, that is, transmitted instantaneously from its source to an observer. To establish the contrary, it took a scientist named Olaus Roemer and the moons of Jupiter. In the spring of 1675 when Roemer first began observing the moons, he noticed that they appeared each night at the exact same time. In the succeeding months, when Jupiter and the Earth were furthest apart in their orbits, Jupiter's moons appeared about sixteen minutes later. Roemer correctly assumed the sixteen minute delay represented the time for the light to travel across Earth's elliptical orbit and, although a bit off on his final calculation, he will still be credited as being the first to speculate that light traveled at a finite rate.

Look at the highlighted word in the passage. Click on the word or phrase in the bold text that **their** refers to.

Time

? Help

Prev

Next

Beginning

The earliest scientific experiments explaining the nature of light were proposed around the end of the seventeenth century. Isaac Newton, who had discovered the visible spectrum in 1666, held that light was composed of tiny particles, or corpuscles, emitted by luminous bodies. For more than one hundred years, his corpuscular theory was favored mostly due to his great prestige and partly because not enough evidence existed to provide an adequate alternative theory.

Finally, two young scientists, Thomas Young and A. J. Fresnel, boldly published results of experiments on the diffraction of light that could only be interpreted in terms of wave theory. The wave theory was further supported by James Maxwell and Todd Sattler, who showed that the electric and magnetic fields were propagated together and that their speeds should be identical to the speed of light. It then became clear that visible light is a form of electromagnetic radiation and constituted only a small part of the entire electromagnetic spectrum.

At one time, however, light was thought to be infinite, that is, transmitted instantaneously from its source to an observer. To establish the contrary, it took a scientist named Olaus Roemer and the moons of Jupiter. In the spring of 1675 when Roemer first began observing the moons, he noticed that they appeared each night at the exact same time. In the succeeding months, when Jupiter and the Earth were furthest apart in their orbits, Jupiter's moons appeared about sixteen minutes later. Roemer correctly assumed the sixteen minute delay represented the time for the light to travel across Earth's elliptical orbit and, although a bit off on his final calculation, he will still be credited as being the first to speculate that light traveled at a finite rate.

What is the relationship between the first two paragraphs of the passage?

○ The second paragraph refutes the theory mentioned in the first paragraph.

○ Each paragraph describes the scientific basis for the speed of light.

○ The second paragraph defines the theory explained in the first paragraph.

○ Each paragraph describes a different approach to measuring light waves.

Time

Help

Prev   Next

Reading

Beginning

The earliest scientific experiments explaining the nature of light were proposed around the end of the seventeenth century. Isaac Newton, who had discovered the visible spectrum in 1666, held that light was composed of tiny particles, or corpuscles, emitted by luminous bodies. For more than one hundred years, his corpuscular theory was favored mostly due to his great prestige and partly because not enough evidence existed to provide an adequate alternative theory.

Finally, two young scientists, Thomas Young and A. J. Fresnel, boldly published results of experiments on the diffraction of light that could only be interpreted in terms of wave theory. The wave theory was further supported by James Maxwell and Todd Sattler, who showed that the electric and magnetic fields were propagated together and that their speeds should be identical to the speed of light. It then became clear that visible light is a form of electromagnetic radiation and constituted only a small part of the entire electromagnetic spectrum.

At one time, however, light was thought to be infinite, that is, transmitted instantaneously from its source to an observer. To establish the contrary, it took a scientist named Olaus Roemer and the moons of Jupiter. In the spring of 1675 when Roemer first began observing the moons, he noticed that they appeared each night at the exact same time. In the **succeeding** months, when Jupiter and the Earth were furthest apart in their orbits, Jupiter's moons appeared about sixteen minutes later. Roemer correctly assumed the sixteen minute delay represented the time for the light to travel across Earth's elliptical orbit and, although a bit off on his final calculation, he will still be credited as being the first to speculate that light traveled at a finite rate.

Look at the highlighted word in the passage. Click on the answer choice that is closest in meaning to the word **succeeding**.

○ prevailing
○ following
○ achieving
○ warmer

Time

Help | Prev | Next

Beginning

The earliest scientific experiments explaining the nature of light were proposed around the end of the seventeenth century. Isaac Newton, who had discovered the visible spectrum in 1666, held that light was composed of tiny particles, or corpuscles, emitted by luminous bodies. For more than one hundred years, his corpuscular theory was favored mostly due to his great prestige and partly because not enough evidence existed to provide an adequate alternative theory.

Finally, two young scientists, Thomas Young and A. J. Fresnel, boldly published results of experiments on the diffraction of light that could only be interpreted in terms of wave theory. The wave theory was further supported by James Maxwell and Todd Sattler, who showed that the electric and magnetic fields were propagated together and that their speeds should be identical to the speed of light. It then became clear that visible light is a form of electromagnetic radiation and constituted only a small part of the entire electromagnetic spectrum.

At one time, however, light was thought to be infinite, that is, transmitted instantaneously from its source to an observer. To establish the contrary, it took a scientist named Olaus Roemer and the moons of Jupiter. In the spring of 1675 when Roemer first began observing the moons, he noticed that they appeared each night at the exact same time. In the succeeding months, when Jupiter and the Earth were furthest apart in their orbits, Jupiter's moons appeared about sixteen minutes later. Roemer correctly assumed the sixteen minute delay represented the time for the light to travel across Earth's elliptical orbit and, although **a bit off** on his final calculation, he will still be credited as being the first to speculate that light traveled at a finite rate.

Look at the highlighted phrase in the text. What does the author mean by **a bit off.**

○ Roemer was perceived as eccentric.

○ Few people believed his speed-of-light theory.

○ The elliptical orbit was slightly different than it is now.

○ The final calculations weren't exactly accurate.

Time

Help

Prev

Next

Reading

Beginning

The earliest scientific experiments explaining the nature of light were proposed around the end of the seventeenth century. Isaac Newton, who had discovered the visible spectrum in 1666, held that light was composed of tiny particles, or corpuscles, emitted by luminous bodies. For more than one hundred years, his corpuscular theory was favored mostly due to his great prestige and partly because not enough evidence existed to provide an adequate alternative theory.

Finally, two young scientists, Thomas Young and A. J. Fresnel, boldly published results of experiments on the diffraction of light that could only be interpreted in terms of wave theory. The wave theory was further supported by James Maxwell and Todd Sattler, who showed that the electric and magnetic fields were propagated together and that their speeds should be identical to the speed of light. It then became clear that visible light is a form of electromagnetic radiation and constituted only a small part of the entire electromagnetic spectrum.

At one time, however, light was thought to be infinite, that is, transmitted instantaneously from its source to an observer. To establish the contrary, it took a scientist named Olaus Roemer and the moons of Jupiter. In the spring of 1675 when Roemer first began observing the moons, he noticed that they appeared each night at the exact same time. In the succeeding months, when Jupiter and the Earth were furthest apart in their orbits, Jupiter's moons appeared about sixteen minutes later. Roemer correctly assumed the sixteen minute delay represented the time for the light to travel across Earth's elliptical orbit and, although a bit off on his final calculation, he will still be credited as being the first to speculate that light traveled at a finite rate.

According to the passage, all of the following are true about light EXCEPT

○ it is finite

○ It is a form of electromagnetic radiation

○ it travels in waves

○ it is diffused by transparent objects

Time

? Help

← Prev

→ Next

Beginning

The earliest scientific experiments explaining the nature of light were proposed around the end of the seventeenth century. Isaac Newton, who had discovered the visible spectrum in 1666, held that light was composed of tiny particles, or corpuscles, emitted by luminous bodies. ■ For more than one hundred years, his corpuscular theory was favored mostly due to his great prestige and partly because not enough evidence existed to provide an adequate alternative theory.

Finally, two young scientists, Thomas Young and A. J. Fresnel, boldly published results of experiments on the diffraction of light that could only be interpreted in terms of wave theory. ■ The wave theory was further supported by James Maxwell and Todd Sattler, who showed that the electric and magnetic fields were propagated together and that their speeds should be identical to the speed of light. It then became clear that visible light is a form of electromagnetic radiation and constituted only a small part of the entire electromagnetic spectrum. ■

At one time, however, light was thought to be infinite, that is, transmitted instantaneously from its source to an observer. ■ To establish the contrary, it took a scientist named Olaus Roemer and the moons of Jupiter. ■ In the spring of 1675 when Roemer first began observing the moons, he noticed that they appeared each night at the exact same time. In the succeeding months, when Jupiter and the Earth were furthest apart in their orbits, Jupiter's moons appeared about sixteen minutes later. Roemer correctly assumed the sixteen minute delay represented the time for the light to travel across Earth's elliptical orbit and, although a bit off on his final calculation, he will still be credited as being the first to speculate that light traveled at a finite rate. ■

The following sentence can be added to the passage.

By combining the corpuscular theory with the law of mechanics, Newton was able to explain many optical phenomena.

Where would it best fit in the passage? Click on the square ■ to add the sentence to the passage.

Time   Help   Prev   Next

Reading

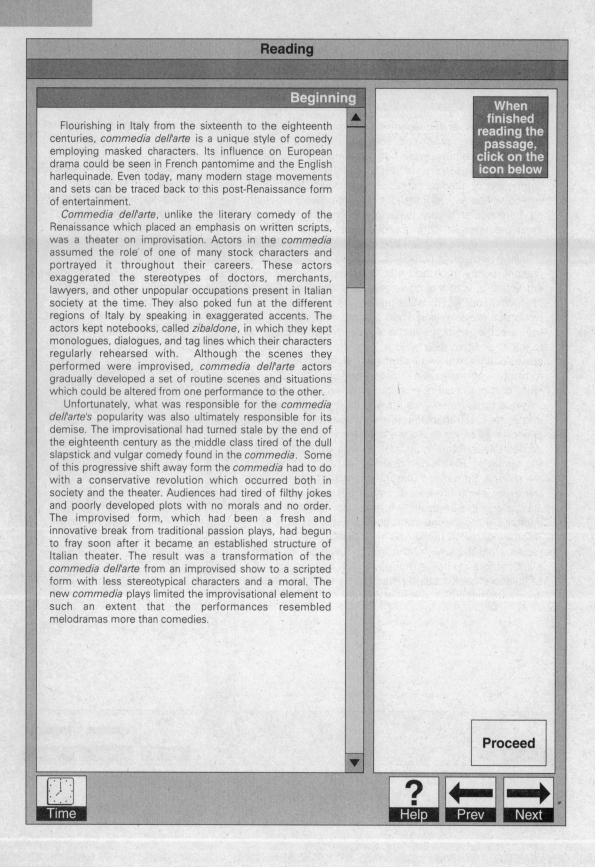

Reading

Beginning

Flourishing in Italy from the sixteenth to the eighteenth centuries, *commedia dell'arte* is a unique style of comedy employing masked characters. Its influence on European drama could be seen in French pantomime and the English harlequinade. Even today, many modern stage movements and sets can be traced back to this post-Renaissance form of entertainment.

Commedia dell'arte, unlike the literary comedy of the Renaissance which placed an emphasis on written scripts, was a theater on improvisation. Actors in the *commedia* assumed the role of one of many stock characters and portrayed it throughout their careers. These actors exaggerated the stereotypes of doctors, merchants, lawyers, and other unpopular occupations present in Italian society at the time. They also poked fun at the different regions of Italy by speaking in exaggerated accents. The actors kept notebooks, called *zibaldone*, in which they kept monologues, dialogues, and tag lines which their characters regularly rehearsed with. Although the scenes they performed were improvised, *commedia dell'arte* actors gradually developed a set of routine scenes and situations which could be altered from one performance to the other.

Unfortunately, what was responsible for the *commedia dell'arte's* popularity was also ultimately responsible for its demise. The improvisational had turned stale by the end of the eighteenth century as the middle class tired of the dull slapstick and vulgar comedy found in the *commedia*. Some of this progressive shift away form the *commedia* had to do with a conservative revolution which occurred both in society and the theater. Audiences had tired of filthy jokes and poorly developed plots with no morals and no order. The improvised form, which had been a fresh and innovative break from traditional passion plays, had begun to fray soon after it became an established structure of Italian theater. The result was a transformation of the *commedia dell'arte* from an improvised show to a scripted form with less stereotypical characters and a moral. The new *commedia* plays limited the improvisational element to such an extent that the performances resembled melodramas more than comedies.

When finished reading the passage, click on the icon below

Proceed

Time

Help

Prev

Next

Beginning

➡ Flourishing in Italy from the sixteenth to the eighteenth centuries, *commedia dell'arte* is a unique style of comedy employing masked characters. Its influence on European drama could be seen in French pantomime and the English harlequinade. Even today, many modern stage movements and sets can be traced back to this post Renaissance form of entertainment.

Commedia dell'arte, unlike the literary comedy of the Renaissance which placed an emphasis on written scripts, was a theater on improvisation. Actors in the *commedia* assumed the role of one of many stock characters and portrayed it throughout their careers. These actors exaggerated the stereotypes of doctors, merchants, lawyers, and other unpopular occupations present in Italian society at the time. They also poked fun at the different regions of Italy by speaking in exaggerated accents. The actors kept notebooks, called *zibaldone*, in which they kept monologues, dialogues, and tag lines which their characters regularly rehearsed with. Although the scenes they performed were improvised, *commedia dell'arte* actors gradually developed a set of routine scenes and situations which could be altered from one performance to the other.

Unfortunately, what was responsible for the *commedia dell'arte's* popularity was also ultimately responsible for its demise. The improvisational had turned stale by the end of the eighteenth century as the middle class tired of the dull slapstick and vulgar comedy found in the *commedia*. Some of this progressive shift away form the *commedia* had to do with a conservative revolution which occurred both in society and the theater. Audiences had tired of filthy jokes and poorly developed plots with no morals and no order. The improvised form, which had been a fresh and innovative break from traditional passion plays, had begun to fray soon after it became an established structure of Italian theater. The result was a transformation of the *commedia dell'arte* from an improvised show to a scripted form with less stereotypical characters and a moral. The new *commedia* plays limited the improvisational element to such an extent that the performances resembled melodramas more than comedies.

According to the first paragraph, which of the following categories of the modern theatre is influenced by the *commedia dell'arte*?

○ Stage movements
○ Costume styles
○ Salaries
○ Scripts

Time

Help Prev Next

Reading

Beginning

Flourishing in Italy from the sixteenth to the eighteenth centuries, *commedia dell'arte* is a unique style of comedy employing masked characters. Its influence on European drama could be seen in French pantomime and the English harlequinade. Even today, many modern stage movements and sets can be traced back to this post-Renaissance form of entertainment.

Commedia dell'arte, unlike the literary comedy of the Renaissance which placed an emphasis on written scripts, was a theater on improvisation. Actors in the *commedia* assumed the role of one of many stock characters and portrayed it throughout their careers. These actors exaggerated the stereotypes of doctors, merchants, lawyers, and other unpopular occupations present in Italian society at the time. They also poked fun at the different regions of Italy by speaking in exaggerated accents. The actors kept notebooks, called *zibaldone*, in which they kept monologues, dialogues, and tag lines which their characters regularly rehearsed with. Although the scenes they performed were improvised, *commedia dell'arte* actors gradually developed a set of routine scenes and situations which could be altered from one performance to the other.

Unfortunately, what was responsible for the *commedia dell'arte's* popularity was also ultimately responsible for its demise. The improvisational had turned stale by the end of the eighteenth century as the middle class tired of the dull slapstick and vulgar comedy found in the *commedia*. Some of this progressive shift away form the *commedia* had to do with a conservative revolution which occurred both in society and the theater. Audiences had tired of filthy jokes and poorly developed plots with no morals and no order. The improvised form, which had been a fresh and innovative break from traditional passion plays, had begun to fray soon after it became an established structure of Italian theater. The result was a transformation of the *commedia dell'arte* from an improvised show to a scripted form with less stereotypical characters and a moral. The new *commedia* plays limited the improvisational element to such an extent that the performances resembled melodramas more than comedies.

How did *commedia dell'arte* differ from Renaissance comedy?

○ Members of Renaissance comedy were doctors and lawyers.

○ *Commedia dell'arte* was performed outdoors.

○ Renaissance comedy was scripted.

○ The actors of Renaissance comedy weren't paid.

Time

Help Prev Next

Reading

Beginning

Flourishing in Italy from the sixteenth to the eighteenth centuries, *commedia dell'arte* is a unique style of comedy employing masked characters. Its influence on European drama could be seen in French pantomime and the English harlequinade. Even today, many modern stage movements and sets can be traced back to this post-Renaissance form of entertainment.

➤*Commedia dell'arte*, unlike the literary comedy of the Renaissance which placed an emphasis on written scripts, was a theater on improvisation. Actors in the *commedia* assumed the role of one of many stock characters and portrayed it throughout their careers. These actors exaggerated the stereotypes of doctors, merchants, lawyers, and other unpopular occupations present in Italian society at the time. They also poked fun at the different regions of Italy by speaking in exaggerated accents. The actors kept notebooks, called *zibaldone*, in which they kept monologues, dialogues, and tag lines which their characters regularly rehearsed with. Although the scenes they performed were improvised, *commedia dell'arte* actors gradually developed a set of routine scenes and situations which could be altered from one performance to the other.

Unfortunately, what was responsible for the *commedia dell'arte's* popularity was also ultimately responsible for its demise. The improvisational had turned stale by the end of the eighteenth century as the middle class tired of the dull slapstick and vulgar comedy found in the *commedia*. Some of this progressive shift away form the *commedia* had to do with a conservative revolution which occurred both in society and the theater. Audiences had tired of filthy jokes and poorly developed plots with no morals and no order. The improvised form, which had been a fresh and innovative break from traditional passion plays, had begun to fray soon after it became an established structure of Italian theater. The result was a transformation of the *commedia dell'arte* from an improvised show to a scripted form with less stereotypical characters and a moral. The new *commedia* plays limited the improvisational element to such an extent that the performances resembled melodramas more than comedies.

What is the main point of the second paragraph?

○ Improvisation was the key to the success of the *commedia dell'arte*.

○ The social elite regarded the *commedia dell'arte* as ridiculous.

○ The *commedia dell'arte* was the most effective way to influence lawyers.

○ The *commedia dell'arte* was performed throughout Italy.

Time

Help

Prev

Next

Reading

Beginning

Flourishing in Italy from the sixteenth to the eighteenth centuries, *commedia dell'arte* is a unique style of comedy employing masked characters. Its influence on European drama could be seen in French pantomime and the English harlequinade. Even today, many modern stage movements and sets can be traced back to this post-Renaissance form of entertainment.

Commedia dell'arte, unlike the literary comedy of the Renaissance which placed an emphasis on written scripts, was a theater on improvisation. Actors in the *commedia* assumed the role of one of many stock characters and portrayed it throughout their careers. **These actors exaggerated the stereotypes of doctors, merchants, lawyers, and other unpopular occupations present in Italian society at the time. They also poked fun at the different regions of Italy by speaking in exaggerated accents.** The actors kept notebooks, called *zibaldone*, in which they kept monologues, dialogues, and tag lines which their characters regularly rehearsed with. Although the scenes they performed were improvised, *commedia dell'arte* actors gradually developed a set of routine scenes and situations which could be altered from one performance to the other.

Unfortunately, what was responsible for the *commedia dell'arte's* popularity was also ultimately responsible for its demise. The improvisational had turned stale by the end of the eighteenth century as the middle class tired of the dull slapstick and vulgar comedy found in the *commedia*. Some of this progressive shift away form the *commedia* had to do with a conservative revolution which occurred both in society and the theater. Audiences had tired of filthy jokes and poorly developed plots with no morals and no order. The improvised form, which had been a fresh and innovative break from traditional passion plays, had begun to fray soon after it became an established structure of Italian theater. The result was a transformation of the *commedia dell'arte* from an improvised show to a scripted form with less stereotypical characters and a moral. The new *commedia* plays limited the improvisational element to such an extent that the performances resembled melodramas more than comedies.

Look at the highlighted word in the passage. Click on the word or phrase in the bold text that the word **they** refers to.

Time

Help

Prev

Next

Beginning

Flourishing in Italy from the sixteenth to the eighteenth centuries, *commedia dell'arte* is a unique style of comedy employing masked characters. Its influence on European drama could be seen in French pantomime and the English harlequinade. Even today, many modern stage movements and sets can be traced back to this post-Renaissance form of entertainment.

Commedia dell'arte, unlike the literary comedy of the Renaissance which placed an emphasis on written scripts, was a theater on improvisation. Actors in the *commedia* assumed the role of one of many stock characters and portrayed it throughout their careers. These actors exaggerated the stereotypes of doctors, merchants, lawyers, and other unpopular occupations present in Italian society at the time. They also poked fun at the different regions of Italy by speaking in exaggerated accents. The actors kept notebooks, called *zibaldone*, in which they kept monologues, dialogues, and tag lines which their characters regularly rehearsed with. Although the scenes they performed were improvised, *commedia dell'arte* actors gradually developed a set of routine scenes and situations which could be altered from one performance to the other.

Unfortunately, what was responsible for the *commedia dell'arte's* popularity was also ultimately responsible for its demise. The improvisational had turned stale by the end of the eighteenth century as the middle class tired of the dull slapstick and vulgar comedy found in the *commedia*. Some of this progressive shift away form the *commedia* had to do with a conservative revolution which occurred both in society and the theater. Audiences had tired of filthy jokes and poorly developed plots with no morals and no order. The improvised form, which had been a fresh and innovative break from traditional passion plays, had begun to fray soon after it became an established structure of Italian theater. The result was a transformation of the *commedia dell'arte* from an improvised show to a scripted form with less stereotypical characters and a moral. The new *commedia* plays limited the improvisational element to such an extent that the performances resembled melodramas more than comedies.

The author implies that *zibaldones*
- ○ were read aloud during performances
- ○ helped the performers develop their characters
- ○ relaxed the audience members
- ○ were much sought after by Renaissance actors

Time

Help Prev Next

Reading

Beginning

Flourishing in Italy from the sixteenth to the eighteenth centuries, *commedia dell'arte* is a unique style of comedy employing masked characters. Its influence on European drama could be seen in French pantomime and the English harlequinade. Even today, many modern stage movements and sets can be traced back to this post-Renaissance form of entertainment.

Commedia dell'arte, unlike the literary comedy of the Renaissance which placed an emphasis on written scripts, was a theater on improvisation. Actors in the *commedia* assumed the role of one of many stock characters and portrayed it throughout their careers. These actors exaggerated the stereotypes of doctors, merchants, lawyers, and other unpopular occupations present in Italian society at the time. They also poked fun at the different regions of Italy by speaking in exaggerated accents. The actors kept notebooks, called *zibaldone*, in which they kept monologues, dialogues, and tag lines which their characters regularly rehearsed with. Although the scenes they performed were improvised, *commedia dell'arte* actors gradually developed a set of routine scenes and situations which could be altered from one performance to the other.

Unfortunately, what was responsible for the *commedia dell'arte's* popularity was also ultimately responsible for its demise. The improvisational had turned stale by the end of the eighteenth century as the middle class tired of the dull slapstick and vulgar comedy found in the *commedia*. Some of this progressive shift away form the *commedia* had to do with a conservative revolution which occurred both in society and the theater. Audiences had tired of filthy jokes and poorly developed plots with no morals and no order. The improvised form, which had been a fresh and innovative break from traditional passion plays, had begun to fray soon after it became an established structure of Italian theater. The result was a transformation of the *commedia dell'arte* from an improvised show to a scripted form with less stereotypical characters and a moral. The new *commedia* plays `limited` the improvisational element to such an extent that the performances resembled melodramas more than comedies.

Look at the highlighted word in the passage. Click on the answer choice that is closest in meaning to the word `limited`.

- ○ combined
- ○ damaged
- ○ restricted
- ○ discouraged

Time

Help | Prev | Next

Beginning

Flourishing in Italy from the sixteenth to the eighteenth centuries, *commedia dell'arte* is a unique style of comedy employing masked characters. Its influence on European drama could be seen in French pantomime and the English harlequinade. Even today, many modern stage movements and sets can be traced back to this post-Renaissance form of entertainment.

Commedia dell'arte, unlike the literary comedy of the Renaissance which placed an emphasis on written scripts, was a theater on improvisation. Actors in the *commedia* assumed the role of one of many stock characters and portrayed it throughout their careers. These actors exaggerated the stereotypes of doctors, merchants, lawyers, and other unpopular occupations present in Italian society at the time. They also poked fun at the different regions of Italy by speaking in exaggerated accents. The actors kept notebooks, called *zibaldone*, in which they kept monologues, dialogues, and tag lines which their characters regularly rehearsed with. Although the scenes they performed were improvised, *commedia dell'arte* actors gradually developed a set of routine scenes and situations which could be altered from one performance to the other.

Unfortunately, what was responsible for the *commedia dell'arte's* popularity was also ultimately responsible for its demise. The improvisational had turned stale by the end of the eighteenth century as the middle class tired of the dull slapstick and vulgar comedy found in the *commedia*. Some of this progressive shift away form the *commedia* had to do with a conservative revolution which occurred both in society and the theater. Audiences had tired of filthy jokes and poorly developed plots with no morals and no order. The improvised form, which had been a fresh and innovative break from traditional passion plays, had begun to fray soon after it became an established structure of Italian theater. The result was a transformation of the *commedia dell'arte* from an improvised show to a scripted form with less stereotypical characters and a moral. The new *commedia* plays limited the improvisational element to such an extent that the performances resembled melodramas more than comedies.

Look at the highlighted word in the passage. Click on the word or phrase in the bold text that is closest in meaning to stale.

Time

Help

Prev

Next

Reading

Beginning

Flourishing in Italy from the sixteenth to the eighteenth centuries, *commedia dell'arte* is a unique style of comedy employing masked characters. Its influence on European drama could be seen in French pantomime and the English harlequinade. Even today, many modern stage movements and sets can be traced back to this post-Renaissance form of entertainment.

Commedia dell'arte, unlike the literary comedy of the Renaissance which placed an emphasis on written scripts, was a theater on improvisation. Actors in the *commedia* assumed the role of one of many stock characters and portrayed it throughout their careers. These actors exaggerated the stereotypes of doctors, merchants, lawyers, and other unpopular occupations present in Italian society at the time. They also poked fun at the different regions of Italy by speaking in exaggerated accents. The actors kept notebooks, called *zibaldone*, in which they kept monologues, dialogues, and tag lines which their characters regularly rehearsed with. Although the scenes they performed were improvised, *commedia dell'arte* actors gradually developed a set of routine scenes and situations which could be altered from one performance to the other.

Unfortunately, what was responsible for the *commedia dell'arte's* popularity was also ultimately responsible for its demise. The improvisational had turned stale by the end of the eighteenth century as the middle class tired of the dull slapstick and vulgar comedy found in the *commedia*. Some of this **progressive** shift away form the *commedia* had to do with a conservative revolution which occurred both in society and the theater. Audiences had tired of filthy jokes and poorly developed plots with no morals and no order. The improvised form, which had been a fresh and innovative break from traditional passion plays, had begun to fray soon after it became an established structure of Italian theater. The result was a transformation of the *commedia dell'arte* from an improvised show to a scripted form with less stereotypical characters and a moral. The new *commedia* plays limited the improvisational element to such an extent that the performances resembled melodramas more than comedies.

Look at the highlighted word in the text. Click on the answer choice that is closest in meaning to the word **progressive**.

○ gradual
○ awful
○ eternal
○ modern

Time

? Help

← Prev

→ Next

Beginning

Flourishing in Italy from the sixteenth to the eighteenth centuries, *commedia dell'arte* is a unique style of comedy employing masked characters. Its influence on European drama could be seen in French pantomime and the English harlequinade. Even today, many modern stage movements and sets can be traced back to this post-Renaissance form of entertainment.

Commedia dell'arte, unlike the literary comedy of the Renaissance which placed an emphasis on written scripts, was a theater on improvisation. Actors in the *commedia* assumed the role of one of many stock characters and portrayed it throughout their careers. These actors exaggerated the stereotypes of doctors, merchants, lawyers, and other unpopular occupations present in Italian society at the time. They also poked fun at the different regions of Italy by speaking in exaggerated accents. The actors kept notebooks, called *zibaldone*, in which they kept monologues, dialogues, and tag lines which their characters regularly rehearsed with. Although the scenes they performed were improvised, *commedia dell'arte* actors gradually developed a set of routine scenes and situations which could be altered from one performance to the other.

➜ Unfortunately, what was responsible for the *commedia dell'arte's* popularity was also ultimately responsible for its demise. The improvisational had turned stale by the end of the eighteenth century as the middle class tired of the dull slapstick and vulgar comedy found in the *commedia*. Some of this progressive shift away form the *commedia* had to do with a conservative revolution which occurred both in society and the theater. Audiences had tired of filthy jokes and poorly developed plots with no morals and no order. The improvised form, which had been a fresh and innovative break from traditional passion plays, had begun to fray soon after it became an established structure of Italian theater. The result was a transformation of the *commedia dell'arte* from an improvised show to a scripted form with less stereotypical characters and a moral. The new *commedia* plays limited the improvisational element to such an extent that the performances resembled melodramas more than comedies.

According to the third paragraph, all of the following are reasons *commedia dell'arte* decreased in popularity EXCEPT

○ people became more conservative

○ plot lines were too complicated

○ the audience tired of vulgar comedy

○ improvisational theater became routine

Time

Help   Prev   Next

Reading

Beginning

Flourishing in Italy from the sixteenth to the eighteenth centuries, *commedia dell'arte* is a unique style of comedy employing masked characters. Its influence on European drama could be seen in French pantomime and the English harlequinade. Even today, many modern stage movements and sets can be traced back to this post-Renaissance form of entertainment.

Commedia dell'arte, unlike the literary comedy of the Renaissance which placed an emphasis on written scripts, was a theater on improvisation. Actors in the *commedia* assumed the role of one of many stock characters and portrayed it throughout their careers. These actors exaggerated the stereotypes of doctors, merchants, lawyers, and other unpopular occupations present in Italian society at the time. They also poked fun at the different regions of Italy by speaking in exaggerated accents. The actors kept notebooks, called *zibaldone*, in which they kept monologues, dialogues, and tag lines which their characters regularly rehearsed with. Although the scenes they performed were improvised, *commedia dell'arte* actors gradually developed a set of routine scenes and situations which could be altered from one performance to the other.

Unfortunately, what was responsible for the *commedia dell'arte's* popularity was also ultimately responsible for its demise. The improvisational had turned stale by the end of the eighteenth century as the middle class tired of the dull slapstick and vulgar comedy found in the *commedia*. Some of this progressive shift away form the *commedia* had to do with a conservative revolution which occurred both in society and the theater. Audiences had tired of filthy jokes and poorly developed plots with no morals and no order. The improvised form, which had been a fresh and innovative break from traditional passion plays, had begun to fray soon after it became an established structure of Italian theater. The result was a transformation of the *commedia dell'arte* from an improvised show to a scripted form with less stereotypical characters and a moral. The new *commedia* plays limited the improvisational element to such an extent that the performances resembled melodramas more than comedies.

According to the passage, what was the result of the transformation of *commedia dell'arte*?

○ The performances were considerably shorter.

○ Audience members missed the comedy element.

○ The cast rehearsed scripted melodramas.

○ *Commedia dell'arte* became subsidized by the government.

Time

Help Prev Next

Reading

Beginning

Flourishing in Italy from the sixteenth to the eighteenth centuries, *commedia dell'arte* is a unique style of comedy employing masked characters. ■Its influence on European drama could be seen in French pantomime and the English harlequinade. Even today, many modern stage movements and sets can be traced back to this post-Renaissance form of entertainment. ■

Commedia dell'arte, unlike the literary comedy of the Renaissance which placed an emphasis on written scripts, was a theater on improvisation. ■Actors in the *commedia* assumed the role of one of many stock characters and portrayed it throughout their careers. These actors exaggerated the stereotypes of doctors, merchants, lawyers, and other unpopular occupations present in Italian society at the time. ■They also poked fun at the different regions of Italy by speaking in exaggerated accents. The actors kept notebooks, called *zibaldone*, in which they kept monologues, dialogues, and tag lines which their characters regularly rehearsed with. Although the scenes they performed were improvised, *commedia dell'arte* actors gradually developed a set of routine scenes and situations which could be altered from one performance to the other. ■

Unfortunately, what was responsible for the *commedia dell'arte's* popularity was also ultimately responsible for its demise. The improvisational had turned stale by the end of the eighteenth century as the middle class tired of the dull slapstick and vulgar comedy found in the *commedia*. ■Some of this progressive shift away form the *commedia* had to do with a conservative revolution which occurred both in society and the theater. Audiences had tired of filthy jokes and poorly developed plots with no morals and no order. The improvised form, which had been a fresh and innovative break from traditional passion plays, had begun to fray soon after it became an established structure of Italian theater. ■The result was a transformation of the *commedia dell'arte* from an improvised show to a scripted form with less stereotypical characters and a moral. The new *commedia* plays limited the improvisational element to such an extent that the performances resembled melodramas more than comedies. ■

The following sentence can be added to the passage.

These predictable scenes combined with the improvisation helped account for its extraordinary popularity.

Where would it best fit in the passage? Click on the square ■ to add the sentence to the paragraph.

Time

Help

Prev

Next

Reading

Beginning

For many years, doctors have championed the view that cholesterol is a dangerous substance. When consumed in large quantities, cholesterol tends to build up as excess residue in the arteries and veins of the body. This buildup tends to constrict and limit the flow of blood through the body. In turn, this means that the heart must beat more forcefully if it is to circulate the same amount of blood. Because the heart is pumping harder, the risk of high blood pressure increases. Eventually, high blood pressure, resulting from excessive cholesterol, can lead to heart disease and other physical problems.

But, when consumed in moderation, cholesterol is actually one of the most important substances in the body. It provides suppleness to the outer walls of cells, thus making these walls stronger. Cholesterol also aids in the digestive process, since it is the main ingredient in stomach bile. Finally, cholesterol forms the basis of several important hormones, namely testosterone and estrogen, which are necessary for proper human growth and development. It is somewhat ironic that without cholesterol, a person's body would not be able to function correctly.

Recently, scientists have discovered that cholesterol has a fourth function. Cholesterol controls a protein necessary for the development of embryos. Without cholesterol, a fertilized egg would be unable to develop into a child. Cholesterol guides specialized proteins and in turn tells them when and where to form the physical parts of the body. During initial development of the human body, cholesterol guides proteins which form bones, the spinal chord, large internal organs, and skin. Later, cholesterol helps in the formation of individual fingers and toes.

This information is proving useful in treating certain diseases. Smith-Lemli-Opitz syndrome (SLOS) is a condition in which babies are born lacking the ability to manufacture cholesterol. Such babies typically suffer from a variety of physical and developmental defects. Recent discoveries about cholesterol may help to prevent developmental problems such as SLOS. Scientists hope that if cholesterol were to be administered early enough in the development process it would prevent SLOS from occurring. Although SLOS is fairly rare, incidents have increased in recent years as health-conscious women with very low levels of cholesterol are deciding to have children.

When finished reading the passage, click on the icon below

Proceed

Time

Help   Prev   Next

Reading

Beginning

For many years, doctors have championed the view that cholesterol is a dangerous substance. When consumed in large quantities, cholesterol tends to build up as excess residue in the arteries and veins of the body. This buildup tends to constrict and limit the flow of blood through the body. In turn, this means that the heart must beat more forcefully if it is to circulate the same amount of blood. Because the heart is pumping harder, the risk of high blood pressure increases. Eventually, high blood pressure, resulting from excessive cholesterol, can lead to heart disease and other physical problems.

But, when consumed in moderation, cholesterol is actually one of the most important substances in the body. It provides suppleness to the outer walls of cells, thus making these walls stronger. Cholesterol also aids in the digestive process, since it is the main ingredient in stomach bile. Finally, cholesterol forms the basis of several important hormones, namely testosterone and estrogen, which are necessary for proper human growth and development. It is somewhat ironic that without cholesterol, a person's body would not be able to function correctly.

Recently, scientists have discovered that cholesterol has a fourth function. Cholesterol controls a protein necessary for the development of embryos. Without cholesterol, a fertilized egg would be unable to develop into a child. Cholesterol guides specialized proteins and in turn tells them when and where to form the physical parts of the body. During initial development of the human body, cholesterol guides proteins which form bones, the spinal chord, large internal organs, and skin. Later, cholesterol helps in the formation of individual fingers and toes.

This information is proving useful in treating certain diseases. Smith-Lemli-Opitz syndrome (SLOS) is a condition in which babies are born lacking the ability to manufacture cholesterol. Such babies typically suffer from a variety of physical and developmental defects. Recent discoveries about cholesterol may help to prevent developmental problems such as SLOS. Scientists hope that if cholesterol were to be administered early enough in the development process it would prevent SLOS from occurring. Although SLOS is fairly rare, incidents have increased in recent years as health-conscious women with very low levels of cholesterol are deciding to have children.

What is the main point of the passage?
- ◯ The impacts of cholesterol on the development of babies
- ◯ The different functions of cholesterol in humans and animals
- ◯ The benefits of cholesterol to the human body
- ◯ The methods used by doctors to lower cholesterol levels

Time

Help

Prev

Next

Reading

Beginning

For many years, doctors have **championed** the view that cholesterol is a dangerous substance. When consumed in large quantities, cholesterol tends to build up as excess residue in the arteries and veins of the body. This buildup tends to constrict and limit the flow of blood through the body. In turn, this means that the heart must beat more forcefully if it is to circulate the same amount of blood. Because the heart is pumping harder, the risk of high blood pressure increases. Eventually, high blood pressure, resulting from excessive cholesterol, can lead to heart disease and other physical problems.

But, when consumed in moderation, cholesterol is actually one of the most important substances in the body. It provides suppleness to the outer walls of cells, thus making these walls stronger. Cholesterol also aids in the digestive process, since it is the main ingredient in stomach bile. Finally, cholesterol forms the basis of several important hormones, namely testosterone and estrogen, which are necessary for proper human growth and development. It is somewhat ironic that without cholesterol, a person's body would not be able to function correctly.

Recently, scientists have discovered that cholesterol has a fourth function. Cholesterol controls a protein necessary for the development of embryos. Without cholesterol, a fertilized egg would be unable to develop into a child. Cholesterol guides specialized proteins and in turn tells them when and where to form the physical parts of the body. During initial development of the human body, cholesterol guides proteins which form bones, the spinal chord, large internal organs, and skin. Later, cholesterol helps in the formation of individual fingers and toes.

This information is proving useful in treating certain diseases. Smith-Lemli-Opitz syndrome (SLOS) is a condition in which babies are born lacking the ability to manufacture cholesterol. Such babies typically suffer from a variety of physical and developmental defects. Recent discoveries about cholesterol may help to prevent developmental problems such as SLOS. Scientists hope that if cholesterol were to be administered early enough in the development process it would prevent SLOS from occurring. Although SLOS is fairly rare, incidents have increased in recent years as health-conscious women with very low levels of cholesterol are deciding to have children.

Look at the highlighted word in the text. Click on the answer choice that is closest in meaning to the word **championed**.

○ supported
○ combated
○ tolerated
○ defeated

Time

 Help Prev Next

Beginning

For many years, doctors have championed the view that cholesterol is a dangerous substance. When consumed in large quantities, cholesterol tends to build up as excess residue in the arteries and veins of the body. **This buildup tends to constrict and limit the flow of blood through the body. In turn, this means that the heart must beat more forcefully if is to circulate the same amount of blood**. Because the heart is pumping harder, the risk of high blood pressure increases. Eventually, high blood pressure, resulting from excessive cholesterol, can lead to heart disease and other physical problems.

But, when consumed in moderation, cholesterol is actually one of the most important substances in the body. It provides suppleness to the outer walls of cells, thus making these walls stronger. Cholesterol also aids in the digestive process, since it is the main ingredient in stomach bile. Finally, cholesterol forms the basis of several important hormones, namely testosterone and estrogen, which are necessary for proper human growth and development. It is somewhat ironic that without cholesterol, a person's body would not be able to function correctly.

Recently, scientists have discovered that cholesterol has a fourth function. Cholesterol controls a protein necessary for the development of embryos. Without cholesterol, a fertilized egg would be unable to develop into a child. Cholesterol guides specialized proteins and in turn tells them when and where to form the physical parts of the body. During initial development of the human body, cholesterol guides proteins which form bones, the spinal chord, large internal organs, and skin. Later, cholesterol helps in the formation of individual fingers and toes.

This information is proving useful in treating certain diseases. Smith-Lemli-Opitz syndrome (SLOS) is a condition in which babies are born lacking the ability to manufacture cholesterol. Such babies typically suffer from a variety of physical and developmental defects. Recent discoveries about cholesterol may help to prevent developmental problems such as SLOS. Scientists hope that if cholesterol were to be administered early enough in the development process it would prevent SLOS from occurring. Although SLOS is fairly rare, incidents have increased in recent years as health-conscious women with very low levels of cholesterol are deciding to have children.

Look at the highlighted word in the passage. Click on the word or phrase in the bold text that **it** refers to.

Time

Help

Prev

Next

Reading

Beginning

For many years, doctors have championed the view that cholesterol is a dangerous substance. When consumed in large quantities, cholesterol tends to build up as excess residue in the arteries and veins of the body. This buildup tends to constrict and limit the flow of blood through the body. In turn, this means that the heart must beat more forcefully if it is to circulate the same amount of blood. Because the heart is pumping harder, the risk of high blood pressure increases. Eventually, high blood pressure, resulting from excessive cholesterol, can lead to heart disease and other physical problems.

But, when consumed in moderation, cholesterol is actually one of the most important substances in the body. It provides suppleness to the outer walls of cells, thus making these walls stronger. Cholesterol also aids in the digestive process, since it is the main ingredient in stomach bile. Finally, cholesterol forms the basis of several important hormones, namely testosterone and estrogen, which are necessary for proper human growth and development. It is somewhat ironic that without cholesterol, a person's body would not be able to function correctly.

Recently, scientists have discovered that cholesterol has a fourth function. Cholesterol controls a protein necessary for the development of embryos. Without cholesterol, a fertilized egg would be unable to develop into a child. Cholesterol guides specialized proteins and in turn tells them when and where to form the physical parts of the body. During initial development of the human body, cholesterol guides proteins which form bones, the spinal chord, large internal organs, and skin. Later, cholesterol helps in the formation of individual fingers and toes.

This information is proving useful in treating certain diseases. Smith-Lemli-Opitz syndrome (SLOS) is a condition in which babies are born lacking the ability to manufacture cholesterol. Such babies typically suffer from a variety of physical and developmental defects. Recent discoveries about cholesterol may help to prevent developmental problems such as SLOS. Scientists hope that if cholesterol were to be administered early enough in the development process it would prevent SLOS from occurring. Although SLOS is fairly rare, incidents have increased in recent years as health-conscious women with very low levels of cholesterol are deciding to have children.

According to the passage, which of the following can be inferred about blocked veins and arteries?

○ They store useful cholesterol residue until the body processes it.

○ They naturally grow stronger with age.

○ They increase the chance of high blood pressure.

○ They produce cholesterol fighting chemicals.

Time

 Help Prev Next

Beginning

For many years, doctors have championed the view that cholesterol is a dangerous substance. When consumed in large quantities, cholesterol tends to build up as excess residue in the arteries and veins of the body. This buildup tends to constrict and limit the flow of blood through the body. In turn, this means that the heart must beat more forcefully if it is to circulate the same amount of blood. Because the heart is pumping harder, the risk of high blood pressure increases. Eventually, high blood pressure, resulting from excessive cholesterol, can lead to heart disease and other physical problems.

➔ But, when consumed in moderation, cholesterol is actually one of the most important substances in the body. It provides suppleness to the outer walls of cells, thus making these walls stronger. Cholesterol also aids in the digestive process, since it is the main ingredient in stomach bile. Finally, cholesterol forms the basis of several important hormones, namely testosterone and estrogen, which are necessary for proper human growth and development. It is somewhat ironic that without cholesterol, a person's body would not be able to function correctly.

Recently, scientists have discovered that cholesterol has a fourth function. Cholesterol controls a protein necessary for the development of embryos. Without cholesterol, a fertilized egg would be unable to develop into a child. Cholesterol guides specialized proteins and in turn tells them when and where to form the physical parts of the body. During initial development of the human body, cholesterol guides proteins which form bones, the spinal chord, large internal organs, and skin. Later, cholesterol helps in the formation of individual fingers and toes.

This information is proving useful in treating certain diseases. Smith-Lemli-Opitz syndrome (SLOS) is a condition in which babies are born lacking the ability to manufacture cholesterol. Such babies typically suffer from a variety of physical and developmental defects. Recent discoveries about cholesterol may help to prevent developmental problems such as SLOS. Scientists hope that if cholesterol were to be administered early enough in the development process it would prevent SLOS from occurring. Although SLOS is fairly rare, incidents have increased in recent years as health-conscious women with very low levels of cholesterol are deciding to have children.

Click on the sentence in paragraph 2 that gives an example of the role cholesterol plays in food consumption.

Time

Help

Prev

Next

Reading

Beginning

For many years, doctors have championed the view that cholesterol is a dangerous substance. When consumed in large quantities, cholesterol tends to build up as excess residue in the arteries and veins of the body. This buildup tends to constrict and limit the flow of blood through the body. In turn, this means that the heart must beat more forcefully if it is to circulate the same amount of blood. Because the heart is pumping harder, the risk of high blood pressure increases. Eventually, high blood pressure, resulting from excessive cholesterol, can lead to heart disease and other physical problems.

But, when consumed in moderation, cholesterol is actually one of the most important substances in the body. It provides suppleness to the outer walls of cells, thus making these walls stronger. Cholesterol also aids in the digestive process, since it is the main ingredient in stomach bile. Finally, cholesterol forms the basis of several important hormones, namely testosterone and estrogen, which are necessary for proper human growth and development. It is somewhat **ironic** that without cholesterol, a person's body would not be able to function correctly.

Recently, scientists have discovered that cholesterol has a fourth function. Cholesterol controls a protein necessary for the development of embryos. Without cholesterol, a fertilized egg would be unable to develop into a child. Cholesterol guides specialized proteins and in turn tells them when and where to form the physical parts of the body. During initial development of the human body, cholesterol guides proteins which form bones, the spinal chord, large internal organs, and skin. Later, cholesterol helps in the formation of individual fingers and toes.

This information is proving useful in treating certain diseases. Smith-Lemli-Opitz syndrome (SLOS) is a condition in which babies are born lacking the ability to manufacture cholesterol. Such babies typically suffer from a variety of physical and developmental defects. Recent discoveries about cholesterol may help to prevent developmental problems such as SLOS. Scientists hope that if cholesterol were to be administered early enough in the development process it would prevent SLOS from occurring. Although SLOS is fairly rare, incidents have increased in recent years as health-conscious women with very low levels of cholesterol are deciding to have children.

Look at the highlighted word in the text. Click on the answer choice that is closest in meaning to the word **ironic**.

- ○ useless
- ○ paradoxical
- ○ biological
- ○ coincidental

Time

Help Prev Next

Reading

Beginning

For many years, doctors have championed the view that cholesterol is a dangerous substance. When consumed in large quantities, cholesterol tends to build up as excess residue in the arteries and veins of the body. This buildup tends to constrict and limit the flow of blood through the body. In turn, this means that the heart must beat more forcefully if it is to circulate the same amount of blood. Because the heart is pumping harder, the risk of high blood pressure increases. Eventually, high blood pressure, resulting from excessive cholesterol, can lead to heart disease and other physical problems.

But, when consumed in moderation, cholesterol is actually one of the most important substances in the body. It provides suppleness to the outer walls of cells, thus making these walls stronger. Cholesterol also aids in the digestive process, since it is the main ingredient in stomach bile. Finally, cholesterol forms the basis of several important hormones, namely testosterone and estrogen, which are necessary for proper human growth and development. It is somewhat ironic that without cholesterol, a person's body would not be able to function correctly.

Recently, scientists have discovered that cholesterol has a fourth function. Cholesterol controls a protein necessary for the development of embryos. Without cholesterol, a fertilized egg would be unable to develop into a child. Cholesterol guides specialized proteins and in turn tells them when and where to form the physical parts of the body. During **initial** development of the human body, cholesterol guides proteins which form bones, the spinal chord, large internal organs, and skin. Later, cholesterol helps in the formation of individual fingers and toes.

This information is proving useful in treating certain diseases. Smith-Lemli-Opitz syndrome (SLOS) is a condition in which babies are born lacking the ability to manufacture cholesterol. Such babies typically suffer from a variety of physical and developmental defects. Recent discoveries about cholesterol may help to prevent developmental problems such as SLOS. Scientists hope that if cholesterol were to be administered early enough in the development process it would prevent SLOS from occurring. Although SLOS is fairly rare, incidents have increased in recent years as health-conscious women with very low levels of cholesterol are deciding to have children.

Look at the highlighted word in the text. Click on the answer choice that is closest in meaning to the word **initial**.

○ early
○ crucial
○ complex
○ aging

Time

Help · Prev · Next

Reading

Beginning

For many years, doctors have championed the view that cholesterol is a dangerous substance. When consumed in large quantities, cholesterol tends to build up as excess residue in the arteries and veins of the body. This buildup tends to constrict and limit the flow of blood through the body. In turn, this means that the heart must beat more forcefully if it is to circulate the same amount of blood. Because the heart is pumping harder, the risk of high blood pressure increases. Eventually, high blood pressure, resulting from excessive cholesterol, can lead to heart disease and other physical problems.

But, when consumed in moderation, cholesterol is actually one of the most important substances in the body. It provides suppleness to the outer walls of cells, thus making these walls stronger. Cholesterol also aids in the digestive process, since it is the main ingredient in stomach bile. Finally, cholesterol forms the basis of several important hormones, namely testosterone and estrogen, which are necessary for proper human growth and development. It is somewhat ironic that without cholesterol, a person's body would not be able to function correctly.

Recently, scientists have discovered that cholesterol has a fourth function. Cholesterol controls a protein necessary for the development of embryos. Without cholesterol, a fertilized egg would be unable to develop into a child. Cholesterol guides specialized proteins and in turn tells them when and where to form the physical parts of the body. During initial development of the human body, cholesterol guides proteins which form bones, the spinal chord, large internal organs, and skin. Later, cholesterol helps in the formation of individual fingers and toes.

This information is proving useful in treating certain diseases. Smith-Lemli-Opitz syndrome (SLOS) is a condition in which babies are born lacking the ability to manufacture cholesterol. Such babies typically suffer from a variety of physical and developmental defects. Recent discoveries about cholesterol may help to prevent developmental problems such as SLOS. Scientists hope that if cholesterol were to be administered early enough in the development process it would prevent SLOS from occurring. Although SLOS is fairly rare, incidents have increased in recent years as health-conscious women with very low levels of cholesterol are deciding to have children.

It can be inferred from the passage that embryonic skin
- ○ covers the veins and arteries
- ○ builds up inside the heart muscle
- ○ forms before the fingers and toes
- ○ produces cholesterol in its cells

Time

Help   Prev   Next

Reading

Beginning

For many years, doctors have championed the view that cholesterol is a dangerous substance. When consumed in large quantities, cholesterol tends to build up as excess residue in the arteries and veins of the body. This buildup tends to constrict and limit the flow of blood through the body. In turn, this means that the heart must beat more forcefully if it is to circulate the same amount of blood. Because the heart is pumping harder, the risk of high blood pressure increases. Eventually, high blood pressure, resulting from excessive cholesterol, can lead to heart disease and other physical problems.

But, when consumed in moderation, cholesterol is actually one of the most important substances in the body. It provides suppleness to the outer walls of cells, thus making these walls stronger. Cholesterol also aids in the digestive process, since it is the main ingredient in stomach bile. Finally, cholesterol forms the basis of several important hormones, namely testosterone and estrogen, which are necessary for proper human growth and development. It is somewhat ironic that without cholesterol, a person's body would not be able to function correctly.

Recently, scientists have discovered that cholesterol has a fourth function. Cholesterol controls a protein necessary for the development of embryos. Without cholesterol, a fertilized egg would be unable to develop into a child. Cholesterol guides specialized proteins and in turn tells them when and where to form the physical parts of the body. During initial development of the human body, cholesterol guides proteins which form bones, the spinal chord, large internal organs, and skin. Later, cholesterol helps in the formation of individual fingers and toes.

This information is proving useful in treating certain diseases. Smith-Lemli-Opitz syndrome (SLOS) is a condition in which babies are born lacking the ability to manufacture cholesterol. Such babies typically suffer from a variety of physical and developmental defects. Recent discoveries about cholesterol may help to prevent developmental problems such as SLOS. Scientists hope that if cholesterol were to be administered early enough in the development process it would prevent SLOS from occurring. Although SLOS is fairly rare, incidents have increased in recent years as health-conscious women with very low levels of cholesterol are deciding to have children.

According to the passage, children born with Smith-Lemli-Opitz syndrome

○ are treated with the hormones estrogen and testoterone

○ are unable to produce healthy levels of cholesterol

○ have difficulty digesting foods rich in cholesterol

○ need diets of cholesterol-free foods

Time

 Help Prev Next

Reading

Beginning

For many years, doctors have championed the view that cholesterol is a dangerous substance. When consumed in large quantities, cholesterol tends to build up as excess residue in the arteries and veins of the body. This buildup tends to constrict and limit the flow of blood through the body. In turn, this means that the heart must beat more forcefully if it is to circulate the same amount of blood. Because the heart is pumping harder, the risk of high blood pressure increases. Eventually, high blood pressure, resulting from excessive cholesterol, can lead to heart disease and other physical problems.

But, when consumed in moderation, cholesterol is actually one of the most important substances in the body. It provides suppleness to the outer walls of cells, thus making these walls stronger. Cholesterol also aids in the digestive process, since it is the main ingredient in stomach bile. Finally, cholesterol forms the basis of several important hormones, namely testosterone and estrogen, which are necessary for proper human growth and development. It is somewhat ironic that without cholesterol, a person's body would not be able to function correctly.

Recently, scientists have discovered that cholesterol has a fourth function. Cholesterol controls a protein necessary for the development of embryos. Without cholesterol, a fertilized egg would be unable to develop into a child. Cholesterol guides specialized proteins and in turn tells them when and where to form the physical parts of the body. During initial development of the human body, cholesterol guides proteins which form bones, the spinal chord, large internal organs, and skin. Later, cholesterol helps in the formation of individual fingers and toes.

This information is proving useful in treating certain diseases. Smith-Lemli-Opitz syndrome (SLOS) is a condition in which babies are born lacking the ability to manufacture cholesterol. Such babies typically suffer from a variety of physical and developmental defects. Recent discoveries about cholesterol may help to prevent developmental problems such as SLOS. Scientists hope that if cholesterol were to be administered early enough in the development process it would prevent SLOS from occurring. Although SLOS is fairly rare, incidents have increased in recent years as health-conscious women with very low levels of cholesterol are deciding to have children.

All of the following are mentioned as functions of cholesterol EXCEPT

○ it makes cell walls stronger
○ it aids in the circulation of blood
○ it aids in human development
○ it guides the creation of bones and organs

Time

Help   **Prev**   **Next**

Reading

Beginning

James Watson, Francis Crick, and Maurice Wilkins are the Nobel prize–winning molecular biologists credited with the discovery of the double helix shape of DNA. DNA, the enzymes that make up the chromosomes and therefore the cells of the body, are linked together in two parallel strands of billions of enzymes which coil around one another. This pattern resembles curled train rails intertwined and twisted around each other to form an over-lapping and spiraled strand of genetic information. This discovery is one of the most significant in the entire field of molecular biology.

Some recent investigations have uncovered evidence that Watson, Crick, and Wilkins were not the sole specialists researching the properties DNA. A British scientist, Rosalind Franklin, may have contributed to crucial experimental work which lead to the discovery of the DNA strand. Franklin spent the first half of her professional career in England where she researched how rodents responded to interbreeding. She later relocated to France soon after the Second World War. Under the guidance of French crystallographer Jaques Mering, who is credited with the first mapping of crystal scaffolding, she learned to design complex models of various chemical compositons. In addition, she perfected a technique for diffracting X-rays. After returning to England in 1951, she began conducting experiments in molecular genetics at King's College, Cambridge University under the critical supervision of James Randal.

At Cambridge, Franklin ingeniously combined her knowledge of X-ray diffraction with chemical and crystal mapping to successfully photograph a rough image of a single strand of DNA. Unfortunately, the equipment she used was substandard and it exposed her to dangerous X-rays. In 1956, Franklin learned she had cancer and died two years later. Some scientists now speculate that the overexposure to dangerous X-rays during the course of her work was actually the cause of her cancer. Subsequently, Franklin's compiled notes were given over to Watson, Crick, and Wilkins who then went on to perfect nucleic acid research. When the three scientists finally did recieve the Nobel Prize, they gave no credit to Franklin for the crucial work she performed which led to the discovery of the double helix shape of DNA.

When finished reading the passage, click on the icon below

Proceed

Time

Help Prev Next

Reading

Beginning ▲

James Watson, Francis Crick, and Maurice Wilkins are the Nobel prize–winning molecular biologists credited with the discovery of the double helix shape of DNA. DNA, the enzymes that make up the chromosomes and therefore the cells of the body, are linked together in two parallel strands of billions of enzymes which coil around one another. This pattern resembles curled train rails intertwined and twisted around each other to form an over-lapping and spiraled strand of genetic information. This discovery is one of the most significant in the entire field of molecular biology.

Some recent investigations have uncovered evidence that Watson, Crick, and Wilkins were not the sole specialists researching the properties DNA. A British scientist, Rosalind Franklin, may have contributed to crucial experimental work which lead to the discovery of the DNA strand. Franklin spent the first half of her professional career in England where she researched how rodents responded to interbreeding. She later relocated to France soon after the Second World War. Under the guidance of French crystallographer Jaques Mering, who is credited with the first mapping of crystal scaffolding, she learned to design complex models of various chemical compositons. In addition, she perfected a technique for diffracting X-rays. After returning to England in 1951, she began conducting experiments in molecular genetics at King's College, Cambridge University under the critical supervision of James Randal.

At Cambridge, Franklin ingeniously combined her knowledge of X-ray diffraction with chemical and crystal mapping to successfully photograph a rough image of a single strand of DNA. Unfortunately, the equipment she used was substandard and it exposed her to dangerous X-rays. In 1956, Franklin learned she had cancer and died two years later. Some scientists now speculate that the overexposure to dangerous X-rays during the course of her work was actually the cause of her cancer. Subsequently, Franklin's compiled notes were given over to Watson, Crick, and Wilkins who then went on to perfect nucleic acid research. When the three scientists finally did recieve the Nobel Prize, they gave no credit to Franklin for the crucial work she performed which led to the discovery of the double helix shape of DNA.

▼

What is the main idea of the passage?

○ How Rosalind Franklin was instrumental in the discovery of the shape of DNA

○ Whether Watson, Crick, and Wilkins were students of the physicist Rosalind Franklin

○ How the double helix shape of the DNA molecule radically altered genetics

○ The dangers of using potentially substandard X-ray equipment

Time

? Help Prev Next

Beginning

James Watson, Francis Crick, and Maurice Wilkins are the Nobel prize–winning molecular biologists credited with the discovery of the double helix shape of DNA. DNA, the enzymes that make up the chromosomes and therefore the cells of the body, are linked together in two parallel strands of billions of enzymes which coil around one another. This pattern resembles curled train rails intertwined and twisted around each other to form an over-lapping and spiraled strand of genetic information. This discovery is one of the most significant in the entire field of molecular biology.

Some recent investigations have uncovered evidence that Watson, Crick, and Wilkins were not the sole specialists researching the properties DNA. A British scientist, Rosalind Franklin, may have contributed to crucial experimental work which lead to the discovery of the DNA strand. Franklin spent the first half of her professional career in England where she researched how rodents responded to interbreeding. She later relocated to France soon after the Second World War. Under the guidance of French crystallographer Jaques Mering, who is credited with the first mapping of crystal scaffolding, she learned to design complex models of various chemical compositons. In addition, she perfected a technique for diffracting X-rays. After returning to England in 1951, she began conducting experiments in molecular genetics at King's College, Cambridge University under the critical supervision of James Randal.

At Cambridge, Franklin ingeniously combined her knowledge of X-ray diffraction with chemical and crystal mapping to successfully photograph a rough image of a single strand of DNA. Unfortunately, the equipment she used was substandard and it exposed her to dangerous X-rays. In 1956, Franklin learned she had cancer and died two years later. Some scientists now speculate that the overexposure to dangerous X-rays during the course of her work was actually the cause of her cancer. Subsequently, Franklin's compiled notes were given over to Watson, Crick, and Wilkins who then went on to perfect nucleic acid research. When the three scientists finally did recieve the Nobel Prize, they gave no credit to Franklin for the crucial work she performed which led to the discovery of the double helix shape of DNA.

Time

Click on the drawing below that most closely resembles the object described in the text.

A   B

C   D

Help   Prev   Next

Reading

Beginning

James Watson, Francis Crick, and Maurice Wilkins are the Nobel prize–winning molecular biologists credited with the discovery of the double helix shape of DNA. DNA, the enzymes that make up the chromosomes and therefore the cells of the body, are linked together in two parallel strands of billions of enzymes which coil around one another. This pattern resembles curled train rails intertwined and twisted around each other to form an over-lapping and spiraled strand of genetic information. This discovery is one of the most significant in the entire field of molecular biology.

Some recent investigations have uncovered evidence that Watson, Crick, and Wilkins were not the **sole** specialists researching the properties DNA. A British scientist, Rosalind Franklin, may have contributed to crucial experimental work which lead to the discovery of the DNA strand. Franklin spent the first half of her professional career in England where she researched how rodents responded to interbreeding. She later relocated to France soon after the Second World War. Under the guidance of French crystallographer Jaques Mering, who is credited with the first mapping of crystal scaffolding, she learned to design complex models of various chemical compositons. In addition, she perfected a technique for diffracting X-rays. After returning to England in 1951, she began conducting experiments in molecular genetics at King's College, Cambridge University under the critical supervision of James Randal.

At Cambridge, Franklin ingeniously combined her knowledge of X-ray diffraction with chemical and crystal mapping to successfully photograph a rough image of a single strand of DNA. Unfortunately, the equipment she used was substandard and it exposed her to dangerous X-rays. In 1956, Franklin learned she had cancer and died two years later. Some scientists now speculate that the overexposure to dangerous X-rays during the course of her work was actually the cause of her cancer. Subsequently, Franklin's compiled notes were given over to Watson, Crick, and Wilkins who then went on to perfect nucleic acid research. When the three scientists finally did recieve the Nobel Prize, they gave no credit to Franklin for the crucial work she performed which led to the discovery of the double helix shape of DNA.

Look at the highlighted word in the text. Click on the answer choice that is closest in meaning to the word **sole**.

○ original
○ last
○ few
○ only

Time | ? Help | ← Prev | → Next

Beginning

James Watson, Francis Crick, and Maurice Wilkins are the Nobel prize–winning molecular biologists credited with the discovery of the double helix shape of DNA. DNA, the enzymes that make up the chromosomes and therefore the cells of the body, are linked together in two parallel strands of billions of enzymes which coil around one another. This pattern resembles curled train rails intertwined and twisted around each other to form an over-lapping and spiraled strand of genetic information. This discovery is one of the most significant in the entire field of molecular biology.

Some recent investigations have uncovered evidence that Watson, Crick, and Wilkins were not the sole specialists researching the properties DNA. A British scientist, Rosalind Franklin, may have contributed to crucial experimental work which lead to the discovery of the DNA strand. Franklin spent the first half of her professional career in England where she researched how rodents responded to interbreeding. She later relocated to France soon after the Second World War. Under the guidance of French crystallographer Jaques Mering, who is credited with the first mapping of crystal scaffolding, she learned to design complex models of various chemical compositons. In addition, she perfected a technique for diffracting X-rays. After returning to England in 1951, she began conducting experiments in molecular genetics at King's College, Cambridge University under the critical supervision of James Randal.

At Cambridge, Franklin ingeniously combined her knowledge of X-ray diffraction with chemical and crystal mapping to successfully photograph a rough image of a single strand of DNA. Unfortunately, the equipment she used was substandard and it exposed her to dangerous X-rays. In 1956, Franklin learned she had cancer and died two years later. Some scientists now speculate that the overexposure to dangerous X-rays during the course of her work was actually the cause of her cancer. Subsequently, Franklin's compiled notes were given over to Watson, Crick, and Wilkins who then went on to perfect nucleic acid research. When the three scientists finally did recieve the Nobel Prize, they gave no credit to Franklin for the crucial work she performed which led to the discovery of the double helix shape of DNA.

It can be inferred from the passage that before World War II, Franklin

○ was uninterested in the genetical science
○ immigrated to the United States
○ worked in England
○ changed her course of study at Cambridge

Time

Help Prev Next

Reading

Beginning

James Watson, Francis Crick, and Maurice Wilkins are the Nobel prize–winning molecular biologists credited with the discovery of the double helix shape of DNA. DNA, the enzymes that make up the chromosomes and therefore the cells of the body, are linked together in two parallel strands of billions of enzymes which coil around one another. This pattern resembles curled train rails intertwined and twisted around each other to form an over-lapping and spiraled strand of genetic information. This discovery is one of the most significant in the entire field of molecular biology.

Some recent investigations have uncovered evidence that Watson, Crick, and Wilkins were not the sole specialists researching the properties DNA. A British scientist, Rosalind Franklin, may have contributed to crucial experimental work which lead to the discovery of the DNA strand. Franklin spent the first half of her professional career in England where she researched how rodents responded to interbreeding. She later relocated to France soon after the Second World War. Under the guidance of French crystallographer Jaques Mering, who is credited with the first mapping of crystal scaffolding, she learned to design complex models of various chemical compositons. In addition, she perfected a technique for diffracting X-rays. After returning to England in 1951, she began conducting experiments in molecular genetics at King's College, Cambridge University under the critical supervision of James Randal.

At Cambridge, Franklin ingeniously combined her knowledge of X-ray diffraction with chemical and crystal mapping to successfully photograph a rough image of a single strand of DNA. Unfortunately, the equipment she used was substandard and it exposed her to dangerous X-rays. In 1956, Franklin learned she had cancer and died two years later. Some scientists now speculate that the overexposure to dangerous X-rays during the course of her work was actually the cause of her cancer. Subsequently, Franklin's compiled notes were given over to Watson, Crick, and Wilkins who then went on to perfect nucleic acid research. When the three scientists finally did recieve the Nobel Prize, they gave no credit to Franklin for the crucial work she performed which led to the discovery of the double helix shape of DNA.

Look at the highlighted word in the passage. Click on the word or phrase in the bold text that **it** refers to.

Time

Help

Prev

Next

Reading

Beginning

James Watson, Francis Crick, and Maurice Wilkins are the Nobel prize–winning molecular biologists credited with the discovery of the double helix shape of DNA. DNA, the enzymes that make up the chromosomes and therefore the cells of the body, are linked together in two parallel strands of billions of enzymes which coil around one another. This pattern resembles curled train rails intertwined and twisted around each other to form an over-lapping and spiraled strand of genetic information. This discovery is one of the most significant in the entire field of molecular biology.

Some recent investigations have uncovered evidence that Watson, Crick, and Wilkins were not the sole specialists researching the properties DNA. A British scientist, Rosalind Franklin, may have contributed to crucial experimental work which lead to the discovery of the DNA strand. Franklin spent the first half of her professional career in England where she researched how rodents responded to interbreeding. She later relocated to France soon after the Second World War. Under the guidance of French crystallographer Jaques Mering, who is credited with the first mapping of crystal scaffolding, she learned to design complex models of various chemical compositons. In addition, she perfected a technique for diffracting X-rays. After returning to England in 1951, she began conducting experiments in molecular genetics at King's College, Cambridge University under the critical supervision of James Randal.

At Cambridge, Franklin ingeniously combined her knowledge of X-ray diffraction with chemical and crystal mapping to successfully photograph a rough image of a single strand of DNA. Unfortunately, the equipment she used was substandard and it exposed her to dangerous X-rays. In 1956, Franklin learned she had cancer and died two years later. Some scientists now speculate that the overexposure to dangerous X-rays during the course of her work was actually the cause of her cancer. Subsequently, Franklin's compiled notes were given over to Watson, Crick, and Wilkins who then went on to perfect nucleic acid research. When the three scientists finally did recieve the Nobel Prize, they gave no credit to Franklin for the crucial work she performed which led to the discovery of the double helix shape of DNA.

According to the passage, to what do scientists attribute Franklin's cancer?
- ○ Radiation from World War II
- ○ Faulty and inadequate equipment
- ○ Genetic inheritance
- ○ Overexposure to dangerous chemicals

Time

? Help

 Prev

 Next

Reading

Beginning

James Watson, Francis Crick, and Maurice Wilkins are the Nobel prize–winning molecular biologists credited with the discovery of the double helix shape of DNA. DNA, the enzymes that make up the chromosomes and therefore the cells of the body, are linked together in two parallel strands of billions of enzymes which coil around one another. This pattern resembles curled train rails intertwined and twisted around each other to form an over-lapping and spiraled strand of genetic information. This discovery is one of the most significant in the entire field of molecular biology.

Some recent investigations have uncovered evidence that Watson, Crick, and Wilkins were not the sole specialists researching the properties DNA. A British scientist, Rosalind Franklin, may have contributed to crucial experimental work which lead to the discovery of the DNA strand. Franklin spent the first half of her professional career in England where she researched how rodents responded to interbreeding. She later relocated to France soon after the Second World War. Under the guidance of French crystallographer Jaques Mering, who is credited with the first mapping of crystal scaffolding, she learned to design complex models of various chemical compositons. In addition, she perfected a technique for diffracting X-rays. After returning to England in 1951, she began conducting experiments in molecular genetics at King's College, Cambridge University under the critical supervision of James Randal.

At Cambridge, Franklin ingeniously combined her knowledge of X-ray diffraction with chemical and crystal mapping to successfully photograph a rough image of a single strand of DNA. Unfortunately, the equipment she used was substandard and it exposed her to dangerous X-rays. In 1956, Franklin learned she had cancer and died two years later. Some scientists now speculate that the overexposure to dangerous X-rays during the course of her work was actually the cause of her cancer. Subsequently, Franklin's compiled notes were **given over to** Watson, Crick, and Wilkins who then went on to perfect nucleic acid research. When the three scientists finally did recieve the Nobel Prize, they gave no credit to Franklin for the crucial work she performed which led to the discovery of the double helix shape of DNA.

Look at the highlighted phrase in the text. What does the author imply by saying that Franklin's notes were **given over to** Watson, Crick and Wilkins?

○ Watson, Crick, and Wilkins continued Franklin's research.

○ Watson, Crick, and Wilkins stole Franklin's research.

○ Watson, Crick, and Wilkins presented Franklin's research to other scientists.

○ Watson, Crick, and Wilkins devoted themselves to Franklin's research.

Time

Help

Prev

Next

Reading

Beginning

James Watson, Francis Crick, and Maurice Wilkins are the Nobel prize–winning molecular biologists credited with the discovery of the double helix shape of DNA. DNA, the enzymes that make up the chromosomes and therefore the cells of the body, are linked together in two parallel strands of billions of enzymes which coil around one another. This pattern resembles curled train rails intertwined and twisted around each other to form an over-lapping and spiraled strand of genetic information. This discovery is one of the most significant in the entire field of molecular biology.

Some recent investigations have uncovered evidence that Watson, Crick, and Wilkins were not the sole specialists researching the properties DNA. A British scientist, Rosalind Franklin, may have contributed to crucial experimental work which lead to the discovery of the DNA strand. Franklin spent the first half of her professional career in England where she researched how rodents responded to interbreeding. She later relocated to France soon after the Second World War. Under the guidance of French crystallographer Jaques Mering, who is credited with the first mapping of crystal scaffolding, she learned to design complex models of various chemical compositons. In addition, she perfected a technique for diffracting X-rays. After returning to England in 1951, she began conducting experiments in molecular genetics at King's College, Cambridge University under the critical supervision of James Randal.

At Cambridge, Franklin ingeniously combined her knowledge of X-ray diffraction with chemical and crystal mapping to successfully photograph a rough image of a single strand of DNA. Unfortunately, the equipment she used was substandard and it exposed her to dangerous X-rays. In 1956, Franklin learned she had cancer and died two years later. Some scientists now speculate that the overexposure to dangerous X-rays during the course of her work was actually the cause of her cancer. Subsequently, Franklin's compiled notes were given over to Watson, Crick, and Wilkins who then went on to perfect nucleic acid research. When the three scientists finally did recieve the Nobel Prize, they gave no credit to Franklin for the crucial work she performed which led to the discovery of the double helix shape of DNA.

In what order does the author discuss Franklin's accomplishments in the passage?
- ○ From the most prominent to the least prominent
- ○ In the order in which they occurred
- ○ According to the scientific journal in which they were published
- ○ The most recent to the earliest

Time

? Help

 Prev

 Next

Writing

Writing

- Read the essay questions carefully.

- Think before you write. Making notes may help to organize your essay.

- It is important to write only in the topic you are given.

- Check your work. Allow a few minutes before the time is up to read over your essay and make changes.

- In the actual test you must stop writing at the end of 30 minutes. If you continue to write, it will be considered cheating.

- If you finish your essay before 30 minutes, click on Next and then on Confirm Answer.

- When you are ready to continue, click on the Dismiss Directions icon.

When finished reading directions click on the icon below

Dismiss Directions

Time

? Help

Answer Confirm

→ Next

Writing

Read the question below and type your response in the box.

Do you agree or disagree with the following statement?
The best education comes from experience, not from a book.
Use reasons and specific examples to support your opinion.

| Cut |

| Paste |

| Undo |

Time

? Help

Answer Confirm

→ Next

Writing

_____

_____

_____

_____

_____

_____

_____

_____

_____

_____

_____

_____

_____

_____

_____

_____

_____

_____

_____

_____

_____

_____

Answer Key

LISTENING SECTION

1. Take some time before deciding

2. She's not responsible for the lost notecards.

3. He probably isn't interested in seeing the play.

4. She forgot about their plans to play racquetball.

5. She's too tired to travel.

6. The work on the laser center should be completed soon.

7. He still hasn't decided on a topic.

8. See if the game was canceled

9. David will not go to the movie.

10. He would prefer to take a taxi.

11. She feels that the room is already too cold.

12. Pete lent her his notes.

13. The twentieth-century painting collection is also small.

14. The journalism classes helped her with her new position.

15. He doesn't have the right skills for debate.

16. The disk could be among some other disks.

17. To clarify a previous lecture on banking

18. To give an example of earlier methods of acquiring goods

19. It was dangerous to carry. It was too heavy.

20. They issued receipts.

21. Dangers facing the Earth's trees

22. Farming, Shelter

23. To give an example of the serious threat natural disasters are to trees

24. Most severe threat = Humans

    Severe threat = Natural disasters

    Least severe threat = Insects and disease

25. Hunting and gathering = Tribal method

    Southern colonial = Manor method

    Pompeii = Brazier method

26. Outdoor kitchens wouldn't increase the indoor temperature.

27. Bathing, Sewing

28. They are used for more than just food preparation.

29. To inform the students of the side effects of smoking

30. To seal peace treaties among tribes

31. The infants are born earlier than expected

32. Recent studies on the dangers of second-hand smoke

33. Heart rate, Circulation

34. They need more to bring about the same effects.

35. The survival techniques of moths

36. Moths are active during the night.

37. They are knobby and feathery.

38. Leaves, Sticks

39. The correct order is:

    The caterpillars weave a communal silk tent.

    A predator threatens the larvae.

    Thousands of larvae begin to wiggle and squirm.

    The larvae release a highly offensive smell.

40. Its legs detach from its body.

41. How various joints differ from each other

42. Ball and socket joint = Shoulder

    Hinge joint = Elbow

    Pivot joint = Neck

43. It allows the greatest range of movement.

44. Ball and socket

45. Picture C

46. It becomes painful and movement is limited.

47. It is replaced by newer information.

48. Associate the name with something ridiculous or absurd.

49. How well the material was stored in the association stage

50. Age, Disuse

STRUCTURE SECTION

1. most plentiful element
2. organization
3. it useful
4. which they
5. included
6. they need
7. attract
8. language native
9. how to go
10. although
11. but account
12. thereby making
13. necessary
14. ranch
15. There are about
16. are children
17. a such
18. were of no use
19. incorporates
20. prevent

READING SECTION

1. The overthrow of established medical tradition
2. prevent
3. They kept the common people from understanding medicine.
4. ridiculous
5. needles
6. often were of no help to their patients
7. chose
8. He educated himself about medicine.
9. doctors were not to share medical information with nonprofessionals

10. dismissed

11. Historical experiments on light and its properties

12. believed

13. He had considerable influence in the scientific world.

14. Publishing their results on light diffraction took a lot of courage.

15. electric and magnetic fields

16. The second paragraph refutes the theory mentioned in the first paragraph.

17. following

18. The final calculations weren't exactly accurate.

19. it is diffused by transparent objects

20. The sentence should be added at the first black square.

21. Stage movements

22. Renaissance comedy was scripted.

23. Improvisation was the key to the success of the *commedia dell'arte*.

24. actors

25. helped the performers develop their characters

26. restricted

27. dull

28. gradual

29. plot lines were too complicated

30. The cast rehearsed scripted melodramas.

31. The sentence should be added to the end of paragraph 2.

32. The benefits of cholesterol to the human body

33. supported

34. heart

35. They increase the chance of high blood pressure.

36. Cholesterol also aids in the digestive process, since it is the main ingredient in stomach bile.

37. paradoxical

38. early

39. forms before the fingers and toes

40. are unable to produce healthy levels of cholesterol

41. it aids in the circulation of blood

42. How Rosalind Franklin was instrumental in the discovery of the shape of DNA

43. Drawing A

44. only

45. worked in England

46. equipment

47. overexposure to dangerous chemicals

48. Watson, Crick, and Wilkins continued Franklin's research.

49. In the order in which they were occurred

How to Score Your Test

HOW TO SCORE YOUR TEST

Calculating your score on the TOEFL CBT is quite a process. However, you can follow the steps below to find your estimated score. Remember that your 30-minute essay is one-half of your total Structure score. Although we know that ETS grades your essay on a scale of 1 to 6, we don't know their exact grading criteria and how they incorporate it into the final Structure score. Therefore, it is impossible to incorporate your Writing score into your final score.

To calculate your estimated score on the diagnostic test, you must first determine how many questions you answered correctly. Fill in the number of correctly answered questions for each section in the spaces below.

Listening Section 1: Number correct _____

Structure Section 2: Number correct _____

Reading Section 3: Number correct _____

Now, find the corresponding raw score range on the Converted Score Range in Chart 1. For example, if you answered 31 questions correctly in a section, your raw score range would be 30–32. After you find the right raw score range for each section, find the converted score range that corresponds to it by moving across that row to the column for the appropriate section. If you answered 31 questions correctly in the Listening Section 1, you would receive a converted score range of 49–51. Convert your scores for all three sections using Chart 1 on the next page.

CONVERTED SCORE RANGES—CHART 1			
Raw Score Range	Listening Section 1	Structure Section 2	Reading Section 3
48–50	64–68		66–68
45–47	61–63		62–65
42–44	58–60		58–61
39–41	56–57		55–57
36–38	53–55		52–54
33–35	50–51		49–51
30–32	49–51		47–48
27–29	48–49		45–46
24–26	46–47		43–44
21–23	44–45		41–42
18–20	42–43	58–68	39–40
15–17	40–42	50–56	36–38
12–14	37–39	44–49	33–35
9–11	33–36	39–43	29–32
6–8	30–32	32–38	26–28
3–5	28–29	24–30	23–25
0–2	25–27	20–22	20–22

SAMPLE CONVERSION

Look at a sample conversion. Below is the number of questions one student

answered correctly on The Princeton Review Diagnostic test:

Listening section 1: 28   Converted raw score range for Section 1: 48–49

Structure section 2: 15   Converted raw score range for Section 2: 50–56

Reading section 3: 38   Converted raw score range for Section 3: 52–54

1. Add together the first number in each of the converted score range. In the sample above, 48 + 50 + 52 = 150.

2. Next, add the last number in each of the converted score range. In the sample above, 49 + 56 + 54 = 159.

3. Multiply each number by 10/3. Round down to the nearest whole number. This will give you a converted score range. For our sample scores: $150 \times 10/3 = 500$. $159 \times 10/3 = 530$. The converted score range is 500–530.

4. Now find the halfway point between your score range. In this case, the halfway point between 500–530 is 515. 515 is now your pre-score.

5. Find your pre-score in the left column of Comparison Chart 2 below. Our pre-score, 515, falls between the range 499–520. Move directly to the right to find the final score range. In this case, 174–190.

6. Find the halfway point between 174–190, which is 182. 182 is your final score.

Comparison Chart 2

Pre-score	Final score range
661–677	228–300
641–661	272–287
621–640	261–271
601–620	251–260
581–600	238–250
561–580	221–237
541–560	208–220
521–540	191–207
499–520	174–190
481–498	158–173
461–480	141–157
441–460	124–140
421–440	111–123
400–420	98–110
381–399	82–97
361–380	71–81
341–360	61–70
321–340	48–60
310–320	40–47

YOUR TURN

Number correct for

Section 1: _____

Section 2: _____

Section 3: _____

Converted score range for Section 1 (refer to chart 1): _____

Converted score range for Section 2 (refer to chart 1): _____

Converted score range for Section 3 (refer to chart 1): _____

ADD first number in each of converted score range sections.

1. _____ + _____ + _____ = _____

ADD second number in each of converted score range sections.

2. _____ + _____ + _____ = _____

MULTIPLY your respective results.

3. _____ $\times \dfrac{10}{3}$ = _____

   _____ $\times \dfrac{10}{3}$ = _____

4. Find the halfway point of your score range _____.

5. Find your pre-score in the left column of Comparison Chart 2 and move directly to the right to find your final score range. Final score range _____.

6. Find the halfway point of your final score range. Final score _____.

About the Author

George S. Miller, a University of Iowa graduate, first became interested in the TOEFL examination during his two-year study abroad in The Peoples' Republic of China. He joined The Princeton Review in 1995 and helped to develop and design the TOEFL CBT course curriculum taught in test prep classes both in the United States and abroad. He also trained other Princeton Review instructors for TOEFL CBT test prep classes and ran his own English as a Second Language school in New York City.

Sadly, our friend George Miller passed away in July 1999. His dedication to this project will always be remembered and appreciated. George will be sorely missed.

TOEFL DIAGNOSTIC SOFTWARE

ABOUT THE SOFTWARE

The drills on the CD-ROM were designed to help you practice for the Reading and Structure sections of the TOEFL. The Reading section is very similar to the actual Computer Based Test, and although the Grammar questions on a real TOEFL are computer adaptive, the linear drills on the disc should still be very useful as you study. We advise making good use of the review features—look at the explanations for questions you missed and determine which sections are giving you the most trouble.

SYSTEM REQUIREMENTS

WINDOWS™

- IBM PC or 100% Compatible (486/66 MHz or higher)
- Windows 3.1, 95, 98
- 8 MB RAM
- 10MB Hard Disk space
- SVGA Monitor (256 Colors)
- Double-speed CD-ROM or faster
- Mouse

MACINTOSH©

- Power PC
- System 7.1 or higher
- 8 MB RAM
- 10MB Hard Disk space
- Double-speed CD-ROM or faster
- Mouse

INSTALLATION AND START-UP

WINDOWS:

Close all other applications
Check that your monitor is set to 256 colors

1. Insert the CD-ROM in your CD-ROM drive
2. From your Start Menu (or File Menu if using Win 3.1), select **Run**
3. Type D:setup and press **Enter**. If your CD-ROM drive is not drive D:, type the appropriate letter)
4. Follow the onscreen instructions until installation is complete.
5. Once setup is complete, if you want to begin immediately, you can check "Yes, I want to run TOEFL Diagnostic now" and select **Finish**. Otherwise, just select Finish.

To run the software later, make sure the CD is in your CD-ROM drive, and simply select **TOEFL Diagnostic** from the *Princeton Review* folder in Programs from the Start Menu (or in the *Princeton Review* Program Group, if you are using Win 3.1)

MACINTOSH:

1. Insert the CD in your CD-ROM drive
2. Double click the TOEFL Diagnostic Installer icon
3. Follow the onscreen instructions until installation is complete.

To run the software, make sure the CD is in your CD-ROM drive, and simply double click the *Tester* icon located in the *TOEFL Diagnostic* folder on your hard drive.

USING TOEFL DIAGNOSTIC TESTS

Each time you launch you TOEFL Diagnostic, you will begin with the Main Menu. This screen contains two sections: **Start** and **Review.**

Taking a Drill: You have your choice of six Reading sections and five Grammar sections. Click on the section you want, then click on **Begin.** Additionally, you have the option of working timed or untimed. Click on the "untimed" box if you wish to work untimed. If you need to review the directions for any type of question or the functions of any of the buttons on your screen, simply click the **Help** button of any active testing screen.

Reviewing a Drill: After you complete a section, it will appear in the **Review a Drill** box. Click on a section you want to review, then click on **Begin.** You may review any question from your drill by clicking on the question number in the **Score Report.** The review mode will show you a green checkmark to indicate the credited response, and show your answer as the darkened oval. To view an explanation for an answer choice, click on the answer (the words in the answer, not on the oval).

If you have any questions, please call our Technical Support Center at (800) 546-2102.

www.review.com

Expert Advice

Talk About It

www.review.com

Pop Surveys

Paying for it

www.review.com

www.review.com

THE
PRINCETON
REVIEW

Getting in

Word du Jour

www.review.com

Find-O-Rama School & Career Search

www.review.com

Finding it

Best Schools

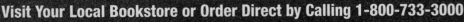

FIND US...

International

Hong Kong
4/F Sun Hung Kai Centre
30 Harbour Road, Wan Chai,
Hong Kong
Tel: (011)85-2-517-3016

Japan
Fuji Building 40, 15-14
Sakuragaokacho, Shibuya Ku,
Tokyo 150, Japan
Tel: (011)81-3-3463-1343

Korea
Tae Young Bldg, 944-24,
Daechi- Dong, Kangnam-Ku
The Princeton Review- ANC
Seoul, Korea 135-280,
South Korea
Tel: (011)82-2-554-7763

Mexico City
PR Mex S De RL De Cv
Guanajuato 228 Col. Roma
06700 Mexico D.F., Mexico
Tel: 525-564-9468

Montreal
666 Sherbrooke St.
West, Suite 202
Montreal, QC H3A 1E7 Canada
Tel: (514) 499-0870

Pakistan
1 Bawa Park - 90 Upper Mall
Lahore, Pakistan
Tel: (011)92-42-571-2315

Spain
Pza. Castilla, 3 - 5º A, 28046
Madrid, Spain
Tel: (011)341-323-4212

Taiwan
155 Chung Hsiao East Road
Section 4 - 4th Floor,
Taipei R.O.C., Taiwan
Tel: (011)886-2-751-1243

Thailand
Building One, 99 Wireless Road
Bangkok, Thailand 10330
Tel: (662) 256-7080

Toronto
1240 Bay Street, Suite 300
Toronto M5R 2A7 Canada
Tel: (800) 495-7737
Tel: (716) 839-4391

locations

Vancouver
4212 University Way NE,
Suite 204
Seattle, WA 98105
Tel: (206) 548-1100

National (U.S.)

We have over 60 offices around the U.S. and
run courses in over 400 sites. For courses and locations
within the U.S. call 1 (800) 2/Review and you will be
routed to the nearest office.